The BiblioPlan Companion, Year One: A Text for

ANCIENT HISTORY

Ancient and Biblical History from Creation to the Fall of Rome

with World Geography

HARDCOVER EDITION

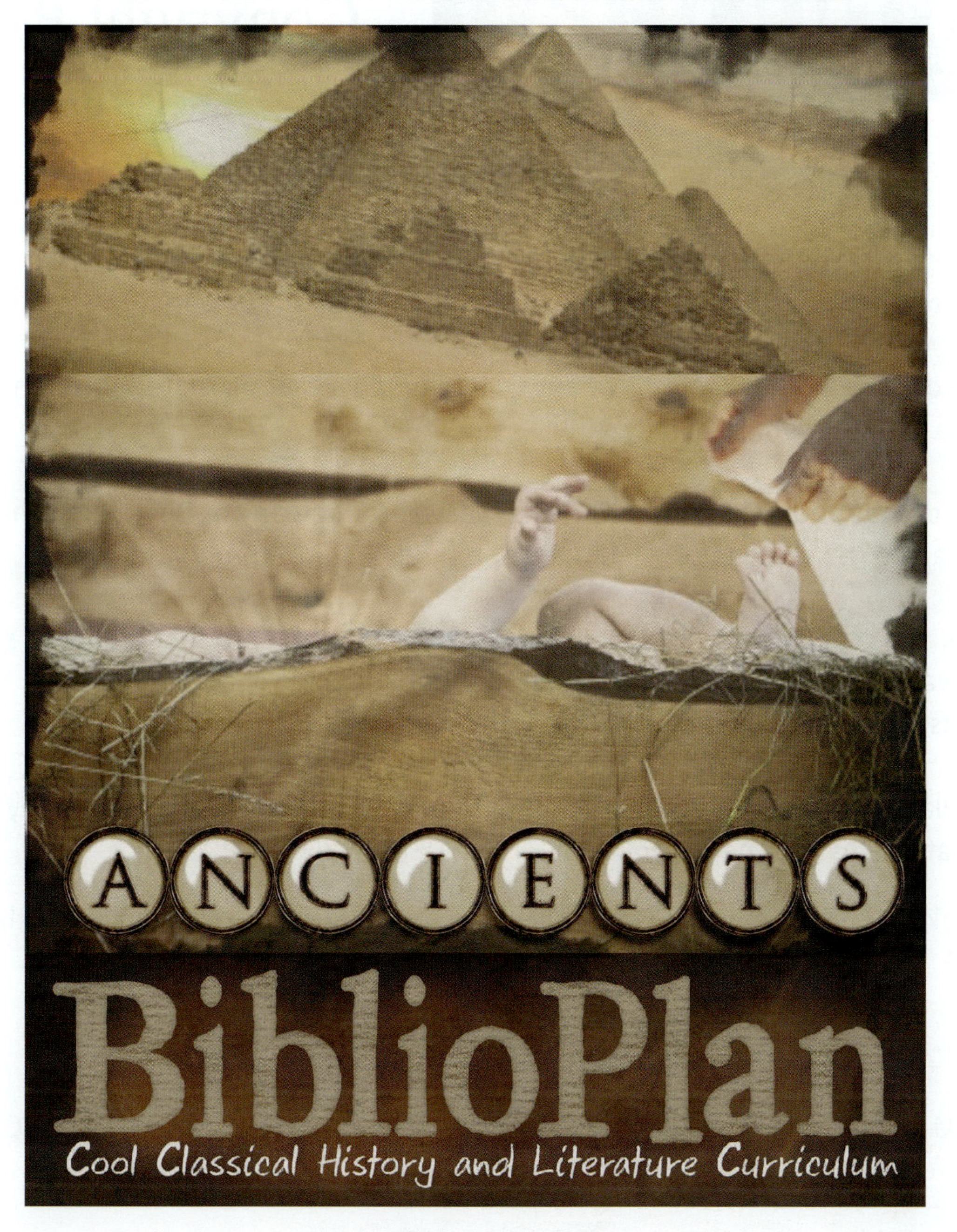

by Rob and Julia Nalle

Published in Palmyra, Virginia by BiblioPlan for Families.

Hardcover Version ISBN 978-1-942405-02-3

Copyright Policy

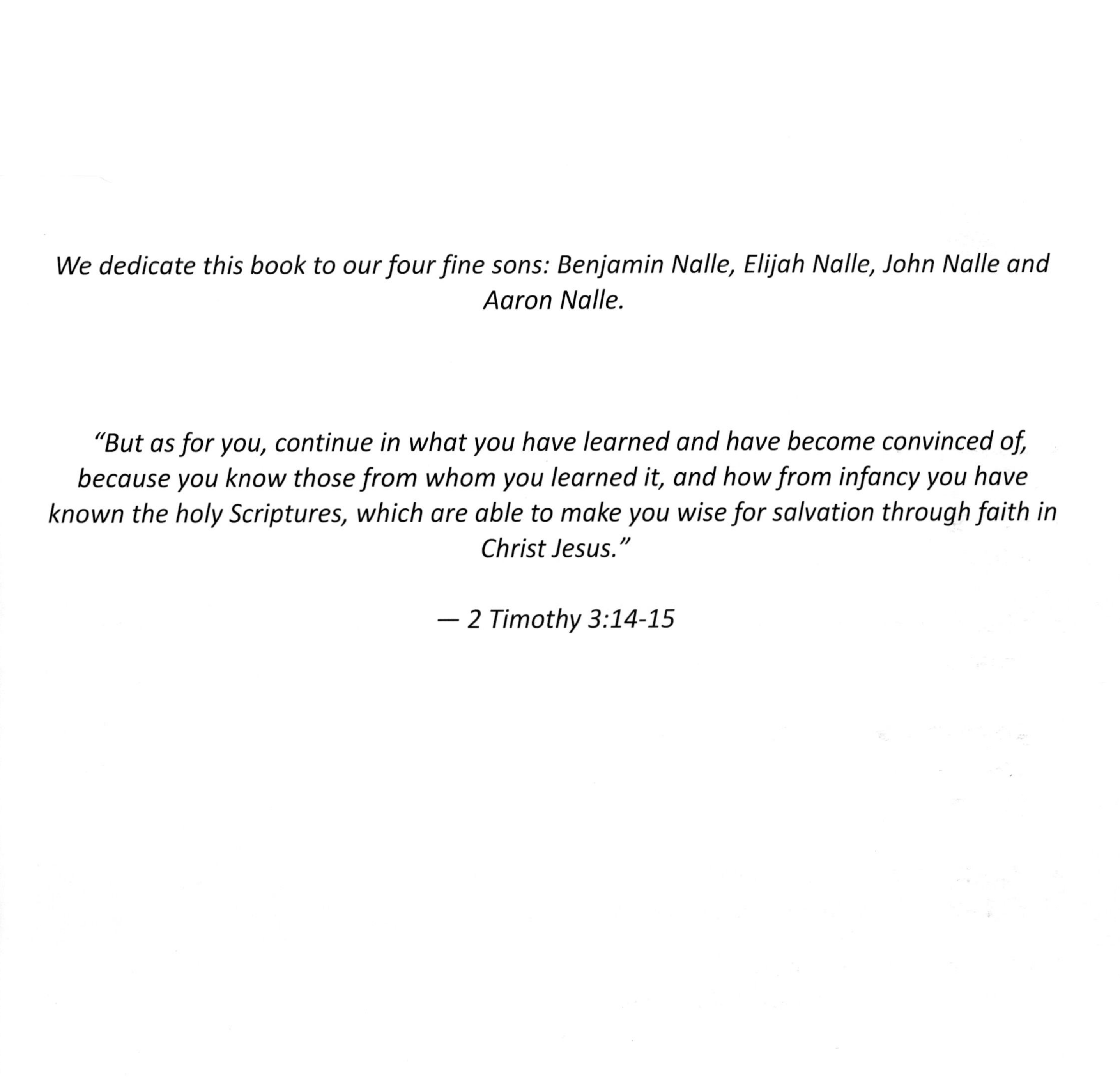

We dedicate this book to our four fine sons: Benjamin Nalle, Elijah Nalle, John Nalle and Aaron Nalle.

"But as for you, continue in what you have learned and have become convinced of, because you know those from whom you learned it, and how from infancy you have known the holy Scriptures, which are able to make you wise for salvation through faith in Christ Jesus."

— 2 Timothy 3:14-15

Welcome to the BiblioPlan Companion!

The BiblioPlan Companion is both a textbook and an enrichment supplement for a four-year, literature-based, Christian-worldview survey of U.S. and World history. BiblioPlan offers four Companions, each with 34 chapters for 34 weeks of study:

YEAR ONE, ANCIENTS covers Ancient and Biblical History from Creation to the Fall of Rome with World Geography

YEAR TWO, MEDIEVAL covers Medieval and Church History from the Fall of Rome through the Renaissance with World Geography

YEAR THREE, EARLY MODERN covers U.S. and World History from 1600-1850 with Missionary Highlights and U.S. Geography

YEAR FOUR, MODERN covers U.S. and World History from 1850-2000 with Missionary Highlights and U.S. Geography

Notes on Scope and Sequence

YEAR ONE, ANCIENTS

For Year One, BiblioPlan's scope is based on the Bible. Because Bible history begins with Creation and ends before the Fall of Rome, the Bible makes an excellent framework for a study of ancient history. We study topics from secular history wherever they fit best with Bible history. For example, topics from Egypt are woven into the stories of Biblical figures who lived in Egypt, patriarchs like Abraham, Joseph and Moses. Most chapters include a section on World Geography.

YEAR TWO, MEDIEVAL

For Year Two, BiblioPlan's scope is heavy on Western European history and Christian church history. The first 15 weeks focus mainly on Europe. The next few weeks examine Asia. From Asia, the scope moves to Africa; then to pre-Columbian America; and then to the European explorers who discovered America. Finally, the scope returns to Europe to cover the Renaissance, the Protestant Reformation and Elizabethan England. Most chapters include a section on World Geography.

YEAR THREE, EARLY MODERN
YEAR FOUR, MODERN

Year Three covers U.S. and World History from 1600 – 1850; and Year Four covers U.S. and World History from 1850 – 2000. Our scope covers U.S. History as chronologically as possible from beginning to end in years Three and Four. Some chapters cover U.S. history exclusively; some are divided between U.S. and World History; and a few cover World history exclusively.

Our scope also covers World History as chronologically as possible, but with one proviso: to avoid the confusion that comes with jumping back and forth from region to region too often, we have organized our studies of Asia, Eastern Europe, Western Europe, the Middle East, Australia, Africa and South America into units. Whatever part of the world we study, we always provide the background students need to understand what came before and what comes next. Most chapters include a section on U.S. Geography, as well as Missionary Highlights on the lives and works of great Christian missionaries.

A Note from the Authors

The BiblioPlan Companion is both a history textbook and a history supplement. As a textbook, it relates the events of history through a combination of narrative prose and timelines. As a supplement, it provides fun facts and concise, detailed summaries of people and events to enrich students' study of history. The Companion is designed to help students find the interesting, fun connections and themes that reappear throughout humanity's story.

The Companion is printed in a color-coordinated style that makes it easy to read and allows students to locate special topics quickly. The black-on-white sections contain the narrative of history in either prose or timeline form. The colored-background sections detail people and events of special interest that we hope will captivate your students and boost their interest in history.

Although the Companion is easy to read, parents and teachers must sometimes choose which portions are appropriate for children of different ages. Of necessity, the Companion sometimes describes deeds from history that were violent, cruel, or motivated by greed or lust. Parents may judge some of the material to be beyond the maturity level of younger readers. We judge the vast majority of this material to be appropriate for independent reading by older middle school and high school students. A few sections have parental warnings, and we advise parents to use their discretion regarding these sections.

A Note on BiblioPlan for Families

BiblioPlan for Families is a classical Christian History and Literature curriculum for homeschoolers, homeschool cooperatives and Christian schools. BiblioPlan offers simple, family-friendly lessons that enrich your children's studies of all of these subjects:

Ancient History	Medieval History	World History
Bible Studies	Church History	Missionary Studies
Geography	Social Studies	U.S. History
Literature	Art	Creative Writing

BiblioPlan's survey of history is divided into four years:

- **Year One: Ancients** covers Ancient and Biblical History from Creation to the Fall of Rome
- **Year Two: Medieval** covers Medieval and Church History from the Fall of Rome to the Renaissance
- **Year Three: Early Modern** covers U.S. and World History from 1600-1850 with Missionary Highlights
- **Year Four: Modern** covers U.S. and World History from 1850-2000 with Missionary Highlights

For each of these years, BiblioPlan offers eight helpful products:

1. The **Family Guide**, a lesson plan that outlines your course of study while providing versatile reading choices and writing assignments for all ages.
2. The **Companion**, a textbook that pulls together each week's lessons while adding plenty of fun and interesting facts to liven up your class time.
3. The **Discussion Guide**, a lesson recap/discussion starter designed to help families and classes get the most

out of the teaching time they spend together.

4. **Cool Histories**, weekly homework assignments based on the lessons in the Family Guide and the Companion.
5. **Hands-On Maps**, weekly map assignments based on the lessons in the Family Guide and the Companion.
6. **Timelines**, flowcharts with cutouts of important historical figures for students to assemble.
7. **Craft Books**, collections of arts, crafts and activities that highlight the lessons in the Family Guide and the Companion.
8. **Coloring Books**, collections of simple sketches from history for the little ones to color.

BiblioPlan's goals are:

- To honor God with every word we write.
- To provide an easy-to-follow curriculum that
    1. allows children of all ages to study the same topics at the same time, making life far easier for parents and teachers; while also
    2. providing history and literature readings that are appropriate for each child's reading level.
- To provide literature, lessons and activities that bring the family together.
- To meet the needs of every family member– big or small, young or old, child or adult.
- To provide supplemental materials such as crafts, activities, hands-on maps, timeline figures and coloring books that are fun for kids, but that also educate by fixing lessons in students' minds.
- To provide an adaptable curriculum with plenty of reading options.
- To provide an affordable curriculum.
- To weave God-honoring Bible lessons into the study of history.

To learn more about BiblioPlan for Families, please visit our website: www.biblioplan.net

Or email: contactus@biblioplan.net

Table of Contents

Chapter 1

Creation and the First People

BIBLE FOCUS

Scripture Spotlight: The Seven Days of Creation

Genesis 1 is the Biblical description of The Creation. It is written in a cyclical, poetic form that adds meaning and helps the hearer remember the story.

Over the first three days, God divides the world in three distinct ways:

Day One - Darkness is divided from light.
Day Two - The waters are divided from the skies.
Day Three - The sea is divided from the land. It is on this day that plants and trees are created.

Over the next three days heavenly bodies, birds and fish, and finally animals are placed into the three divisions, in the same order:

Day Four corresponds with Day One - The sun, moon and stars are placed in the darkness and light.
Day Five corresponds with Day Two - The fish and birds are placed in the waters and the skies.
Day Six corresponds with Day Three - Animals are placed on the land. On this day the Lord also makes man and gives him the charge to rule over the fish, birds and animals, and gives the plants to man as his food.

After each of the first five days of the Creation, God sees that all of his Creation is "good." After man is created on the sixth day, God sees that his Creation is "Very Good!"

On <u>Day Seven</u>, with His work complete, God rests. Day seven completes the two cycles of three, and leaves the hearer to contemplate all that God has done. Before Creation, the earth was "formless and void," but after Creation, it teems with varieties of life and beauty that tell of God's goodness and power.

ANCIENT HISTORY FOCUS

ANCIENT HISTORY'S BEGINNINGS

Ancient history is not as clear cut as more modern history (which is not very clear cut at all). The events and dates of ancient history are murky and disputed. Nearly everyone can agree on the hour and day on which Abraham Lincoln was assassinated, as well as who shot him. In the most ancient times, though, there were no means or traditions for recording important events, so little is known of them.

The two main views on the origins of life are Creation and Evolution. Evolutionists believe that humankind and everything we see are products of natural changes and chance. According to this view, every living thing changed, mutated, and evolved very gradually over a period of millions of years. Therefore Evolutionists must add millions of years to their timeline of ancient history in order to allow time for the evolutionary process. In the evolutionary timeline, the beginnings of man date back two million or more years, with modern Homo Sapiens appearing about 150,000 years ago. According to this timeline, the Ice Age ends and the first farming activity begins at around 10,000 B.C. The first major city to appear was Jericho, at around 7,000-8,000 BC.

Most Creationists, on the other hand, believe in a relatively "Young Earth." According to this view, history begins at Creation and the timeline can be understood from the Bible. The strictest Young Earthers insist that God created the entire universe in 7 consecutive 24-hour days. The Young Earth timeline places Creation around 6000 - 4000 B.C., just 6,000 - 8,000 years ago. In between Evolutionism and Young Earth Creationism are several blends and compromises, such as "Old Earth Creationism" and "Theistic Evolution," each with its own timeline.

FASCINATING FACTS: Jericho

Jericho is the first known ancient city, built somewhere between 10,000 - 6,000 BC. Jericho has continuously maintained a population all the way from ancient times through the present, although after Joshua destroyed the city it was left bare except as a camp. Today it is part of the Palestinian territories, located near the Jordan River in the West Bank.

Jericho originally consisted of city walls, a shrine and a tower with an internal staircase. Surrounding Jericho are naturals walls consisting of Mt. Nebo to the east and the Central Mountains to the west. With the Dead Sea to the south, Jericho sat in the center of natural fortifications that kept it well protected from invasion. By Joshua's time, the city walls had been strengthened and expanded and the city was prosperous. Jericho benefits from an abundance of water sources. The Jordan River is only four miles to the east, and the Central Mountains provide underground tributaries that flow into the city.

<u>Definitions:</u>

History: A written chronological record of past events and developments.

Historian: An individual who studies, records, and comments on history using documents, letters, journals and other artifacts.

Paleontology: The science of prehistoric life, often studied by examining fossils.

Paleontologist: A scientist who studies fossils to understand prehistoric life.

Anthropology: The science of the origins and social relationships of human beings.

Archaeology: The scientific study of the ancient past through the examination of artifacts.

Archaeologist: A scientist who studies artifacts and learns from them.
Artifact: A tool, weapon or object of historical significance that is usually discovered at an archaeological site.

FASCINATING FACTS: The History of Archaeology

LE HISTORIE DEL BIONDO, DA LA DECLINAtione de l'imperio di Roma, insino al tempo suo (che ui corsero circa mille anni).
Ridotte in Compendio da Papa Pio: e tradotte per Lucio Fauno in buona lingua Volgare.

IN VENETIA. M D XLIII.
Co'l Priuilegio del summo Pontefice Paulo III. & dello Illustriss. Senato Venetiano per anni dieci.

The science of Archaeology really began during the Age of Enlightenment in the 17th and 18th centuries A.D., even though excavations of ancient monuments had already been taking place for thousands of years. In ancient times, grave robbers raided the tombs of the pharaohs for the treasures buried in them, but they were more interested in the artifacts' value than in their historical significance.

In the early 15th century, Flavio Biondo created a guide to the ruins of ancient Rome. Biondo is considered the founder of archaeology.

In the 18th century, Johann Joachim Winckelmann began a systematic study of the past. Winckelmann is considered the founder of modern archaeology because his approach was based on detailed observations of artifacts. Thomas Jefferson became another "father of archaeology" when he used a systematic approach in the excavation of a Native American burial mound on his Virginia property in 1784.

Napoleon Bonaparte also earned archaeological credit by taking scientists along on his Egyptian campaign to study Ancient Egypt. In 1799, Napoleon's men discovered a unique carved stone slab at a place called Rosetta with the same text written in three languages, including hieroglyphic (the written language of ancient Egypt) and classical Greek. Because Greek is still in use, the Rosetta Stone became the key to translating long-forgotten hieroglyphics, and therefore the key to Egyptology.

FASCINATING FACTS: The Archaeologist

An archaeologist searches for artifacts and uses them to understand life and events in ancient times. The archaeologist does not seek treasures to sell; his goal is to learn about the ancient past. Archaeologists are not like paleontologists, who study prehistoric animal and plant life using the fossil record. Archaeologists deal with items that are related to people. (Photo to the left courtesy of Mario Modesto Mato)

An archaeologist conducts excavations to study the past using a very systematic approach:

Step 1, RESEARCH: An archaeologist must first research an area to learn as much as possible about the site before any excavation.
Step 2, PERMIT: An archaeologist must obtain a license or a permit from the local government granting him permission to excavate a site.
Step 3, MAPPING: An archaeologist must survey the site and map it. He must divide the site into squares or units (called site grids) and mark them with string so that when artifacts are found, their exact location can be fixed.
Step 4, EXCAVATION: At the site, the archaeologist digs carefully into the soil using many different tools. He may use a shovel to remove the top layer. As he moves closer to possible artifacts, he uses trowels or picks to remove soil without damaging anything. When an artifact is uncovered, the archaeologist carefully digs around the artifact before removing it from the ground. He also filters the soil through screens in order to pick up the tiniest items of interest.
Step 5, NOTE-TAKING: Pictures and videos are taken during the dig, and the archaeologist keeps careful notes in order to keep a record of where and when any artifacts are found during the excavation.
Step 6, BAGGING: Each artifact is placed into a separate bag. Each bag is labeled with the artifact's exact location.

Step 7, SITE NOTEBOOK: The archaeologist puts all his notes into the site notebook. These notes include location, process, items discovered, drawings, graphs, maps and more.
Step 8, ANALYSIS: The artifacts are taken to a laboratory and carefully cleaned. They are sorted and analyzed. The analysis may take years.
Step 9, REPORTING: The archaeologist publishes a report of his findings.

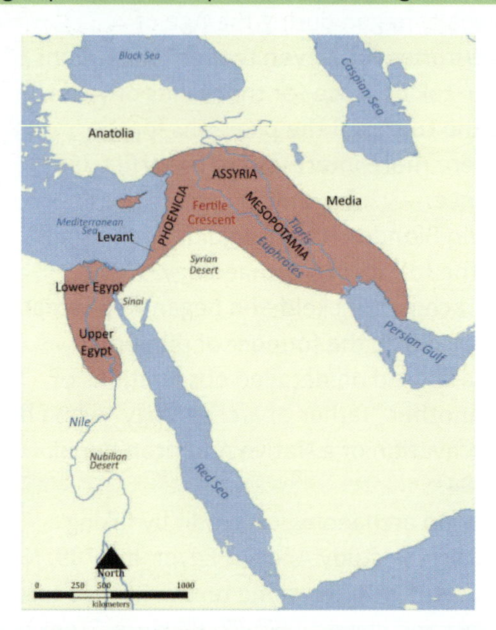

FASCINATING FACTS: The Fertile Crescent

The Fertile Crescent is a quarter moon shaped region stretching from the Mediterranean Sea to the Persian Gulf. It contains parts of modern-day Jordan, Israel, Syria, Turkey, Iraq, Iran and Kuwait. The Tigris and Euphrates Rivers lie along the Fertile Crescent, and these two unpredictable rivers provide a lifeline of water to the area. The strip of land between the two rivers was called Mesopotamia, which means "between the rivers." (see map)

FASCINATING FACTS: The Shaduf

A shaduf (or shadoof) is a primitive irrigation device that originally appeared in ancient Mesopotamia. Water is dense and therefore heavy, especially in the amounts needed for irrigating crops. The seesaw-like design of the shaduf uses a lever and a counterweight to enable a farmer to lift water out of a river or a shallow well without having to lift all of the water's weight. The device consists of a frame with a crossbar which supports a long pole. The long end of the pole holds a bucket on a rope, while the short end holds a counterweight. The farmer swings the bucket down into the water to fill it, raising the counterweight. Then the counterweight helps him raise the full bucket. The rope is long enough to allow him to empty the bucket into an irrigation channel. If the counterweight and pole lengths are correct, the shaduf cuts the effort required to lift the filled bucket in half.

Although the shaduf is a primitive machine, it is still used in Africa and Asia. Where modern equipment is available, irrigation is performed with electric, gas or diesel pumps.

ANCIENT NOMADS

The nomads were tribal wanderers, hunters and herdsmen who moved from place to place in search of grass for their herds. Nomads traveled with the seasons, following the wild game and grass that they needed to live. When they had depleted an area of food, they would move on to another area. They lived in either tents or caves, depending upon the location. Nomad hunters killed their prey using stone-tipped spears or primitive bows and arrows. Some ancient nomads painted pictures on cave walls. The first nomads began to appear in the Fertile Crescent around 8500-6500 BC.

Eventually, the nomads began to make more permanent settlements in the Fertile Crescent, establishing the first farms. Farmers dug canals from the Tigris and Euphrates rivers for irrigation, raised animals for meat, built permanent homes and banded together in communities in order to protect each other against raiders.

GEOGRAPHY FOCUS

The Seven Continents

DID YOU KNOW...

- The globe has seven continents: Africa, Antarctica, Asia, Australia, Europe, North America, and South America.
- Every continent except Antarctica is inhabited.
- About 70% (seven tenths) of the globe is covered with water, and about 30% is covered with land.
- The equator is an imaginary line that divides the earth into two sections, the Northern Hemisphere and the Southern Hemisphere. "Hemisphere" means "half-globe."

FASCINATING FACTS: The Globe

Ancient people long believed that the earth was a flat disk with water encircling it. But the flat earth theory did not explain the movement of the sun, moon and stars, and so ancient scholars began to theorize that the earth was actually a globe. Around 250 BC, a Greek mathematician named Eratosthenes set out to calculate the diameter of the earth by using the measured angle of elevation to the sun from two locations a known distance apart. His calculated diameter was off by only about 76 miles. One should never underestimate the intelligence of the ancient Greeks!

The earliest globe was created in 150 BC by a Greek scholar, Crates of Mallus. Crates' globe was naturally quite different from the modern globe, as only a small part of the earth had been explored.

Chapter 2

The Early Egyptians and Noah

BIBLE FOCUS

GIANTS OF THE FAITH: Noah

Noah and the Flood

Variations of the Biblical Flood story are found in many cultures and on every continent. Although the stories differ in their details, it is significant that there are so many stories about a worldwide flood. The deluge was so massive and world-changing that it is remembered by cultures around the world millennia later. The Flood divides history: before the Flood (in *antediluvian* times), even the Bible tells almost nothing of human history except that the people grew wicked. After the Flood, some recording of human events begins.

One difference between the Bible account and others is that according to the Bible, God himself starts the Flood and then ends it after 40 days. In most other tales, an evil god starts the flood and a good god ends it. As always, the Bible emphasizes that there is only one God and that He is good. The evil that other cultures blame on gods, the Bible blames on sinful humans.

The Biblical flood story begins in Genesis 6.

Verse 5 is key: **"The Lord observed the extent of human wickedness on the earth, and he saw that everything they thought or imagined was consistently and totally evil" (New Living Translation).**

Contrast that with verse 9: **"Noah was a righteous man, the only blameless person living on earth at the time, and he walked in close fellowship with God."**

The contrast between Noah and the rest of the human race is important. Noah was everything that God desired in a man, as God lays out in Micah 6:8:

"The Lord has told you what is good, and this is what He requires of you: to do what is right, to love mercy, and to walk humbly with your God."

The rest of the human race was so corrupt that God decided to act:

"Now God saw that the earth had become corrupt and was filled with violence. God observed all this corruption in the world, for everyone on earth was corrupt. So God said to Noah, "I have decided to destroy all living creatures, for they have filled the earth with violence. Yes, I will wipe them all out along with the earth!"

Only Noah and his family would be saved by faith.

SCRIPTURE SPOTLIGHT: Rain

Some Bible scholars believe that it had never rained anywhere on earth before the Flood. These scholars point out the following:

- Genesis 2:6 says that **"Springs came up from the ground and watered all the land."** This indicates that perhaps the earth was watered through springs and not rain, although the timing is uncertain.
- Hebrews 11:7 may indicate that Noah had never seen rain. **"By faith Noah, when warned about things not yet seen, in holy fear built an ark to save his family"** (Of course, he had also never seen a worldwide flood).
- The fact that the rainbow, given after the flood to mark God's covenant with Noah, is such a new phenomenon may also indicate that it had never rained.
- The fact that Noah was mocked by others as he built the ark may indicate that the idea of rain and a flood was ludicrous and unprecedented in their minds.

God gave Noah the specifications for building the ark and told him who and what to take with him. God promised to protect Noah throughout the flood, making a covenant with Noah that is the first covenant in scripture:

"But I will establish my covenant with you, and you will enter the ark—you and your sons and your wife and your sons' wives with you" (Gen. 6:18, NIV)

God's covenant places Him in sharp contrast with the other so-called gods of the Ancient Near East, who never made covenants with humans.

SCRIPTURE SPOTLIGHT: Two by Two or Seven?

Noah's Ark, oil on canvas painting by Edward Hicks

In Genesis 6:19 Noah is instructed to **"bring into the ark two of all living creatures, male and female, to keep them alive with you. Two of every kind of bird, of every kind of animal and of every kind of creature that moves along the ground will come to you to be kept alive."**

Then in 7:2-3 he is told to **"Take with you seven of every kind of clean animal, a male and its mate, and two of every kind of unclean animal, a male and its mate, and also seven of every kind of bird, male and female, to keep their various kinds alive throughout the earth."**

Why are there two different instructions? Why does God tell Noah to take the animals two by two and then tell him to take seven of every kind of clean animal just a few verses later?

The key to understanding the passage lies in the understanding of clean and unclean animals. In the Bible, clean animals are animals that are considered good for food and fit for sacrifices. The sacrifice of clean animals was pleasing to God. God instructs Noah to bring along seven of every kind of clean animal to fulfill both of these purposes. Noah and his family would need to survive after the flood; they would need clothing, shelter and food. The clean animals would help provide these things. They would be the beginnings of Noah's new collection of livestock, with perhaps cows and goats for milk and meat, chickens for eggs, sheep for wool, and so on.

After Noah and his family left the ark, they built an altar and made a sacrifice to God. The animals for that sacrifice were the **"animals and birds that had been approved for that purpose"** (8:20). Some of the clean animals had been set aside for the sacrifice.

After the humans and animals went into the ark, the Lord shut them in. This is also unique to the Biblical flood story. Although other cultures' stories told of boats, it was always a man who closed the door. In the Bible story, God closed the door.

God then loosed the torrents of rain until even the mountains were flooded. In other flood accounts, the gods became terrified at the forces unleashed. Some of them cowered or cried out. In the Biblical account, however, God remained fully in control. After 40 days and nights, the rain stopped and the waters began to recede:

"But God remembered Noah and all the wild animals and livestock with him in the boat. He sent a wind to blow across the earth, and the floodwaters began to recede. The underground waters stopped flowing, and the torrential rains from the sky were stopped" (Genesis 7:24-8:2).

Noah sent out birds from the ark to see if they could find any dry land, first a raven, then a dove three different times. Birds also appear in other flood stories. The second time the dove returns, it brings Noah an olive leaf.

FASCINATING FACTS: The Olive Tree

The Olive tree is one of the oldest cultivated trees in the Near East. An evergreen, the olive tree has been a symbol of peace, fertility, purity and power for thousands of years. To the Greeks it symbolized peace and prosperity. They dedicated the olive to the goddess Athena and made olive-leaf crowns to adorn the heads of their Olympic champions. In the Bible, the olive tree is one of the most often-mentioned plants. Olive oil is used for anointing, cooking and healing. Jesus ascended to heaven from the Mount of Olives in Acts 1, and according to Zechariah 14:4, the Lord will return to the Mount of Olives at the end of time.

Then the Lord spoke to Noah and told him to leave the ark. One of his first deeds was to build an altar to the Lord and offer a sacrifice. Other flood accounts also mention sacrifices, but in those, the sacrifice was meant to feed the gods because the flood had destroyed their food. In the Biblical account, Noah sacrificed as an act of worship. The Lord smelled the sacrifice and was pleased with Noah's heart.

Finally, the Lord made a covenant with Noah that he would never again destroy the earth with a flood. The Lord placed a rainbow in the sky and said:

"I am giving you a sign of my covenant with you and with all living creatures, for all generations to come. I have placed my rainbow in the clouds. It is the sign of my covenant with you and with all the earth. When I send clouds over the earth, the rainbow will appear in the clouds, and I will remember my covenant with you and with all living creatures. Never again will the floodwaters destroy all life. When I see the rainbow in the clouds, I will remember the eternal covenant between God and every living creature on earth." Then God said to Noah, "Yes, this rainbow is the sign of the covenant I am confirming with all the creatures on earth." (Genesis 9:12-17)

GEOGRAPHY FOCUS

The Nile River Hieroglyphics

THE NILE RIVER

The Nile River is one of the two longest rivers in the world (the other is the Amazon River in South America). The Nile flows from the high mountains in central Africa (modern Uganda) to the Nile Delta (Egypt) and the Mediterranean Sea. This south-to-north flow is reversed from the more typical north-to-south flow, so the Nile may be said to run backwards. Much of Egypt is desert country, so the Nile River is a great source of food and life for Egypt.

The Nile lies in a green valley called the "Black Land" which is far more fertile than the rest of the country, the "Red Land." The Black Land is the center of life in Egypt. The Nile provided the Ancients with water, food and even transportation, as boats could travel up and down the Nile. Each year the snow and heavy rain in the mountains to the south would send a torrent of water downriver, causing the banks of the Nile to flood between June and September. When the floods receded, a thick rich mud (silt) was left behind which provided excellent soil for crops. Since this mud was the only fertile ground in Egypt, the Ancient Egyptians had to live along the Nile in order to survive.

Ancient Egypt was divided into two regions: Upper Egypt was in the south, and its king wore a White Crown; while Lower Egypt was in the north, and its king wore a Red Crown. In 1898, archaeologists discovered a two-sided Egyptian palette that dated back to around 3000 BC. The palette shows King Menes (sometimes called Narmer) on both sides. On one side, he wears the white crown of Upper Egypt, while on the other side, he wears the red crown of Lower Egypt. Based on this palette, Narmer is credited with uniting the two regions into one kingdom and is considered the first King of all Egypt.

ANCIENT HISTORY FOCUS

FASCINATING FACTS: The Ice Age

Evolutionists and Creationists both believe that there was an Ice Age. Scientists have collected mountains of evidence that ice covered Canada, parts of the United States, parts of Asia, Europe, the mountains of Africa and South America and the tropics. Where Evolutionists and Creationists disagree is on the timing of the Ice Age.

Evolutionists date the Ice Age's beginning at around 2 million years ago, and its ending at around 11,000 BC. Evolutionists hold to the theory of Uniformitarianism, which suggests that landforms on the Earth developed over long periods of time through slow geological changes instead of catastrophic processes like earth-wide floods.

EVROPE IN THE AGE OF ICE

Creationists reject uniformitarianism and believe that the earth's landforms were shaped by short, sudden and violent events, chief among them the great Flood. They believe that the waters of the Flood came both above and below ground, as scripture says (see Genesis 7:11). According to this view, waters bursting out of the ground might have caused earthquakes, volcano eruptions and massive changes in the earth's crust. Volcanic ash and dust might have spewed into the atmosphere, creating an "anti-greenhouse" effect that brought on the Ice Age.

FASCINATING FACTS: Major Gods of Egypt

Painting of Pharaoh by Jeff Dahl

The Ancient Egyptians had over 700 gods and goddesses over their long history, although at one time, under Pharaoh Akhenaton (Amenhotep IV), they only worshiped one god, Aten. Aten was the light force of the sun and was originally part of the sun god Ra. When Akhenaton died, the Egyptians went back to worshiping their many gods.

The gods were divided into two categories: household gods and gods of the region or nation. Household gods were worshiped in the home. The two best-known were Bes (god of marriage and love, protector against snakes) and Tauter (goddess of childbirth).

Among the regional or national gods, the following were the most popular:

- **Anubis (god of the dead):** He held the scales on which the heart was weighed.
- **Bastet (cat goddess):** She was a daughter of Ra and is usually shown with a feline head on a woman's body.
- **Geb (green god of Earth):** He was a fertility god who laid the egg from which the sun was hatched. His laughter caused earthquakes. He often witnessed the weighing of the heart.
- **Hathor (goddess of the moon and children):** She was either the wife or mother of Ra, depending upon the tradition.
- **Horus (falcon god):** He was the protector of Pharaoh.
- **Isis (goddess of love):** Isis was wife of Osiris and was worshiped all over Egypt.
- **Nut (goddess of sky and stars):** Nut was the mother of gods.
- **Osiris (god of the dead):** He is dressed like the pharaohs with the ram's horn on his crown and his lower body mummified. He judges the dead in the underworld.
- **Ra (god of the sun):** Ra ruled everything as the king of the gods.
- **Set: god of chaos and evil.**

The Ancient Egyptians believed that when a pharaoh died, certain burial customs were necessary to ensure that he would attain immortality after death since they considered the pharaoh to be a god. These customs included mummification, the casting of spells and placing around the body items that the person would need in the afterlife.

The Embalming

Photo courtesy of Joshua Sherucii: Mummy in Vatican

The embalming process took exactly 70 days under the following procedure:

1. The embalmers washed the body with sweet-smelling palm wine and rinsed it with water from the Nile.
2. The body was taken to a tent called the 'ibu' or the "tent of purification."
3. A hook was inserted into the nose, smashing the brain. The body was turned over and the brain fluid drained out.
4. A cut was made into the side of the body in order to remove the stomach, liver, lungs and intestines. The heart was left in the body for weighing by Anubis. The other organs were cleaned and stored in Canopic jars (see below). The Canopic jars were packed with Natron (see below) to dry the organs out.
5. Natron was packed around the body and inside the body cavity. The body was covered and left for forty days in order to dry it out.
6. After 40 days, the Natron sacks were removed and the body was again washed with water from the Nile River.
7. The body was anointed with spices, oils, herbs and resins to keep it sweet smelling and the skin pliable.
8. The body was stuffed with cloth and straw (soaked in the oils and perfumes and resins) and shaped back to its normal size. Any open wounds were covered with wax and a decorated metal ornament was placed over

the wax as a symbol of protection.

9. The body was painted. Men were painted red, and women were painted yellow.
10. The body was wrapped with layers of linen cloths coated with resin. Hundreds of yards of linen were needed for the wrapping. The toes and fingers were wrapped separately. Often the cloths had spells written on them to protect the deceased, and jewels and amulets were placed among the wrappings. This process took about 13 days.
11. Finally, the body was covered with a sculpted death mask. Gold and precious jewels were inlaid into the mask.

The Opening of the Mouth Ceremony

After the mummy was prepared, a priest would utter a spell and touch the mummy with a blade. This ceremony gave the mummy the ability to breathe in the afterlife. The priest would also utter spells over the limbs to grant them movement in the afterlife.

The Burial

The prepared body was placed into up to three coffins. The coffins were made out of different materials, including gold and wood. The coffins were then taken to the burial chamber and placed in an outer coffin called a sarcophagus that was carved from stone. Everything that the body needed in the afterlife was placed inside the burial chamber, including books, tools and furniture.

FASCINATING FACTS: Natron

Natron was a salt mixture harvested from dry lake banks in Ancient Egypt. Modern chemists know it as hydrated sodium carbonate. Natron had numerous uses in ancient times: It was used as a cleaning product, as a soap (blended with oil), and as a toothpaste and mouthwash. It was also used to treat minor injuries, to dry fish and meat and to bleach clothing. It was one of the ingredients combined to make a blue dye, and it was also mixed with sand and lime for glass and pottery making by the Romans.

In the process of Egyptian mummification, Natron was used to absorb water and dry out the body.

FASCINATING FACTS: Canopic Jars

Photo Courtesy of Captmondo: British Museum

When a Pharaoh died, the body was preserved in a process called mummification. The major organs in the body were removed and placed in four separate canopic jars. The heart was left in the body, as it was considered the seat of the soul. The Egyptians believed that the heart would be weighed by the god Anubis. He would use the feather of truth, and if the heart weighed too much, it would be used as food for the monster Ammit.

The canopic jars were decorated with the heads of the Four Sons of Horus. The Four Sons of Horus were the guardians of the internal organs. They would in turn be protected by companion goddesses.

Son of Horus	Protects	Head	Point on Compass	Protected by goddess
Imsety	Liver	Human	South	Isis
Hapy	Lungs	Baboon	North	Nephthys
Duamutef	Stomach	Jackal	East	Neit
Qebehseneuf	Intestines	Falcon	West	Selkis

Chapter 3

Early Writing, the Sumerians and Babel

BIBLE FOCUS

SCRIPTURE SPOTLIGHT: The Tower of Babel

After the flood, the Lord commanded Noah and his family to

"Be fruitful and increase in number; multiply on the earth and increase upon it" (Genesis 9:7).

Genesis 10 contains the genealogy of Noah's sons.

In Chapter 11, instead of spreading over the earth as God had commanded them, Noah's descendants apparently migrated together to the area between the Tigris and Euphrates. There they plotted to build a tower that would reach the heavens, the Tower of Babel. This tower was probably in the form of a *ziggurat*, a multi-leveled, pyramid-like tower with ramps and stairs. At the top would have been a temple for the gods.

Their motive for building the tower seems to have been similar to the temptation in the Garden of Eden: they wanted to be like gods themselves, or perhaps to build a great nation that could somehow resist God's demands.

"Come, let us build ourselves a city," they said, "with a tower that reaches to the heavens, so that we may make a name for ourselves and not be scattered over the face of the whole earth" (Genesis 11:4).

They resented and resisted God's command to spread out and inhabit all of the earth.

Although their tower reached up to the heavens, God still had to come down from the heavens to see their city:

"But the LORD came down to see the city and the tower that the men were building" (Genesis 11:5).

Their attempts at earthly greatness didn't quite measure up to God's greatness.

When the Lord saw the tower, he found another way to enforce his will that they scatter over the earth:

"'If as one people speaking the same language they have begun to do this, then nothing they plan to do will be impossible for them. Come, let us go down and confuse their language so they will not understand each other.' So the Lord scattered them from there over all the earth, and they stopped building the city" (Genesis 11:6-8).

When the Lord says, "nothing... will be impossible for them, it means not that they could succeed in becoming gods and threaten God himself, but that no level of sinfulness was beyond them. The earth's new inhabitants were following in the footsteps of the old, spiraling downward into sin and rebellion. The Lord had promised not to send another flood to eradicate the people, but their sin was becoming intolerable. By confusing their language and forcing them to spread out, God was punishing their sin and enforcing their obedience.

FASCINATING FACTS: Stonehenge

Photo Courtesy of garethwiscombe: Stonehenge

Stonehenge is one of the most recognizable and famous sites in the world. It is located in Wiltshire, England and could date back to as early as 3,000 BC. Stonehenge consists of earthworks surrounding a circular setting of large standing stones. The layout involved sophisticated math on the part of its builders. Stonehenge was built using two different types of stones: the bluestones, which were not found in that part of England and had to be transported from over 200 miles away, and the Sarsen stones, which weighed up to 25 tons each. How the people of that day managed to lift and move such heavy stones is a mystery in itself.

Although more than 900 stone rings exist in the British Isles, Stonehenge is by far the most impressive and best known. No one knows exactly who built Stonehenge, or for what purpose; but it has often been theorized that it played a role in druidic religious practice. Archaeological evidence suggests that it was a burial ground, but it may also have been an altar, an astronomy tool (since it is aligned to many astronomical events) or even a gallows. Some connect Stonehenge to King Arthur, and even suggest that it may have been built by Arthur's sorcerer mentor, Merlin.

HIEROGLYPHICS

Ancient Egyptian funerary stela, Ashmolean Museum by ChrisO

The English language uses an alphabet of 26 letters. These letters represent sounds that are combined to form words (This type of alphabet is called "phonetic" because the letters represent sounds).

Ancient Egypt used a different system of writing entirely. Instead of a phonetic alphabet, the Egyptians used a system of over 2,000 *hieroglyphic* characters, each of which represented a common object. The hieroglyph could represent the object pictured, the sound of the object's name or an idea associated with the object (This type of writing, in which the characters represent an idea, is called "ideographic"). Hieroglyphics were written in rows or columns and could be read backward or forward, depending on the direction the animals or figures were facing. Hieroglyphics were used mainly by priests. The earliest hieroglyphic writing dates back to 3,200 BC.

As the written language developed and more Egyptians began to use it, simplified forms developed. The priests used a day to day script that abbreviated the picture signs considerably; this form is known as *hieratic*. Another form, used for non-religious purposes, was called *demotic*. The Rosetta Stone, found in 1799, contains parallel writing in both hieroglyphic and demotic forms, as well as classical Greek. This made the Rosetta Stone the key to translating long-forgotten hieroglyphics.

The Egyptians carved their writing into stone, which took a considerable amount of time but allowed their writings to be preserved for a very long time. Eventually, the Egyptians began to make a form of paper called papyrus.

FASCINATING FACTS: Papyrus

Papyrus is a reedy plant that grows along the Nile River Valley. Egyptians used papyrus reeds to make boats, mats, baskets, sandals and more. Papyrus was used for food and was burned for fuel. Its greatest use, though, was in the making paper.

To make paper, the Egyptians cut the stalks of the papyrus plant and soaked them in water until they decomposed. Then they laid the stalks next to each other, crisscrossing them in layers, and pounded them flat until they were mashed together into one piece. They left the resulting sheet to dry under weights for several days. Finally, they polished the sheet with a stone in order to make it smooth for writing.

CUNEIFORM

The area between the Tigris and Euphrates Rivers was called Mesopotamia (*Mesopotamia* means "between two rivers"). The Sumerians who lived in southern Mesopotamia used a form of writing called *cuneiform*. Like hieroglyphics, cuneiform used pictures (or ideograms) instead of a phonetic alphabet. Cuneiform was used for over 30 centuries, but it underwent considerable changes over that time: the earliest cuneiform consisted of simple pictures, but the later had a more abstract look. By the time of the Romans, cuneiform had been completely replaced by a phonetic alphabet.

The Sumerians wrote on tablets of wet clay using long reeds to make their markings. The reed was known as a *stylus*. When the clay hardened, the writing became permanent.

The word "cuneiform" comes from two Latin words: cuneus (wedge) and forma (shape). This refers to the wedge-shaped forms of the later cuneiform characters. As cuneiform writing developed, the number of characters decreased from about 1,000 to about 400.

FASCINATING FACTS: Archaeological Periods of the Ancient Near East

The Ancient Near East is considered the cradle of civilization. Agriculture, writing, pottery, the wheel, governments, laws, empires, slavery and warfare all originated in this area, which we call today the Middle East. Following is the standard time-line that most archaeologists use for the Ancient Near East:

Stone Age (Neolithic and Chalcolithic)	~ 8500 – 3300 BC
Early Bronze Age	~ 3300 – 2000 BC
Middle Bronze Age	~ 2000 – 1550 BC
Late Bronze Age	~ 1550 – 1200 BC
Iron Age	~ 1200 – 586 BC
Persian Period	~ 586 – 330 BC
Hellenistic (Greek) Period	~ 330 – 63 BC
Roman Period	~ 63 BC – 330 AD
Byzantine Period	~ 330 AD – 640 AD

FASCINATING FACTS: Cylinder Seals

Cylinder seals were small cylinders used to impress royal seals or other symbols onto ancient "documents" made of wet clay. The earliest cylinder seals date back to around 3500 BC.

The cylinders themselves were made of hard materials like stone, ivory, glass, wood, bone or baked clay. Into the surfaces of these cylinders, the ancients carved designs, scenes or symbols that conveyed certain messages. A king might roll his cylinder seal onto a document as a sign of royal approval; while a priest might use his seal as a sign of religious authority. Cylinder seals were easy to carry, and could even be worn as jewelry.

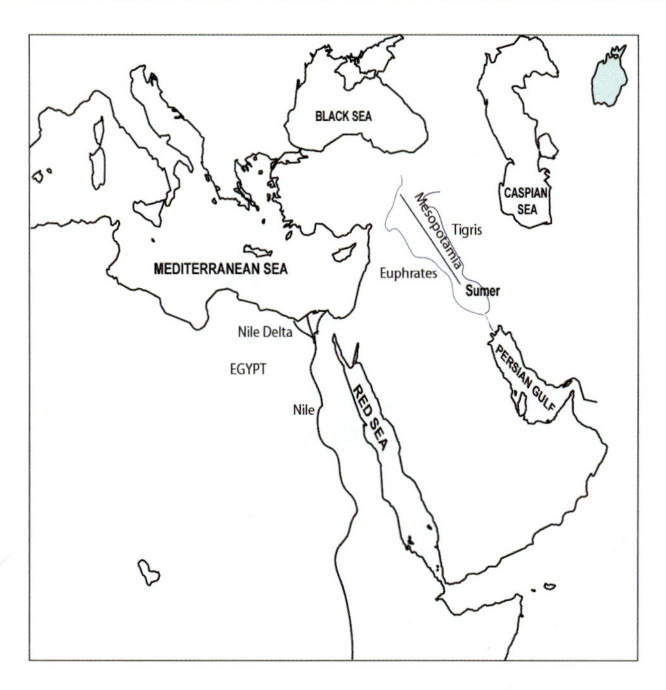

THE SUMERIANS

The Sumerians were the first to arrive in southern Mesopotamia, somewhere around 3000 BC. Around 2800 BC, the Akkadian people moved into the area and the two cultures blended into one. In the earliest times, the land was divided into city-states, each of which had its own ruler or king. Around 2334 BC, the city-states were united under an Akkadian king named Sargon.

FASCINATING FACTS: Sargon in the Basket from *The Sargon Legend*

"Sargon, strong king, king of Agade, am I.
My mother was a high priestess, my father I do not know.
My paternal kin inhabit the mountain region.
My city (of birth) is Azupiranu, which lies on the bank of the Euphrates.
My mother, a high priestess, conceived me, in secret she bore me.
She placed me in a reed basket, with bitumen she caulked my hatch.
She abandoned me to the river from which I could not escape.
The river carried me along: to Aqqi, the water drawer, it brought me.
Aqqi, the water drawer, when immersing his bucket lifted me up.

Aqqi, the water drawer, raised me as his adopted son.
Aqqi, the water drawer, set me to his garden work.
During my garden work, Istar loved me (so that) 55 years I ruled as king."

Brian Lewis' *The Sargon Legend* (American Schools of Oriental Research, 1978).

TERRIBLE TYRANTS: Sargon

Sargon reigned as King of ancient Mesopotamia for 56 years, from 2334-2279 BC. He was the strongest leader of his time period and the founder of the Mesopotamian military tradition.

After being abandoned as a baby, set afloat in a basket made of reeds, and rescued by a gardener, Sargon earned the position of cup-bearer to Ur-Zababa, King of Kish, a Sumerian city-state. The cup-bearer's job was to serve drinks at the royal table. The cup-bearer held a position of high trust, as it was his job to guard against any attempted poisoning of the king's cup. Often the cup-bearer would be required to drink the wine before serving it, thus ensuring that it was safe for the king to drink. Since the cup-bearer was often in the king's presence and held the king's trust, he had great influence in the king's court.

According to at least one story, Sargon used this influence to turn Kish's military against Ur-Zababa and replace him as king. By this time, there was already some unity among the Sumerian city-states, but Sargon was not satisfied with reigning over only a part of Mesopotamia. He eventually conquered all of southern Mesopotamia, as well as modern Syria, Anatolia (Asia Minor or modern day Turkey) and western Iran. Sargon understood military tactics, including choosing the high ground for fighting.

Sargon was able to subdue and control such a vast area through the organization of his military. He had a well-developed system in which he appointed 5,400 Akkadian-speaking leaders to posts throughout his empire. They ruled as military dictators, putting down revolts and forbidding protests against Sargon. The leaders collected taxes from the working class to support their armies. Because Sargon kept the peace in such a large area, trade flourished during his reign, and tin and copper for his bronze weapons was readily available.

GEOGRAPHY FOCUS

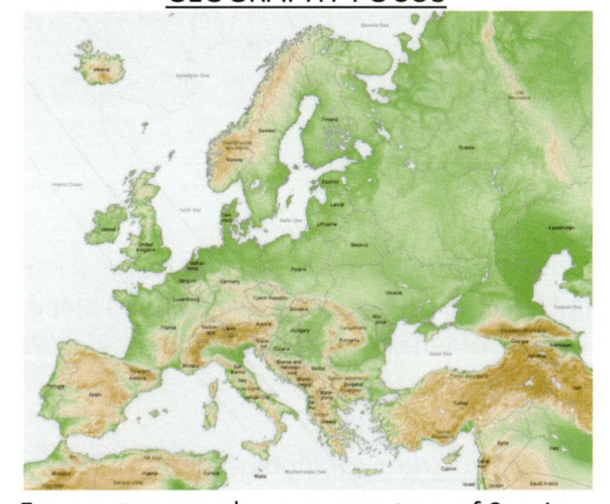

Europe topography map courtesy of San Jose

Dividing ASIA from EUROPE

DID YOU KNOW...

- The raised sections on the globe indicate the major mountain ranges.
- The accepted dividing line between Europe to the west and Asia to the east is the Ural Mountain Range.
- Where the Ural Mountains die out north of the Caspian Sea, the Ural River continues the dividing line between Europe and Asia.
- The Caucasus Mountain Range, which runs between the Caspian Sea and the Black Sea, forms the accepted boundary between Europe to the north and Asia to the south.

Chapter 4

Abraham

BIBLE FOCUS

INTERESTING INDIVIDUALS: Terah

Abram's father Terah was from the line of Noah's son Shem. The name "Terah" was associated with the moon, "yareah," and thus the moon-god. Only after he was 70 years old did Terah have his three sons, Abram, Nahor and Haran-- infertility may have been a family trait in the line of the Patriarchs. Terah's son Haran died early, leaving behind his own son, Lot, Abram's nephew. Terah had several wives, one of whom bore a daughter named Sarai, whom Abram later married (Genesis 20:12). Thus Abram married his own half-sister (this becomes important in some scripture stories). Nahor married another daughter of Terah (Genesis 1:29). A granddaughter of that marriage was Rebecca, who married Isaac, Abram's son. Intermarriage between family members was very common in those days.

Terah was an idol worshipper, as is reported in Joshua 24:2:

"Joshua said to all the people, This is what the LORD, the God of Israel, says: 'Long ago your forefathers, including Terah the father of Abraham and Nahor, lived beyond the River and worshiped other gods.'"

Abram did not learn about the one God from his father Terah.

Terah was also a merchant and, according to some Jewish traditions, a maker of idols. After Haran died, Terah decided to leave Ur (see below) and move his family to Canaan. Exactly why is uncertain: He may have wanted to leave the place where his son had died, or he may have fled an invasion of Ur by a barbaric mountain people known as the Guti. Another theory is that Abram received his call from God while the family was still in Ur and that Abram convinced Terah to move. Acts 7:2-3 supports this idea, although Genesis 12:1-4 indicates that Abram set out from Haran after receiving the call there. The timing of the call is uncertain. Some scholars believe that Abram could have received the call at Ur and convinced Terah to come along, but once Terah arrived in the bustling city of Haran, he chose to stay and Abram had to leave him there.

Terah died in Haran at the age of 205 years.

GIANTS OF THE FAITH: ABRAHAM

ABRAM'S JOURNEY - Genesis 12 and 13

When God called Abram to leave his country, his people and his father's house, He didn't tell Abram where he was supposed to go.

SCRIPTURE SPOTLIGHT: Genesis 12: 2-3

Abraham's call from God had seven elements:

1. **"I will make you into a great nation**	(from Abraham's seed would come a great nation)
2. **and I will bless you;**	(Abraham would enjoy material prosperity)
3. **I will make your name great,**	(Abraham's name would be renowned beyond his lifetime)
4. **and you will be a blessing.**	(God's blessing would be based on Abraham's name and seed)
5. **I will bless those who bless you,**	(God would prosper those who blessed Abraham and his seed)
6. **and whoever curses you I will curse;**	(God would punish those who cursed Abraham and his seed)
7. **and all peoples on earth will be blessed through you."**	(Through Abraham's seed, God would provide a future blessing: the Messiah)

In obedience, Abram took his family and his brother's son Lot and set off. He probably followed a common trade route toward Canaan. At Shechem (see map below), the Lord suddenly appeared to Abram and promised him all of the land around him. Abram was obviously on the right road! In a worshipful response, Abram built the Lord an altar.

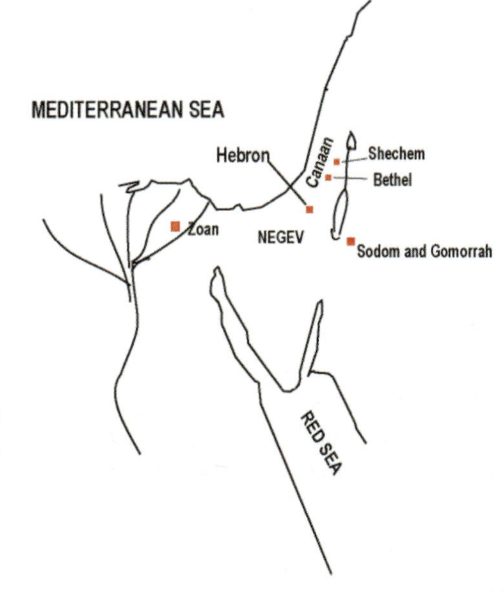

Abram traveled next to Bethel, where he built the Lord another altar (see map). He moved down to the Negev area and remained there until a famine struck. Then he moved on to Zoan, Egypt (see map), which was on the lush Nile Delta.

Here he had an encounter with the Pharaoh, who fell in love with Abram's wife Sarai. Knowing how beautiful Sarai was, Abram was prepared for this. He had instructed Sarai to say that she was Abram's sister (which was half true) in order to keep her suitors from killing him to get to her. The ploy worked, and Abram benefited financially from Pharaoh because Sarai had Pharaoh's favor. But the Lord afflicted Pharaoh and his family with a disease, which caused him to re-think keeping Sarai in his household. Whatever the disease was, it was apparent to Pharaoh that it was a direct result of keeping Sarai. He sent both Abram and Sarai away, and Abram left Egypt a wealthy man.

Abram and Lot returned to the Negev and lived as nomads for a time. They eventually settled in Bethel, where they had built an altar before. Their flocks and herds grew so large that the land could no longer support both wealthy men at once, so they decided to split up. Lot chose an area around the Jordan River, near the city of Sodom (see map). Abram chose Canaan. The Lord appeared to Abram after Lot's departure and reaffirmed his promises that Canaan would be his and that he would have offspring. Abram and his family settled in Hebron and built another altar to the Lord there.

REAFFIRMING THE COVENANT - Genesis 15

Years passed, and Abram and Sarai were still childless. When the Lord appeared to Abram a fourth time in a vision, Abram pointed out the obvious, that he still had no sons. The Lord re-affirmed his promise that Abram would have a son. In Abram's fifth encounter, the Lord again promised him the land of Canaan.

Abram's persistent faith shines through in Genesis 15:6: **"Abram believed the Lord, and he credited it to him as righteousness."**

SARAI'S SOLUTION - Genesis 16

After ten years in Canaan without a son, Sarai's desperation reached a climax, so she offered her servant Hagar to Abram in the hope that Hagar would bear a child in her place. This was common practice in those days; it is mentioned in both the Code of Lipit-Ishtar (a Sumerian law code from around 1800 B.C.) and an Old Assyrian Marriage contract (from around the same time). According to custom, the child born in this way would belong to Abram and Sarai, not to the servant.

FASCINATING FACTS: Code of Lipit-Ishtar concerning Surrogate Mothers

"If a man's wife has not borne him children but a harlot from the public square has borne him children, he shall provide grain, oil and clothing for that harlot. The children which the harlot has borne him shall be his heirs, and as long as his wife lives the harlot shall not live in the house with the wife."

Hagar became pregnant, and was quite proud of the fact that she would bear a child when Sarai could not. Already distraught over her own inability to bear children, Sarai could not stand Hagar's taunts. She began to mistreat Hagar.

FASCINATING FACTS: Sarai's Punishment of Hagar

After Hagar taunted Sarai, Abram gave Sarai permission to do with Hagar as she wished (Gen. 16:6). Ancient law allowed for punishment of a female slave who was insolent toward her mistress: the mistress could clean out the slave's mouth. According to the code of Ur-Nammu (around 2000 BC), "If a man's slave-woman, comparing herself to her mistress, speaks insolently to her, her mouth shall be scoured with 1 quart of salt."

Sarai's abuse forced Hagar to run away. But as she rested beside a spring in the desert, an angel appeared to Hagar (this is the first appearance of an angel in scripture). The exchange between the angel and Hagar is evidence of a loving God who cares for the weak and helpless. The angel told Hagar to return to Sarai and submit to her, but comforted her with the promise that she would bear a son named Ishmael and that his descendants would be too numerous to count.

INTERESTING INDIVIDUALS: Ishmael

Ishmael was Abram's first son. His name, chosen by the Lord, means "God hears." Abram was 86 years old when Ishmael was born. Although Sarai later bore Abram the son that God had promised him, Abram retained a special place in his heart for his first-born, Ishmael. The renamed Abraham pleads with God for Ishmael in Genesis 17:18:

"If only Ishmael might live under your blessing."

The Lord hears Abraham's plea for Ishmael. He promises that Ishmael will be the father of 12 rulers (paralleling the twelve tribes of Israel) and that his descendants will be a great nation.

When Ishmael was around 13 years old, the renamed Sarah bore Isaac, the true son of God's promise. The old jealousy resurfaced, and Sarah demanded that Abraham send Ishmael and Hagar away so that Ishmael could never share Isaac's inheritance. Abraham was upset because he cared for Ishmael, but God promised that he would take care of Ishmael.

So Abraham sent Hagar and Ishmael away with a small supply of food and water (see picture). When their supplies ran out, Hagar laid Ishmael in the shade of a bush to die. But Ishmael cried out, and God heard his cry. An angel again spoke words of comfort to Hagar, repeating the promise that a great nation would rise from Ishmael. A well appeared, and Hagar gave her son water. God cared for Hagar and Ishmael, and Ishmael grew into manhood, becoming an expert archer.

Hagar found Ishmael an Egyptian wife (Hagar was herself Egyptian), and together they had 12 sons. He also had two daughters, one of whom married Esau (Isaac's son). Ishmael reappears in Genesis 25 at Abraham's burial: Isaac and Ishmael together entomb their dead father in a cave. Ishmael was 137 years old when he himself died.

In the Islamic religion, Ishmael is considered a prophet and the father of the Arab people. Islamists believe that it was Ishmael, not Isaac, whom Abraham nearly sacrificed in the story from Genesis 22.

Thirteen more years passed, and Sarai remained childless. Abraham was 99 years old. Suddenly, the Lord appeared to Abraham a sixth time, this time naming himself El-Shaddai ("all-sufficient God," usually translated "God Almighty"). He commanded Abram to "walk before me and be blameless" (Genesis 17:1) and reaffirmed his covenant with Abram. He also changed Abram's name to Abraham, which means "father of a multitude of nations." Sarai's name was changed to Sarah ("princess"), and she too received God's blessing.

FASCINATING FACTS: Name Changes for Sarai and Abram

Sarai and Abram were both named by Terah, who worshipped the Sumerian moon god Sin. "Sarai" was the name of the moon-god's female consort. The meaning of the name "Abram" is unknown, but it may also have been associated with the moon god.

When God fulfilled his promise by causing Sarai to conceive, upholding his covenant with them, he gave each of them a new name that contained part of his name, YHWH. God was in effect bringing the couple into his family, and renaming them for their true father. They were transferring allegiance from the 'god' of their father, Terah, and covenanting with the God of the ages-- YHWH.

As a sign of the covenant, God commanded that Abraham and all the males in the household should be circumcised. Abraham obeyed God, and from that time forward Abraham, Ishmael, Isaac and all Jewish men bore the mark of circumcision.

In a seventh encounter with God, Abraham and Sarah were visited by three men in Genesis 18. The three men turned out to be angels, or perhaps even the Lord Himself in disguise (Can you think of a reason why the Lord might appear as three strangers?). When they told Abraham that Sarah would have a child, she laughed, perhaps in both joy and disbelief.

A year later, at the age of ninety, Sarah had a son whom they named Isaac (Genesis 21: 1-7):

"Now the LORD was gracious to Sarah as he had said, and the LORD did for Sarah what he had promised. Sarah became pregnant and bore a son to Abraham in his old age, at the very time God had promised him. Abraham gave the name Isaac to the son Sarah bore him. When his son Isaac was eight days old, Abraham circumcised him, as God commanded him. Abraham was a hundred years old when his son Isaac was born to him.

Sarah said, "God has brought me laughter, and everyone who hears about this will laugh with me."

And she added, "Who would have said to Abraham that Sarah would nurse children? Yet I have borne him a son in his old age."

FASCINATING FACTS: Isaac and laughter

Isaac's name means "laughter." The name is a play on words. Isaac's birth to a dried-up old couple like Abraham and Sarah was a source of disbelieving mirth at least 3 times in Genesis:

In Genesis 17:17, Abraham fell facedown and laughed after hearing that he would become a father at the age of 100.

In Genesis 18:12, Sarah eavesdropped on Abraham and the Lord/angels, and when they said she would have a son within the year, she laughed to herself. When the Lord asked her later why she laughed, she was frightened and denied laughing.

In Genesis 21: 6, after Isaac was born, Sarah said:

"God has brought me laughter, and everyone who hears about this will laugh with me."

God's ability to fulfill this most unlikely-seeming promise was a great testimony to His power over human life. God proved that He could do the impossible, and he proved it in an area that had marked Sarah's entire life: the bearing of children.

The story of Isaac continues in Chapter 5.

ANCIENT HISTORY FOCUS

FASCINATING FACTS: Ziggurats

Photo courtesy of Hardnfast: Ancient ziggurat at Ali Air Base Iraq

Ziggurats were ancient Mesopotamian structures comparable to Egyptian pyramids. They were terraced step pyramids with sloping walls and up to seven platforms at different levels. Each platform had a core made from common brick. The facings were made of fired bricks, which were often glazed with different colors or decorated with writings. The platforms were linked by stairways. A ziggurat was usually found in the center of a city, surrounded by a temple complex.

A Mesopotamian city's ziggurat was considered the city god's dwelling place. The top of the ziggurat housed the temple for the city god. Only priests were permitted on the ziggurat, and they were responsible to feed and care for the god.

FASCINATING FACTS: Ur

Ur was an ancient Sumerian city at the southern end of the Euphrates River, close to the Persian Gulf, making it an excellent location for trading goods. In its day it was one of the largest cities in the world, the central hub of a great number of city-states in the Sumerian empire.

The principle deity worshiped at Ur was the Sumerian moon god Nanna (or Nannar), known as Sin in Akkadian. Nanna was depicted as a wise old man with a flowing beard and four horns. Nanna's shrine was contained in the Great Ziggurat of Ur; this was thought to be the place on earth where Nanna chose to dwell. His supposed bedchamber was at the ziggurat's summit, and each night a woman was chosen to sleep on the bed there to provide Nanna with companionship. The Great Ziggurat of Ur was the religious and administrative center of Ur during Abraham's time.

The Sumerians of Ur believed that their purpose on earth was to serve their gods. Since they considered their kings to be gods, they made human sacrifices when a king died; this was their final service to their god-king. The king was buried at the lowest level of his burial chamber, and his attendants would group themselves around him and sacrifice themselves by drinking a poison. Other human sacrifices would be layered above the king and his attendants, sometimes even in several layers of bodies with layers of dirt between them. The number of victims varied from twelve to eighty. At the very top was the chief sacrifice, usually the Queen. Finally, a chapel was erected on top of the tomb. This system made the death of a king a terribly sad occasion. The additional sacrifices assured that the king's death would be greatly mourned, if not for his own sake, then for the sakes of all of those who died along with him.

GEOGRAPHY FOCUS

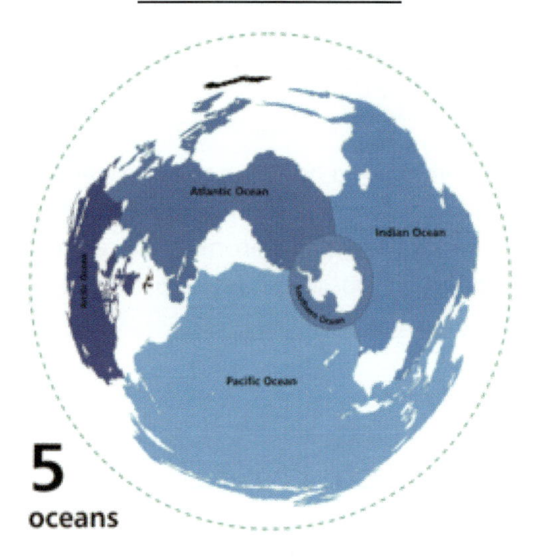

The Oceans of the Earth

DID YOU KNOW...

- There are five oceans: the Atlantic Ocean, the Pacific Ocean, the Indian Ocean, the Arctic Ocean and the Southern Ocean.
- The Southern Ocean surrounds Antarctica. It is a fairly recent addition, and may not appear on older maps. Its definition is disputed, but some people define it as the body of ocean water south of the globe's 60th parallel south.
- The oceans have no defined boundaries. They are all interconnected. Some people refer to all five together as the World Ocean.

Chapter 5

Hammurabi and Isaac

BIBLE FOCUS

GIANTS OF THE FAITH: ISAAC

Genesis 21: 1-21

When Abraham was 100 years old, Sarah bore him a son whom they named Isaac (see Chapter 4). On the day Isaac was weaned (possibly three to five years old), Abraham threw a party.

FASCINATING FACTS: Weaning

"Weaning" is of course the end of a child's nursing stage, but in the Ancient Near East it was more than this-- it was a milestone in a child's life. In those days a great many children died in infancy, so it was a cause for joy when a child survived to his or her weaning. Therefore weaning feasts were common.

At the party, Sarah saw Ishmael 'mocking' Isaac (v. 9) and told Abraham to get rid of the boy and his mother. What exactly Ishmael was doing is unclear. It may have angered Sarah simply to see Ishmael playing with Isaac as an equal-- Sarah wanted it to be clear that Isaac was the favored son who would receive all of the inheritance (v. 10). Ishmael may have mocked or ridiculed Isaac, or perhaps hurt him. The Apostle Paul indicates in Galatians 4:29 that Ishmael persecuted Isaac. Whatever happened, Abraham sadly sent Ishmael and his mother away (see Chapter 4 for more on Ishmael).

Genesis 22

Some time later, the Lord appeared to Abraham and told him to take Isaac to the region of Moriah (the location is unknown but the name may mean "ordained/considered by God") to sacrifice him as a burnt offering.

SCRIPTURE SPOTLIGHT: THE TESTING - Genesis 22:1-19

In Genesis 22:2, God asks Abraham to sacrifice his son Isaac as a burnt offering. In a burnt offering, the entire animal being offered is cut up into pieces and consumed by fire. God's request was beyond shocking; it was outrageous. Although Abraham was no doubt familiar with the idea of human sacrifice from his time in Ur, it had no part in his new faith. Furthermore, the request simply made no human sense: why would God make him wait for so long for this son and make so many promises about him, only to require the boy's life in sacrifice now? Abraham was used to facing difficult tasks requiring great faith-- he has already left his home and family to go into an unknown country, and he has sent away his first-born Ishmael-- but this task is by far the hardest and most dreadful.

The story emphasizes Abraham's great faith: He offers no objection or comment, but simply sets out to obey. Perhaps his reaction is simply beyond what words can tell. He and Isaac set off the next morning with a donkey and two servants. Abraham offers no explanation of what is happening to the servants or to Isaac. After three days of traveling, they approach the mountain that God has designated for the sacrifice. Abraham says to his servants,

"Stay here with the donkey while I and the boy go over there. We will worship and then we will come back to you" (Genesis 22:5).

Abraham's words seem strange in light of what he means to do. He implies that both he and Isaac will return when Isaac won't, and he says nothing about a sacrifice, despite having gathered wood for a burnt offering. He may have been concealing the truth from the servants to keep them from interfering. He also avoids calling his son by name, perhaps to detach himself from what he is about to do.

When they are finally alone, Isaac asks his father the obvious question:

"Father?"

"Yes, my son?" Abraham replies.

"The fire and wood are here," Isaac says, "but where is the lamb for the burnt offering?"

"God himself will provide the lamb for the burnt offering, my son," replies Abraham (Genesis 22:7).

When they reach the site, Abraham builds the altar and arranges the firewood. Then he binds his son and lays him on the altar. No words are exchanged, and there is no record of a struggle. Isaac is trusting his father and Abraham is trusting his God. Abraham raises his knife and is preparing to kill Isaac when an angel cries out from heaven:

"Abraham! Abraham!"

"Here I am," he replies.

"Do not lay a hand on the boy," he said. "Do not do anything to him. Now I know that you fear God, because you have not withheld from me your son, your only son."

Probably weeping for joy, Abraham sees a ram caught in the thicket and uses it as a burnt offering in the place of Isaac. He names the mountain "The Lord Will Provide" because God did indeed provide the sacrifice, just as Abraham had told Isaac. Abraham's great faith has survived God's testing, and God is tremendously pleased with Abraham. God swears by Himself that Abraham and his seed will be blessed because Abraham obeyed God and did not love his son Isaac more than he loved God.

Genesis 24: Isaac and Rebekah

After the testing, Abraham and Isaac return home. Sarah dies at the age of one hundred twenty-seven, and Abraham buys a cave from the Hittites so that he can bury Sarah in the land of promise (Genesis 23).

Abraham realizes that the end of his life is approaching, and he doesn't want Isaac to marry a Canaanite. Therefore he sends his servant on a quest for a match for Isaac in the longest chapter in the book of Genesis.

AMAZING ANCIENTS: The Servant

The Bible does not report the name of the servant Abraham sends in search of Isaac's match. It might have been Eliezer, the servant mentioned in Genesis 15:2-3 who was Abraham's heir before Isaac was born. Whoever he was, he was trusted with a tremendous responsibility: to find an acceptable match for Isaac in another country where he knew no one, and then convince the girl to leave her home, family and life far behind to come with him and marry a man she had never seen. His task was impossibly daunting.

This unnamed "servant" was no mere servant; rather, he was a trusted steward with full knowledge of all of Abraham's affairs. He was as loyal as if he were Abraham's own brother, and he certainly shared Abraham's faith in God. His prayers and deeds throughout the story demonstrate his faith. The story of finding Isaac's match is this servant's story.

SPOTLIGHT ON SCRIPTURE: The Promise

The servant promised to find a wife for Isaac from Abraham's own family back in Mesopotamia. Abraham made him seal his promise in an extremely personal way: the servant had to place his hand on Abraham's privates. The sign of God's covenant with Abraham was circumcision, and both Abraham and this most trustworthy servant had been circumcised. By placing his hand on the area that was circumcised, and by swearing in the name of the God who created the heavens and the earth, the servant was binding himself to Abraham's God. The lands where the servant would travel were filled with the gods of those lands. Abraham wanted to be certain that the servant would not turn aside from the true God.

The servant promised that he would not let Isaac marry a Canaanite, but that he would find a match from Abraham's family. Abraham also wanted to be certain that Isaac and Isaac's seed would not be corrupted. A Canaanite girl would bring her gods into the marriage. Abraham set a standard that would be upheld many years later, when Joshua led the Israelites into the Promised Land:

"Be careful not to make a treaty with those who live in the land; for when they prostitute themselves to their gods and sacrifice to them, they will invite you and you will eat their sacrifices. And when you choose some of their daughters as wives for your sons and those daughters prostitute themselves to their gods, they will lead your sons to do the same" (Exodus 34:15-16).

Finally, Abraham wanted to be certain that Isaac would not go back to Mesopotamia. The servant asks what to do if the girl will not return with him: should he take Isaac to her? Abraham insists that Isaac must remain in the Promised Land. If the girl refuses to come, Abraham says, the servant will be released from his promise. But he assures the servant that God will provide.

THE QUEST

The servant sets out with 10 camels carrying great quantities of supplies and gifts. This caravan is meant to impress upon Abraham's family that Abraham has become wealthy. When the servant reaches northern Mesopotamia (most likely near Haran, where Abraham had said goodbye to his family years before), he stops near a well.

The well was a most natural place for a traveler to go. Both he and the camels need water from the well, and it is also a gathering place for the townspeople, which makes it a good place to meet locals and learn who is who. The servant knows that it was customary for young unmarried women to draw their water in the evening, and he hopes to meet Isaac's match at the well. To that end, he prays a very bold and specific prayer.

FASCINATING FACTS: The Servant's Test

The servant asks the Lord to show him which girl he should choose for Isaac according to the following plan:

- He will ask an unmarried girl at the well to give him a drink from her jar.
- The chosen girl must not only give the servant a drink, but also offer to water his camels. In this way, the servant would know the Lord's choice for Isaac.

The servant's requests were not simple. According to the social customs of the time, young unmarried girls did not speak to men outside of their homes, much less to foreigners. Most girls would have turned away or been offended if a man spoke directly to them. Furthermore, drawing water was a lot of work. The jar was heavy, and Rebekah had already put in a full day's labor.

Nevertheless, Rebekah fulfills all of the prayer's requirements. She draws water for the servant, then offers to water the camels until they are full (which requires a great deal of water). She also turns out to meet other requirements: she is part of Abraham's family (his niece, so the servant has hit pay dirt), she is unmarried, and she is beautiful (not on the list but definitely a plus). God goes beyond the servant's requests in such a bountiful way that the servant has to bow down and worship.

When the servant realizes that Rebekah is God's choice for Isaac, he gives her gold bracelets for her arms and a ring for her nose. These gifts let Rebekah and her family know that he is hoping to arrange a marriage. She immediately tells her mother and her brother, Laban, what has happened. Laban is highly interested in this servant of a rich master, so he goes out to the well and invites the servant to dinner. The servant tells Abraham's story to Laban and Rebekah's father, Bethuel.

After hearing the long story, both Laban and Bethuel agree that Rebekah will make a good match for Isaac. Although they say that the decision is in the Lord's hands, their motivation is probably at least partly financial. If so, it works out well for them, because upon their agreement, the servant lavishes extravagant gifts on the family. Rebekah is not consulted about her own marriage, which is normal for a patriarchal culture.

Once the deal is made, the servant wants to take Rebekah and return to Abraham immediately, but Laban and Rebekah's mother ask him to delay.

"Let the girl remain with us ten days or so; then you may go" (Genesis 24:55).

"Ten days or so" in this context probably means ten months to a year. The servant knows that Abraham is weak, and wants to return right away. This time, the family consults Rebekah, and she agrees to go with the servant immediately.

When Rebekah and the servant arrive in the Negev, Isaac sees them from afar. He heads in their direction, and Rebekah sees him. She asks the servant who the approaching man is, and when she finds that he is her intended husband, she properly veils her face. Isaac and Rebekah are married in Sarah's tent. Their fairy-tale love story plays out beautifully:

"So she became his wife, and he loved her; and Isaac was comforted after his mother's death" (Genesis 24:67).

CRITICAL COMPARISONS between Hagar/Ishmael (Genesis 21) and Abraham/Isaac (Genesis 22)

Here are some interesting parallels between the Genesis stories of Ishmael and Isaac:

- 21:12 - God orders Ishmael to leave — 22:2 - God orders Isaac's sacrifice

(Most likely both boys were about the same age when the events happened, in their late teens)

- 21:14 - Leave in the morning with supplies — 22:3 - Leave in the morning with supplies
- 21:16 - Ishmael is about to die — 22:10 - Isaac is about to be sacrificed
- 21:17 - Angel calls to Hagar — 22:11 - Angel calls to Abraham
- 21:18 - Ishmael will be a great nation — 22:17 - Isaac's descendants will be innumerable
- 21:19 - God provides a well — 22:13 - God supplies a ram

ANCIENT HISTORY FOCUS

AMAZING ANCIENTS: HAMMURABI - 1792 BC

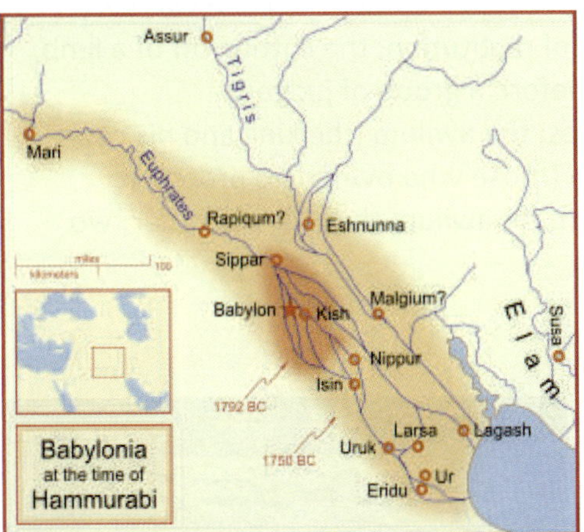

Ancient Babylon is about 55 miles south of present day Baghdad in Iraq. King Hammurabi inherited Babylon from his father in 1792 BC. Hammurabi began to expand his kingdom by taking the city of Kish and other small neighboring cities. He then formed alliances with a large northern kingdom and smaller cities in the south. He was a cautious king: he took his time about building up his army and patiently waited for his opportunity to expand his kingdom. When he finally made his move, he was able to gain control over a tremendous area stretching through southern Mesopotamia from Mari to Ur (see map).

THE CODE OF HAMMURABI

Hammurabi managed his vast kingdom by controlling the trade routes along the rivers and into the Persian Gulf. To maintain order, he developed a well-known book of laws called the Code of Hammurabi. The Code contained 282 laws and was written in Akkadian (the common language of his people) on 12 tablets.

FASCINATING FACTS: The Stele

In addition to the tablets, the Code of Hammurabi was also carved into an eight foot high black stele (a large stone monument) and displayed in public so that all could see it (although relatively few were sufficiently educated to actually read it). At the top of the stele is a carving that depicts Hammurabi receiving the laws from the god Shamash. Shamash was the sun god, and one of his attributes was justice. Just as the sun chased away darkness, so Shamash supposedly exposed wrong and injustice to the light.

Because of Hammurabi's well-known focus on law, the early founders of the United States chose to include a depiction of Hammurabi (along with 23 other lawgivers) on several U.S. government buildings, including a marble bas-relief on the United States Capitol (see picture) and a frieze on the Supreme Court building.

The stele was taken from Babylon in a battle against the Elamites and was lost for centuries. It was rediscovered in Iran in 1901, and now resides in the Louvre Museum in Paris.

The Prologue carved into the stele:

"When Anu the Sublime, King of the Anunaki, and Bel, the lord of Heaven and earth, who decreed the fate of the land, assigned to Marduk, the over-ruling son of Ea, God of righteousness, dominion over earthly man, and made him great among the Igigi, they called Babylon by his illustrious name, made it great on earth, and founded an everlasting kingdom in it, whose foundations are laid so solidly as those of heaven and earth. Then Anu and Bel called by name me, Hammurabi, the exalted prince, who feared God, to bring about the rule of righteousness in the land, to destroy the wicked and the evil-doers; so that the strong should not harm the weak; so that I should rule over the black-headed people like Shamash, and enlighten the land, to further the well-being of mankind."

Hammurabi's laws were sorted into groups: he had laws to govern business, labor, personal property, real estate, and family life. The laws were strict and harsh, and placed responsibility for crimes not only on the criminals, but also in some cases on anyone who might possibly have prevented a crime. The code was very specific, especially in the area of punishments. These included payment of restitution, the cutting off of a limb, enslavement, and of course death. The death sentence required a trial before a group of judges.

The Code of Hammurabi divided the population into three classes: the awilum (the king and his court, landowners, high officials, craftsmen and professionals), the muskingum (those who owned no property, beggars) and the wardum (slaves). Penalties for offenses were less severe for awilum than for the other two classes.

SOME OF HAMMURABI'S LAWS:

- If any one steals the property of a temple or of the court, he shall be put to death, and also the one who receives the stolen thing from him shall be put to death.
- If any one receive into his house a runaway male or female slave of the court, or of a freedman, and does not bring it out at the public proclamation of the major domus, the master of the house shall be put to death.
- If fire break out in a house, and some one who comes to put it out cast his eye upon the property of the owner of the house, and take the property of the master of the house, he shall be thrown into that self-same fire.
- If any one be too lazy to keep his dam in proper condition, and does not so keep it; if then the dam break and all the fields be flooded, then shall he in whose dam the break occurred be sold for money, and the money shall replace the corn which he has caused to be ruined.
- If conspirators meet in the house of a tavern-keeper, and these conspirators are not captured and delivered to the court, the tavern-keeper shall be put to death.
- If any one fail to meet a claim for debt, and sell himself, his wife, his son, and daughter for money or give them away to forced labor: they shall work for three years in the house of the man who bought them, or the proprietor, and in the fourth year they shall be set free.

FASCINATING FACTS: Mesopotamian Pottery

Photo courtesy of Fabien Dany: Iran Bastan

Pottery is among the most abundant of ancient artifacts because it was widely used and lasts practically forever. It was inexpensive to make, and when it was broken, the discarded pieces remained for centuries to be discovered by archaeologists.

In the area of Mesopotamia, the broken dishes were often decorated with geometric designs. The base was either creamy white or buff in color, and the geometric designs were painted in black (now faded) or reddish brown. The vessels came in all shapes and sizes, and were used not only for eating, but also for transporting and storing food.

FASCINATING FACTS: The Babylonian Calendar

The Babylonians were people of the moon, as the Egyptians were people of the sun. The Babylonian sun god Shamash was an offspring of the moon god Nannar, and so the sun was subordinate to the moon. This thinking carried over into their calendar.

The Babylonian calendar was based on 12 lunar months, each named for a different god. Because the actual time between full moons is 29.53 days, 12 lunar months added up to a year of 354 days. This was 11 days short of a true solar year, so occasionally the Babylonians inserted an extra month (by decree from the king) to make up the difference. Later, they devised more complex schemes to keep the months consistent with the seasons of the year.

The year began in the spring and was divided into three sections: beginning, middle and end. Instead of having a set number of days, each month began on the day when the priests observed a new crescent moon at sunset. For the Babylonians (and later the Hebrews and Muslims) the day began at sunset rather than sunrise.

The Hebrews adopted the Babylonian calendar during the 6th century BC (500-600 BC) during their time in Babylonian captivity.

GEOGRAPHY FOCUS

Photo courtesy of Hansueli Krapf: Portugal-Porto Moniz

The Seas of the Earth

DID YOU KNOW…

- Seas are smaller than oceans, but are still very large. Most are directly connected to the oceans and contain salt water like the oceans (with a few exceptions).
- Most seas are surrounded by land in three directions and are connected to an ocean in the fourth direction (again, there are exceptions).
- The globe contains about 100 seas (different people count them differently).
- Examples of large seas are the Mediterranean Sea, the Caribbean Sea, the Arabian Sea and the South China Sea.
- The words "ocean" and "sea" are often used interchangeably. We will stick with the common convention of five oceans: Pacific, Atlantic, Arctic, Indian and Southern.

Chapter 6

The Assyrians, Gilgamesh and Jacob

BIBLE FOCUS

GIANTS OF THE FAITH: JACOB

FASCINATING FACTS: Isaac Trivia

The Bible tells little about Isaac that is not contained in either Abraham's story or Jacob's story. He acts as a transition figure between the other two patriarchs. But there are interesting facts about Isaac that set him apart from his father Abraham and his son Jacob:

1. Both Isaac and his brother Ishmael receive their names from God, and unlike Abram and Jacob, Isaac keeps his name.
2. Isaac never leaves the Promised Land. Both Abraham and Jacob live in Haran for a period of time, but Isaac always lives in the land of Canaan.
3. Isaac has only one wife and is faithful to her, despite 20 years of childlessness.
4. Isaac is a tiller of the soil. He puts down roots both agriculturally and literally.
5. Isaac lives longer than either Abraham or Jacob, to the ripe old age of 180.

THE LIFE AND TIMES OF JACOB

- **Genesis 25:19-21**: Isaac and Rebekah were married when Isaac was 40 years old. When he turned sixty, he prayed to the Lord for his barren wife. The Lord heard, and Rebekah became pregnant with twins. This was the second generation of patriarchs in which childlessness was a problem.

- **Genesis 25:23**: The twins wrestled in Rebekah's womb. Rebekah prayed to the Lord and He told her:

"Two nations are in your womb,
and two peoples from within you will be separated;
one people will be stronger than the other,
and the older will serve the younger."

- **Genesis 25:24-26**: Rebekah gave birth to twins. The first was full of life, with a full head of red hair and a ruddy complexion. They named him Esau, which meant "hairy"; he was also called Edom, which meant "red." The second was born grasping his brother's heel. This one they named Jacob, which could mean "he grasps the heel," or in a figurative sense "deceiver." Isaac definitely displayed his sense of humor in the naming of his sons.

- **Genesis 25:17-28**: As the boys grew up, the parents chose favorites. Isaac favored Esau, the wild, boisterous, manly child who hunted and roamed outside. Rebekah favored Jacob, the quiet, thoughtful child who stayed at home.

FASCINATING FACTS: Sibling Rivalry in the Bible

So far in Scripture we have encountered three pairs of brothers in which the younger was favored over the older: Cain and Abel, Isaac and Ishmael and now Jacob and Esau. The pattern doesn't end here. Other prominent younger brothers will be chosen over their older brothers as we move through the history of God's people: Joseph, Benjamin, David and Solomon.

- **Genesis 25:29-34**: One day Esau returned home from his roaming ravenously hungry. Jacob had made a red stew from a lentil plant that was plentiful in that area. Esau begged Jacob for some of his stew. Instead of simply giving it to Esau, Jacob decided to try to sell it to him. Jacob's price for the meal was Esau's birthright.
  Esau's hunger may not have been trivial: There was a famine in the land (Genesis 26:1). Esau's roaming may have been a fruitless hunting trip, in which he was trying to bring home food for the family in lean times. Jacob's stew was made from lentils (plants), not meat. Jacob may have orchestrated this encounter, knowing how hungry Esau would be and how little food was available to him. Esau agreed to Jacob's terms and ate his dinner, in the process turning his back on his rights as the firstborn son.

FASCINATING FACTS: The Birthright

Traditionally, the firstborn son had two advantages over his younger brothers: he would receive two portions of the inheritance to their one (for example, if there were three sons, the estate would be divided into four parts, and the firstborn would receive two while each younger son would receive one), and he would be head of the house. As head of the house, the firstborn would be responsible for any unmarried sisters (this is why Rebekah's brother Laban was part of the negotiations with Abraham's servant), for maintaining the younger brothers, for the care of any widows or orphans and for the affairs of the household. Double portions of the inheritance included double land. For Jacob and Esau, this meant that the one who had the birthright would get twice as much of the Promised Land as the other.

SCRIPTURE SPOTLIGHT: The Blessing in a Seven-Part Drama

Genesis 27:1-46 and 28:1-9

As blind, elderly Isaac nears the end of his life, he decides to get his affairs in order. He calls his son Esau in to give him his blessing as the firstborn son.

Act One: Isaac and Esau
Isaac calls his favored son Esau into his tent and tells him to bring some of Isaac's favorite foods for a blessing feast. Esau readily agrees, gathers his weapons and sets off for the wilderness. Rebekah overhears all of this.

Act Two: Rebekah and Jacob
Rebekah calls her favored son Jacob and tells him to prepare his father's favorite foods in Esau's place so that he can masquerade as Esau. Jacob readily agrees, scheming with his mother about how to pass himself off as Esau. He gathers his pots and pans and sets to work.

Act Three: Rebekah and Jacob
Jacob brings the food to Rebekah. She dresses him in Esau's clothes and covers him with goatskins to make his skin hairy.

Act Four: Isaac and Jacob
Jacob brings his food to blind Isaac, who is suspicious but takes it and eats it. Then Isaac touches and smells Jacob and is convinced that he is Esau. He gives him this blessing:

"May God give you of heaven's dew
And of earth's richness—
An abundance of grain and new wine.
May nations serve you
And peoples bow down to you.
Be lord over your brothers,
And may the sons of your mother bow down to you.
May those who curse you be cursed
And those who bless you be blessed."

Jacob leaves the tent in triumph.

Act Five: Isaac and Esau
Later, Esau brings his food to Isaac, who is shocked and dismayed to realize that he has been deceived. Both realize that Isaac has given Jacob the firstborn's blessing and placed him above Esau. Esau begs to be blessed, but Isaac has only this prophecy for Esau:

"Your dwelling will be
Away from the earth's richness,
Away from the dew of heaven above.
You will live by the sword
And you will serve your brother.
But when you grow restless,
You will throw his yoke
From off your neck."

Esau is outraged at all of this and threatens to kill Jacob. Rebekah, whose deceit has broken her relationship with her firstborn, is now terrified that she will also lose Jacob to Esau's wrath. She wants Jacob to go live with her brother Laban back in Haran until Esau cools off, but she doesn't have the authority to send him herself. So she tells Isaac she's afraid that if Jacob remains in Canaan, he might marry one of the local Hittite women.

Act Six: Isaac and Jacob
Isaac calls Jacob to his side and tells him to go back to Northern Mesopotamia and choose one of Laban's daughters to be his wife. Jacob leaves with his father's blessing.

Act Seven - Esau - After Esau hears that Jacob is leaving to marry within the clan and that Isaac has again blessed his brother, Esau realizes that his Canaanite wives are not acceptable to his father. He marries his uncle Ishmael's daughter (his cousin), in hopes that this will improve his father's opinion of him.

- **Genesis 28:10-15** - Jacob sets off for Haran. One night he lies down to sleep with a stone for a pillow. As he dreams, he has a vision of a heavenly stairway with God at the top and angels climbing up and down (perhaps he envisioned something like a ziggurat). In the vision, the Lord makes the same promises to Jacob that He has made to Abraham and Isaac before him:

"I am the LORD, the God of your father Abraham and the God of Isaac. I will give you and your descendants the land on which you are lying. Your descendants will be like the dust of the earth, and you will spread out to the west and to the east, to the north and to the south. All peoples on earth will be blessed through you

and your offspring. I am with you and will watch over you wherever you go, and I will bring you back to this land. I will not leave you until I have done what I have promised you."

- **Genesis 28: 16-22** - Jacob is changed by his vision. When he awakens, he acknowledges God for the first time in his life. He vows to the Lord that he will follow Him if God will care for him. He names the site of the vision Bethel ("house of God"), setting up his stone pillow as a pillar to mark the site and anointing it with oil.

- **Genesis 29:1-30** - Jacob arrives near Haran, where he goes directly to the well and asks a shepherd where he can find Laban. They point out a beautiful woman who happens to be Laban's daughter, Rachel. Jacob greets her with a kiss as a member of his family.

FASCINATING FACTS: Comparisons and contrasts between Jacob and Abraham's Servant

Jacob's journey in search of a bride parallels the journey of Abraham's servant in some ways:

Servant arrives in Haran with riches	Jacob arrives in Haran with nothing
Servant goes straight to the well	Jacob goes straight to the well
Servant is at the well in the evening	Jacob is at the well at noon
Servant encounters Rebekah at the well	Jacob encounters Rachel at the well
Servant finds out Rebekah is family	Jacob finds out Rachel is family
Rebekah waters servant's camels	Jacob waters Rachel's sheep
Servant rejoices and gives bracelets	Jacob rejoices and gives kiss
Rebekah runs home to tell her mother and Laban	Rachel runs home to tell Laban
Servant is invited home and negotiates for Rebekah	Jacob is invited home and negotiates for Rachel
Servant pays the bride price and Laban is satisfied	Jacob has no bride-price except his labor
Servant refuses to stay when invited	Jacob stays for 14 years, gaining two wives, sisters Rachel and Leah

SCRIPTURE SPOTLIGHT: Jacob's Children

Genesis 29: 31-35, 30: 1-24 and 35:16-18

The rivalry between the sisters was evident within a year of their wedding days. Leah begins to bear sons, but Rachel is barren (this is yet another generation of infertility). The battle of the sons begins....

SON #	NAME	MOTHER
1.	Reuben (means *He has seen my misery*)	Leah
2.	Simeon (means *One who hears*)	Leah
3.	Levi (means *attached*)	Leah
4.	Judah (means *praise*)	Leah
5.	Dan (means *He has vindicated*)	Rachel's servant Bilhah
6.	Naphtali (means *my struggle*)	Rachel's servant Bilhah
7.	Gad (means *good fortune*)	Leah's servant Zilpah
8.	Asher (means *happy*)	Leah's servant Zilpah
9.	Issachar (means *reward*)	Leah
10.	Zebulon (means *honor*)	Leah
11.	Joseph (means *may He add*)	Rachel
12.	Benjamin (means *son of my right hand*)	Rachel (she dies in childbirth)

Note: Before Rachel died she named her son Benjamin "Ben-Oni," which means *son of my trouble*. Jacob changed his name to Benjamin, *son of my right hand*.

Genesis 31- 33 continues the story of Jacob (and Esau).

- **Genesis 30:25-43** - Having served Laban for 14 years, Jacob has paid for his wives and wants to go home. Laban begs him to stay and tells Jacob that he may name his wages. Jacob feels that all of his work has gone to build up Laban's flocks, and he wants to build a flock of his own. At Jacob's suggestion, Laban agrees to give Jacob any sheep and goats which are spotted or speckled.

  Most of the sheep are white, and most of the goats are dark brown or white, so Jacob is apparently asking for only a small number of sheep and goats. But Jacob is an expert breeder, and he has God's help. He somehow manages to ensure that all of the best sheep and goats are born spotted or speckled. For his part, Laban tries to remove all of the spotted sheep so that Jacob will get nothing. Jacob proves to be the better of the two schemers, and his flock of spotted sheep grows large and strong.

- **Genesis 31** - Jacob takes his wives, his children and all of his livestock and secretly leaves Laban to return to Canaan. Unknown to Jacob, Rachel steals her father's household idols. Laban pursues them like thieves, but God tells Laban in a dream not to harm Jacob. When Laban catches up, he searches for his idols, but cannot find them because Rachel is sitting on them. Finally, Jacob and Laban agree to part ways.

- **Genesis 32:1-21** - Having dispensed with the disgruntled family member behind him, Jacob turns his attention to the one in front of him. He has not forgotten how he left matters with Esau. Hoping to appease Esau, he sends a message ahead to tell Esau that he is returning to Canaan. The messengers return to tell Jacob that Esau is approaching with 400 men. In real fear, Jacob divides his party into two groups so that Esau can't destroy all of them at once. He also prepares large gifts of sheep, goats, cattle and camels for Esau, sending them ahead in groups a good distance apart.

- **Genesis 32:22-32** - Jacob lags behind the rest of his group, waiting to see the results of all of his gifts to Esau. In the night, he has an odd encounter with a stranger and wrestles with him until morning. As dawn breaks and the stranger finds that Jacob will not be overpowered, the **stranger dislocates Jacob's hip with a touch**. Unable to fight, Jacob still refuses to let go unless the stranger blesses him. The stranger asks Jacob his name, and then tells him that Jacob will no longer be his name. From now on, he will be known as "Israel," which means *He struggles with God*. When Jacob asks the stranger's name in return, the stranger replies, "Why do you ask my name?" **Jacob realizes that he has wrestled with God**.

- **Genesis 33** - Jacob meets Esau. Just as Rebekah planned, Esau is no longer bitter toward Jacob. Twenty years have passed.

ANCIENT HISTORY FOCUS

ASSYRIA

When Hammurabi began to take over Mesopotamia, he had two large kingdoms to overcome. To the south was King Rim-Sin, who controlled the area around the cities of Ur and Uruk. To the north was Shamshi-Adad, who controlled the area from Mari and Assur down to Sippar (see map). Realizing that the northern king was stronger, Hammurabi formed an alliance with Shamshi-Adad and moved south against Rim-Sin.

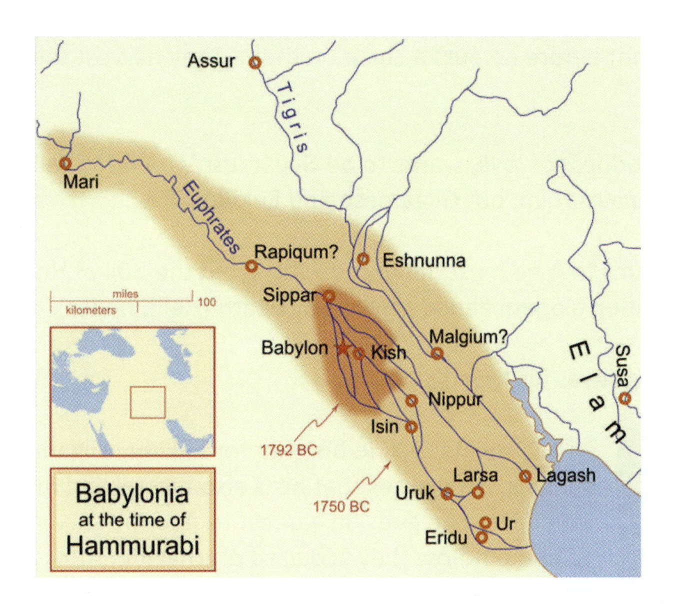

SHAMSHI-ADAD

Shamshi-Adad (who reigned from about 1813-1780 BC) gained his power the hard way. His father, who ruled Mari, had left the throne to his brother, so Shamshi-Adad had to scratch his way to the top. After some failed attempts and a time in exile, Shamshi-Adad established his kingdom in the town of Ekallatum. His next move was against the king of Assur. Assur (or Ashur) was an important commercial and religious center in the region. By controlling Assur, Shamshi-Adad controlled the trade routes into Anatolia (modern day Turkey). Next, he took Mari, gaining control over the trade routes into Syria. Control and taxation of trade routes means wealth for a ruler. Shamshi-Adad built one of the most powerful nations of his time. At the height of his power, he controlled a triangular region around Nineveh, Assur and Mari. He called his nation "Assyria," and appointed his sons as lesser kings, one in Mari and the other to the north.

Shamshi-Adad was a proud man. He claimed the title "King of All" and built temples for his gods, whom he believed had blessed him. He was a strong leader who created terror in nearby kingdoms by brutally killing the leaders of conquered cities and displaying their heads on stakes.

After Shamshi-Adad died, Hammurabi overtook first Mari, then Assur. Hammurabi became the "King of All." When Shamshi-Adad's sons died, Assyria disappeared from the map for over 100 years.

AMAZING ANCIENTS: GILGAMESH

Gilgamesh was the fifth king of Uruk, which he ruled around 2700 BC. Because numerous tales about him survive in the *Epic of Gilgamesh,* Gilgamesh is the best-known of all ancient heroes. These tales probably began as Sumerian oral legends and poems, which were later inscribed on 12 tablets by an Assyrian king named Ashurbanipal (who reigned from 668-627 BC). The tablets were rediscovered in a library in Nineveh.

FASCINATING FACTS: *The Epic of Gilgamesh*

Tablet I: Gilgamesh, builder of the city of Uruk with its magnificent ziggurats, orchards and fields, begins as a cruel king-- part god, part human, and possessed of super-human strength. The god Anu creates Enkidu, a wild man, to stop Gilgamesh. Enkidu is sidetracked by a trapper and learns the ways of humans.

Tablet II: When Enkidu finally meets Gilgamesh, they fight. Gilgamesh wins, but the two become friends and agree to go on a quest to cut cedar trees in Southern Iran (What else?).

Tablets III-V: Gilgamesh and Enkidu pursue their quest to cut the cedars, but they run into trouble with a demon named Humbaba. They

defeat and kill Humbaba, but not before he puts a curse on them. They harvest the trees, using some of them for Uruk's city gate.

Tablet VI: Ishtar, the goddess of love, wants to be Gilgamesh's lover. When he rejects and insults her, she sends the Bull of Heaven against him, but Gilgamesh and Enkidu kill it.

Tablet VII: Enkidu dreams that he must die because he killed the Bull of Heaven. He grows ill. After Enkidu suffers for 12 days, reciting a poem about a House of Death (Hell), he dies.

Tablet VIII: Gilgamesh grieves his friend's death.

Tablets IX-X: In his grief for Enkidu, Gilgamesh stops bathing and shaving. He realizes that he is also mortal and must one day die. Unable to accept this, he goes on a quest to find the survivors of the Great Flood, hoping to find out how they acquired eternal life. After a long and complex journey he reaches Utnapishtim, who is supposedly a Flood survivor.

Tablet XI: Utnapishtim tells Gilgamesh the Babylonian version of the Flood, and then tells him that if he remains awake for six days and seven nights (the length of the Flood, according to Utnapishtim), then Gilgamesh will become immortal. Gilgamesh tries, but instead ends up sleeping for six solid days. Next, Utnapishtim tells Gilgamesh about a plant found at the bottom of the ocean that will give him eternal life if he can find and eat it. Gilgamesh succeeds in finding the plant, but is afraid to eat it, so he brings it back to Utnapishtim for positive identification. On the way back, a snake eats his plant and becomes immortal. Gilgamesh loses his chance at eternal life.

Tablet XII: This "appendix" to the tale tells of items given to Gilgamesh by Ishtar in Tablet VI. Also, the spirit of Enkidu returns with a dire report about life in hell.

FASCINATING FACTS: Ancient Games

The ancients loved to play games as much as we do. One game they played was a form of backgammon (photo at right), which dates back to around 3,000 BC. In 2004, archaeologists found a backgammon board made of ebony wood with playing pieces carved from turquoise and agate. It even had dice.

There is an even older table game called Senet (photo at left courtesy of Deror Avi: A Senet game from the tomb of Amenhotep III - the Brooklyn Museum), or the Game of Thirty Squares. A Senet game was found in ancient Egyptian burial tombs dating back to 3,500 BC. Archaeologists are unsure exactly how Senet was played, although its name means "the game of passing." The game board was a grid with three rows of ten squares each.

FASCINATING FACTS: Cone Mosaics

Sumerians used clay "nails" or cones to create mosaics on walls and pillars in and around their buildings. They painted the nail heads red, black or white and pushed them into wet plaster. By placing them close together in geometric patterns, they created beautiful mosaics. One example of an Uruk temple cone mosaic resides in a German museum (see picture).

GEOGRAPHY FOCUS

The Rivers of the Earth

DID YOU KNOW...

- Rivers are bodies of flowing fresh water. They may contain some salt water near their mouths where they empty into a salty ocean or sea.
- Antarctica is the only continent that lacks rivers.
- Rivers flow into other rivers, a lake, a sea or an ocean.
- Ancient civilizations sprang up along major rivers because the rivers provided fresh water, fertile soil, fish and sanitation. They also provided transportation and trade routes.
- In modern times, rivers still provide for all of those needs. They have also become a source of hydroelectric power.
- Africa's Nile River is the longest river in the world; but South America's Amazon River carries more water than any other river.

The world's five longest rivers are:

1. The Nile River (Africa)
2. The Amazon River (South America)
3. The Yangtze River (Asia)
4. The Mississippi and Missouri Rivers (North America)
5. The Yellow River (Asia)

Photo courtesy of Dr Marian Muste, University of Iowa: Amazon River

Chapter 7

Joseph

BIBLE FOCUS

GIANTS OF THE FAITH: JOSEPH

FASCINATING FACTS: Joseph

- Joseph was the eleventh son of Jacob, but only the first child of Rachel, the wife Jacob loved best. Rachel had to wait many years before she finally conceived Joseph, and she died giving birth to her second child, Joseph's younger brother Benjamin.
- Joseph was Jacob's favorite son, at least partly because he was Rachel's.
- The story of Joseph covers chapters 37-50 in the book of Genesis. It is one of the longest stories in the Bible, far longer than the creation story or the flood story.
- The Lord does not speak directly to Joseph as He did to Abraham, Isaac and Jacob; there are no direct revelations or miracles in Joseph's story. Yet God's guiding hand is apparent throughout the story, and Joseph is quick to acknowledge God's part in what happens to him.
- Joseph's sons Manasseh and Ephraim became the fathers of two of the nation of Israel's twelve tribes. Each of his brothers gets only one tribe. In this way Joseph receives a double portion of the inheritance. What might this mean?

The story of Joseph is rich, filled with twists and turns that make the hearer want to laugh, cry, mourn, cringe and rejoice. It is beautifully written, designed to impress its exquisite detail on the hearer's memory. It begins in the land of Canaan, and ends in the land of Egypt. This entire section's central character is Joseph, except for chapter 38, which covers Judah and Tamar (This chapter is optional; use family discretion).

The story begins with Jacob's family in Hebron (see map).

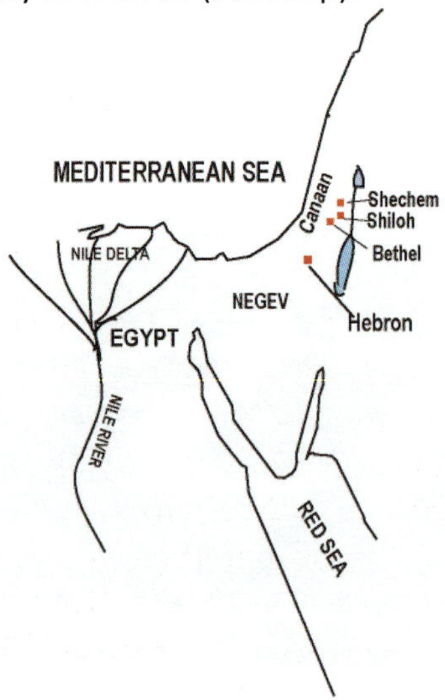

TROUBLE WITH THE BROTHERS (Genesis 37)

Part One: Sibling Rivalry Turns To Hate (Genesis: 37:1-11)

The practice of choosing favorites in Abraham's family line began with Abraham (Ishmael and Isaac), and continued when Isaac favored Esau and Rebekah favored Jacob. The same thing happened in Jacob's family. In Chapter 6 we learned about the births of Jacob's twelve sons and of the rivalry between their mothers. That rivalry did not end when the boys were born, but was passed down to the sons. Rachel was Jacob's favorite wife, and so her firstborn son, Joseph, became Jacob's favorite son, even though he was eleventh in line. The other brothers noticed this, and grew jealous and bitter against Joseph. The events of verses 1-11 bring this hatred to a head.

Event One: While keeping the sheep with several of his brothers (those closest to him in age), Joseph brings his father a bad report about something his brothers were doing wrong. After this incident, whatever it is, Joseph is no longer a shepherd, but stays at home with his father.

Event Two: Jacob (Israel) gives Joseph a richly colored robe. The robe is probably similar to those worn by royalty-- long, colorful and finely made. This special robe symbolizes Joseph's importance in the family. When the brothers see Joseph's robe, they hate him for it.

Event Three: Joseph has two dreams that seem to mean that he will rule over his brothers and all of his family. When he tells his brothers of these dreams, they become extremely jealous and begin to contemplate murdering Joseph.

SCRIPTURE SPOTLIGHT: Two Dreams

In Genesis 37: 5-11, Joseph tells of two dreams.

In his **first dream**, his sheaf of grain stands straight, while his brothers' sheaves of grain bow down to it.

In his **second dream**, the sun and moon (representing his parents) and eleven stars (his 11 brothers) bow down to him. The dreams cause Joseph's brothers to hate him all the more. When he tells his father the second dream, Jacob rebukes him in shock.

Jacob and the brothers all ask the same basic question: "Will we bow down to Joseph as our ruler?" Living as shepherds as they do, none of them can foresee how they might one day bow to Joseph. In fact, the dreams are true: they will all be subject to Joseph in Egypt, and Joseph will receive the birthright as the firstborn. Many years later, when Moses blesses the tribe of Joseph (Deuteronomy 33: 13-17), he speaks of Joseph as the "prince among his brothers" and like a "firstborn bull." Like a firstborn son, Joseph receives a double portion of the Promised Land through his two sons, Manasseh and Ephraim.

Part Two: The Siblings Get Even (Genesis 37: 12-36)

The brothers take their flocks to Shechem to graze (see map). They would move the flocks constantly as they used up the available pasture and water. Apparently oblivious to his other sons' hatred of Joseph, Jacob sends Joseph to check on the brothers. When Joseph arrives in Shechem, they have already moved on to Dothan. He catches up to them there. When the brothers see Joseph approaching, wearing his royal robe, they seethe with rage and plot to kill him. The firstborn, Reuben, intervenes and convinces the others not to kill Joseph. His plan is to throw Joseph into a dry cistern (an open water storage pit), from which he later hopes to rescue him. As firstborn, Reuben is responsible for his brothers and their actions, and he doesn't want murder set to his account. He does not, however, try to quell the brothers' anger or speak in Joseph's defense. His hatred of Joseph is just as great as theirs.

The brothers strip Joseph of his robe and throw him into the dry cistern. Reuben leaves and the other brothers sit down to eat, probably within earshot of Joseph's frantic pleas for help and mercy.

Joseph Sold by his Brothers

When a caravan of Midianites (or Ishmaelites) ride by on their way to Egypt, Judah convinces the other brothers to retrieve Joseph from the cistern and sell him to the Midianites. In this way, he says, they won't have Joseph's blood on their hands, and they will get some money for him into the bargain. They sell their brother into slavery for twenty pieces of silver. Joseph goes with the Midianites, probably kicking and screaming.

Reuben returns to find the cistern empty and his brother gone. He tears his clothes in grief, not about what happened to Joseph, but about what will happen to Reuben himself when his father finds out. The brothers formulate a plan: they stain Joseph's robe with blood from a goat, then take it home and show it to Jacob, who believes that his son has been killed by a wild animal.

JOSEPH IN EGYPT (Genesis 39-41)

Part One: Joseph in Potiphar's house (Genesis 39)

Potiphar, a captain of the Egyptian guard, buys Joseph from the Ishmaelites. Now Joseph is far from his home without a single friend or family member. But he is not alone: Yahweh is with him.

SCRIPTURE SPOTLIGHT: God's Presence, the Theme of Genesis 39

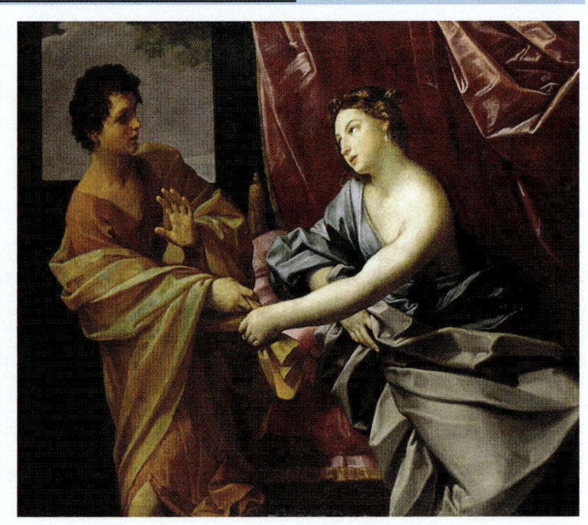

Genesis 39 begins and ends with bold statements about God's presence with Joseph. Joseph is sold to Potiphar, the captain of the Egyptian guard, and begins his life in exile. But

"God was with him,"

and all that Joseph touched was blessed, so Potiphar placed Joseph in charge of the entire household.

Then a problem arose with Potiphar's wife. Because Joseph was an attractive young man, she wanted to be romantically involved with him; but when he refused and ran from her, she was insulted and accused him of behaving indecently toward her. Potiphar believed his wife's story, and had Joseph thrown into jail.

But again, **"God was with him,"**

and all that Joseph touched was blessed, so the prison warden put Joseph in charge of the entire prison.

Part Two: Joseph in Prison (Genesis 40)

A cupbearer and a baker from Pharaoh's court get themselves into trouble and wind up in Joseph's prison. After a time, both men become upset about their disturbing dreams. They have seen dreams interpreted in Pharaoh's court, and they share the common belief that certain dreams are sent by various Egyptian gods as visions of the future. When they tell Joseph that they long for an interpreter, Joseph says, "Do not interpretations belong to God? Tell me your dreams." Thus Joseph declares to them his faith in the one God.

SCRIPTURE SPOTLIGHT: Two More Dreams (Genesis 40)

In his dream, the **chief cupbearer** sees a grapevine with three branches filled with grapes. The cupbearer takes the grapes, squeezes them into Pharaoh's cup and presents the cup to Pharaoh.

In his dream, the **baker** sees himself carrying three baskets of bread on his head for the Pharaoh, but birds were eating the bread out of the basket.

Joseph interprets the cupbearer's dream to mean that in three days, on Pharaoh's birthday, he would be restored to his position as chief cupbearer.

Joseph interprets the baker's dream to mean that in three days, he will be executed.

Both of these things happen just as Joseph predicts.

Joseph asks the cupbearer to tell the Pharaoh about him after he is restored to the court, but the cupbearer forgets, so Joseph remains in prison.

Part Three: Joseph Rises to Power (Genesis 41:1-45)

Two more years pass, and Joseph is still in prison. Then Pharaoh has two dreams.

SCRIPTURE SPOTLIGHT: Pharaoh's Two Dreams

Pharaoh has two dreams that neither the magicians nor the wise men of Egypt can interpret:

In **dream one**, seven fat cows come out of the Nile River and graze on the banks. Then seven emaciated cows come out and stand beside the fat cows. The emaciated cows then eat the fat cows, yet are unchanged in appearance.

In **dream two**, seven healthy heads of grain are growing on a single stalk. Beside them, seven other heads of grain are being scorched by the wind so that they are thin and barren. Then the thin heads of grain swallow the healthy heads.

After everyone else fails to interpret Pharaoh's dream, the cupbearer finally remembers Joseph and tells Pharaoh about the Hebrew boy who correctly interpreted his own dream. Pharaoh immediately sends for Joseph.

Before Joseph gives Pharaoh the interpretation, he gives credit to God:

"God will give Pharaoh the answer he desires."

Then he tells Pharaoh this: The seven healthy cows and the seven healthy heads of grain stand for seven good years. The seven emaciated cows and the seven thin heads of grain stand for seven years of famine. God is going to bring seven years of abundance to Egypt, but they will be followed by seven years of famine, and Egypt must prepare itself during the good years for the bad years to follow.

Realizing that the Spirit of the Lord is with Joseph, Pharaoh makes him his second in command (this is the third time that Joseph has been placed over everything his master owns).

Pharaoh gives Joseph three items to wear: **a signet ring**, which allows Joseph to sign orders in the name of Pharaoh; **fine linen of the same sort that would later be used in the Tabernacle**; and a **gold chain**. The gold chain was a well known Egyptian symbol, one of the highest distinctions a Pharaoh could bestow. Joseph also receives a chariot and rides before the people, who bow in his presence. Finally, Joseph receives a wife. Joseph is now 30 years old and has been in Egypt for 13 years.

Part Four: Joseph as Ruler (Genesis 41: 46-57)

Joseph begins to travel throughout Egypt, gathering and storing enormous amounts of grain from each city. During this time before the famine he has two sons, Manasseh (God has made me forget) and Ephraim (God has made me fertile).

SCRIPTURE SPOTLIGHT: Manasseh and Ephraim (Genesis 48)

Joseph's two sons provide yet another example of a younger son winning out over an older. When Jacob finally arrives in Egypt (later in the story), he adopts Joseph's two sons into his own family, giving them a share of the inheritance as if they were Jacob's own sons. As Jacob (Israel) prepares to bless the two boys, he places his right hand on Ephraim, the younger son, and his left hand on Manasseh, the older. This is backwards: the right hand signifies the firstborn. Jacob has to cross his arms to do this.

Joseph tells his father that his hands are backwards, and that Manasseh is older:

"No, my father, this one is the firstborn; put your right hand on his head."

Jacob responds:

"I know, my son, I know. He too will become a people, and he too will become great. Nevertheless, his younger brother will be greater than he, and his descendants will become a group of nations.

He blessed them that day and said,
'In your name will Israel pronounce this blessing:
'May God make you like Ephraim and Manasseh.'
So he put Ephraim ahead of Manasseh."

In fulfillment of Jacob's blessing, Ephraim became the most dominant of the tribes in the Kingdom of Israel and the name Ephraim became synonymous for the entire Kingdom.

When the famine arrives as Joseph predicted, Egypt is prepared. Joseph begins to ration the grain, first to Egyptians and then to foreigners who begin to travel to Egypt to buy grain.

THE BROTHERS IN EGPYT (Genesis 42-45)

Back in Canaan, Jacob's family is feeling the famine's effects. When he hears that Egypt has grain for sale, Jacob sends the brothers to buy some.

The next several chapters cover the brothers' two journeys to Egypt. The two journeys are parallel in some ways.

First Journey:	Second Journey:
• The 11 brothers travel to Egypt to buy grain (Benjamin stays at home with Jacob).	• The 11 brothers travel to Egypt to buy grain (they bring Benjamin along, as well as double payment because their first payment was returned to them).
• The 11 brothers approach Joseph, Pharaoh's second in command, and bow before him.	• The 11 brothers arrive in Egypt, tell their story to Joseph's steward and then bow before Joseph when they meet him.
• Joseph recognizes his brothers, but they do not recognize him.	• Joseph recognizes Benjamin, but the brothers still do not recognize him.
• Joseph accuses them of being spies and throws them in prison for three days.	
• Joseph weeps.	• Joseph weeps.
• Joseph keeps Simeon and sends the rest away, demanding that they come back with Benjamin.	

• Joseph orders their sacks filled and their silver (money) returned.	• Joseph orders their sacks filled and their silver returned. He adds his personal silver cup to Benjamin's sack.
• The 10 brothers leave Egypt, but soon realize that their silver has been returned to their sacks.	• The 11 brothers leave Egypt, but soon realize that their silver has been returned and that Benjamin has Joseph's cup.
• The 10 brothers tell their father that Simeon has been kept captive and that they must take Benjamin back with them.	
• Jacob grieves the loss of Joseph, Simeon and now Benjamin.	
	• Fearing trouble over the cup, the 11 brothers return to Egypt. Joseph demands Benjamin as his slave in payment for the supposed theft. Judah begs for mercy and offers himself in Benjamin's place.
	• Joseph weeps.
	• Joseph reveals himself to his brothers.

FASCINATING FACTS: Forgiveness for the Brothers

For twenty years, Joseph has been estranged from his family. His father has thought him dead, and his own brothers have sold him into slavery. So when he sees his brothers, Joseph does not immediately reveal his identity. He needs to know for sure what sort of men his brothers have become.

- The Accusation: Joseph accuses them of being spies three times, then puts them in prison for three days so that he can watch them. The brothers reflect that this hardship must be God's punishment for their horrible treatment of Joseph all of those years ago. Joseph weeps upon hearing of their remorse.

- Simeon held hostage: Joseph holds Simeon to see whether the others will come back for him or simply abandon him. Back in Canaan, the brothers beg Jacob to allow Benjamin to return with them so that they can rescue Simeon. Reuben even offers his own sons to his father as a sacrifice if they fail to bring Benjamin back. But Jacob will not bargain for Benjamin, the only surviving son of his favorite wife Rachel. Only when the family begins to starve again does Jacob relent.

- The Silver: In yet another test, Joseph returns the brothers' silver to see what they'll do with it. Years ago, they had sold him for 20 pieces of silver. Joseph wants to see how they handle having their treasures returned. If they keep quiet about it, he will know that they still love money more than their brothers. But when they return, they bring the silver back.

- The Meal: When the brothers return with Benjamin, Jacob welcomes them and releases Simeon. He still does not reveal himself to them. He eats with them, questions them about their father and makes sure that Benjamin has the best of everything. In preparation for his final test, he plants his personal silver cup in Benjamin's sack for the return journey.

- The Final Test: Joseph sends his steward after the departed brothers, and he finds the cup in Benjamin's sack. The brothers return, and Joseph sets them a final test: Because Benjamin stole the cup, Joseph says, Benjamin must become his slave. The rest may go free. Instead of agreeing, Judah offers himself in Benjamin's place. In a beautiful speech, Judah tells Joseph of the special love that Jacob has for Benjamin and his lost Joseph as the sons of his favorite wife. Yet Judah is no longer bitter over this. His love for his father and his desire to do what is right overrides his hatred and bitterness. He begs for his father to be allowed to keep this boy whom he loves more than any of the rest.

When Joseph finally believes in his brothers' change of heart, he breaks down and weeps once more, then finally reveals himself to them. He forgives them and offers them this absolution for their sin:

"...it was not you who sent me here, but God."

He sends them back to Canaan with carts so that they can bring Jacob and the rest of the family back to Egypt to ride out the famine.

FASCINATING FACTS: Judah

Judah was the fourth son of Leah but by the end of the Joseph story, the leadership for the family has been passed on to him. Reuben lost his place as firstborn when he slept with his father's slave, Bilhah (Genesis 35). Simeon and Levi lost favor for their revenge in Genesis 34 against the Shechemites. In Jacob's blessing of his sons, he passes over the first three sons (Genesis 49:3-12) and gives Judah the firstborn blessing, saying, "Your father's sons will bow down to you."

In fulfillment of this blessing, Judah's tribe became one of the strongest and it eventually became the southern kingdom when Solomon died (Kingdom of Judah). Out of Judah's line, Jesus was born.

FASCINATING FACTS: Jesus' Genealogy to this point

Abraham - Isaac - Jacob - Judah and Tamar

JACOB GOES TO EGYPT (Genesis 46-50)

All through Joseph's long story, God speaks directly only once, and it is not to Joseph. When the brothers return a second time from Egypt and tell them that Joseph has invited the entire family there, God speaks to Jacob, reassuring him that his promises to Jacob will remain with him in Egypt (Genesis 46:2-4). The great nation promised to Abraham, Isaac and Jacob will still be fulfilled. God also promises that Jacob will not be left in Egypt, but that his body will be brought back to the Promised Land:

"And God spoke to Israel in a vision at night and said, "Jacob! Jacob!"
"Here I am," he replied.
"I am God, the God of your father," he said. "Do not be afraid to go down to Egypt, for I will make you into a great nation there. I will go down to Egypt with you, and I will surely bring you back again. And Joseph's own hand will close your eyes."

When Jacob arrives in Egypt, his family receives the best land. During the famine, other Egyptians are forced to sell their land to the Pharaoh in exchange for food. But thanks to Joseph, Jacob's family prospers and grows in their new land.

SCRIPTURE SPOTLIGHT: Jacob's Bones

Jacob wanted to be buried in the Promised Land, not in Egypt. God had promised Jacob that He would bring him back to Canaan, so after he blessed his sons, he instructed them about what to do with his remains (Genesis 49:29-31):

"Then he gave them these instructions: 'I am about to be gathered to my people. Bury me with my fathers in the cave in the field of Ephron the Hittite, the cave in the field of Machpelah, near Mamre in Canaan, which Abraham bought as a burial place from Ephron the Hittite, along with the field. There Abraham and his wife Sarah were buried, there Isaac and his wife Rebekah were buried, and there I buried Leah.'"

When Jacob died, Joseph took his father's body back to Canaan and buried him in the cave along with Abraham and Isaac, just as his father asked.

SCRIPTURE SPOTLIGHT: Joseph's bones

After Jacob dies, Joseph reaffirms his forgiveness to his brothers. He then makes them promise to return his body to the Promised Land. This promise is not fulfilled until the time of Moses, 300 years later. When Moses took the children of Israel out of Egypt, he

"Took the bones of Joseph with him because Joseph had made the sons of Israel swear an oath. He had said, 'God will surely come to your aid, and then you must carry my bones up with you from this place'" (Exodus 13:19).

Later, Joshua buries Joseph's bones:

"And Joseph's bones, which the Israelites had brought up from Egypt, were buried at Shechem in the tract of land that Jacob bought for a hundred pieces of silver from the sons of Hamor, the father of Shechem. This became the inheritance of Joseph's descendants" (Joshua 24:32).

ANCIENT HISTORY FOCUS

FASCINATING FACTS: Paddle Dolls

Ancient Egyptian paddle dolls are the earliest known toys. They were flat, wooden dolls shaped like paddles. Their hair was made from short strings of clay or wooden beads. Their clothes were carved into the wood or painted on.

Paddle dolls had no legs. This omission may have been intended to keep the dolls from running away, as many paddle dolls have been discovered in tombs. Their purpose there may have been to provide the pharaoh with protection, entertainment or companionship in the afterworld.

Chapter 8

Egypt's Middle Kingdom

ANCIENT HISTORY FOCUS

EGYPTIAN PYRAMIDS

The Ancient Egyptians believed that their dead went on to another life in the afterworld, and that the soul could live on only if the body was preserved from breaking down. Therefore they went to great lengths to preserve the body of the deceased, and also to protect it from thieves. Buried with the body were treasures that the deceased would need in the next world. These unwatched treasures were of great interest to grave robbers.

During the Old Kingdom, the Egyptians buried their dead in "mastaba" tombs. These were flat, rectangular structures with sloping sides, built of brick or stone. The body was placed deep in a sealed chamber, accompanied by all the comforts of home. The builders of the mastaba went to great lengths to hide the entrance in order to protect the deceased. They used false doors, filled the shaft with stones, or created an elaborate system of sliding doors to keep the sarcophagus safe from grave robbers.

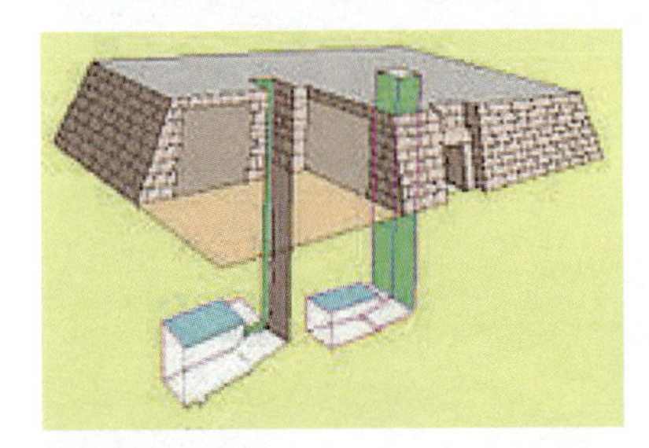

As Egypt's wealth and empire grew, the pharaohs' opinions of themselves grew as well, and the mastaba was no longer good enough for the gods they considered themselves to be. They began to build pyramid tombs with pointed tops that reached to the sky. The earliest known pyramid is the Pyramid of Djoser.

EGYPT'S OLD KINGDOM (3000 - 2100 BC)

FASCINATING FACTS: The Pyramid of Djoser

The oldest known Egyptian pyramid is the Pyramid of Djoser, built around 2630 BC for King Djoser of the 3rd Dynasty. It was a step pyramid 62 meters (203 feet) tall, located near present-day Cairo. It was designed to serve as a gigantic stairway so that the deceased pharaoh could make his way up to the heavens.

The Pyramid of Djoser was built by Imhotep, an architect, builder and sculptor who was so well revered that he was deified by later Egyptians. His pyramid was remarkable for both its size and its innovative use of dressed stone. Imhotep began with a mastaba tomb (see above), then added another mastaba on top of it, followed by four more for a total of six levels. The result was the first step pyramid made entirely of stone.

Around Djoser's pyramid, Imhotep built a complex of buildings that resembled pharaoh's palace and its surrounding buildings. Many of them were fakes, shell buildings decorated on the outside and filled with rubble. It is assumed that this complex was built so that when King Djoser died, his palace and buildings would go with him into the afterlife. The entire complex was enclosed by a 30 foot wall with 14- 15 entrances, only one of which was functional. The scale of this work is almost unimaginable.

Under the structure was an elaborate maze of tunnels, chambers, galleries and shafts that totaled over 3 ½ miles long. These were built both for religious purposes and to discourage grave robbers from stealing the pharaoh's treasures. A 90-foot shaft led to the burial chamber. Despite all of this, by the time of the 3rd Dynasty, all that was left of Djoser's remains and treasures was his mummified left foot.

THE GREAT PYRAMID OF GIZA (2550 BC)

Photo courtesy of Nina Aldin Thune: Kheops pyramid

The largest pyramid of all is the Great Pyramid of Giza, built for King Khufu (Cheops) of the 4th Dynasty. Part of an immense complex of monuments to the dead known as a *Necropolis* ("city of the dead"), the Great Pyramid measures 756 feet on each side and weighs almost 6 million tons. It took over 20 years to build, and during construction it required about 800 tons of stone per day (Imagine bringing in 40 large modern dump truck loads per day-- without dump trucks!). At 480 feet high, it was the tallest man-made structure for over 3,800 years. It remains substantially intact today, although it has lost its smooth outer layer of casing stone and its *pyramidion,* a large apex stone.

Inside the pyramid were three chambers: a King chamber, a Queen chamber, and an unfinished chamber deep inside. Surrounding the Great Pyramid were smaller buildings including temples, mastaba tombs for court nobles and even four smaller pyramids.

Beside the Great Pyramid sits a statue, the Great Sphinx of Giza. It is aligned with the Pyramid, and the most popular theory holds that it was commissioned by Khufu as a guardian for the tombs. Carved from the bedrock, it has the body of a lion and the head of a king or a god. It remains the largest statue in the world at 65 feet high and 240 feet long.

Because the Sphinx sits in the desert, it has been buried by sandstorms several times since its creation thousands of years ago. Its head has been battered by the sand, and its original paint wore off long ago except for a bit around one ear. Most unfortunately, the Sphinx has lost its nose. Endless theories have grown up around the loss of the nose. One suggests that a Muslim fanatic chopped it off after catching Egyptian peasants making offerings to the Sphinx in hopes of a good harvest in 1378 AD. If this is true, he must have built a tall scaffold first, because the nose sits at least 40 feet high (but perhaps the sphinx was half buried in sand at the time?). Supposedly, the fanatic was hanged. This story is impossible to verify, and is only one of several. No one really knows how the Sphinx lost its nose.

EGYPT'S MIDDLE KINGDOM (2040 BC - 1782 BC)

As the Old Kingdom of Egypt declined (3000 - 2100 BC), the kingdom split into dozens of independent states. This period of time is known as the First Intermediate Period. The Middle Kingdom began with the 11th Dynasty in 2040 BC, but Egypt's real reunification began under Pharaoh Amenemhet I and the 12th Dynasty in 1991 BC.

Photo courtesy of John Campana: Funerary relief of Amenemhet I from El-Lisht

Amenemhet I was not of royal lineage. Instead, he was a powerful military general who managed to take the throne and establish Egypt's 12th Dynasty. Amenemhet I ruled Egypt from 1991 to 1962 BC. He used several tactics to reunify Egypt: He moved his capital close to the all-important Delta area; he instituted a military draft to increase the size and power of his army; and he centralized power under his government, limiting the power of Egypt's nobles. He also built a string of fortresses called "The Wall of the Prince" along the eastern Delta to protect Egypt's border with Asia. Egypt prospered under Amenemhet I.

Amenemhet I expanded his empire by pushing his army south into exotic Nubia, gaining control of Nubian trade routes.

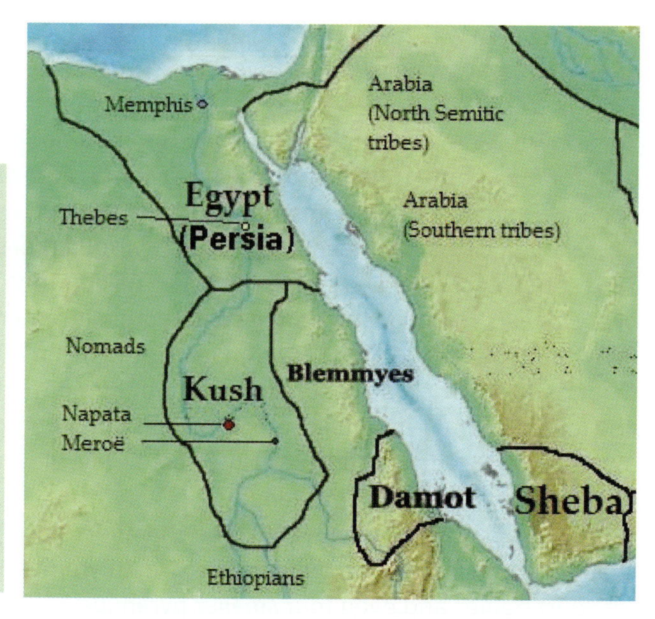

FASCINATING FACTS: Nubia

In ancient times, Nubia (Kush on the map) was an independent African kingdom situated in modern Sudan and southern Egypt. It was one of the earliest black civilizations, and was a land of great wealth. The Nubians traded exotic animals, ivory, gold and ebony to the Egyptians. Nubia was conquered by Egypt during Amenemhet I's reign and renamed *Kush*. Amenemhet erected forts along the Nile to protect his captured territory. Kush was held by Egypt for so long that the Nubians began to consider themselves Egyptians.

Late in his reign, Amenemhet I established a successful co-regency with his son Senusret I, which lasted for 10 years. Around 1962 BC, Amenemhet I was assassinated (by his own guards?) and his son took the throne. The 12th Dynasty reigned from around 1991 - 1802 BC.

BIBLE FOCUS

A Possible Overlay of the Twelfth Dynasty with the Biblical Story

No one can say with certainty exactly how the Bible narrative fits in with what is known of Egyptian history, but here is one possible overlay:

Amenemhet I (reigned 1991 BC – 1962 BC)	1991 BC: Abraham dies
Senusret I (reigned 1971 BC – 1928 BC)	1930 BC: Jacob travels to Haran
Amenemhet II (reigned 1929 BC – 1895 BC)	1899 BC: Joseph taken to Egypt
Senusret II (reigned 1897 BC – 1878 BC)	1886 BC: Joseph released; 1879 BC: famine begins
Senusret III (reigned 1878 BC – 1843 BC)	1876 BC: Jacob moves to Egypt; 1859 BC: Jacob dies
Amenemhet III (reigned 1842 BC – 1797 BC)	1806 BC: Joseph dies
Amenemhet IV (reigned 1798 BC – 1790 BC)	
Sobekneferu (reigned 1790 BC - 1782 BC)	

THE HYKSOS TAKE OVER EGYPT

The 12th Dynasty of Egypt reached its peak under Amenemhet III. His son Amenemhet IV succeeded him, but he reigned for only one year and died without an heir. Amenemhet IV's wife, Queen Sobekneferu, took the throne, but the Pharaohs' power grew weak under her. This was the beginning of a new period in Egyptian history called the Second Intermediate Period (1782-1570).

During this Intermediate Period between the end of the Middle Kingdom and the beginning of the New Kingdom, the Hyksos invaded the eastern part of the Nile Delta. They had moved into Egypt earlier, but when the Egyptian dynasties weakened, the Hyksos seized power in 1663 BC and ruled Egypt as the 15th Dynasty.

FASCINATING FACTS: The Hyksos

The Hyksos were a people group of Semitic-Asiatic descent who first settled in northern Egypt during the 12th Dynasty. Their name meant "king-shepherds." In battle, the Hyksos used new weapons that the Egyptians had never seen before, the horse and chariot and the compound bow. They also introduced improved battle axes and advanced techniques to fortify their cities.

At the height of their power, the Hyksos ruled most of Lower Egypt and part of Upper Egypt. They ruled for about 150 years and probably had a friendly relationship with the Israelites, who lived in their region.

The Hyksos did not move into southern Egypt, but instead made alliances with the Nubians, who were by this time reestablishing their own kingdom apart from the Egyptians. Between the territories of the Hyksos and the Nubians, the Egyptians maintained control of the city of Thebes and its surrounding area (see map below). Conflict between the Egyptians and the Hyksos eventually led to the demise of the Hyksos Dynasty. Around 1567 BC, Ahmose I of the 18th Dynasty defeated the Hyksos and reunited Egypt once again. This was the end of the Second Intermediate Period and the beginning of the New Kingdom.

THE ISRAELITES BECOME SLAVES

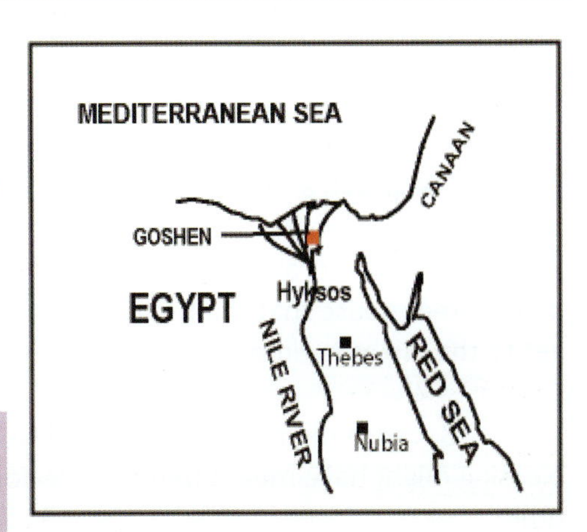

The Israelites began their time in Egypt at the end of the Book of Genesis as a family of seventy. Thanks to the influence of Joseph, they were given the land of Goshen, a fertile part of the Nile Delta. In the first chapter of the Book of Exodus they **"filled the land"** so extensively that **seven words** are used to describe their growth (Exodus 1:7):

"And the children of Israel were fruitful, and increased abundantly, and multiplied, and waxed exceeding mighty; and the land was filled with them."

FASCINATING FACTS: How many Israelites?

Exodus 1 doesn't say exactly how many Israelites there were when the Exodus began; but it does say that the entire land of Goshen (a region in Egypt's Nile Delta) was "filled with them." In the second year after the Israelites fled Egypt, Moses ordered a count (census) of all able-bodied Israelite men older than twenty (Numbers 1). The total was 603,550. This number did not include women, children, or Levite men (priests from the tribe of Levi, who did not fight). Taking all of these into account, the entire population may have been as many as two million or more. All of this population growth, from 70 to perhaps 2 million, took place in the 400 years that separated Jacob and Moses. The Jewish population's growth rate of just over 3 percent probably astounded the Egyptians. The Hebrews had obviously reversed their earlier infertility problems.

When the Hebrews' numbers grew large enough to alarm the Egyptians, Pharaoh ordered their midwives to kill all Hebrew baby boys in an attempt to slow down their rapid growth.

Exodus says that when a new king arose over Egypt, he became concerned about the Israelites' great numbers. This "new king" could have been a new Dynasty, possibly that of the Hyksos, who rose to power around 1663 BC. It could also have been Ahmose I of the 18th Dynasty, who drove the Hyksos out in 1567 BC. This second explanation makes some sense: after Ahmose I succeeded in driving out one set of Semitic invaders (the Hyksos), he might have been quick to view a second set of Semitic people (the Hebrews) as a threat.

This Pharaoh decided to do something about the problem of the Hebrews, so he conscripted them into slavery. The Bible indicates that he forced them to build two great cities, Pithom and Rameses. But this did not slow their growth.

FASCINATING FACTS: Pithom and Rameses

The cities of Pithom and Rameses appear frequently in ancient Egyptian writings, but Pithom is mentioned only once in the Bible (Exodus 1:11). The name *Pithom* means "House of Atum." In ancient Egyptian theology, Atum was the creator and finisher of the world, one of the most important Egyptian deities. Pithom is a lost city; no one knows where it lay, although various theories have been presented.

Rameses is mentioned four times in the Bible. In Genesis 47:11, *Rameses* is used in place of *Goshen* to indicate where the Israelites lived in Egypt. The city the Hebrews built was probably located in the northeastern Nile Delta in the choicest part of the land of Egypt. Ancient Egyptian poems extol the city's beauty and majesty. Rameses was also the name of several New Kingdom Pharaohs.

So Pharaoh increased the Hebrews' work load, and their lives became bitter. **Another series of seven words**, all from the Hebrew root meaning "to serve" or "to work," are used in the next three verses to indicate how oppressed they were (Exodus 1: 12-14):

"But the more they were oppressed, the more they multiplied and spread; so the Egyptians came to dread the Israelites and worked them ruthlessly. They made their lives bitter with hard labor in brick and mortar and with all kinds of work in the fields; in all their hard labor the Egyptians used them ruthlessly."

Even though the Israelites were forced to work in the harshest of conditions, they continued to multiply, and Pharaoh became all the more concerned about this growing threat. Finally, he took the barbaric step of calling in Shiphrah and Puah, two Hebrew midwives, and instructing them that they were to watch at the time of birth and kill any male Hebrew children. But Shiphrah and Puah were good Hebrew women, and as midwives they loved mothers and children. Even though they risked death by disobeying Pharaoh, they didn't kill the boys, making the excuse that the Hebrew women were too quick with their deliveries and that they were unable to get to the births in time.

Because the midwives refused to help Pharaoh exterminate Hebrew children, God blessed them. This blessing might have meant that the previously barren midwives could bear children of their own for the first time:

"So God was kind to the midwives and the people increased and became even more numerous. And because the midwives feared God, he gave them families of their own" (Exodus 1: 20-21).

FASCINATING FACTS: Midwifery

Midwives are women whose primary job is to help pregnant women deliver babies. Ancient Egyptian midwives held positions of prestige. Shiphrah and Puah were probably overseers of a large guild of midwives, as they could not have cared for the entire Israelite population alone.

Pregnant woman used a birthing stone or brick decorated with painted scenes of the birthing process. The woman would stand, kneel or squat over the brick and the midwife would position herself in front of the mother to catch the baby.

Exodus 1 ends with Pharaoh taking matters into his own hands, ordering "all his people" to throw every boy born into the Nile. Since Pharaoh was considered a god, his orders could not be ignored. He now had the entire nation of Egypt working to fulfill his goal of decreasing the Israelite population.

TIMELINE OF EGYPT'S OLD, MIDDLE AND NEW KINGDOMS

KINGDOM	ROUGH DATES	IMPORTANT PHARAOHS	DYNASTIES
Old Kingdom	3000 BC - 2100 BC	Djoser, Khufu	3 - 8
First Intermediate Period			9 - 10
Middle Kingdom	2040 BC - 1782 BC	Amenemhet I, Amenemhet III	11 - 12
Second Intermediate Period		(the Hyksos)	13 - 17
New Kingdom	1570 BC - 1070 BC	Ahmose I, Rameses II	18 - 20
Third Intermediate Period			21 - 25

GEOGRAPHY FOCUS

The Deltas of the Earth

DID YOU KNOW…

- A delta is the low, watery land that forms near a river's mouth. Delta soil tends to be rich and fertile.
- Delta land is partly formed from silt and soil that flowing river water carries along with it from places farther upstream.
- Deltas received their name from the Greek historian Herodotus, who noticed that the Nile Delta was shaped like the Greek letter Delta (a triangle).
- There are several large and well-known deltas, including the Ganges Delta (the world's largest), the Indus Delta, the Rhine Delta, the Danube Delta, the Volga Delta, the Mississippi Delta and the Yangtze Delta.
- The area where the Israelites lived and thrived before the Exodus was part of the Nile Delta.

Chapter 9

Egypt's New Kingdom

ANCIENT HISTORY FOCUS

EGYPT'S NEW KINGDOM (1570 – 1070 BC)

Ahmose I's expulsion of the Hyksos marked the beginning of the New Kingdom and the 18th Dynasty. This was a period of prosperity, a renaissance in art, massive building projects, increased foreign trade and conquest of nearby lands. Many of Egypt's best-known pharaohs were part of the 18th Dynasty. It was Egypt's golden age.

At the beginning of the 19th Dynasty, Egypt continued its rise to power. The Great Ramesses II was this Dynasty's most notable pharaoh. He reigned for 67 years, making peace with the Hittites and bringing peace and prosperity to the region. His successors could not maintain his kingdom, and by the end of the 19th Dynasty, Egypt was beginning to fall into chaos.

In the 20th Dynasty, Ramesses III made some headway by protecting the country from foreign invasion, but internal corruption and social turmoil prevented him from restoring Egypt to its former glory. From his death through the end of the 20th Dynasty, Egypt divided itself into factions.

The 18th Dynasty (1570 – 1292 BC)

Ahmose I 	Best known for ridding the country of the Hyksos.
Amenhotep I 	Continued his father's work, maintaining dominance over Nubia and the north. He was the first pharaoh to separate his tomb from his temple in order to protect his tomb from grave robbers. Other pharaohs followed this practice throughout the New Kingdom.

<table>
<tr>
<td>Thutmose I
</td>
<td>Either a military commander under Amenhotep I or a son from a lesser wife. It is possible that Thutmose I also reigned as co-regent before Amenhotep I died. During his reign he pushed Egypt's borders deep into Nubia. It was rumored that he personally fought the Nubian chief and brought the body back to Thebes hanging from the end of his boat. Thutmose I also extended his power into Canaan, fighting against the Hyksos all the way to the Euphrates River (see map).

Thutmose I was the first pharaoh to be buried in the Valley of the Kings.</td>
</tr>
<tr>
<td>Thutmose II</td>
<td>Thutmose II was only a third son of his father Thutmose I, but took the throne when his father died either because his older brothers had died or because he carried his father's name. He married his half-sister Hatshepsut to improve his royal position. He held the throne for fourteen years, maintaining the policies of his father.</td>
</tr>
<tr>
<td>Queen Hatshepsut
</td>
<td>One of only three queens to rule Egypt, Hatshepsut was ambitious and single-minded. Her father was Thutmose I, and she married her half-brother Thutmose II. She may have gained governing experience during her husband's reign. When her husband died, his son Thutmose III (who was not her son, but her step-son), took the throne. But because he was so young, Hatshepsut took control of the government as his regent. Hatshepsut reigned for 20 years, claiming full rights to the throne for two reasons: because her father wanted her to take the throne, and because she was the offspring of the god Amun, who spoke to her and affirmed that she was to be the pharaoh.

As pharaoh, Hatshepsut was often seen wearing the traditional pharaoh garb, including the head cloth adorned with the cobra and the false beard. She is best known for funding expeditions into Africa and commissioning hundreds of building projects throughout Egypt.

Hatshepsut is regarded by many scholars as the most likely candidate for the "Pharaoh's daughter" who rescued Moses from his papyrus basket in the Nile river and raised him as her son (Exodus 2:1-10).</td>
</tr>
</table>

Thutmose III 	Thutmose III spent the first 21 years of his "reign" watching from the sidelines as his step-mother ruled as pharaoh. When she died, he ruled in his own right for over 30 years. As soon as he came to full power, he erased his step-mother's name on many of her monuments. He immediately began a series of military conquests, engaging in at least 17 campaigns throughout his long reign. Under his rule, Egypt expanded north into Northern Syria and south deep into Nubia. Egypt's empire was at its largest under Thutmose III. His son Amenhotep II co-ruled with him for his last few years as Pharaoh. If Hatshepsut was indeed Moses's rescuer, then Thutmose III would be the Pharaoh who sought to kill Moses after Moses killed the Egyptian slave master for beating the Hebrew slave (Exodus 2:11-15). If so, he would have known Moses as a child, and they might possibly have been raised in the same household. Moses fled to Midian and lived there in exile for about 40 years. Sometime during that 40 years, that pharaoh died, enabling Moses to return to Egypt.
Amenhotep II 	Amenhotep II reigned as pharaoh for 23 years after his father died. He continued his father's military campaigns, especially in Syria. During one such campaign, Amenhotep captured and executed seven Syrian princes, then hung their bodies in the temple at Thebes. Amenhotep was reputedly extremely athletic, and stories abounded about his prowess in bow hunting and rowing. If Hatshepsut was Moses's rescuer and Thutmose III was the one who threatened Moses, then Amenhotep II would be the Pharaoh of the Exodus, the one who endured the 10 plagues and hardened his heart repeatedly, the one who gave the Hebrews permission to leave and then pursued them to the Red Sea/Reed Sea (Exodus 7-14).
Thutmose IV 	Thutmose IV reigned for about 9 years, spending most of his reign building up government bureaucracy and cutting the size of the military. Thutmose IV is best known for the *Dream Stele*, a carved stone that sits between the paws of the Great Sphinx. Thutmose IV claimed that as a prince, he once fell asleep between the paws of the Great Sphinx and had a dream there. In the dream, a god told him that he would be pharaoh if he cleared the sand from around the Sphinx. As pharaoh, Thutmose IV cleared away the sand and restored the Great Sphinx, finally commissioning the Dream Stele to sit between its paws and relate the story of the dream. Some have suggested that the story of the dream sounds like an elaborate effort to make Thutmose IV's shaky claim to the kingship more solid. It is known that Thutmose IV was not Amenhotep's oldest son. Is it possible that the firstborn son, the one with the legitimate claim to the throne, died in the Plague on the Firstborn, the tenth of the Lord's plagues on the Egyptians (Exodus 11)?

Amenhotep III 	Amenhotep III's 38-year reign was peaceful. He spent his time building monuments and encouraging the arts. Trade flourished during his reign, and he ensured peace with foreign countries by marrying his daughters to their kings. Amenhotep III is still on a very short of the richest people of all time.
Amenhotep IV (Akhenaten) 	Amenhotep IV was a younger son of Amenhotep III, but he too succeeded his father after an older brother died. The primary focus of his 17 year reign was the establishment of a monotheistic (believing in one god) religion in Egypt. Egyptians had always been polytheists (believing in many gods), but Amenhotep IV sought to change this and bring the focus of worship onto the sun-god, Aten (Aten means disk). Because his name associated him with a different god, Amun, Amenhotep changed his name to Akhenaten, which meant "servant of Aten." Akhenaten saw himself as an intermediary between the Aten and the people. He forced the priests of other gods to disband, and he removed the names of other gods from their temples. None of these changes endured, however. After Akhenaten died, all of the monuments he had built were demolished and his name was erased. Every effort was made to wipe out the records of Amenhotep, the "heretic pharaoh," and little was known of him in modern times until the rediscovery of Amarna, the city he built for Aten. Polytheism was restored under Tutankhamen. Akhenaten's wife was the famously beautiful Nefertiti.
Smenkhkare (Neferneferuaten)	Smenkhkare reigned for 3 years after Akhenaten died. Exactly who he was is uncertain: He may have been Akhenaten's wife Nefertiti, his brother or a son-in-law. Whoever he was, he allowed the monotheistic religion of Akhenaten to gradually collapse, slowly restoring Egypt's old gods to their previous place.
Tutankhamen 	Tutankhamen is the most famous pharaoh of all in modern times because his tomb was discovered, entirely undisturbed by grave robbers, by Howard Carter in the Valley of the Kings in 1922. He is popularly known as King Tut, and his burial mask is the best-known image of ancient Egypt. Tutankhamen was originally named Tutankhaten ("living image of Aten") by his father, the Aten-focused Akhenaten. After his father died, he changed his name to Tutankhamen, which meant "living image of Amun." Amun was the god for whom his father was originally named. Despite his modern fame, Tutankhamen actually reigned for only nine years, most of them assisted by regents and advisers. The "boy king" died at around sixteen years of age, possibly murdered by his own advisers at just the time when he might have begun to reign in his own right. His reign was just long enough to complete Egypt's restoration to polytheism.

Ay 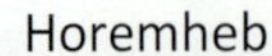	Ay took the throne after Tutankhamen died. He was Grand Vizier to Tutankhamen, and although it is unknown exactly what his family ties were (he might have been Tutankhamen's uncle), he was apparently the best qualified to take the throne in the absence of a dynastic heir. He reigned for four years, and spent that time solidifying the restoration of polytheism.
Horemheb 	The last pharaoh of the 18th Dynasty, Horemheb, was the military adviser to Tutankhamen. Like Ay, he was apparently judged to be best qualified to assume the throne in the absence of a legitimate heir. Horemheb was responsible for returning power to the central government, restoring the pharaoh's role and fully restoring the worship of Amun. He reigned for somewhere between thirty and sixty years. He, too, had no heirs, so he appointed his military commander, Paramessu, as heir to his throne. Paramessu changed his name to Ramesses I and started a new Dynasty. The reign of Ahmose I and his heirs died with Tutankhamen, and the 18th Dynasty was at an end.

The 19th Dynasty (1293 – 1185 BC)

Ramesses I 	Ramesses I was the founder of one of Egypt's most powerful dynasties. He began as Paramessu, Horemheb's military commander. When Horemheb produced no heirs of his body, he named Paramessu as his heir. After Paramessu assumed the throne, he took the name Ramesses ("born of Ra"). Because he was already an old man when he took the throne, his reign lasted for just two years; but during this time, he opened trade routes into the Sinai and led campaigns into Syria.
Seti I 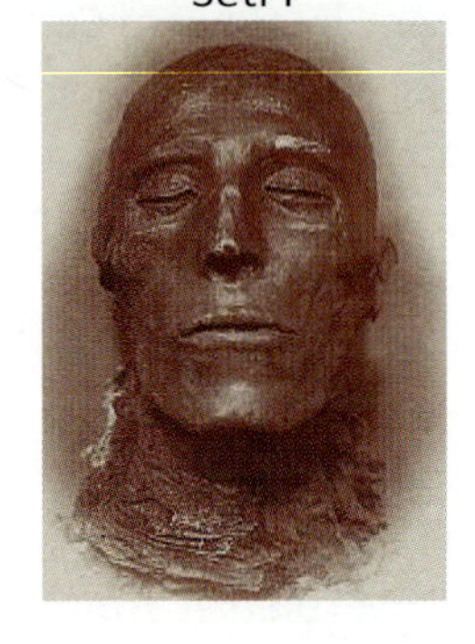	Like his father Ramesses I, Seti was an accomplished military leader. During his 12-15 year reign he warred against Palestine, brought Damascus under Egyptian control, fought in Nubia and Libya and reconciled with the Hittite kings in the region. Art and architecture flourished during his reign.

Ramesses II 	Ramesses II (Ramesses the Great) is considered one of Egypt's most important rulers. He ruled longer than any other pharaoh except for Pepi II. By the end of his reign, his name had been carved into many, many monuments, statues and temples. His victorious campaigns against the Hittites in Syria led to a lasting peace with them. Ramesses II had over 200 wives and concubines, and possibly fathered as many as 96 sons and 60 daughters. His favorite wife was Nefertiti. Ramesses II is another pharaoh whom some believe might have been the pharaoh of the Exodus. Egyptian records never mention the Exodus, and the Bible does not give a precise chronology, so the truth remains unclear.
Merneptah 	Merneptah assumed the throne when Ramesses II died around the age of 90. Merneptah reigned for ten years. He maintained his father's hard-won peace with the Hittites, and even sent them food when a famine struck their land. He led military expeditions in Nubia and Libya.
Amenmesse 	It is uncertain exactly when Amenmesse ruled and whether his rule was even legitimate. It is possible that he assumed his half-brother Seti II's throne in the middle of his reign and tried to depose him. Legitimate or not, he ruled for only around three years, and little is known of his activities as pharaoh.
Seti II 	Seti II's reign was short and relatively uneventful. He led campaigns in Nubia and the Sinai and possible had to manage his half-brother's attempt to take his throne.

Siptah 	Siptah was in his early teens when he took the throne and was probably subject to the co-regency of his step-mother Tawosret and an advisor named Chancellor Bay. He died in his late teens after only six years on the throne.
Tawosret	Tawosret assumed the throne after her step-son Siptah died. She ruled a total of seven years, six of them as co-regent with Siptah, before she died. The 19th Dynasty was in steep decline, and some believe that either Chancellor Bay or Setnakhte may have had Tawosret executed.

The 20th Dynasty (1185 – 1070 BC)

Dynasty 20 began with the three-year reign of Setnakhte. Little is known of his reign except that he restored law and order to Egypt, which was in decline at the end of the 19th Dynasty. Setnakhte dated his reign from the time of Seti II, as if the reigns of Siptah and Tawosret never happened.

Ramesses III followed Setnakhte, and he is considered the last great king of Egypt. Ramesses III defended Egypt against the Libyans and Sea People, and Egypt was stable under his leadership. After Ramesses III, a series of other Ramesses (8 in all) held power, but economic and social struggles sent the country into a downward spiral. After the 20th Dynasty, Egypt returned to chaos and the Third Intermediate Period began.

GEOGRAPHY FOCUS

PHASCINATING PHARAOH PHACTS: The Valley of the Kings

The Valley of the Kings is a valley in Egypt which sits across the Nile from the city of Thebes, Egypt's capital for most of the 18th Dynasty era. The Valley of the Kings was the designated place for the tombs of the New Kingdom's pharaohs and important nobles. The valley holds more than 60 tombs and chambers, including the famous tomb of King Tut, which Egyptologist Howard Carter rediscovered intact in 1922.

Chapter 10

The Exodus

BIBLE FOCUS

GIANTS OF THE FAITH: MOSES

MOSES AS A BABY (Exodus 2:1-10)

Moses was born to a man and woman from the line of Levi, the Hebrew tribe of priests. His birth came at a time of great danger, when Pharaoh had demanded that any boy born to a Hebrew woman must be thrown into the Nile River. Moses' mother concealed him for as long as she could, but Moses was a healthy and robust baby, and he could not be hidden forever. When he was three months old, his mother decided she would have to entrust his life to God.

So she made a basket of papyrus reeds and sealed it with tar and pitch so that it would float. **The Hebrew word translated "basket" here actually means "ark," and is the same word used for Noah's ark.** Moses' mother lovingly placed him in his little saving ark and positioned his older sister, Miriam, to watch over him. She placed the ark among the reeds along the riverbank, so that it wouldn't be swept away.

Pharaoh's daughter came down to the river to bathe, as was her custom. She saw the basket among the reeds and sent a servant to bring it to her. As soon as she saw Moses, she knew that he was one of the condemned Hebrew babies. In defiance of her father, she immediately decided to keep Moses. Since he was still of nursing age, Miriam came out of hiding and quickly offered to bring "one of the Hebrew women"-- her mother-- to nurse the baby. So Moses was saved from Pharaoh's death sentence by Pharaoh's own daughter, and was able to remain with his mother until he was weaned (3-5 years old).

FOUR ABUSE STORIES (Exodus 2:11-25)

Moses grows up as the son of Pharaoh's daughter, but he knows of his origin as a child of Hebrew slaves. He goes out to where his people are working to see what their lives are like. What he sees breaks his heart.

Three times in this section of Exodus, Moses encounters someone abusing someone else. All three times, Moses responds to the abuse with action. His compassion and concern for people who are helpless is clear in all three situations.

Abuse	Response	Result
1) Egyptian abusing Hebrew	Moses kills Egyptian	Moses turns away from life of privilege

"He saw an Egyptian beating a Hebrew, one of his own people. Glancing this way and that and seeing no one, he killed the Egyptian and hid him in the sand." (Exodus 2: 11-12)

2) Hebrew abusing Hebrew	Moses confronts the abuser	Moses is forced to flee

"The next day he went out and saw two Hebrews fighting. He asked the one in the wrong, 'Why are you hitting your fellow Hebrew?' The man said, 'Who made you ruler and judge over us? Are you thinking of killing me as you killed the Egyptian?' Then Moses was afraid and thought, 'What I did must have become known.' When Pharaoh heard of this, he tried to kill Moses, but Moses fled from Pharaoh and went to live in Midian, where he sat down by a well." (Exodus 2:13-15)

3). Shepherds abusing girls   Moses comes to their rescue   Moses gains a wife

"Now a priest of Midian had seven daughters, and they came to draw water and fill the troughs to water their father's flock. Some shepherds came along and drove them away, but Moses got up and came to their rescue and watered their flock." (Exodus 2:16-17)

4.) The section of abuse and response ends with increased abuse of the Israelites by a new Pharaoh. (Since Moses was raised in the old Pharaoh's household, he must have known the new Pharaoh; they may possibly have been raised as cousins or even brothers). The Israelites begin to cry out to God, and a compassionate God hears their cry.

"During that long period, the king of Egypt died. The Israelites groaned in their slavery and cried out, and their cry for help because of their slavery went up to God. God heard their groaning and he remembered his covenant with Abraham, with Isaac and with Jacob. So God looked on the Israelites and was concerned about them." (Exodus 2: 23-24)

Key Focus in this section: IN THE SAME WAY THAT MOSES RESPONDED TO ABUSE - GOD ALSO RESPONDED.
THE OPPRESSED DID NOT GO UNNOTICED BY HIM. WHEN THEY CRIED OUT, HE LISTENED!

FASCINATING FACTS: The Midianites

Moses ran to Midian after he fled Egypt. The Midianites were descendants of Abraham, just as Moses was:

"Abraham took another wife, whose name was Keturah. She bore him Zimran, Jokshan, Medan, Midian, Ishbak and Shuah. Jokshan was the father of Sheba and Dedan; the descendants of Dedan were the Asshurites, the Letushites and the Leummites. The sons of Midian were Ephah, Epher, Hanoch, Abida and Eldaah. All these were descendants of Keturah." (Genesis 25:1-4)

The Hebrews' relationship with the Midianites was originally friendly, so Moses was warmly welcomed into the family of Jethro (in red in the picture), the priest and judge of Midian. Moses married one of Jethro's daughters, and they had two sons, Gershom and Eliezer (Exodus 18:2-4).

When the Hebrews left Egypt, good relations between the Midianites and the Hebrews continued. In Exodus 18, Jethro helped Moses set up a court system similar to the one he used as priest and judge of Midian. Together they brought offerings to God, and together they praised God for all that He had done for the Hebrews.

The next time the Midianites turn up in Scripture, however, they have become enemies of Israel: they are conspiring with the Moabites to curse Israel through Balaam (Numbers 22:4-7). From this point forward, the Midianites and the Israelites are enemies, until finally Gideon defeats the Midianites (Judges 6-7).

FASCINATING FACTS: Three sets of 40 years for Moses

According to Acts 7, Moses was 40 years old when he fled to Midian. He spent the next 40 years in Midian, fathering two sons before he encountered the burning bush and returned to Egypt. Later, Moses led the Israelites through their wanderings in the wilderness for another 40 years. When this final set of 40 years was over, Moses died.

MOSES ENCOUNTERS GOD (Exodus 3-4)

For forty years, Moses has been living in Midian, quietly raising a family and working for his father-in-law. He takes his sheep to the area of Mount Horeb to find good pasture. It is here that he has his first encounter with God.

FASCINATING FACTS: Horeb and Sinai

The place names "Mount of Horeb" and "Mount Sinai" seem to be interchangeable in the Bible. Horeb may have referred to the mountain region in the Sinai Peninsula, while Sinai may have referred to the mountain peak itself. Mount Sinai is the site of three very important encounters with God: Moses first meets God there, and later receives the Ten Commandments there; and it is on this same mountain that God speaks to the prophet Elijah in a "still small voice" (I Kings 19).

Moses sees a bush on the mountain that burns, but is not consumed. Curious, he goes to investigate. Suddenly, God begins to speak to Moses from the burning bush. God calls Moses' name and tells him to remove his sandals (probably made from papyrus or leather) because he is standing on holy ground. Removing one's shoes when entering a home or a sacred place was the common practice for the day. God was telling Moses to remove his shoes, not because the place or the area was holy, but because God Himself was there.

Moses falls **face down** and hides his face in fear **expecting judgment to come.**

"Do not come any closer," God said. "Take off your sandals, for the place where you are standing is holy ground." Then he said, "I am the God of your father, the God of Abraham, the God of Isaac and the God of Jacob." At this, Moses hid his face, because he was afraid to look at God." (Exodus 3: 5-6)

Then God tells Moses that the cries of the Israelites have reached his ears and He is going to rescue them. He wants Moses to go to Pharaoh and demand the release of his people. Moses is shocked that God wants him to be his people's rescuer, and wants to know, "Why me?"

Throughout this chapter, God tells Moses who He is in **five different ways**:

3:6: God tells Moses "I am the God of Abraham, Isaac and Jacob"
3:14: God tells Moses "I AM WHO I AM" (or "I WILL BE WHAT I WLL BE")
3:15: Moses is instructed to tell the Israelites that God is the "Lord, the God of your fathers - The God of Abraham, Isaac and Jacob"
3:16 Moses is instructed to tell the elders that God is the "Lord, the God of your fathers - The God of Abraham, Isaac and Jacob"
3:18: Moses is instructed to tell Pharaoh that God is "the Lord, the God of the Hebrews"

Moses is reluctant to go, and starts listing reasons why he is the wrong person to go and no one will ever believe him. In response, God provides Moses with a series of signs that he can use to prove God's power and authority:

1. God changes Moses' staff into a snake, and when Moses grabs the snake by the tail, it changes back into a staff (never try that at home!).
2. God causes Moses' hand to become diseased and then heals it.
3. God tells Moses that if anyone still doesn't believe him, he may pour water from the Nile on the ground and it will turn to blood.

Moses still wavers, saying that he has never been a speechmaker. Even after God promises to give Moses the right words, Moses begs God to send someone else. God is angry, but allows Moses' brother Aaron to speak in Moses' place. Moses will remain the leader of the Israelites.

FROM BAD TO WORSE (GENESIS 5-6)

Back in Egypt, Moses and Aaron approach Pharaoh and ask that he allow the Israelites to go into the desert for three days to worship God. Pharaoh refuses, saying that he doesn't know or fear the God of the Hebrews. Instead, he increases the Israelites' work load by making them gather their own straw for brickmaking. When they can't fulfill their brick quotas, they are beaten, and they blame Moses for bringing more trouble upon them.

In turn, Moses blames God, saying "you have not rescued your people at all." But God renews his promise and again tells Moses who He is in **four different ways**:

"God also said to Moses, 'I am the LORD. I appeared to Abraham, to Isaac and to Jacob as God Almighty, but by my name the LORD I did not make myself known to them. I also established my covenant with them to give them the land of Canaan, where they lived as aliens. Moreover, I have heard the groaning of the Israelites, whom the Egyptians are enslaving, and I have remembered my covenant.

Therefore, say to the Israelites: 'I am the LORD, and I will bring you out from under the yoke of the Egyptians. I will free you from being slaves to them, and I will redeem you with an outstretched arm and with mighty acts of judgment. I will take you as my own people, and I will be your God. Then you will know that I am the LORD your God, who brought you out from under the yoke of the Egyptians. And I will bring you to the land I swore with uplifted hand to give to Abraham, to Isaac and to Jacob. I will give it to you as a possession. I am the LORD.' "

When Moses and Aaron approached Pharaoh again, they used one of the signs that God had given them: Aaron threw down his staff and it turned into a snake (notice that he did not use sorcery or chants, but simply threw it down). But the Egyptian court magicians were also able to turn their staves into snakes by their secret arts. Aaron's snake consumed the magicians' snakes, but Pharaoh was not impressed.

FASCINATING FACTS: Rods into Snakes

The Ancient Egyptians loved their snakes. A favorite was the rearing cobra with its distinctive hood spread. The Pharaoh often wore a headdress resembling the cobra's hood for protection and as a symbol of royalty.

For the Egyptian court magicians, duplicating Aaron's miracle was easy. With certain snakes, it is possible to pinch a pressure point on the neck so that they stiffen like a staff until they are released and thrown to the ground. Snake charmers around the world still perform this trick today. The real shocker of the day came when Aaron's snake ate the magicians' snakes.

THE PLAGUES (Exodus 7:14-24 - 12:1-51)

When the signs failed to convince Pharaoh, God began a series of ten plagues on the Egyptians, both to convince Pharaoh to release them and to prove His power and authority to the Israelites. The plagues would also demonstrate God's superiority to the Egyptian gods.

The plagues are usually divided into four groups, three groups of three plagues each and one final, climactic plague. The first three plagues affected all of Egypt. After that, the plagues spared the area around Goshen (where the Israelites lived).

PLAGUE	WARNING	TIME	RESPONSE	EGYPTIAN GOD
1. BLOOD	YES	MORNING	PHARAOH'S HEART WAS HARDENED	Hapi, Knum, Osiris
2. FROGS	YES	NONE	PHARAOH HARDENED HIS HEART	Heqt
3. LICE/GNATS	NO	NONE	PHARAOH HARDENED HIS HEART	Kheper, Geb
4. INSECTS	YES	MORNING	PHARAOH HARDENED HIS HEART	Kheper, Amon-Ra
5. LIVESTOCK	YES	NONE	PHARAOH'S HEART WAS HARDENED	Apis (bull), Hathor (cow)
6. BOILS	NO	NONE	LORD HARDENED PHARAOH'S HEART	Imhotep, Serapes, Thoth
7. HAIL	YES	MORNING	PHARAOH HARDENED HIS HEART	Nut (sky goddess)
8. LOCUSTS	YES	NONE	LORD HARDENED PHARAOH'S HEART	Seth, Nepri, Thermuthis
9. DARKNESS	NO	NONE	LORD HARDENED PHARAOH'S HEART	Ra (Sun god)
10. DEATH	YES	NONE	PHARAOH LET THE ISRAELITES GO	PHARAOH

PLAGUE	OUTCOME
1. Blood	• All the water in the Nile and in the streams, reservoirs, ponds and even buckets and jars was changed to blood. All of the fish in the Nile died as a result. • The Magicians replicated this plague by their secret arts. • **Pharaoh turned his back on Moses and went into the palace.**
2. Frogs	• The frogs were so numerous that they were everywhere: in the houses, in the bedrooms and in all of the food. After Moses prayed, their dead carcasses were everywhere and the smell was sickening. • The Magicians also made frogs appear by their secret arts, but they couldn't remove the Lord's frogs. • Pharaoh begged Moses to remove the frogs, and promised to let the Israelites go to offer sacrifices to God if he succeeded. • **After the frogs disappeared, Pharaoh hardened his heart.**

3. Lice/Gnats	• The lice (or gnats) descended upon everyone, people and animals. • The Magicians were unable to replicate this plague and acknowledged God's hand. • **Pharaoh would not listen.**
4. Insects	• The insects (flies or beetles) swarmed everywhere, eating whatever they could and probably spreading disease wherever they went. • This plague affected only the Egyptians; the Land of Goshen, where the Israelites lived, was spared. • Pharaoh tried to negotiate, suggesting that the Israelites could worship God in Egypt, but Moses stood firm, insisting that they must go to the desert. Pharaoh agreed to let them go if Moses would pray to have the insects removed. • **After the insects were removed, Pharaoh changed his mind.**
5. Livestock	• The livestock of the Egyptians-- cows, sheep, goats, camels, horses and donkeys--died. • This plagued affected only the Egyptians; the livestock of the Israelites was spared. • **Pharaoh's heart was unchanged.**
6. Boils	• Open boils covered all the Egyptians and their animals. • The Magicians were unable to heal themselves from this plague and were ashamed at the impotence of their gods. They could not stand in Moses' presence. • **Pharaoh's heart was unchanged.**
7. Hail	• The worst hailstorm ever known to man until that time hit Egypt, tearing up trees and destroying flax and barley that were ready to be harvested. • The land of Goshen was spared, and so were some Egyptians who were becoming convinced of the Lord's power and heeded the warning. • Pharaoh admitted that he had sinned against the Israelites, and begged Moses to stop the hail. Moses agreed to pray to God, even though he recognized that Pharaoh wasn't truly repentant. • **When the hail was over, Pharaoh once again hardened his heart.**

8. Locusts	• Immense swarms of locusts completely wiped out the rest of the crops and stripped the land. • Pharaoh's officials began to beg Pharaoh to let the Israelites go. • Pharaoh tried to compromise with Moses, offering to allow only the Israelite men to go. Moses refused and brought on the locusts. • It is uncertain whether the land of Goshen was spared. • Pharaoh agrees again that he has sinned and begs Moses to pray. • **After Moses prays and the locusts leave, the Lord hardens Pharaoh's heart.**
9. Darkness	• Impenetrable darkness covered Egypt for three days. • The land of Goshen was not covered in darkness. • Usually before judgment in Scripture, there is a period of silence. This darkness symbolizes that silence. The ninth plague is the set-up for the tenth and final plague. • Pharaoh agreed that the Israelites could go and worship, but insisted that they could not take their animals. • Moses refused, and Pharaoh ejected him from the palace, threatening him with death if he should ever return. • **The Lord hardened Pharaoh's heart.**
10. Death	• The firstborn son in every family, slave or free, died-- except for those that heeded the warning and marked their doorframes. • **After Pharaoh's firstborn son died, he sent the Israelites away in his grief**. • Laden with gifts of gold, silver and cloth from the Egyptians, the Israelites began their great Exodus from Egypt.

SCRIPTURE SPOTLIGHT: The Passover (Exodus 11-12)

The final plague, the killing of the firstborn sons, was the most shocking of all. It may be interpreted as a judgment on Pharaoh for killing the Hebrew boys at the beginning of Exodus. It is a powerful reminder that God is the master of life and death, and that what He gives, He may also take away.

After the plague of Darkness, Moses warns Pharaoh that at midnight, all of the firstborn sons in Egypt will die, but the firstborn sons of Israel will be spared. Pharaoh's heart has been hardened by God, and so he does not listen to Moses.

The story of the Passover is one of the most important in Jewish history; many Jewish traditions have their roots in Passover night. Accordingly, the narrative of events stops here briefly for a section on the procedures for Passover night, instructions for future celebrations of Passover and a new Jewish calendar.

FASCINATING FACTS: The Jewish Calendar (Exodus 12:1-2)

God directs the Israelites to abandon the Egyptian calendar and adopt a new system. The Passover would now begin their new year. Their new calendar would be a first step toward creating a new society as a free people. The Egyptian calendar was built around the Egyptian gods and three festivals: the festival of the gods, the festival of the kings and the festival of the dead. The new Jewish calendar was based not on mythology or seasonal changes, but on an historic event. This was unheard of in the ancient world.

SCRIPTURE SPOTLIGHT: Procedures for Passover (Exodus 12: 3-13)

Lamb - The Israelites were to take a year old male lamb without blemish and slaughter it at twilight. They were to take some of the blood and spread it on the doorframes of their houses. They were then to roast the lamb over a fire.

Herbs - For the Passover meal, they were to eat bitter herbs, most likely a salad made up of lettuce and other stemmed plants.

Unleavened Bread - They were also to eat unleavened bread, a flat cake that could be prepared quickly because it didn't need to rise.

No leftovers - They were not to save food from the Passover meal, but were either to consume everything or burn it up. This was in keeping with food that has been used for an offering.

Loins girded - The normal dress for an Israelite was a long flowing garment. When a person needed to move quickly, he would grasp the garment at the bottom and pull it up to the waist, tucking it in the belt. This allowed for easy maneuvering.

Sandals and staff - The Israelites were to be prepared to leave as soon as they were given the signal, so they were to eat with sandals on and staff in hand. Usually the sandals were removed inside the house and the staff was kept near the door, to be taken up as one left; but the Israelites were not to leave the house until morning (12:22). This highlights their urgent waiting on the Lord and their readiness to follow.

SCRIPTURE SPOTLIGHT: The Feast of Unleavened Bread (Exodus 12: 14-20)

Before they even had their first Passover, Moses gave the Israelites instructions for how to celebrate the Passover and the Feast of Unleavened Bread each year thereafter. They had not even won their release yet, but God in His power and Sovereignty could establish a yearly commemoration of the Passover even before it actually happened.

Moses and the Israelites did as instructed. They placed the blood on their doors, readied themselves in their houses and waited for the Lord's Passover.

"At midnight the LORD struck down all the firstborn in Egypt, from the firstborn of Pharaoh, who sat on the throne, to the firstborn of the prisoner, who was in the dungeon, and the firstborn of all the livestock as well. Pharaoh and all his officials and all the Egyptians got up during the night, and there was loud wailing in Egypt, for there was not a house without someone dead." (Exodus 12: 29-30)

Anguished, Pharaoh told Moses and Aaron to leave. The Egyptians helped the Israelites, piling gifts on them in an attempt to get rid of them as soon as possible. The movement of that many people, together with livestock and supplies, in such a short period of time was a miracle in and of itself!

The Israelites journeyed from Rameses to Succoth, led by the Lord who went ahead of them in a pillar of cloud during the day and a pillar of fire at night. They did not journey toward the shores of the Mediterranean, because the Israelites were not yet ready for battle against the mighty Philistines. Instead, the Lord led them on a more southerly route, but their ultimate goal was the promised land of Canaan.

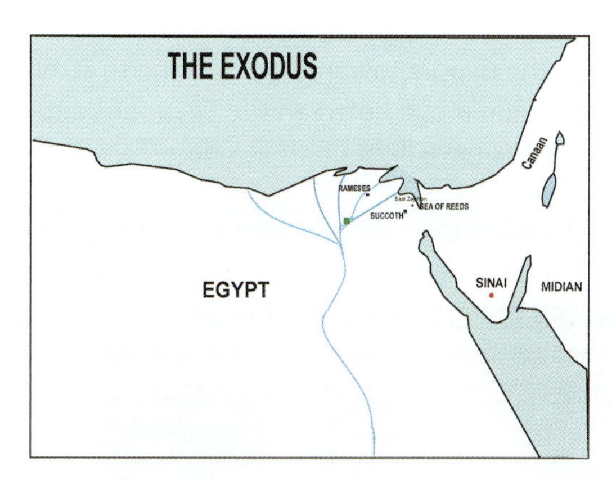

Back in Egypt, Pharaoh began to have second thoughts about letting the Israelites go, and thoughts of blame and vengeance entered his mind. He gathered a chariot-borne army to chase down the Israelites. By this time the Israelites were camped next to the Sea of Reeds at Baal Zephon (see map).

FASCINATING FACTS: The Crossing of the Reed/Red Sea

There has been much debate over the years regarding which sea the Israelites crossed and precisely where they crossed. Traditionally, the name of the sea was translated as "Red Sea," but more recently it has often been translated as "Reed Sea." Modern Biblical scholars generally agree that the Israelites crossed the Sea of Reeds, although some still believe that they crossed at the northernmost tip of the Red Sea.

Some have theorized that the crossing was not miraculous, but that the heavy Egyptian chariots got stuck in the mud while the Israelites waded across a swamp on foot. But Scripture says that they:

"Went through the sea on dry ground with a wall of water on their right and on their left" (Exodus 14:22).

The Parting of the Sea is foundational to the Jewish and Christian faiths, and cannot be lightly brushed aside. As Eugene Merrill says:

"The crossing of Israel, which immediately preceded the drowning of the Egyptian chariotry, cannot be explained as a wading through a swamp. It required a mighty act of God, an act so significant both in scope and meaning that forever after in Israel's history it was the paradigm against which all of his redemptive and saving work was measured. If there was no actual miracle of the proportions prescribed, all subsequent reference to the Exodus as the archetype of the sovereign power and salvific grace of God is hollow and empty."
(Merrill, Kingdom of Priests, Baker Book House, Grand Rapids, 1987)

According to Scripture, Pharaoh brings six hundred of his best chariots to pursue the Israelites, as well as other horses, officers and troops. When the Israelites see the terrible Egyptians approaching, they cry out to the Lord and blame Moses in the same breath.

"Was it because there were no graves in Egypt that you brought us to the desert to die? What have you done to us by bringing us out of Egypt? Didn't we say to you in Egypt, 'Leave us alone; let us serve the Egyptians'? It would have been better for us to serve the Egyptians than to die in the desert!" (Exodus 14: 11-12)

The Lord tells Moses to move the people towards the sea and to stretch out his hand over the sea. Then the angel of the Lord and the pillar of cloud move between the Egyptians and the Israelites so that the Egyptians cannot see the Israelites, but the Israelites have light on their side.

"Then Moses stretched out his hand over the sea, and all that night the LORD drove the sea back with a strong east wind and turned it into dry land. The waters were divided, **and the Israelites went through the sea on dry ground, with a wall of water on their right and on their left.**

The Egyptians pursued them, and all Pharaoh's horses and chariots and horsemen followed them into the sea. During the last watch of the night the LORD looked down from the pillar of fire and cloud at the Egyptian army and threw it into confusion. He made the wheels of their chariots come off so that they had difficulty driving. And the Egyptians said, "Let's get away from the Israelites! The LORD is fighting for them against Egypt."

Then the LORD said to Moses, "Stretch out your hand over the sea so that the waters may flow back over the Egyptians and their chariots and horsemen." Moses stretched out his hand over the sea, and at daybreak the sea went back to its place. The Egyptians were fleeing toward it, and the LORD swept them into the sea. The water flowed back and covered the chariots and horsemen—the entire army of Pharaoh that had followed the Israelites into the sea. Not one of them survived." (Exodus 14: 21-28)

<u>GEOGRAPHY FOCUS</u>

<u>The Red Sea</u>

DID YOU KNOW….

- The Red Sea forms the dividing line between the continents of Africa and Asia.
- The Red Sea is connected to the Indian Ocean through the Gulf of Aden and the Arabian Sea.
- No one knows the origin of the Red Sea's name. Some believe that it was named for the reddish, mineral-rich mountains nearby. Others believe that it was named for seasonal red flowers that bloomed near the water's surface.
- The Ancients used the Red Sea as a trade route to the Indian Ocean.
- Because no rivers feed fresh water into the Red Sea, it is one of the saltiest bodies of water in the world.

Chapter 11

The Law and the Wilderness

BIBLE FOCUS

GRUMBLING AND COMPLAINING (Exodus 15:22-27, 16 and 17:1-7)

After the Israelites crossed the Red/Reed Sea, leaving Egypt and slave life behind (picture above is a depiction of the Israelites in slavery), one might assume that their gratitude to the Lord would never end--especially in light of all of the miracles they had seen. But these were former slaves who had been beaten and battered throughout their entire lives, and they were crippled in body and spirit. After living a regimented lifestyle in which every waking moment was ordered, they suddenly found themselves free in the desert without homes or a lasting supply of food or water. They were terrified. They knew little of the God of Moses, and they cared mainly about the present and their own basic needs: food, water and shelter. Furthermore, they had just left behind the threat of attack from Egypt, and would soon face the terror of the Amalekites. They were helpless and completely dependent upon God as their provider and protector.

God provided water for them twice: at Marah, He made the bitter water drinkable, and in the desert, He made water flow from a rock. Centered between the water stories is the story of Manna (food from heaven). In all three situations, God proves His love for these grumbling, faithless people. His providence was not dependent upon their good behavior.

SCRIPTURE SPOTLIGHT: Manna from Heaven

Soon after God provides water, the people begin to grumble that their food is running out. They have been out of Egypt for over a month, and the food they brought along with them is now gone. They begin to cry out against Moses and Aaron (note that they leave God out of their complaining), wishing they were back in Egypt where there was meat in every pot, along with cucumbers, melons, leeks, onions and garlic (Numbers 11:5).

The Lord heard their complaining, but He loved them enough to overlook their lack of faith. He provided both meat and bread for them in the form of quail and the bread from heaven that came to be known as "manna."

Exodus 16:11 "The LORD said to Moses, 'I have heard the grumbling of the Israelites. Tell them, 'At twilight you will eat meat, and in the morning you will be filled with bread. Then you will know that I am the LORD your God.' "

The quail came only once, but the manna came every day (except on the Sabbath) throughout their forty years in the desert. Manna was "white like coriander seed and tasted like wafers made with honey" (Exodus 16:31). It fell with the dew overnight, and could be gathered in the morning.

The instructions for handling manna were as follows:

- They were to gather manna in the morning, enough for the entire day.
- They were to gather only enough for the people living in their tent.
- They were not to gather extra and keep it overnight; when some of them tried anyway, they found that it spoiled and became filled with maggots.
- They were to gather double portions on the sixth day so that they could rest on the seventh day, the Sabbath. On that night, they could keep it and it wouldn't spoil.

Note the following:

- Manna from heaven was a daily reminder of God's love and provision for his people. They were completely dependent upon a loving God. This was in sharp contrast with their former lives as slaves, in which they were dependent upon the Egyptians (who were anything but loving).
- They had come out of a world in which rest and leisure were non-existent. Only the Egyptians rested; slaves did not rest. Yet from the time of creation, God had established the idea of working for six days and resting on the seventh. By providing manna for only six days, God was establishing the Sabbath and giving these runaway slaves their first taste of real freedom-- the freedom to rest.

In Joshua 5:11-12, just before the Israelites enter the promised land of Canaan, they celebrate Passover. The next day they eat unleavened bread and roasted grain, the produce of Canaan. No more manna fell from the sky.

THE AMALEKITES (Exodus 17:8-16)

Before the Israelites arrive at Sinai, they are forced to deal with an attack from the Amalekites. The Amalekites may have been descendants of Esau (Esau's son Eliphaz had a concubine who bore him a son named Amalek in Genesis 36:12), which would mean that they were related to the Israelites. The Amalekites attacked from the rear (Deuteronomy 25:18), killing off the weak and helpless. Moses sent Joshua to do battle with the Amalekites while he himself stood on a hill with his staff held high, where the Israelites could see him. As long as the staff was in the air, the Israelites had the upper hand; but whenever Moses lowered the staff, the Amalekites did better. Aaron and Hur held Moses' tired arms up throughout the day so that Joshua and the Israelites could defeat the Amalekites.

FASCINATING FACTS: Raising of the Rod/Hand

It is interesting to note that in both the defeat of the Egyptians at the Red/Reed Sea and the defeat of the Amalekites, Moses had to lift his rod/hands as a tangible sign to the people of God's power over their enemies.

After the sea crossing, a song was sung in praise of God and His mighty acts: "Your right hand, O Lord was majestic in power. Your right hand shattered the enemy" (Exodus 15:6).

After the victory over the Amalekites, Moses built an altar and called it "The LORD is my Banner. He said, 'For hands were lifted up to the throne of the LORD'" (Exodus 17:15-16a).

SCRIPTURE SPOTLIGHT: What Happened to the Amalekites?

God declared that because the Amalekites had attacked Israel, they would eventually would be wiped off the face of the earth. Before that happened, though, God used the Amalekites to punish Israel's rebellion.

The Amalekites in the Bible:

- Numbers 14: 43-45 - The Amalekites and Canaanites attacked the Israelites, and won because the Israelites had sinned against the Lord.
- Judges 3:13 - The Amalekites and Ammonites joined with the Moabites against Israel, and won because Israel had sinned against the Lord.
- Judges 6:3 - The Amalekites and Midianites attacked the Israelites, ruining their crops, because the Israelites had sinned against the Lord.
- I Samuel 15: 1-9 - Saul is instructed to completely destroy the Amalekites because of their attacks on the Israelites, but Saul sins and loses favor with God.
- I Samuel 27: 8-9 - David fights and begins to cut down on the Amalekites' numbers.
- I Samuel 30 - The Amalekites raid David's camps and kidnap his wives and sons. David goes after the Amalekites and kills all but 400 young men.
- I Chronicles 4:43 - The Amalekites are completely destroyed during the time of Hezekiah.

MOUNT SINAI

The Israelites have been out of Egypt for three months when they arrive at Mount Sinai. In preparation for establishing his covenant with the Israelites, God gives them three days in which to consecrate themselves before He meets with them. God's desire to have a relationship with His people WAS COMPLETELY UNIQUE, AND HIS COVENANT WITH THEM WAS UNIQUE. Covenants were not uncommon in the ancient world, but a covenant between God and his people was something new. God wanted to live among them, care for them, guide them and protect them. He planned to be their God, their King and their Judge. In order to establish that relationship, God had to set up boundaries to govern their behavior: God's law.

SCRIPTURE SPOTLIGHT: The Law

When people talk about the Law that God gave Moses, they are usually referring to the Ten Commandments. But God also gave Moses 603 other laws in addition to the Ten Commandments, for a total of 613. These laws can be divided into three categories: civil (or judicial), moral and ceremonial.

- **Civil and judicial laws** deal with conflicts between citizens, disputes over property rights and personal injuries.
- **Moral laws** protect the helpless, such as slaves, widows, orphans and aliens. These laws were unique to God's law, nearly unheard of in other law codes.
- **Ceremonial laws** included tabernacle regulations, instructions for different types of sacrifices, and rules regarding cleanliness and holiness.

The laws were part of a Covenant between God and the Israelites in which He promised to be their God and they became His special, chosen people (Exodus 19:5-6):

"Now if you obey me fully and keep my covenant, then out of all nations you will be my treasured possession. Although the whole earth is mine, you will be for me a kingdom of priests and a holy nation."

Moses ascended Mount Sinai, where God gave him the Law over a period of forty days. First came the overarching Ten Commandments, then the moral and civil laws and finally the ceremonial laws. The moral and civil laws provided the Israelites for the first time with a guidebook for a righteous life. Right and wrong as defined by God Himself are laid out in the Ten Commandments and the moral and civil laws. God wants his children to live holy, righteous lives. He wants them to be upright in their dealings with other people. And He wants them to share His care and concern for the weak and helpless, which is evident throughout His laws.

CRITICAL COMPARISONS between Biblical Laws and Other Ancient laws

There are quite a number of differences between the laws God gave to Moses and the laws written for other ancient cultures, such as the Code of Hammurabi:

- The laws were given by God Himself and not a human king.
- The laws were given orally first and then written down, instead of the other way around.
- Many of the laws are designed so that God can have a relationship with His people.
- The laws defined no separate social classes; all were considered equal.
- One person could not be punished for the crime of another person.
- Punishments were generally less brutal and tended to fit the crime.
- Only one punishment was allotted for a crime, instead of numerous punishments.
- The death penalty was used sparingly.
- Slaves were to be treated with kindness.
- Slaves were to work for only six days, just like the rest of the household.
- Hebrew slaves were to be freed after seven years.
- The laws were built around relationships instead of property.
- Human life ranked higher than property.
- The helpless were to be protected.
- Care was to be given to the stranger or alien.
- The practice of charging interest on loans was banned.
- One was expected to look out for the needs of others, even one's enemies.
- The dignity of the poor and helpless was to be protected.
- Each person was to learn the law; education was important.

After the moral and civil laws, the Lord gave instructions for the building of His tabernacle (a sort of mobile temple) and then gave the ceremonial laws and holiness laws. The tabernacle was to be God's dwelling place among them, but if the Israelites wanted to be close to God, they would have to make themselves holy:

"Be holy because I, the Lord your God, am holy" (Leviticus 19:2).

God was going to dwell among them, so they would have to learn how to behave, appear and worship in His presence.

FASCINATING FACTS: Ancient Temples

The Israelites were very familiar with temples, since Egypt was filled with gods. Each city had a temple for its particular god. Ancient temples were usually large and majestic, and also quite stationary, since most gods were tied to their localities (see picture). They were often built using slave labor, and cost vast amounts of money. Temples generally stood higher than the surrounding buildings and houses so that they could be seen from afar. They were complex and opulent in design, filled with rooms including kitchens, storage rooms, and priests' rooms, as well as inner and outer courtyards and a holy place at the center housing the idol. This holy place often had windows so that people could peek in and see the god sitting on his throne.

The holy place, or throne room, contained a throne for the idol. The typical throne was lavish, and often had cherubim on both sides and a footstool in front. The throne room also had dressers for the god's clothes, a table with eating utensils, lamps, incense and a bed. The temple was the god's house, and the priests' job was to feed, dress and care for the god. The focus of the temple was on meeting the god's every need.

The idols themselves were dressed in expensive clothing, which was changed according to the rituals and laws surrounding that god. The gods were typically fed at least twice daily with vast amounts of the best food available. The food was displayed on the table in a picturesque style, with musicians performing for the god's pleasure. Then the table was cleared, and the god was given water to wash his/her hands. The food from the god's table would then be given to the king, the only one worthy to partake.

FASCINATING FACTS: The Tabernacle

The Tabernacle was very different in substance and purpose from the ancient temples. Although it contained some of the same items as other temples-- a Holy of Holies for God Himself, a Holy Place for the priests, courtyards, incense, candlesticks, food and basins for washing-- the tabernacle was quite different.

- God did not reside in the tabernacle in order to have the people meet His needs. God did not need to be fed, clothed or washed.
- The Holy of Holies contained only an ark and a lid called the Mercy Seat.
- No idol sat in the Holy of Holies.
- God did not need light, a bed, a dresser for His clothes, a throne or a table for food. All of these items were in the Holy Place for the Priests to use.
- The Tabernacle was not stationary, but portable.
- God was not confined to the Tabernacle.
- When the Tabernacle was packed up for travel, God would go in front of the people to guide them.
- The Tabernacle was simple and inexpensive, designed to be easy to build and move-- yet the presence of God made the Tabernacle priceless.
- God was willing to live in a tent, just as His people were living in tents. He did not need a dwelling that stood over and above those of His people; He resided among them. God desired His people to KNOW Him.
- No food was ever brought before God for Him to "taste or consume."
- The sacrifices God required were simple compared to the sacrifices of the Near Eastern world gods.
- God didn't need to wash His hands. The basin of water was used by the priests to wash themselves for purification and cleansing.
- To enter God's presence was a reverent and holy act. Only the High Priest could enter the Holy of Holies, and even he entered only once a year. There were no windows to allow others to peek inside.
- There was no class system. The tabernacle was available to everyone. Special offerings were available so that even the poor could participate.
- God did not need clothing, so the laws regarding clothing covered only what the priests wore, not what God wore.

INSIDE THE TABERNACLE

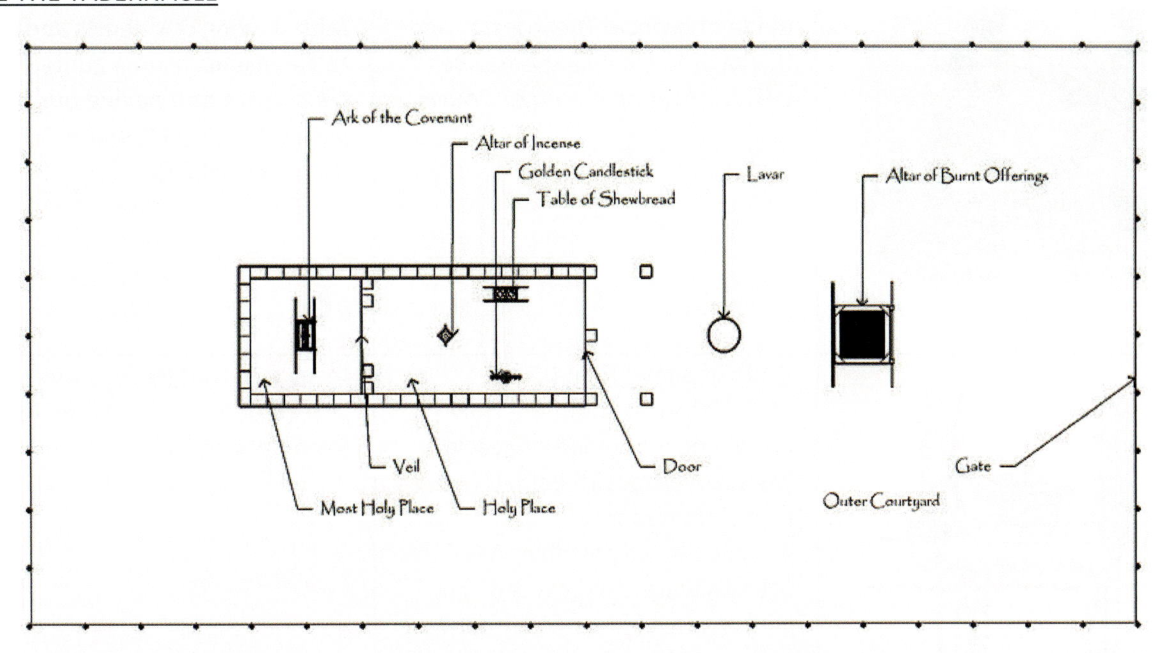

The Tabernacle was separated into sections: the Outer Courts, the Holy Place and the Holy of Holies. The Holy Place and the Holy of Holies were enclosed in a tent, and the entire tabernacle with its courtyard was surrounded by a fence.

The Holy Place and the Holy of Holies were covered with hangings of blue, purple and crimson linen (colors of royalty) that could be seen only from the inside. The linen covered a tough layer of black curtains made of goat's hair. Over all of this was a tent layer made of ram's skin, followed by another layer of skin on top. From the outside, the tent of the tabernacle looked like any other tent, with the layers of skin providing protection from the elements.

Altar of Burnt Offerings (Exodus 27:1-8): This was made of acacia wood covered with bronze. All of the utensils were also covered with bronze. This altar was designed to be carried, which was unheard of in the ancient world. The sacrifices on the altar covered the unintentional sins of the Israelites so that they could be clean.

"The blood of goats and bulls and the ashes of a heifer sprinkled on those who are ceremonially unclean sanctify them so that they are outwardly clean. How much more, then, will the blood of Christ, who through the eternal Spirit offered himself unblemished to God, cleanse our consciences from acts that lead to death, so that we may serve the living God!" (Hebrews 9:13-14; see also Mark 14:24, Hebrews 10, I Peter 1: 18-19 and 2 Corinthians 5:21)

	Laver or Basin for Washing (Exodus 30: 17-21): This was made of bronze. The priests used the laver to cleanse themselves before entering the Inner Courts.	**"Let us draw near to God with a sincere heart in full assurance of faith, having our hearts sprinkled to cleanse us from a guilty conscience and having our bodies washed with pure water." (Hebrews 10:22)**
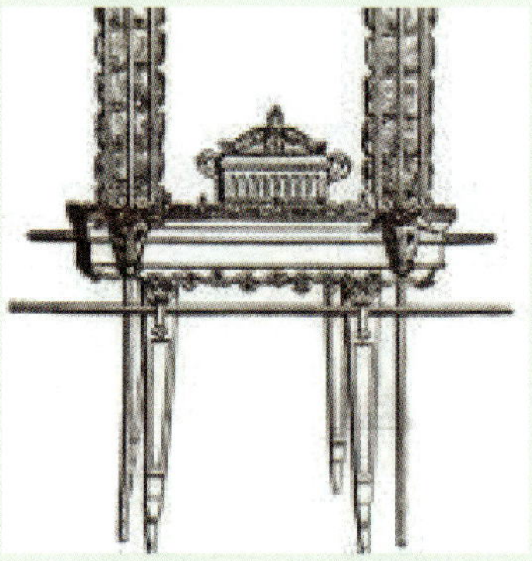	Table of Shewbread (Exodus 25:23-30): This sat in the Holy Place, and was made of acacia wood covered with gold. Like the rest of the tabernacle, it was designed to be portable. All of the utensils were also covered in gold. Twelve loaves of bread were placed on the table each Sabbath, in two rows of six each. The bread was not food for God, but stood as a reminder of the covenant God made with the twelve tribes of Israel and of Israel's dependence upon God the Provider.	**Jesus said that He was the "bread of life" who came down from heaven (John 6:35, 48-51).**
	Lampstand or Menorah (Exodus 25:31-40): This was made of pure gold and had seven lamps. It gave light for the priests.	**Jesus said that He was the "light of the world" (John 8: 12).**
	Altar of Incense (Exodus 30: 1-10): This was made of acacia wood covered with gold. It sat in the Holy Place and was burned twice a day by the priests.	**Psalm 141: 1-2 indicates that our prayers are like incense to the Lord. In Revelation 5:8 and 8:3, an angel of the Lord offers incense and *the prayers of the saints* before the throne.**
	Veil (Exodus 26:31-35): This was made of wool and linen and decorated with cherubim. It separated the Holy Place from the Holy of Holies.	**When Jesus died on the cross, the veil in the temple (the permanent structure that replaced the tabernacle) in Jerusalem was torn in two (Matthew 27:51).**

	Ark (Exodus 25: 10-22): The ark was a chest made of acacia wood covered with gold inside and out. Its gold cover, the "Mercy Seat," featured two golden cherubim facing each other. The Lord spoke to Moses from above the Mercy Seat, between the two cherubim- - just where the idol's throne would have been in a god's temple (How does this show the difference between God and the other so-called gods?). Inside the ark were the two stone tablets containing the Ten Commandments.	**John 1:14 says of Jesus that "The Word became flesh and made his dwelling ("tabernacled") among us. We have seen his glory, the glory of the One and Only, who came from the Father, full of grace and truth."**

NOTE: God showed Moses the design of the Tabernacle on Mount Sinai. According to the Book of Hebrews, Moses actually saw a heavenly tabernacle, and what God told the Israelites to build was a copy of this heavenly tabernacle:

"Make this tabernacle and all its furnishings exactly like the pattern I will show you." (Exodus 25:9)
"See that you make them according to the pattern shown you on the mountain." (Exodus 25:40; see also Exodus 26:30, Numbers 8:4, Acts 7:44, Hebrews 8 and 9)

THE GOLDEN CALF (Exodus 32-33:6)

While Moses was on the mountain receiving the laws, the Israelites were getting restless. They were frightened by a God they could not see, and wanted to fashion for themselves an image that made sense to them-- an idol like those the Egyptians had. They made a calf idol that may have been modeled on the Egyptian bull god, Apis. When Moses saw the image, he broke the stone tablets in anger.

SPYING OUT THE LAND (Numbers 13: 13-14)

The Israelites eventually left Sinai and headed toward Canaan. They stopped in the Desert of Zin, at Kadesh, just on the edge of the Promised Land. Twelve men, one from each tribe, were chosen to explore the land and bring back a report. They were given a long list of things to study, including living conditions, locations of towns, soil conditions, people and produce. The scout from the tribe of Ephraim was Hoshea son of Nun. Hoshea was actually Joshua, who would later lead the people into Canaan. Moses changed his name to Joshua, which means "The Lord saves."

The scouts traveled through Canaan for forty days and then returned, bringing with them grapes, pomegranates and figs from the Promised Land. Their report began on a positive note, as they had seen that the land was rich and fertile. But the report soon turned into a frightening list of all of the different people who lived in the land and how strong and overwhelming they were. The listening Israelites became frightened at their stories, which became more gruesome and exaggerated as they went on. Two of the scouts remained positive, but the other ten spread doubt among the people. The Israelites began to question their ability to conquer the Promised Land, and demanded new leadership.

In response, Moses and Aaron immediately **fell face down** in front of everyone. The people's doubting response was a direct assault on God's leadership and promises, and Moses and Aaron were **preparing themselves for the judgment they were sure was coming** (Numbers 16:4, 22, 45; 20:6).

When judgment didn't come right away, Caleb and Joshua (the two good scouts) began pleading for the Israelites to move into the land, telling them to trust that God would do all that He had promised and would take care of them. When the people started talking about stoning their leaders, the Lord stepped into the argument.

Moses interceded for the people before the Lord, and although He forgave their sins, He did not allow them to enter the Promised Land. The Israelites would now be forced to wander in the wilderness until all of the adults then living had died. Only their children then under twenty years of age would be allowed to enter the land, along with Caleb and Joshua.

In rebellion, the people decided to go into the Promised Land and take possession of a part of it themselves, without Moses' blessing; but they were beaten back by the Amalekites and the Canaanites. So they wandered grumbling in the wilderness for forty years. Throughout this time of rebellion the Lord cared for them, provided for them and continued to guide them.

WATER FROM THE ROCK (Numbers 20:1-13 and 27:12-14)

After a time, the Israelites arrived back in the Desert of Zin, at Kadesh. Moses and Aaron's sister Miriam dies and is buried here. There was a lack of water where they were camped, and the quarreling began. The Israelites began to moan about their hard luck, wishing for the good old days in Egypt, yet also longing for the figs, grapes and pomegranates of the Promised Land.

Again realizing that **judgment on the grumbling Israelites was likely**, Moses and Aaron **fell face down** on the ground. The **Lord's presence filled the place**, and He instructed Moses to:

1. Take the rod
2. Gather the people
3. Speak to the rock

Then water would pour from the rock.

Instead, Moses:

1. Took the rod
2. Gathered the people
3. Spoke to the people
4. Struck the rock

Still, water poured from the rock.

But the Lord was angry with Moses. With the people gathered in a solemn assembly before the rock, Moses was to speak to the rock, asking for water so that God could demonstrate His provision for the people's needs. Instead, Moses spoke to the people himself, striking the rock as though he was providing the water himself. Moses elevated himself into God's place, and so the brothers lost their right to go into the land of promise.

The Lord did allow Moses to see the promised land before he died from the Abarim mountain range, but he was never allowed to enter (Numbers 27:12-14 and Deuteronomy 32: 48-52).

SCRIPTURE SPOTLIGHT: The Ten Commandments

The Ten Commandments found in Exodus 20 and again in Deuteronomy 5 were spoken by God to Moses on Mount Sinai/Horeb and then carved by God into two stone tablets (Deut. 5: 22).

When Jesus was asked in Matthew 22: 36-40 (and in Mark 12: 28-34) which Commandment was the greatest, He said,

"'Love the Lord your God with all your heart and with all your soul and with all your mind.' This is the first and greatest commandment. And the second is like it: 'Love your neighbor as yourself.' All the Law and the Prophets hang on these two commandments."

The first part of Jesus' response comes from Deuteronomy 6:5, and the second part was from Leviticus 19:18.

These two verses summarize the Ten Commandments: The first 3 (or 4) Commandments have to do with loving God, while the last 7 (or 6) involve loving others. The Sabbath Commandment (number 4) can go both ways. It is a day of rest in which we can focus on loving God, but it is also a day to rest and to allow others to rest. It is a day to restore relationships, enjoy family and enjoy our Creator. Interestingly enough, it is not a day for God to rest while the people serve Him, as it would have been with the other gods of the ancient world. It is the people who rest on the Sabbath.

The Commandments:

No other gods
No idols
Respect God's name
Rest on Sabbath
Respect your parents
Do not murder
Do not commit adultery
Do not steal
Do not lie
Do not covet

FASCINATING FACTS: Feast of Tabernacles (Sukkoth)

The Jewish Feast of Tabernacles comes from Leviticus 23:33-44. The festival was to be observed on the fifteenth day of the Hebrew month of Tishri, which falls either in September or October on the modern calendar. The people were to erect booths (Sukkoth) according to the law in Leviticus:

"On the first day you are to take choice fruit from the trees, and palm fronds, leafy branches and poplars, and rejoice before the LORD your God for seven days. Celebrate this as a festival to the LORD for seven days each year. This is to be a lasting ordinance for the generations to come; celebrate it in the seventh month. Live in booths for seven days: All native-born Israelites are to live in booths so your descendants will know that I had the Israelites live in booths when I brought them out of Egypt. I am the LORD your God."

The celebration commemorates the Israelites' time in the wilderness and is also associated with the end of year harvest. On the first day and the eighth day, the Israelites were to present burnt offerings to the Lord. On all of the days between, the people were to live in booths, which were simple shelters made of branches. The booths were often decorated with pictures and verses.

GEOGRAPHY FOCUS

The Deserts of the Earth

DID YOU KNOW...

- Deserts receive very little rainfall. Their dry ground is very susceptible to temperature change, so deserts tend to be extremely hot during the day and extremely cold at night.
- Some deserts are always hot, and some are always cold.
- The largest hot desert in the world is Africa's Sahara desert.
- The continent of Antarctica is the largest and coldest desert in the world.
- Other large deserts are the Gobi (in China), the Australian, the Patagonian (in southeast South America), the Atacama (on the west coast of South America) and the Kalahari (on the southeast tip of Africa).
- Deserts are home to very little plant and animal life.
- Many desert animals are nocturnal (active only at night) in order to avoid the extreme heat of the day.
- About 20% of the Earth's land is dry desert land.
- Deserts are found on every continent.

Chapter 12

Ancient India, China and Conquering Canaan

ANCIENT HISTORY FOCUS

The earliest known civilizations in the world all centered around one of four river valleys:

- the Tigris-Euphrates River Valley, which lies in what is now Iraq;
- the Nile River Valley, which lies in what is now Egypt;
- the Yellow River Valley, which lies in what is now China; and
- the Indus River Valley, which lies in what are now Pakistan, Afghanistan and India.

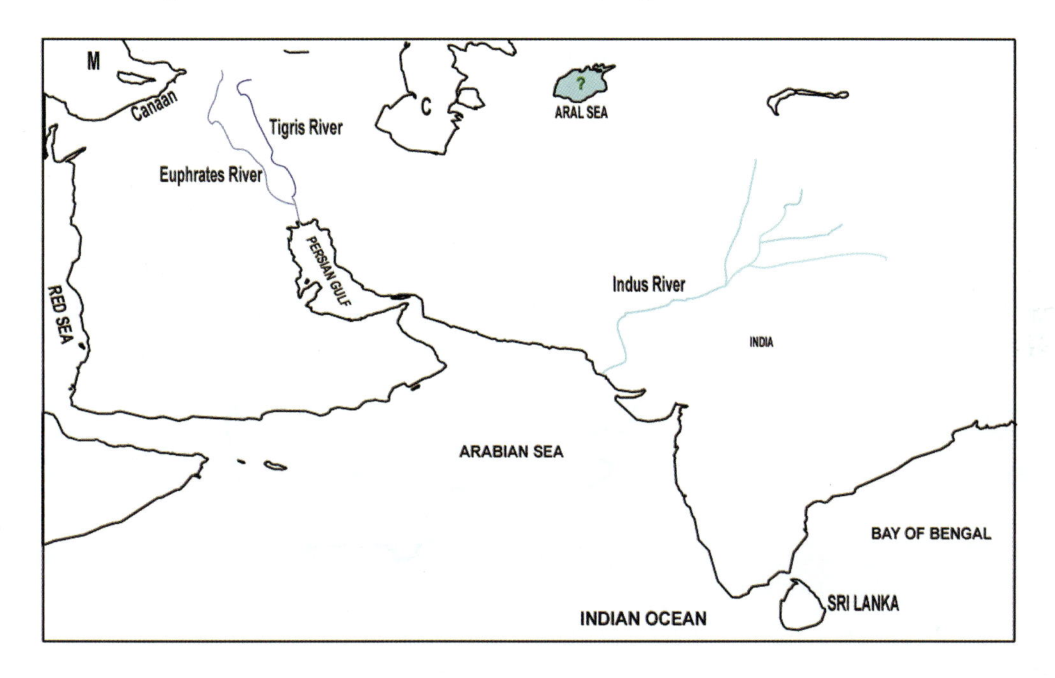

ANCIENT INDIA

Around 2500 BC, people began to settle along the Indus River Valley (along the Indus River) in the area of modern Pakistan, Afghanistan and India. The civilization that emerged and flourished during this time period (2500-1750 BC) became known as the Harappan Civilization, named after their city of Harappa. Another of the Harappans' major cities was Mohenjo-Daro. Both of these cities were built around a central citadel and were quite well organized. The citadels in the Indus Valley are the oldest known structures of that style.

Harappans spoke a language called Dravidian, which is still spoken today in parts of India, Bangladesh, Pakistan, Iran and Sri Lanka. The Harappans were a literate people: in their writing, they used a collection of over 400 distinct Indus symbols, similar in form to hieroglyphs. These symbols have been found on seals, tablets and pots.

From archaeological evidence, it is known that the Harappan people made spears, arrowheads and knives of copper and bronze, lived in multi-story stone houses, used irrigation systems to water their fields, and had sanitary sewer systems. They grew wheat, barley, peas, melons and sesame. They were the first to grow cotton for the production of cloth. They domesticated the elephant and used its ivory. They traded with the people of Mesopotamia and Sri Lanka, and had a generally flourishing civilization.

Around 1750 BC, the Harappan civilization began to disappear from the Indus River Valley. The reasons for the Harappans' decline are uncertain. One theory is that another civilization, the Indo-Aryans, invaded the valley and took over the Harappans' territory, driving them into southern India. Another theory is that the climate around the Indus River changed, drying out the Harappans' valley and forcing them to move on. Whatever may have happened to the Harappans themselves, their language, Dravidian, moved into southern India. Some of the peoples of southern India still speak Telugu and Tamil, languages that are based on Dravidian. In northern India, Indo-European languages replaced Dravidian.

ANCIENT CHINA

The first civilizations in China grew up around the Yellow River and the Yangtze River, just as civilizations in Egypt, Mesopotamia and India grew up near the major rivers.

Little is certain about China before 2200 BC, and it is difficult to separate reality from myth. The history/legend that remains tells of a succession of sovereign-sages and emperor-heroes from about 2852 BC to 2205 BC. Some of these are listed here:

	Fu Xi: According to legend Fu Xi, the Heavenly Sovereign, and his sister Nuwa, the Earthly Sovereign (see picture), were survivors of the Great Flood. Fu Xi is credited with teaching the Chinese about fishing nets, hunting, music and the institution of marriage. He created the Eight Trigrams, which were the basis for Chinese writing. He is depicted as a human being with the body of a snake.

Shennong: Shennong was considered the god of farming, as he taught the people how to grow crops in order to avoid killing animals. He also taught the people which herbs were most useful for curing diseases.

INTERESTING CHINESE RELIGIONS: Chinese Folk Religion

Pangu and Nuwa, the Creators

Chinese Folk Religion is a collection of ancient beliefs that some Chinese have held for centuries. Like some other ancient religions, Chinese Folk Religion is polytheistic, believing in many gods. Among these gods are the creator god Pangu and the mother goddess Nuwa.

According to one Chinese creation story, before the beginning of the world, Pangu awakened inside a chaotic, egg-like mass that contained all of the matter that would make up heaven and earth. The Chinese call this mass *Hundun*; some also call it the "World Egg." When Pangu was born, he split the World Egg in two. The bright, lightweight parts of the World Egg formed the heavens, and the dark, heavy parts of the World Egg formed the earth. Later, when Pangu died, his body formed parts of the heavens and the earth as well.

According to another Chinese creation story, the mother goddess Nuwa molded the Chinese people out of yellow Chinese clay and gave them life. The people whom Nuwa fashioned with great care became nobles; while the people whom she made more carelessly became commoners. Nuwa also protected her people by saving the earth from destruction. When a war between the gods caused the four poles that held up the heavens to collapse, Nuwa replaced those poles with four new poles that she fashioned from the legs of a giant sea turtle named *Ao*.

Ancestor Worship

Some of the other gods of Chinese Folk Religion are actually ancient rulers whose legends became so powerful that the Chinese began to worship them as gods. The process of becoming a god is known as "apotheosis," and the worship of once-living ancestral heroes is known as "ancestor veneration" or "ancestor worship." Two of China's most venerated ancestors are (1) Fuxi, who taught the Chinese people to feed themselves by hunting and fishing (picture shows Fuxi intertwined with Nuwa); and (2) Shennong, who taught the Chinese people to feed themselves by growing grain. Any other worthy ancestor may also be honored as a god and worshipped at an altar.

In China, proper respect for one's ancestors and parents is known as "filial piety," the duty that sons owe to their fathers. Filial piety is perhaps the most important part of Chinese folk religion. The Chinese take their duty to their parents extremely seriously; to neglect one's parents is one of the most shameful things one can do. Even when one's parents are dead, their spirits still need care and nourishment, so the Chinese feed their dead parents' spirits by making offerings at their altars. By continuing to do their duty to their parents even after they are gone, the Chinese hope to win their parents' approval-- and their blessings-- from beyond the grave.

Huang-di: Huang-di, also known as the Yellow Emperor, is credited with uniting all of the tribes into one empire. He is also considered the ancestor of the Han Chinese. It is believed that he ruled around 2695 BC. His reign was a time of Chinese achievements in medicine, architecture and arithmetic. His wife, Lei Zu, is credited with teaching the Chinese how to weave silk from silkworms. Huang-di is an important figure in two of China's religions, Taoism and Confucianism.

	Yao: Yao was a benevolent and wise ruler who reigned for 100 years, according to some legends. When he grew old, he did not name any of his sons as his successor, but instead named Shun, a young man who was well known for his high moral values despite being abused by his family. Yao gave both of his daughters to Shun in marriage and placed his sons under Shun's leadership.
	Shun: Legend has it that Shun grew up under the cruel control of his step-mother and step-brother. Although he was badly mistreated, he maintained his gentle personality, and people were drawn to him. Yao chose Shun as his successor, and Shun ruled with integrity and justice. Like Yao, Shun did not choose his own son to succeed him, but instead gave the throne to Yu, who became the founder of the Xia Dynasty.

The Xia Dynasty (reigned 2205 – 1766 BC, dates are disputed)

THE XIA DYNASTY

The Xia Dynasty was the first Chinese dynasty, reigning from 2205-1766 BC. It was established by Yu the Great, who received the throne from Shun. Yu the Great spent years of his life building dams and canals to control the Yellow River's frequent, crop-destroying floods (according to legend). In all, the dynasty included 17 Xia emperors and lasted for more than 4 centuries. Under the Xia Dynasty, the Chinese began using bronze, stone and bone to make tools.

The last emperor of the Xia Dynasty, Jie, lived a selfish and self-indulgent life. He oppressed the people and abused his power, even executing some of his own advisers. Jie was overthrown in a revolution led by Shang Tang, who then became the founder of the Shang Dynasty.

FASCINATING FACTS: The Nine Tripod Cauldrons

According to legend, after Yu the Great finally managed to bring China's constantly-flooding rivers under control, he divided China into nine provinces (nine is an important number to the Chinese). Then Yu or his son demanded a tribute payment of rare, valuable bronze from each of the provinces' nine governors. From these bronze tribute payments, the kings of the Xia Dynasty fashioned nine large, heavy and ornate three-legged cauldrons, also known as *dings*. For centuries, China's kings used the nine tripod cauldrons as vessels for offering burnt sacrifices to their gods or to their ancestors.

Over the centuries, the nine tripod cauldrons became important symbols of Chinese royalty. In order to prove that one was the rightful king of China, one had to possess the nine cauldrons. Whenever China's kings and dynasties moved their capitals from city to city, the nine cauldrons moved with them.

It may have been during one of these moves that the nine cauldrons were lost (the one in the picture is a reproduction). Sometime during the Warring States Period that came at the end of the Zhou Dynasty, China's treasured nine cauldrons simply disappeared. Some have theorized that the heavy cauldrons sank to the bottom of a deep river during some dangerous river crossing. Others have suggested that a late Zhou Dynasty king may have tried to prop up his dying government or line his pockets by melting the cauldrons down and minting coins from their copious bronze.

The Shang Dynasty (reigned 1766 – 1122 BC, dates are disputed)

THE SHANG DYNASTY

The Shang Dynasty was the second Chinese dynasty, reigning from 1766-1122 BC. It was established by Shang Tang, who overthrew Emperor Jie of the Xia Dynasty. The Shang Dynasty included about 30 kings and lasted for more than 6 centuries. This dynasty used an unusual form of succession: instead of passing from father to son, the kingdom sometimes passed from eldest brother to youngest brother.

The time of the Shang Dynasty is known as China's Bronze Age, because the Shang people developed bronze weapons, vessels, and fittings for their chariots. Their farming implements were primitive, though, as metal was scarce in China. The Shang also developed a written language and left behind numerous examples of their writing, the most common of which are on oracle bones used for divination (see pictograph section below).

In their spiritual lives, the Shang practiced a form of ancestor worship. They also worshipped the "Shang Ti," a god who ruled over the lesser gods of the sun, moon, wind and rain. When a Shang king died, slaves and prisoners of war were often sacrificed and buried with him.

The Shang Dynasty ended when the cruel and tyrannical Shang Zhou, the last Shang king, committed suicide after his army was routed by the conquering Zhou army.

FASCINATING FACTS: Pictograms

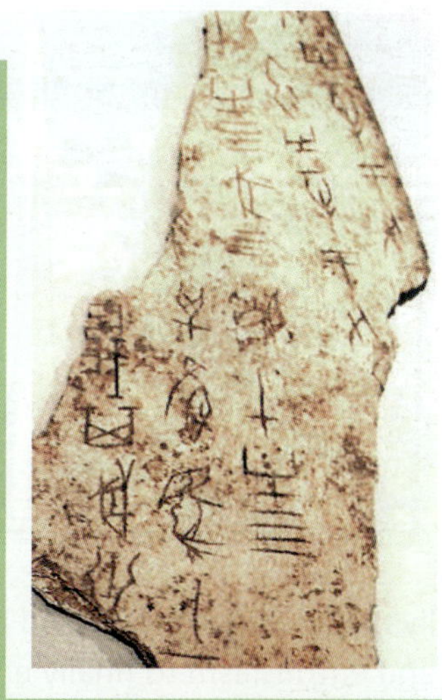

Pictograms date back to the Shang dynasty in China. In pictogram writing, pictures take the place of an alphabet in representing words. Pictograms may look like the object they represent, or they may picture something that suggests the idea of the word they represent. Pictograms were used in both early cuneiform and hieroglyphic writing.

It was during the Shang Dynasty that the Chinese first began to carve pictograms on oracle bones. The oracle bones were pieces of bone or turtle shell that were heated until they cracked, then inscribed with pictures using a bronze pin. These early pictograms were answers to questions asked of the gods (divination), and included predictions about the weather, culture, economy, politics and more from that period.

Pictograms remain in use in everyday life today, especially on signs and at sporting events.

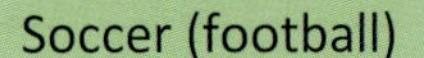
Soccer (football)

Golf

Handicapped
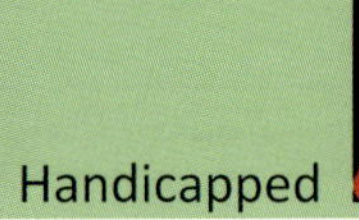

Deer Crossing

FASCINATING FACTS: Rice

Rice has been a staple food in Asia for thousands of years. Archaeologists have found evidence of rice from as early as 2500 BC around the Yangtze River basin. Rice is so important in China that the word "rice" is synonymous with food.

A Chinese myth says that after the Great Flood, when all living things were destroyed and animals were scarce, food was hard to find. One day, a dog approached some Chinese people in a flooded field. Caught in the dog's fur were some yellow seeds. The Chinese planted the seeds in the flooded soil, and rice grew.

BIBLE FOCUS

THE ISRAELITES IN CANAAN: JOSHUA, JUDGES AND RUTH

THE BOOK OF JOSHUA

GIANTS OF THE FAITH: JOSHUA

The Israelites of the Exodus wandered in the wilderness for forty years after leaving Egypt, punished for their lack of faith that God would help them win the promised land of Canaan.

After forty years, all of the adults who were over the age of twenty at the time of the Exodus were dead-- except for Joshua and Caleb, Moses' two good scouts. A new generation of Israelites had emerged, a generation toughened by years of wilderness living. They had little or no memory of their brutal treatment in Egypt (so they didn't have the baggage of being former slaves) and had the privilege of seeing God's provision for them (manna) on a daily basis. Among those who did remember Egypt, most were too young to remember the Egyptian gods, so their faith in Yahweh was untainted. They were an excited, energetic group of men and women who had waited for their entire lives to move into the land promised to their ancestors. Their sorrow over Moses' death was offset by their joy and enthusiasm to finally enter the Promised Land. Their Conquest of Canaan finally happened, possibly around 1400 BC.

The Book of Joshua begins with the death of Moses and ends with the death of Joshua. It begins with a promise from God that He will be with the Israelites, and ends with the Israelites' pledge to follow God. As the book opens, God encourages Joshua with these words:

"No one will be able to stand up against you all the days of your life. As I was with Moses, so I will be with you; I will never leave you nor forsake you." (Joshua 1:5)

As the book closes, Joshua affirms to the Israelites that God has been with them and exhorts them to choose to follow Him. In answer, they pledge themselves to God:

"Then the people answered, 'Far be it from us to forsake the LORD to serve other gods! It was the LORD our God himself who brought us and our fathers up out of Egypt, from that land of slavery, and performed those great signs before our eyes. He protected us on our entire journey and among all the nations

through which we traveled. And the LORD drove out before us all the nations, including the Amorites, who lived in the land. We too will serve the LORD, because he is our God.'" (Joshua 24: 16-18)

The remainder of the Book of Joshua can be divided into two major sections: the conquest and the dividing of the land.

THE CONQUEST (Joshua 1-12)

In order to enter the Promised Land, the Israelites had to cross the Jordan River. The river was at flood stage when they set out to cross, so the Lord parted the Jordan for them just as he had parted the Reed/Red Sea (Joshua 3-4).

Joshua already had two spies in Jericho, the first Canaanite city he planned to attack (Joshua 2). The spies brought back the news that the Canaanites were terrified of the Israelites and the God they served. While in Jericho, these spies had been protected by a woman named Rahab who risked her life to save them from discovery.

GIANTS OF THE FAITH: Rahab

Rahab is an unusual and interesting Bible character. Just before the Israelites' conquest of Canaan, she protects two Israelite spies from discovery, revealing a profound understanding of their God in the process. Through her bargain with them, she secures her own protection, and she finally ends up in Jesus' genealogy!

Joshua sends two spies into Canaan to learn whatever they can. They enter Jericho and end up in Rahab's house. Although she is often known as Rahab the harlot, it is actually uncertain why the spies come to her house. When the king's men come looking for spies, the townsmen know that she has visitors, so they tell her to bring them out. Instead, she lies and sends the king's men on a wild goose chase out of town. Then she helps the spies over the wall and out of town, but not before delivering a beautiful statement of faith:

"For the LORD your God is God in heaven above and on the earth below" (Joshua 2: 11b).

In return for her help, the spies promise to spare her life when the Israelites come to conquer Jericho. This promise is fulfilled:

"But Joshua spared Rahab the prostitute, with her family and all who belonged to her, because she hid the men Joshua had sent as spies to Jericho—and she lives among the Israelites to this day" (Joshua 6:25).

Rahab's name doesn't appear again in scripture until the New Testament. She is listed in the Gospel of Matthew as the mother of Boaz, who married Ruth (from the Book of Ruth). This makes her one of Jesus' ancestors. She appears once more in the Book of Hebrews in a famous chapter sometimes called the faith "hall of fame." She joins a list of ancients who acted on their faith in God without ever seeing what they hoped for:

"By faith the prostitute Rahab, because she welcomed the spies, was not killed with those who were disobedient" (Hebrews 11:31, see also James 2:25).

After crossing the Jordan River, the Israelites build a monument from twelve stones taken from the bed of the Jordan. Then Joshua has all of the men circumcised to reaffirm their covenant with God, and they celebrate Passover.

After the Passover meal, they eat produce from Canaan, and the **manna from heaven finally stops after 40 years** (Joshua 4 and 5:1-14).

The rest of the conquest section includes the following stories of interest to read:

Joshua 5:13-6: The total destruction of Jericho. The walls come down without any fighting!
Joshua 7: Defeat at Ai because of Achan's sin, and Achan's punishment
Joshua 8: 1-29: The total destruction of Ai
Joshua 8: 30-35: Joshua renews the covenant with God by making new stone tablets containing the law God gave to Moses (to replace the ones Moses broke).
Joshua 9: The Gibeonites dress up as foreigners and make a treaty with Joshua, who is deceived by their ruse.
Joshua 10: The five southern kings of the Amorites band together against the Gibeonites, who now have a treaty with Israel. Israel attacks the Amorite kings, and the sun stands still so that the Israelites have enough daylight to destroy the Amorites. Joshua kills all five of the kings and then conquers their southern cities.
Joshua 11: Joshua turns north and overcomes the northern cities. Hazor is totally destroyed (like Ai and Jericho).
Joshua 12: A list of 31 kings defeated by Joshua

CRITICAL COMPARISONS between Joshua and Moses

There are several interesting similarities between Moses and Joshua:

- Both are called by God directly, and He promises each that He will never leave him.
- Both become the instrument that God uses to speak to His people.
- Both lead the Israelites across water that has been parted by God.
- Both have encounters with God in which they are told to remove their shoes.
- Both present to the people stone tablets with the law written on them.
- Both are given tasks that are impossible for a mere man.
- Both witness God's mighty acts of power over nature
- Both appear in Hebrews 11, the faith "hall of fame."

SCRIPTURE SPOTLIGHT: The Brutality of the Conquest

In both Joshua and Judges, the Israelites are charged not merely to drive out the inhabitants of the Promised Land, but to destroy them. This includes men, women and children. These demands seem shocking and brutal, and some question God's fairness in directing the Israelites to do all of this killing. Some wonder how a God of love and mercy could command the killing of all alike, even children. In response, consider the following:

- God is the Creator, Judge and Ruler of the earth. He alone holds life in His hands.
- As Judge, God has the right to decide when any nation has reached a level of sin that cannot be condoned. The sins of the Canaanites had reached that level. Their sins are mentioned in Leviticus 18:1-24, which refers to gross sexual sins and child sacrifice.
- The destruction committed by the Israelites was an act of **DIVINE** judgment. Israel became the instrument of God's judgment. It was not their idea.
- The Israelites did not destroy the Canaanites because they themselves were righteous, but because the Canaanites were utterly sinful (Deuteronomy 9).
- God was not arbitrary in His judgment. He warned the Israelites that they would meet the same fate if they did not obey Him.
- Finally, the Israelites did not fully complete God's instructions, but allowed exceptions, and this eventually led to their own demise. They intermarried with the Canaanites, began to worship the Canaanite gods, and therefore were eventually driven out of the land themselves.

DIVIDING THE LAND (Joshua 13-22)

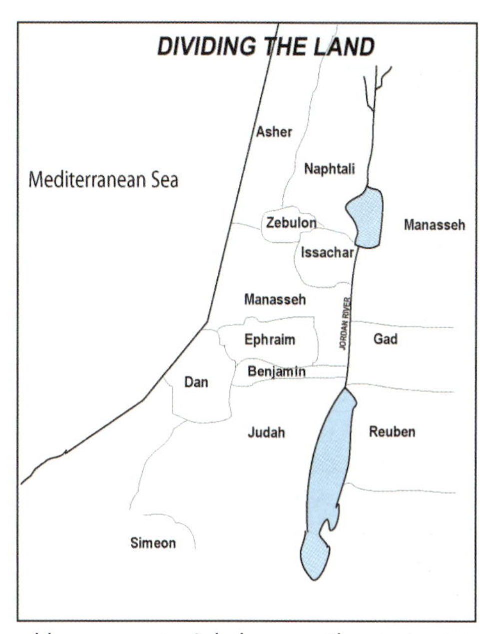

There were actually thirteen Israelite tribes. Jacob had twelve sons, but he also adopted Joseph's two sons, Manasseh and Ephraim; so Joseph received a double portion of his father's estate, a firstborn's portion.

But there was another special provision for the tribe of Levi, the priestly tribe: they were not given a separate division of land, but instead received towns within each of the other tribes' divisions so that they could live and minister among the people. Therefore the land was still divided into twelve sections on both sides of the Jordan River (see map), even though there were thirteen tribes.

THE BOOK OF JUDGES

The Book of Judges is filled with shocking stories and strange heroes. It chronicles the descent of the Israelites into sin and disobedience and the ever-faithful presence of God. Typical Sunday School lesson material chooses the major heroes (or judges) from the book of Judges and focuses on their stories and eventual victories. But this misses the overall point of the book.

The theme of Judges centers on the **sinfulness of man** and the **faithfulness of God**. Judges tells the story of Israel's slide into ever-deeper levels of sin and faithlessness.

Judges covers approximately 300 years of Israel's history, roughly from 1360-1085 BC (the exact dates are disputed). It begins with the death of Joshua, which forces a transition for Israel, because it is without a national leader like Moses or Joshua for the first time since the Exodus. The tribes begin to fall into a cyclical pattern: wherever a tribe fails to drive out the Canaanites, its people stop following God's law and begin to worship the Canaanite gods. Then God allows the Israelites' enemies to punish them. When their suffering grows too great, they remember their covenant with God and cry out for His deliverance, and God raises up a "judge" to deliver them. At first the Israelites return to God quickly after briefly falling away, but by the time of Gideon (Judges 6), their descent into chaos is more evident.

A judge was a military leader and a hero, but could also be a prophet or a decider of disputes. The judge could come from any tribe, and in this most patriarchal society, there was even one female judge (Deborah). There were thirteen judges, seven of whom are considered major judges (heroes).

The Seven Major Judges:

OTHNIEL (Judges 3:7-11): The Israelites did evil before the Lord, thus a king from the north attacked and enslaved them for eight years. **They cried out to God**, and **He raised up Othniel** who became Israel's judge and drove out the invaders. The land was at peace for forty years.

EHUD (Judges 3: 12-30): The Israelites did evil before the Lord, so the king of Moab, the Ammonites and the Amalekites attacked Israel and held it captive for eighteen years. **They cried out to God**, and **He raised up Ehud (a left-handed man)** who killed the king of Moab with his sword and drove out the invaders. The land was at peace for eighty years.

DEBORAH (Judges 4): The Israelites did evil before the Lord, thus the king of Hazor with his mighty chariots attacked Israel and oppressed them for twenty years. **They cried out to God**, and **He raised up Deborah**. She picked Barak to lead the army, but he wanted Deborah to go with him. She agreed, but prophesied that a woman would get the glory for the victory. In the end it was a woman named Jael who killed the king of Hazor. The land was at peace for forty years.

GIDEON (Judges 6 - 8): The Israelites did evil before the Lord, thus the Midianites oppressed the Israelites to such an extent that they had to hide in caves. **They cried out to God**, and **He raised up Gideon**. Gideon protested at first, but eventually tore down his family's altars and led a tiny group of Israelites against the vast army of Midianites and drove them out. Then the Israelites begin to bicker with Gideon. Although the story ends on a positive note, because the land was at peace for forty years, strife among the Israelites themselves is becoming evident. The Israelites ask Gideon to become their king, believing that Gideon himself has saved them and not God. Although Gideon refuses, he does allow them to make for him a garment (ephod) of gold that the Israelites worshipped.

ABIMELECH (Judges 9): The Israelites did evil before the Lord. Abimelech, one of Gideon's sons from a concubine, **raises himself** up as Israel's king. He kills all of his brothers but one, Jotham, who puts a curse on Abimelech. God causes Israelites to fight against Israelites in this shocking story. In the end, Abimelech was defeated by a woman (although his armor-bearer deals the final blow).

JEPHTHAH (Judges 10:6 - 12:7): The Israelites did evil before the Lord, and the Philistines and the Ammonites oppressed them for eighteen years. **They cried out to God**, but **He did not believe them**; so they tore down their foreign gods and **cried out to God** again. **He raised up Jephthah**, the son of a prostitute who had been rejected by his family (God has an interesting way of choosing heroes). In the midst of Jephthah's victory (with God's power), he makes a shocking vow to sacrifice whatever comes through his door first upon his return home. As it turns out, Jephthah's only child, a daughter, becomes the sacrifice. The story deteriorates from there, and Israelites again fight against Israelites.

SAMSON (Judges 13 - 16): The Israelites did evil before the Lord, thus the Philistines oppressed them for forty years. **The Lord raised up Samson (note that the Israelites did not cry out to God yet He still cared for them).** The story of Samson is the longest story in Judges, covering three chapters. Samson is born to Godly parents who raise him as a Nazirite, set apart for God from birth. According to the Nazirite vow, Samson can never drink anything alcoholic, never eat anything unclean and never cut his hair.

Despite this great beginning, Samson is in fact another unlikely hero. He is spoiled and selfish, living for his own pleasure despite his Nazirite vow. Against his parents' advice, he chooses a Philistine wife. Despite this, God uses him in a mighty way against the Philistines, empowering him with tremendous physical strength to defeat them again and again. A later wife, Delilah, brings Samson down in the end: she tricks Samson into revealing that his uncut hair (the sign of his vow to God) is the secret of his strength. Then she brings in men to subdue him in secret and has one of them cut Samson's hair while he sleeps. Samson is captured and his eyes are gouged out, and then he is forced to turn a millstone for the amusement of his captors. In the end, a humbled and contrite Samson prays to God to allow his strength to return for one last battle. God answers his prayer, and with a last burst of strength, Samson collapses a temple on the Philistines.

Israel's Descent into utter chaos (Judges 17-21)

The remainder of Judges (chapters 17-21) tells two sordid tales of Israel's godlessness. They were a nation without a king or a prophet, and **no longer worshipped God as a nation**. Most had turned to the foreign gods of the Canaanites.

The first sordid tale tells how one man makes his own idol and shrine, hiring his own personal priest to tend it. Then the Danites (from the Israelite tribe of Dan), who should know better, steal his idol and his priest for their own use.

The second tale is even worse than the first (chapters 19-21 - parental guidance on this section). The Israelites have failed to live up to their covenant with God under the judges, and have declined into chaos and godlessness as a result.

The book of Judges ends by saying,

"In those days Israel had no king; everyone did as he saw fit."

This is a lead-in for what follows in the Book of Samuel, in which God chooses a prophet who finds a king for Israel.

THE BOOK OF RUTH

GIANTS OF THE FAITH: RUTH

The Book of Ruth is a breath of fresh air after the sad events of Judges. It is a wonderful story of faith, loyalty and love. It **begins with Naomi**, a widow whose husband and sons have died, leaving her without hope of heirs to carry on the family name. It **ends with this same Naomi** holding in her lap a grandson who will be an **ancestor of Jesus**.

The book is divided into six sections. There are similarities between the first and sixth sections, the second and fifth sections and the third and fourth sections. This literary scheme is called a "chiasm," and it is found throughout the Scriptures. Since most ancient people could not read, they learned the Scriptures by hearing, and the stories were often written in the familiar form of a chiasm so that the hearers could more easily remember them.

Naomi's sorrow (Ruth 1:1-5): Naomi and her husband are from the line of Judah. When a famine strikes the land, they move to the country of Moab. Although they are in a foreign land, they remain Godly people and do not embrace the gods of the foreigners. The story opens with the deaths of Naomi's husband and both of her sons. She is left alone with two widowed daughters-in-law in the foreign land of the Moabites. Both girls are Moabites.

The choice (Ruth 1:6-22): When the famine is over, Naomi packs up to go home. On the road home, she realizes that she has nothing to offer her sons' wives, so she tells them to go back to their own mothers' homes so that they can perhaps find other husbands. At first they both refuse, but when Naomi appeals a second time, one of the girls (Orpah) agrees to leave. The second girl, Ruth, chooses to stay with Naomi, even though it means leaving her home. She has seen the beauty of Naomi's righteous life and faith, and she declares her own love for Naomi and faith in God:

"Don't urge me to leave you or to turn back from you. Where you go I will go, and where you stay I will stay. Your people will be my people and your God my God."

The two women arrive in Bethlehem. Back among her own people, Naomi tells of her sorrow and loss. Naomi and Ruth are destitute and alone.

Ruth meets Boaz (Ruth 2): The Old Testament law provided that at harvest time, the fields were not to be picked entirely clean so that the poor, foreigners and widows could go behind the harvesters and glean whatever was left (Lev. 19:9 and Deut. 24:19). Ruth goes out alone (and lonely) to glean in the fields, and ends up in the field of Boaz, a kinsman of her dead husband. Hope has arrived. Boaz arrives and sees Ruth, praises her for her faithfulness to Naomi and blesses her for it. He arranges things so that she will find more to glean than the average widow. He also invites her to eat with the group instead of alone, places protection around her and gives her extra portions of food. When she returns home she tells Naomi everything. When she realizes that Boaz is a kinsman redeemer (see below), Naomi gives praise to God that He has not forgotten them.

Ruth proposes to Boaz (Ruth 3): Naomi encourages Ruth into action. She sends her to the threshing floor (where the harvested wheat is separated from the straw by threshing) so that she can indicate to Boaz that she wants him to redeem her. Naomi tells Ruth to wait until Boaz is asleep, then uncover his feet and lie down at them. Ruth obeys. Boaz wakes up and sees Ruth, praises her for her faithfulness and blesses her for it, arranges a meeting with the other potential kinsman redeemer, invites her to stay with him for the night, places protection around her and gives her extra portions of food. When Ruth returns home she tells Naomi everything.

The choice (Ruth 4: 1-12): Boaz goes to the town gate (where business was usually conducted) and offers Naomi's land to the other, more closely related kinsman redeemer in the presence of a group of ten elders. At first the kinsman redeemer wants the land, but when he realizes that Ruth comes along with it, he refuses. Now that his way is clear, Boaz chooses to redeem the land, and Ruth along with it.

Before the elders and all of the people, Boaz pledges himself to Ruth, and she is no longer alone or destitute.

Naomi's joy (Ruth 4: 13-22): Boaz and Ruth marry, and she conceives and has a son, continuing the line of her dead husband. Naomi is no longer alone, but now has a grandchild from her husband's line to love and cherish.

FASCINATING FACTS: The Kinsman Redeemer

Under the Law of Moses, if a poor person was forced to sell his property or to sell himself into slavery, his nearest kin were allowed to step in and buy back whatever he sold. This buyer was known as the "kinsman redeemer." Also, if a family member died without an heir, the kinsman redeemer could carry on his name by marrying his widow and rearing any son in the name of the widow's dead husband, his kinsman (Leviticus 25:25, 48; Deuteronomy 25:5, Genesis 38:8).

Both of these factors came into play in Ruth's story. She was a widow and had borne her husband no heir, so she needed a kinsman redeemer to carry on her husband's name. Also, because she was a woman, she was part of her dead husband's "estate" along with his other property (Ruth 4:4-5). So when Naomi made it known that she was selling her sons' land, it was understood that Ruth went along with it. In this way God provided for the widows-- as long as faithful Israelites like Boaz upheld the law.

A Final Note about Judges and Ruth

The Book of Judges begins with hope and deteriorates into despair, closing with the pronouncement that Israel had no king. The Book of Ruth, on the other hand, begins with despair that changes to hope. Ruth closes with a genealogy, and the last name listed is that of Israel's greatest king (yet to be born in Ruth's day).

FASCINATING FACTS: Jesus' Ancestors up to this point

Abraham - Isaac - Jacob - Judah and Tamar - Perez - Hezron - Ram - Amminadab - Nahshon - Salmon and Rahab - Boaz and Ruth - Obed - Jesse - King David

GEOGRAPHY FOCUS

FASCINATING FACTS: Cinnamon

Cinnamon is a spice that comes from the dried bark of the laurel tree, and it has been well known since ancient times. The best variety of cinnamon comes from Sri Lanka, the large island that lies just southeast of India. A more common variety grows wild in China, and this variety is more familiar in the United States. Because cinnamon does not grow in Africa, West Asia or Europe, the ancient peoples of the Mediterranean world considered it rare and valuable. Cinnamon's first mention in the Bible comes in Exodus 30:23, where it appears as an ingredient in a sacred anointing oil.

The ancients used cinnamon for several purposes: as a food preservative, as medicine for colds and flu, as a way to cover up foul odors and as a digestive aid. It was used in embalming because of its preservative qualities. It also was used in oil form to treat infections and to improve circulation. It was a pain reducer, had a calming effect (especially for birthing mothers) and decreased nausea and vomiting.

Chapter 13

Ancient Africa, Saul and David (Part I)

ANCIENT HISTORY AND GEOGRAPHY FOCUS

FASCINATING FACTS: The Sahara Desert

The Sahara Desert in North Africa is the largest hot desert in the world, covering over 3,500,000 square miles. Stretching from the Red Sea in the east to the Atlantic Ocean in the west, it encompasses 11 modern day countries. Its land forms range from sand dunes to stone plateaus, dry valleys, salt flats and gravel plains. It is one of the hottest regions in the world, reaching temperatures over 122 degrees Fahrenheit.

But the Sahara was not always hot and dry. Archaeologists have found evidence that the Sahara once had grass, trees and animals, indicating that it was once wet and fertile. Could the Great Flood have changed the climate of the Sahara?

Interesting facts about modern-day countries in the Sahara Desert region:

EGYPT: 99% of the Egypt's population lives on only 5.5 % of its total land area. The rest is mostly desert.
SUDAN: Sudan is the largest country in Africa.
LIBYA: 90% of Libya is in the Sahara Desert.
CHAD: Chad is often called the "Dead Heart of Africa." The northern third of Chad lies in the Sahara.
TUNISIA: 40% of Tunisia lies in the Sahara Desert.
ALGERIA: 80% of Algeria lies in the Sahara Desert.
NIGER: 80% of Niger lies in the Sahara Desert.
MOROCCO: Much of the Sahara Desert's population lives in coastal Morocco, which has 34 million people.
MALI: Most of Mali lies in the Sahara Desert and receives little rainfall.
WESTERN SAHARA: A disputed territory still claimed by Morocco, Western Sahara is one of the most sparsely populated areas in the world.
MAURITANIA - 75% of Mauritania lies in the Sahara Desert.

GEOGRAPHY OF AFRICA

Today, Africa is divided into 53 countries plus the Western Sahara. Its climate ranges from hot and dry deserts (brown areas on map above) to grasslands (light green areas) to rain forests (dark green areas).

Despite the hostility of the Saharan environment, all of Africa's known ancient civilization grew up in or near it. Little is known of any ancient Africans who lived below the Sahara Desert. Unlike the Egyptians, they left no writing or artifacts behind.

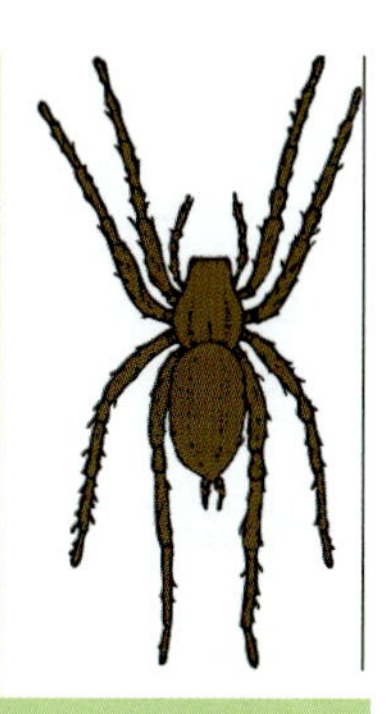

FASCINATING FACTS: Anansi the Spider

Anansi the spider is a popular animal trickster from West African mythology. Although he is a spider, he is able to change his appearance in order to oppose the gods and wreak havoc on humans. Anansi sometimes appears as a rabbit, a human or a fox.

In some West African mythology, Anansi is known as the creator of the world and as the one who taught man how to plant and grow crops for food. Some also know him as a messenger between man and the sky god Nyame.

Anansi is known by several names in Africa, the Caribbean and the United States: Anase, Kweku, Ananse, Anancy and Aunt Nancy.

BRER-RABBIT AND THE TAR BABY

In one of the Anansi stories, the spider fights with a tar baby (a child's doll made of tar) and gets stuck to the tar. There is a well-known African-American tale that has a similar plot, and probably has roots in the Anansi story: *The Tale of Br'er Rabbit*. Joel Chandler Harris compiled *Br'er Rabbit* and other tales into a collection called *Uncle Remus, His Songs and His Sayings* in 1881. Harris' fictional character Uncle Remus was a kindly old slave who loved to tell stories to the children on the plantation. Br'er Rabbit, or Brother Rabbit, was his main character. Like Anansi the spider, Br'er Rabbit was a trickster who was always getting others into trouble, especially Br'er Fox and Br'er Bear.

In *Br'er Rabbit and the Tar Baby*, it looks like Br'er Rabbit has met his match. Br'er Fox finds a lump of tar and dresses it up as a boy doll, then leaves it in Br'er Rabbit's path. When the tar baby refuses to answer Br'er Rabbit's greeting, he gets angry and strikes it, and gets stuck in the tar. Then Br'er Fox comes along and finds Br'er Rabbit stuck to the tar baby, unable to move. Br'er Fox has caught Br'er Rabbit at last, and starts to consider how to dispose of him. In an early example of reverse psychology, Br'er Rabbit pleads with Br'er Fox NOT to throw him in the briar patch. Br'er Fox immediately tosses him into the briar patch. But the briar patch is a rabbit's home ground, and Br'er Rabbit gleefully hops away. Br'er Fox has been foiled again.

BIBLE FOCUS

SAMUEL, SAUL AND DAVID - I and II Samuel

The Bible books of I Samuel and II Samuel are really two parts of one long Book of Samuel. They cover the prophet Samuel and the first two kings of Israel, Saul and David. Taken as a whole, the books of Samuel can be divided into five main sections: Samuel the prophet, Saul as king, David's beginnings, David in hiding, and David as king (covered in II Samuel). This week we will examine I Samuel, which covers Samuel, Saul and David before he becomes king.

Possible Timeline for Saul, David and Solomon

1360-1085 BC: The period of the Judges
1051 BC: Saul's reign begins
1040 BC: David is born
1011 BC: Saul and his three sons are killed on Mount Gilboa; David is anointed king of Judah.
1004 BC: David is anointed king of Israel; David moves capital to Jerusalem.
971 BC: Solomon's reign begins
931 BC: Israel divides into two separate kingdoms

GIANTS OF THE FAITH: SAMUEL THE PROPHET (I Samuel 1-7)

The rise of Samuel begins a new era in the history of Israel, ending the era of the judges. Samuel is the bridge between the two eras. He is the prophet who anoints the first two kings of Israel, and he is the last of Israel's great judges.

SAMUEL'S BIRTH (1 Samuel 1:1-2:11)

If you are keeping up with our chiasms, this section has one: the first section corresponds to the last, the second corresponds to the fourth and the third section stands alone in the center as the climactic event:

Hannah prays to the Lord (I Samuel 1:1-11): Samuel's mother Hannah is the favorite wife of her husband, but she is barren-- just as in the patriarch stories of Abraham and Sarah, Isaac and Rebekah, and Jacob and Rachel. As in those stories, the rivalry between Hannah and her husband's wife Peninnah grows brutal (remember Sarah versus Hagar and Rachel versus Leah). Hannah is desperate to have a child, and so when she is at Shiloh (the home of the tabernacle), she prays to God. Hannah vows that if the Lord will give her a child, she will give him back to the Lord and raise him according to the Nazirite vow, never cutting his hair.
Hannah and Eli (I Samuel 1: 12-18): Eli the priest sees Hannah praying and thinks she is drunk, but when she tells him what she is praying for, he blesses her.
Samuel is born (I Samuel 1:19-23): Hannah gives birth to Samuel and keeps him with her until he is weaned. This is the climax of the story and the reason for its telling.
Hannah and Eli (I Samuel 1: 24-28): Hannah returns to Shiloh and tells Eli that her prayers were answered. The Lord has given her a son, whom she is now giving back to the Lord.
Hannah praises the Lord (I Samuel 2: 1-11): Hannah offers praise and thanksgiving for God's faithfulness.

A FUN CONTRAST BETWEEN SAMUEL AND THE SONS OF ELI THE PRIEST
I Samuel 2:12-26 - 3

This section is written in another literary style, the parallel style. In parallel writing, the writer tells a story about first one item in a pair, then the other, back and forth. Like the chiasm, parallel writing is used often in the Scriptures, especially in poetry. It is fun to hear and helps the audience to remember the story. It also highlights contrasts (differences) between one thing and another.

In this case the pair consists of Eli's sons on the one hand and Hannah's son Samuel on the other. Eli is the priest at the tabernacle, and his sons are being groomed to take his place; but they are wicked and unworthy of the job. Samuel is their opposite, devoted to the Lord from birth.

The wickedness of Eli's sons (I Samuel 2:12-17): Eli's sons treat the sacrifices offered at the tabernacle with contempt, greatly displeasing the Lord.

Samuel's service (I Samuel 2: 18-21): Samuel is reverent, pleasing the Lord. The Lord blesses Samuel's mother Hannah with more children.

Eli is told of his sons' wickedness (I Samuel 2: 22-25): Eli rebukes his sons when he hears how they have displeased the Lord.

Samuel's maturity (I Samuel 2: 26): Samuel continues to give the Lord pleasure as he grows and matures.

Prophecy against Eli's sons (I Samuel 2: 27-36): A prophet comes and predicts that Eli and his sons will die because of the sons' wickedness.

Samuel's call (I Samuel 3: 1-10): The Lord calls to Samuel in his sleep. Unused to hearing the Lord, Samuel thinks that Eli is calling him from the next room. After the third call, with some help from Eli, Samuel answers the Lord's call.

Prophecy against Eli's sons (I Samuel 3: 11-18) The Lord tells Samuel that all of Eli's family will be judged for the wickedness of his sons. Samuel reports this to Eli, who sadly responds, "He is the LORD; let Him do what is good in his eyes."

Samuel as Prophet (I Samuel 3: 19-21): The Lord is with Samuel and speaks to all of Israel through Samuel.

TROUBLE WITH THE ARK (I Samuel 4-7)

The Israelites were constantly at war with the Philistines, who lived in the southern part of Canaan along the Mediterranean Sea (the area now known as Gaza). In I Samuel 4, the Philistines defeat the Israelites in a major battle. Four thousand Israelites are killed in the fighting, and the elders begin to question why God brought them defeat. They decide to send to Shiloh for the Ark of the Covenant, hoping that it will bring them victory. Eli's sons bring the ark to the battle. But instead of bringing victory, the ark brings destruction. Israel suffers an even worse loss in which 30,000 soldiers are killed, including Eli's sons. The Philistines capture the ark, which is lost to Israel for a time. Eli, who has been worried about the ark, dies when he receives the news.

But the Philistines do not find the ark to be a blessing. Wherever the ark goes, the Philistines are afflicted with tumors or death. When it is placed in the temple of the Philistine god Dagon, the Dagon idol mysteriously falls on its face overnight. After the Philistines restore it to its place, it mysteriously collapses a second time, and this time it breaks. Finally, the Philistines decide to return the ark to the Israelites.

After the ark's return, Samuel calls on the people to repent, give up their foreign gods and worship God alone. After they purify themselves, Samuel leads them to victory over the Philistines, and peace settles on the land. In Samuel's old age, he appoints his sons as judges in his place; but like Eli's sons, Samuel's sons are wicked before the Lord.

The people began to cry out for a king to replace Samuel.

SAUL, ISRAEL'S FIRST KING (I Samuel 8 - 15)

The Israelites wanted what other nations had: a strong leader who would unite and protect them. They already had such a leader, God Himself. But their sin was driving a wedge between them and God. By choosing a king, they were rejecting God's leadership. God instructed Samuel to warn them about life under a king, about heavy taxes and the loss of their freedom, but they would not listen. So God finally told Samuel to find them a king.

THE LORD CHOOSES SAUL (I Samuel 9 - 10)

This section contains another chiasm, in which the first division is similar to the last:

Description of Saul (Samuel 9: 1-2): Saul was the son of Kish, a Benjamite. He was handsome and also a head taller than any other Israelite.

Lost donkeys (I Samuel 9: 3-3-14): Saul and his servant set out to find the family's donkeys, which had wandered away. Donkeys were indispensable to a family in those days. Saul looked in three places, but could not find them. Before turning for home, he decided to ask the seer (prophet) if he could tell him where the donkeys had wandered.

God chooses Saul (I Samuel 9:15-27 and 10:1): The Lord had told Samuel that a man would come to him from the tribe of Benjamin. When Saul showed up, the Lord told Samuel that he was the chosen king. Samuel told

Saul that the Lord had chosen him to lead the Israelites. Saul protested that he was unworthy, but Samuel anointed Saul and gave him a blessing.

Three signs given (I Samuel 10: 1-8): Saul received three signs to confirm that he was the chosen king:

1. Two men would meet him at Rachel's tomb and tell him that the donkeys were found.
2. Three men would meet him at Bethel (Jacob's place) with three goats, three loaves of bread and some wine. They would give him two of the loaves.
3. Saul would encounter a group of prophets at Gibeah (Saul's home). The Spirit of the Lord would come upon Saul and he would prophesy with the prophets.

Three signs fulfilled (I Samuel 10: 9-16): By the time Saul arrived home, all three signs had been fulfilled. His family was shocked to see him prophesying.

God chooses Saul through lot (I Samuel 10: 16-21a): Samuel assembled Israelites from every tribe. He drew lots, and Saul was chosen as king.

Lost Saul (I Samuel 10: 21b-22): Saul couldn't be found, so they asked the Lord where he was hiding.

Description of Saul (I Samuel 10: 23-27): Saul stood before them, a head taller than any of the other Israelites. Despite the signs and ceremony, some doubted his ability to lead Israel.

HIGH PRIEST IN ROBES AND BREASTPLATE. —Lev. viii, 8.

FASCINATING FACTS: Casting lots

When the priests of Israel needed to know God's choice in some decision, they sometimes used the method of casting lots. The High Priest carried sacred stones known as Urrim and Thummim in a container inside his breastplate. The stones were cast, and the Lord made them fall as He wished. It is not known what the stones looked like or how the outcome of the cast was determined, but the priests interpreted what they saw, and the authority of the stones was not questioned.

SAUL AS KING (I Samuel 11-15)

I Samuel 11: Saul's time as king begins well. When the Israelites of Jabesh-Gilead (from the tribe of Manasseh, east of the Jordan) are threatened by the Ammonites (who say they will gouge out the right eye of every man), they call for help. Saul is still living on the family farm, more like a judge than a king. Nevertheless he calls upon all Israelites to fight with him, sending a piece of his family ox to each of the twelve tribes. With three hundred and thirty thousand men, Saul defeats the Ammonites. Now that he has proved his leadership ability, the people confirm Saul as king.

I Samuel 12: Old Samuel steps down as leader of the Israelites, but not before he rebukes them and demonstrates God's power and might by bringing down thunder and rain during the dry season. Even though Israel has rejected God as its King, Samuel promises to pray for the Israelites and exhorts them to follow God.

I Samuel 13: Saul quickly begins to prove that he is not God's man. He offends the Lord by not waiting for Samuel to make an offering before a battle against the Philistines. Instead, he hastily makes his own offering so that he can conduct the battle in his own time. The Lord is angered, and decides that He will not establish his kingdom through Saul's line.

I Samuel 14: Saul's son Jonathan and his armor-bearer rout a group of Philistines, setting off a panic throughout the Philistine camp. Saul and the rest of the army join in the battle and defeat the Philistines, but the victory loses its sweetness when Jonathan eats honey, not realizing that Saul has placed a curse on any man who eats before the Philistines are routed.

I Samuel 15: Saul is commanded to attack the Amalekites and destroy them completely, everyone and everything. Instead of obeying the Lord, Saul follows his own wisdom, saving the best of the livestock and letting the Amalekite king live. Samuel confronts Saul and tells him that the Lord has rejected Saul as king for disobeying God's commands. Samuel leaves Saul and does not meet with him again.

GIANTS OF THE FAITH: DAVID, PART ONE (I Samuel 16-31)

I Samuel 16: Samuel is saddened by the turn of events with Saul. Samuel himself is no longer in a position to lead Israel, and Saul has failed miserably as Israel's first king. But then the Lord sends Samuel to Bethlehem to anoint a new king from the house of Jesse. Samuel is worried because he knows Saul is watching his every move, so God arranges a meeting between Samuel and Jesse.

Jesse begins to roll out his sons for Samuel's inspection. **Samuel is impressed with Jesse's eldest son, but the Lord tells him not to be swayed by outward appearance-- it is the heart that matters**. We have already seen the Lord reject the firstborn several times. So Jesse continues to exhibit son after son, and one by one they are all rejected. Now the story takes a fun and unexpected turn. Familiar with such stories, the hearer expects the seventh son to be chosen because seven and twelve represent completion in scripture. **Instead, the seventh son is also rejected, and we are left with no more sons.** Finally, Jesse is forced to bring in the youngest son, the one no one else would choose, the sheep herder who is not even present for the meeting. But the Lord often chooses the ones no human would expect. This youngest son is David, and he is the Lord's choice to replace Saul. Samuel anoints David, and the Spirit of the Lord comes upon him.

In contrast, the Spirit of the Lord has left Saul, who has become tormented in his thoughts. Seeking comfort, Saul brings in musicians to play for him. David is an accomplished harpist and singer, and Saul loves his music. So David, who has just been anointed to replace Saul, is brought into the palace to play pleasing music **for the king he will replace**.

There is another interesting contrast between David and Saul: When Saul first appears in I Samuel 9, he has lost his donkeys. This is our first picture of Israel's chosen first king-- **an incompetent shepherd**. Our first picture of David, on the other hand, is of a shepherd who doesn't leave his sheep even when a man as important as Samuel comes to town. **David is the shepherd who cares for and protects his sheep, like a later shepherd, Jesus**.

FASCINATING FACTS: The Philistines

The Philistines, who were in constant conflict with the Israelites during this time, lived in southwest Canaan along the Mediterranean Sea and in the Shephelah. The Shephelah was the area between the coast and the mountains of Judea. Whoever controlled the Shephelah controlled the region, and most of the Israelite/Philistine battles were fought in the Shephelah.

It is unclear exactly where the Philistines came from. Some theories suggest that they were the 'Sea Peoples' of Crete known in Egyptian lore, who attacked Egypt around 1293-1185 BC (during the 19th Dynasty). The Sea People were repulsed by Ramesses III around 1182-1151 BC (during the 20th Dynasty). They resettled in Canaan, and the Israelites were unable to remove them.

The Philistines had five major cities: Gaza, Ashkelon, and Ashdod on the Mediterranean coast, and Ekron and Gath in the Shephelah. The Philistine cities were joined in a confederacy in which the city rulers all had equal power.

The Philistines worshipped many gods, some of which they adopted from Canaanite traditions. Their chief god was Dagon, believed to have the body of a fish and the head of a man.

The Philistines were skilled at making pottery and were master iron workers. Since the Israelites were still using bronze, their weapons were inferior, and they suffered a great disadvantage in battle.

In modern language, a "philistine" is a low or despised person who knows nothing of refined culture or art, or one who destroys or despises culture or art.

DAVID AND GOLIATH (I Samuel 17)

While David is still a boy, the Philistines and the Israelites are again at war in the Shephelah. The Philistines trot out a nine foot tall warrior named Goliath, who is armed to the teeth and quite intimidating.

Goliath challenges any Israelite to face him in single combat, winner take all: If the Israelite wins, the Philistines will be the Israelites' slaves, but if Goliath wins, the Israelites will be the Philistines' slaves. The shocking challenge puts the Israelites at a loss, for no one wants to be responsible for enslaving his entire people, and Goliath appears unbeatable.

Enter David: Sent by his father to carry food to his three older brothers at the battle, David hears Goliath's challenge (it is repeated daily) and wants to know why no one has accepted it. In simple faith David says:

"Who is this uncircumcised Philistine that he should defy the armies of the living God?" (I Samuel 17: 26b)

Eliab, David's oldest brother, rebukes him harshly. He accuses David of having a wicked heart, the very thing that kept the Lord from choosing Eliab as king. But Eliab has watched his younger brother anointed in his place, and he is jealous of David.

David presents himself to Saul and offers to fight Goliath, reassuring him that since he has killed lions and bears, he can also kill this third monster. Accepting the offer, Saul offers David his armor, which is made of iron just like Goliath's. Among the Israelites, only Saul has armor like Goliath's (I Samuel 13:22). David refuses the armor, selects five stones for his sling and approaches Goliath.

Goliath curses David by his gods, mocks him for his lack of weaponry and jeers him. David responds that he doesn't need weapons. In another statement of his great faith, David says to Goliath:

"This day the LORD will hand you over to me, and I'll strike you down and cut off your head. Today I will give the carcasses of the Philistine army to the birds of the air and the beasts of the earth, and the whole world will know that there is a God in Israel. All those gathered here will know that it is not by sword or spear that the LORD saves; for the battle is the LORD's, and he will give all of you into our hands." (I Samuel 17: 46-47)

Then David slings a stone at Goliath so hard that it "sinks into his forehead," either knocking him out or killing him outright. If the stone didn't kill him, what comes next certainly does: David uses Goliath's sword to cut off the giant's head and offers the head to King Saul. The Philistine army disintegrates, and Israel's army chases them all the way back to Ekron and Gath.

DAVID IN SAUL'S COURT (I Samuel 18 - 20)

I Samuel 18 - 20 relates David's fall from grace with Saul.

I Samuel 18: The chapter begins with Jonathan's pledge of friendship to David. Their relationship is more like father to son than brother to brother, as Jonathan is much older than David. Jonathan gives David his royal robe, which indicates that Jonathan understands that David is the one that God has chosen to lead Israel. As King Saul's son, Jonathan is a contender for Saul's throne himself, **so his yielding to David is an act of true friendship and self-denial**.

David continues to sing and play for Saul, but his renown has made Saul jealous of him. In fits of rage, Saul twice tries to spear David, but David eludes his throws each time. Later, David moves up in military rank and has a following that surpasses Saul's. Saul becomes consumed with thoughts about how to get rid of David. One of his strategies is to offer his daughter Merab to David if David will agree to lead many battles; his hope is that David will die in battle. But David refuses to marry Merab.

When Saul discovers his second daughter, Michal, loves David, he decides to try the same strategy with a new daughter. He offers Michal to David in exchange for one hundred Philistine foreskins (ouch). To get the foreskins, David will have to kill the Philistines, and Saul hopes that David will die trying. But David succeeds, bringing not one hundred but two hundred Philistine foreskins. The arranged marriage takes place.

INTERESTING INDIVIDUALS: Michal

Although Michal married David with her father's blessing, Saul later took her away from David and gave her to another man, probably because she helped David escape (see picture) when Saul was pursuing him. After Saul's death, David demanded that Michal be returned to him. He may have done this out of love (Michal's husband also loved her deeply-- see 2 Samuel 3:16), but he may also have felt that his marriage to Saul's daughter legitimized his own claim to the throne.

I Samuel 19: Jonathan is able to keep Saul off of David for a while, but it doesn't last. Saul tries to kill David once again, but this time he escapes with Michal's help. Saul sends out a group of soldiers to capture David. The group encounters old Samuel in a group of prophets, and somehow the spirit of prophecy gets into the soldiers themselves so that they begin to prophesy. Saul's next group has the same problem. Finally Saul himself goes after David, and he too starts to prophesy.

I Samuel 20:- In a beautiful story of loyalty and love, Jonathan goes against his mad father and helps David escape. As a contender for Saul's throne and a king's son, Jonathan has every reason to be jealous of David; yet, remarkably, his care and concern for David and his faith that God has chosen rightly overrides his own feelings of loss. Before David leaves, he vows to show kindness to Jonathan's family no matter what happens. He fulfills this promise in II Samuel 9.

DAVID AS A FUGITIVE (I Samuel 21-31)

Realizing that it is no longer safe to remain anywhere near Saul, David flees for his life.

I Samuel 21 - 22: David flees, receiving help from a priest who gives him the showbread from the Tabernacle to eat and provides a safe place for his family to live. Coming along in pursuit, Saul kills the priest and his entire family for helping David.

I Samuel 23: David saves the town of Keilah from the Philistines. When Saul sends his forces to Keilah, David flees. Jonathan finds David and encourages him in the Lord (see picture).

I Samuel 24:- Saul seeks shelter in the very cave in which David is hiding, but doesn't see David. When Saul goes to sleep, David has a chance to kill him and end his nightmare of exile. But David never seriously considers killing Saul, whom he still considers to be Israel's anointed king. Instead, David cuts off a piece of the royal robe to prove that he was in the cave and had the chance to kill Saul. When Saul realizes the mercy David has shown him, he acknowledges that David will be the next king and begs David to spare his family. David swears an oath, and Saul leaves.

I Samuel 25:- David and Abigail meet and marry.

GIANTS OF THE FAITH: Abigail (I Kings 25)

This story is like a breath of fresh air in the midst of conflict, war and betrayal. While hiding in the desert, David meets a wealthy man named Nabal (his name means "fool") and his beautiful, intelligent wife Abigail.

David asks Nabal to provide his men with provisions. This is an honorable request: most bands like David's would simply steal what they wanted, but David does not want to pillage from fellow Israelites, so instead he asks politely.

Nabal refuses David's request for food, insulting him and his family and insinuating that David must be a runaway slave. After the Goliath incident, even a "fool" certainly should have known David's story. Nabal may have felt that it was safe to insult David because David was out of favor with the king. But when David hears of Nabal's insults, he rises up in anger, ready to slaughter Nabal and his household.

Abigail finds out that Nabal has just made the mistake of his life, so she decides to intervene for her foolish husband. She loads the requested provisions onto some donkeys and sets out to meet David. Approaching him, she bows to the ground and accepts her husband's blame on her shoulders. She argues that killing Nabal, a fellow Israelite, would be a stain on David's conscience for the rest of his life. Abigail acknowledges that David will be king, and reminds him that it is the Lord who fights his battles.

Her wise words win David over.

David realizes that he did not consult the Lord when he set out against Nabal, and his motives are impure. Instead of being offended by these warnings from a mere woman, David praises God for His intervention, blesses Abigail and sends her home in peace.

Abigail runs home and tells her husband everything. Nabal is safe from David for the time being. But the Lord has other plans: Nabal has a stroke and dies ten days later.

When David hears that Nabal has died, he realizes anew that it really *is* the Lord who fights his battles. **David rescues Abigail from widowhood by marrying her**.

I Samuel 26: This chapter parallels I Samuel 24. David has another chance at a sleeping Saul's life, but only takes his spear and jug. Saul again realizes that David has had a chance to kill him and has refrained.

I Samuel 27: David moves into Gath, a Philistine city, and convinces the king that he is on the Philistines' side. Basing himself in Gath, he quietly goes on raids against Philistine towns, but kills every Philistine in each targeted town so that the King of Gath never finds out what he is doing.

THE DEATH OF SAUL (I Samuel 28 - 31)

This section is another chiasm in which the first section matches the fifth section and the second section matches the fourth section. The center section stands alone as the climax.

The Witch of Endor predicts Saul and his sons will die (I Samuel 28): Saul consults the Witch of Endor to find out if he will defeat the Philistines who are gathering their forces against him. She brings up Samuel from the dead (see picture), and Samuel tells Saul that he and his sons will die on the battlefield the next day.

Meanwhile, David is marching behind the Philistines toward the battle with Saul. He has convinced the Philistine king that he will fight with the Philistines.

David's family is taken by the Amalekites (I Samuel 29 - 30: 1-6): The Philistine king sends David away after his men grow afraid that David will betray them (they are probably quite right). David and his men return home to find that the Amalekites have taken their wives and children and burned their town.

David defeats the Amalekites (I Samuel 30: 7-17): The Amalekites have attacked, murdered and betrayed the Israelites ever since they left Egypt. The Lord has promised that they will be utterly destroyed, but the fulfillment of that promise has long been delayed. David and his men finally fulfill the Lord's curse on the Amalekites.

David's family is rescued from the Amalekites (I Samuel 30: 8-31): David recovers his family, his two wives and everything else the Amalekites have taken.

Saul and his sons die (I Samuel 31): In the battle on Mount Gilboa, the Philistines kill Saul's three sons, including David's great friend Jonathan. Saul is badly wounded himself, and doesn't want to fall into the hands of the enemy. He pleads with his armor-bearer to kill him so that the Philistines won't toy with him; but the man refuses, so Saul kills himself.

FASCINATING FACTS: The Timbrel (often translated Tambourine)

The Timbrel was an ancient percussion instrument used for worship. Like a simple tambourine, the timbrel was a disc with bells or metal discs fastened around it and decorated with ribbons. It could be shaken or tapped with the hand. In the Bible, the timbrel was used in celebration, worship and praise (Exodus 15: 20; 2 Samuel 6: 5; Psalm 81:2), most often by women.

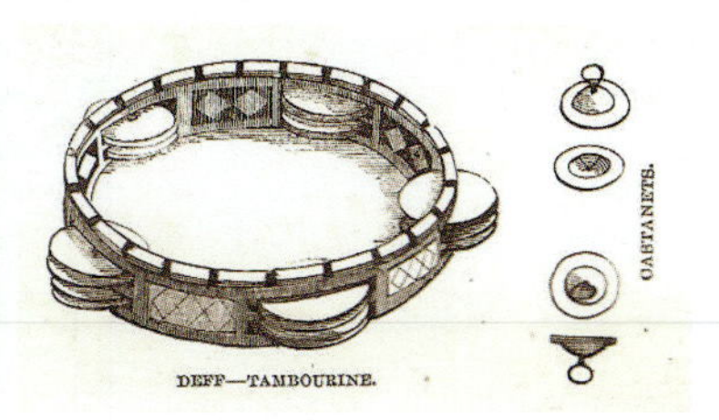

Chapter 14

The Phoenicians, David (part II) and Solomon

GEOGRAPHY FOCUS

The Mediterranean Sea

DID YOU KNOW…

- *Mediterranean* means "middle of the earth" in Latin.
- The Mediterranean Sea is known as the "cradle of civilization." It was the home of several important ancient civilizations, including the Minoans, the Mycenaeans, the Greeks and the Romans.
- It is surrounded by land except at its westernmost point, where the narrow Strait of Gibraltar connects it to the Atlantic Ocean.
- It contains numerous islands. The five largest are Sicily, Sardinia, Corsica, Cyprus and Crete.
- Its water is salty and warm.
- Its shape on the map is said to resemble that of a duck in flight.
- It is one of the most heavily traveled seas in the world.

ANCIENT HISTORY FOCUS

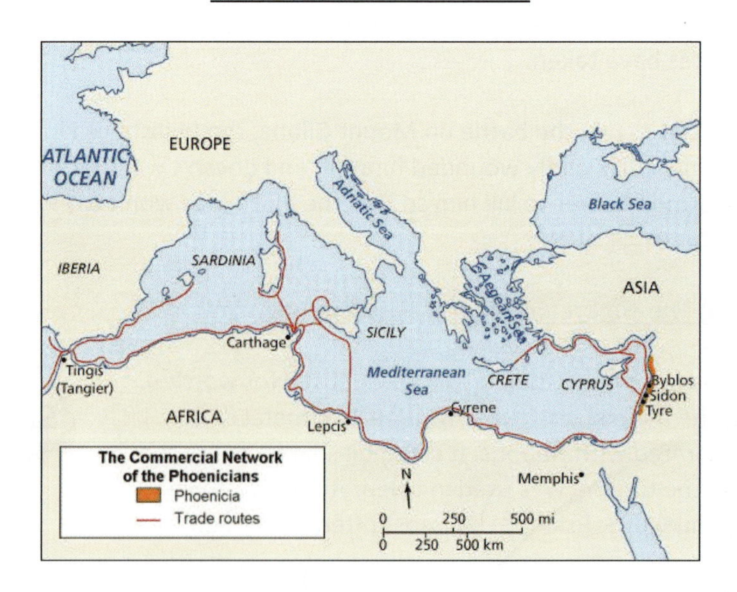

THE PHOENICIANS

The Phoenicians lived along the coast of what is today western Lebanon. In Greek, "phoenicia" means "red-purple," and the Greek poet Homer gave the Phoenicians their name. If this people group had a name for itself, it is unknown; Phoenicians spoke of themselves as citizens of their particular city-state: Tyrians from Tyre, Sidonians from Sidon, or Carthaginians from Carthage. The Old Testament refers to them as "Sidonians" or "Canaanites."

Possible Timeline of Phoenician History:

3000 BC: First known Phoenician settlements appear
2000 BC: Phoenician alphabet is invented
1600 BC: Conflict between Egyptians and Phoenicians
1500 BC: Phoenicians begin to trade with foreign cities
1400 BC: Phoenicians and Egyptians establish commercial treaties
1200 BC: Tyre becomes the chief Phoenician trading city
980 BC: Hiram, king of Tyre, forms an alliance with David and Solomon
854 BC: Phoenicia falls to Assyria
725 BC: The city of Tyre defeats the Assyrians in history's first recorded naval battle
695 BC: Spain, which was originally colonized by Phoenicians, becomes an independent Phoenician kingdom
612 BC: Most of Phoenicia comes under the control of Nebuchadnezzar (Tyre remains independent)
538 BC: Persia conquers all of Phoenicia (including Tyre)
333 BC: Alexander the Great conquers all of Phoenicia except Tyre. After a seven month siege, Tyre falls to Alexander the great and Phoenicia is integrated into the Seleucid kingdom

The Phoenicians were known as great traders. The land around northern Canaan was poor for agriculture, but the location was ideal for trade. With mountains to the east and the sea to the west, the cities were well protected. Lebanon had abundant cedar and pine trees, and these were in high demand for building all around the Mediterranean Sea. The Phoenicians also traded wine, metalwork, glass, salt, fish, purple (or "phoenicia") cloth, fine linen, wood carvings and slaves.

The Phoenicians established trading colonies throughout the Mediterranean. Their largest and most strategic was Carthage in North Africa (modern-day Tunisia - founded in 814 BC). Because their livelihood was based on sea trade, the Phoenicians became the best shipbuilders of the ancient world. Their oar-driven ships were well constructed from the famous Lebanese cedar trees. Their simplest vessel, the galley, was powered by a single deck of oarsmen. They eventually modified the galley into a new invention, the bireme.

FASCINATING FACTS: The Phoenician Bireme

The galley was powered by a single deck of oarsmen who sat on benches on either side of a central aisle. The oars had to move in time as a unit so that they would not tangle with each other, so a drummer on the oar deck beat time. The oarsmen were often slaves.

The Phoenicians improved the galley by creating the bireme, which had two decks of oarsmen. The second deck sat just above the first deck and required a longer set of oars. A bireme might have 40 or more oars in the water.

The Phoenicians created a system of writing involving phonetic symbols instead of pictograms. These Phoenician symbols later became the basis for the Greek alphabet.

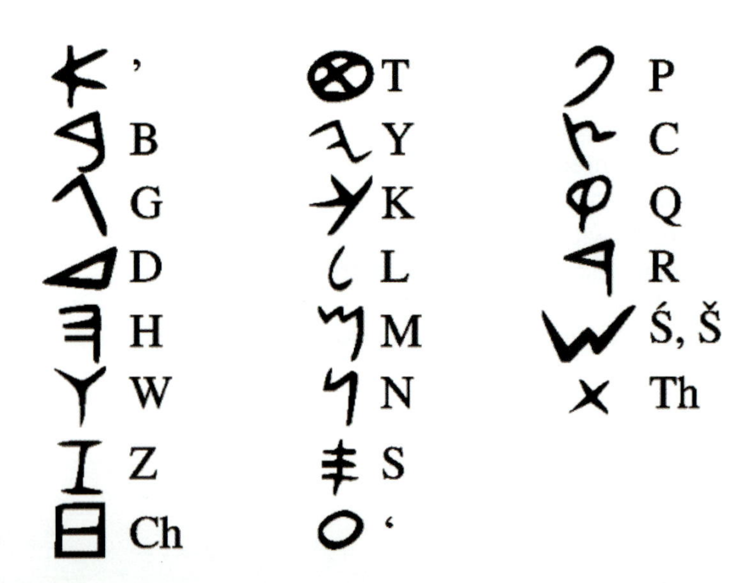

<u>FASCINATING FACTS: The Phoenician Alphabet</u>

Unlike hieroglyphics or Cuneiform, which used pictograms, the Phoenician alphabet used combinations of 22 phonetic symbols to represent words. This clever economy was a marked improvement over pictogram languages with their hundreds or thousands of symbols. Each of the 22 symbols represented a consonant sound. The vowel sounds were not written, but implied or understood. The first letter had the Semitic name “aleph,” the second letter “beth,” and so on. When the Greeks adapted the Phoenician alphabet to their own language, they added vowels. “Aleph” became “alpha,” “beth” became “beta,” and so on. From these first two letters come the word “alphabet.” Our own English alphabet is a descendant of that same Phoenician alphabet.

But while hieroglyphics and cuneiform were written in enduring clay, most Phoenician writing was done on Egyptian papyrus, which of course disintegrated over the ages. Relatively little Phoenician writing survives. But the legacy of the literate Phoenicians lives on: The Phoenician city of Byblos was known for its papyrus. When the Greeks translated the Hebrew Scriptures, they called the book “Byblos” (Bible).

The Phoenicians supplied King Solomon with the building materials for the Temple he built in Jerusalem. Solomon and King Hiram of Tyre negotiated terms for the cedar and pine logs in I Kings 5: 6-11:

Solomon: **"So give orders that cedars of Lebanon be cut for me. My men will work with yours, and I will pay you for your men whatever wages you set. You know that we have no one so skilled in felling timber as the Sidonians."**

When Hiram heard Solomon's message, he was greatly pleased and said, "Praise be to the LORD today, for he has given David a wise son to rule over this great nation." So Hiram sent word to Solomon: "I have received the message you sent me and will do all you want in providing the cedar and pine logs. My men will haul them down from Lebanon to the sea, and I will float them in rafts by sea to the place you specify. There I will separate them and you can take them away. And you are to grant my wish by providing food for my royal household."

In this way Hiram kept Solomon supplied with all the cedar and pine logs he wanted, and Solomon gave Hiram twenty thousand cors of wheat as food for his household, in addition to twenty thousand baths of pressed olive oil. Solomon continued to do this for Hiram year after year.”

The Phoenician religion was similar to that of the surrounding polytheistic cultures. They seemed to have borrowed their system of gods and goddesses from Egypt, Canaan, Babylon, Assyria and Persia. Their primary god was El, also known as Baal, whom they believed to be the protector of the universe.

Perhaps the most infamous Phoenician in the Bible was the hated Jezebel, the wife of King Ahab of Israel. Jezebel was zealous about her Baal worship, and she turned Ahab and Israel away from the worship of the Lord. She ordered the murders of several prophets of the Lord (I Kings 18:4), and tried to have the great prophet Elijah killed (I Kings 19: 1-3) after he killed some of Baal’s prophets. After Elijah’s well-known victory over the Baal prophets, Jezebel was tossed out a window and dogs ate her flesh (II Kings 9: 30-37).

FASCINATING FACTS: Phoenician Purple

The Phoenicians, whose name means "red-purple," developed the ability to extract a purple dye from the mucus of the murex, a tropical sea snail. This dye became a symbol of royalty because it was rare, expensive and difficult to make. One pound of dye might require up to 60,000 snails. This dye was used extravagantly in Solomon's temple and on the Israelite High Priest's clothing. Alexander the Great wore Phoenician purple, as did some of the Egyptian and Roman emperors.

FASCINATING FACTS: Phoenician Glass

The Roman historian Pliny tells how glass was invented: A group of Phoenician sailors were camping on a beach. They lit a fire and placed their cooking pots on blocks of natron (soda) that they had brought with them. When they woke up the next morning, they discovered that the heat of the fire had fused the sand and the natron together into glass.

Whether or not this story is true, the ingredients are correct. To make glass, sand and soda (or lye) are mixed, crushed and melted in a furnace. Lime is sometimes added for strength, and other additives can provide color. When the mixture melts into liquid glass, it can be shaped using a blowing iron or poured into a mold.

The Phoenicians produced three kinds of glass: transparent, colorless glass (for mirrors, non-descript bottles and other common uses), translucent, colored glass (for elegant bottles, jugs and vases) and opaque glass (similar to porcelain and used for vases and other items).

BIBLE HISTORY

Possible Timeline for Saul, David and Solomon

1360-1085 BC: The time of the Judges
1051 BC: Saul's reign begins
1040 BC: David is born
1011 BC: Saul and his three sons are killed on Mount Gilboa. David is anointed king of Judah (the southern kingdom)
1004 BC: David is anointed king of all Israel. David moves his capital to Jerusalem
961 BC: Solomon's reign begins
922 BC: Israel divides into two kingdoms

GIANTS OF THE FAITH: DAVID (Part II) - II Samuel

II Samuel details David's time as the king of Israel. It covers his rise in power first in Judah and then in Israel (II Samuel 1-8). It ends with David's sin and the consequences of his actions (II Samuel 9-24).

DAVID'S RISE

David Laments Saul's death (II Samuel 1)

After Saul's death, David proved that he was a true man of God by forgiving every grievance against the king who had pursued him, threatened him, betrayed him and tried to kill him again and again. **David firmly believed that Saul was Israel's anointed king, chosen by God, and he was always faithful to his king.** No matter what Saul did, David was respectful in his presence. David deeply loved Saul's son and swore an oath to protect Saul's family line. David sang for Saul, fought for Saul, and killed for Saul. After his passing, David honored Saul and his three sons with a lament.

David becomes king over Judah and Israel (II Samuel 2 - 5: 1-3)

With Saul dead, David is anointed king over Judah in the southern city of Hebron, the largest Hebrew city at that time. In an effort to unite the kingdom, David immediately begins to reach out to those who were loyal to Saul. But not all of Saul's friends died with him: Abner, Saul's former army commander, has not forgotten how Saul felt about David. Instead of supporting David, Abner installs Saul's son Ish-Bosheth (the name means "man of shame") on the throne of Israel. Never a fighter or a leader, Ish-Bosheth is not a good candidate for his father's throne.

Conflict between the northern tribes and the southern tribes erupts as Abner leads the northern army against the southern army under David's nephew, Joab. In an attempt to limit bloodshed, the two sides agree to settle the conflict by allowing twelve warriors from each side to fight it out. Unfortunately, the battle ends almost as soon as it begins with all twenty-four warriors killed!

This fiasco settles nothing, and fierce fighting breaks out. Joab is victorious; Abner's forces are defeated and begin to retreat. But when Joab's younger brother chases Abner and won't be warned off, the more experienced Abner ends up killing him. Another battle of revenge begins, until Abner finally pleads with Joab to stop the bloodshed.

As the war between the house of Saul and house of David continues, David grows stronger. His following increases, and so does his family. His list of wives and sons grows as David forms alliances with surrounding kingdoms and important families through his many marriages (II Samuel 3:2-5).

Living up to low expectations, Ish-Bosheth commits an act of colossal stupidity: he accuses his primary supporter Abner of sleeping with his concubine. If this were true, it would constitute an attempt to steal the throne from Ish-Bosheth, because in those days, whoever controlled the harem controlled the kingdom. Insulted and disgusted, Abner withdraws his support from Ish-Bosheth and aligns himself with David. He informs David of his change of heart and uses his influence to convince the elders of Israel to back David as well. Abner travels south to Hebron, where David welcomes him warmly.

But Joab has not forgotten that Abner killed his younger brother. When Joab finds Abner in Hebron, he kills him. This hot-headed move from Joab at such a critical political moment drives a permanent wedge between Joab and David. David curses Joab's family and goes into mourning for Abner. There is great danger that the murder of Abner will prevent the reuniting of the kingdoms. But David's grief is convincing, and the northern tribes begin to think of David as a worthy king.

When he hears that he has lost his commander, Ish-Bosheth becomes terrified for his life; but he doesn't fret for long: two of his commanders soon kill him and carry his head to David. They expect to be rewarded, but they have forgotten David's promise to protect Saul's family line. Instead of being pleased, David is furious and has the men killed. Finally, David becomes the anointed king of all Israel.

INTERESTING INDIVIDUALS: Mephibosheth

Saul still has one more potential heir after the death of Ish-Bosheth, a grandson named Mephibosheth. Jonathan's son Mephibosheth is five years old when his father and grandfather are killed in battle. In those days, potential heirs to the throne were often killed by the king's rivals upon the king's death. When Mephibosheth's nurse hears of Saul's death, she fears that something like this is afoot, so she rushes to remove the child from harm's way. Unfortunately, in her haste she drops the child, permanently crippling both of his feet. Still, Mephibosheth escapes and is raised by a wealthy family who keeps his identity quiet.

In order to fulfill his oath to Jonathan, David begins to inquire if anyone in Saul's family is still alive. He summons Ziba, Saul's house servant, who tells him of Mephibosheth. David brings the young man before him and vows that he will protect him and care for him. David gives him his grandfather Saul's estate and invites him to eat at his table with him as part of his family (II Samuel 9).

Later, Ziba convinces David that Mephibosheth is out to steal his throne. In response, David transfers Saul's estate from Mephibosheth to Ziba, which makes the servant a wealthy man and leaves Mephibosheth destitute (II Samuel 16: 1-4).

Later yet, Mephibosheth appears before David, dirty and in mourning. He begs David to believe that he never wanted to take David's throne. Now uncertain what to believe, David divides the estate between Ziba and Mephibosheth. But Mephibosheth refuses his half, saying that he is content to be with David (II Samuel 19: 24-29).

The last Biblical mention of Mephibosheth comes in II Samuel 21, when David protects him against the Gibeonites who seek revenge against Saul and his heirs.

David's early reign (II Samuel 5: 6-25-10)

As soon as David became king, he set out for Jerusalem in order to make it his capital. Jerusalem was a wise choice. It bordered the southern tribe of Judah, but technically lay within the tribe of Benjamin, so its location united the two kingdoms. David took the city from the Jebusites (a tribe of Canaanites) with little trouble, despite their taunts. Jerusalem became "The City of David." With cedar logs from the Phoenician king, he built a palace for himself and filled it with more wives, concubines and children (II Samuel 5: 6-16).

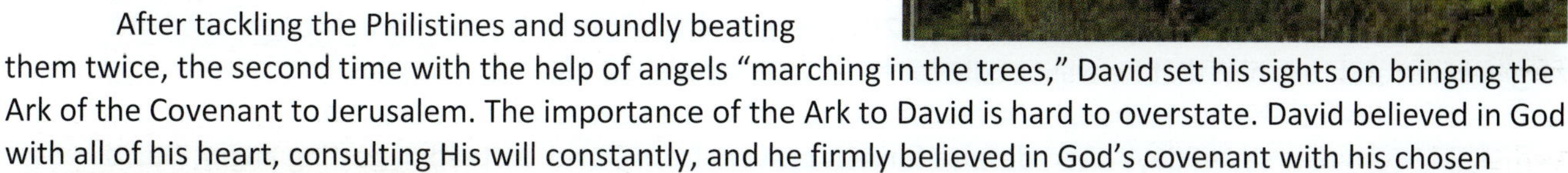

After tackling the Philistines and soundly beating them twice, the second time with the help of angels "marching in the trees," David set his sights on bringing the Ark of the Covenant to Jerusalem. The importance of the Ark to David is hard to overstate. David believed in God with all of his heart, consulting His will constantly, and he firmly believed in God's covenant with his chosen people, Israel. The Ark was the most powerful symbol of that covenant. David was extremely excited about bringing the Ark to Jerusalem and re-establishing the unified Israel as a nation under God.

Unfortunately, the first attempt ended in disaster. The Lord's instructions for handling the Ark were forgotten, and the handlers put the ark in an ox cart (this was their first mistake). When it began to wobble, a non-Levite named Uzzah reached out to steady it (second mistake) and was immediately struck down by God. The Ark's handlers were irreverent and suffered the consequences.

The second attempt worked. This time, Levites carried the ark properly, according to the law given in Numbers 4:15. This allowed it to be brought safely into the city, where David celebrated by dancing in the streets. David's next wish was to build a temple for the Ark in Jerusalem, but the Lord told him that this would be a job for his son and heir.

With the Lord's help, David conquered and subdued the nations around him, building Israel into a great nation (II Samuel 8 and 10).

DAVID'S DOWNFALL

David's Sin with Bathsheba

Older now, David sends his army out to battle against the Ammonites while he stays home to rest. After an afternoon nap one day, David goes out on the roof of his house and sees a beautiful woman bathing on a nearby roof. He finds out that she is Bathsheba, the wife of Uriah, a fine warrior in David's army. But David has grown used to having whatever he wants in the way of women, so he sends for her and she becomes pregnant with his child.

When David finds out about her pregnancy, he attempts a cover-up: He commands Uriah's return so that the husband can have an opportunity to make his wife pregnant himself. **But Uriah is maddeningly upright and refuses to go to his wife, arguing that since his men cannot go to their wives on the battlefield, neither will he at home.** This is in accordance with David's usual standards (I Samuel 21:5): when his men are in battle, they are not to be involved with women.

Frustrated, David carries the cover-up one horrible step farther: he sends a message to Joab commanding him to place Uriah on the front line so that he will die in battle. The new strategy works: Uriah dies and widows Bathsheba. David quickly marries Bathsheba, who has become his favorite, so that he can acknowledge their son.

When this sad, sorry tale is over, the prophet Nathan appears before David with an interesting story. What if, asks Nathan, there was a wealthy man with many sheep who took a poor man's only lamb for his own supper? What should we do to such a man? Caught up in the story, David replies excitedly that we should kill such a man and is ready to strap on his weapons and go find the villain. Nathan convicts David with a chilling pronouncement: **"Thou art the man!"** David has many wives, but Uriah had only one. Not satisfied with all of God's blessings, protection and possessions, David has essentially murdered a righteous man in order to take from him the one thing he had.

For this sin, David's family will be shaken to the core. The son born to Bathsheba will die and his sons will pay for his transgression. His own wives will be harmed.

David's response is complete and true repentance. Confronted with his own sin, he offers no excuses and no lies. **He realizes that according to the law, there is no sacrifice that he can offer for his sins; the penalty is death (Leviticus 20:10, 24:17, Deuteronomy 22:22).** Because David is truly repentant, though, the Lord forgives him and tells him that he will not die for his sins (II Samuel 12:13).

He is not off the hook, though. David still has to suffer the consequences of his sin. David and Bathsheba's son dies seven days later, despite fervent prayers from David. Instead of getting angry, David worships the Lord.

David and Bathsheba have a second son who receives two names: Solomon ("His Peace") and Jedidiah ("loved by God"). It is interesting that the dead son was unnamed, while the second son receives two names.

After all of this, David goes back to the sort of thing kings are supposed to do: fighting for his people against the Ammonites. Only now, some of his sons are old enough to generate trouble of their own.

Amnon's sin, Absalom's revenge (II Samuel 13)

Amnon is the firstborn son of David and stands to inherit the throne. Like a number of these stories, Amnon's is rated about PG-13. He finds himself falling in love with his step-sister Tamar. With the help of a friend, Amnon devises a plan to trick Tamar into being alone with him: he will pretend to be ill and request that his dear sister Tamar be sent to care for him. Taken in by the ruse, David himself sends Tamar in to care for her brother. When they are alone, he ignores her pleas and rapes her. Even after this, the situation might have been salvaged: Tamar tells Amnon that he must now ask for her hand in marriage. He would not be refused. But after his shameful crime is done, Amnon finds that he hates Tamar now more than he supposedly loved her before, and sends her away. Tamar is no longer marriageable and is left in a state of destitution.

Absalom, David's third son and Tamar's full brother, finds out about Amnon's crime against Tamar. Absalom brings Tamar into his house and cares for her as a kinsman-redeemer. Two years later, a vengeful Absalom has his men kill Amnon. Killing Amnon has its political advantages too, though. With Amnon's death, Absalom is first in line to inherit his father's throne. Afterwards, Absalom flees.

FASCINATING FACTS: Daniel, David's Second Son

Amnon was David's firstborn son, followed by Daniel and then Absalom. Although he was third in birth order, Absalom was apparently second in line for the throne (after Amnon).

The son in the middle was Daniel, born to Abigail. For some reason, Daniel was passed over in the line of succession. It is possible that even though Daniel was born to David, he was actually the son of Nabal, Abigail's deceased former husband. If this were true, Daniel would inherit his true father's considerable estate, but would have no part in David's. For whatever reason, Daniel was not in line to inherit David's throne.

David reconciles with Absalom (II Samuel 14)

David grieves over the loss of Absalom, and so his commander, Joab, devises a plan to reconcile the pair. His tactic with David is a bit like Nathan's: he sends an actress to David in the role of a widow with a story about her two fictitious sons. According to her story, one of her sons has killed the other just as Cain killed Abel. The murdering son has run away, and she wants to bring him back, but fears for his life if he returns. David believes her story and issues an order to protect the murdering son. "Not one hair of your son's head will fall to the ground," he says (II Samuel 14:11b). Then she reveals her true mission: to secure protection for Absalom so that he can return and be reconciled to David.

David agrees to allow Absalom's return, but refuses to see him face to face. Just as Cain was allowed to live, but not to remain in the Lord's presence, Absalom remains cut off from his father and the line of succession. Eventually, however, David relents.

Civil War and Absalom's death (II Samuel 13-21)

Discontent at his exclusion from the line of succession, Absalom resolves to take the throne by force. After four years of careful planning, he raises a revolt at Hebron, claims kingship over the city, and divides the kingdom. Caught unprepared and defenseless, David is forced to flee Jerusalem, leaving a priest and 10 of his concubines in charge of the city.

After several betrayals, counter-betrayals and near misses, Absalom enters Jerusalem and rapes his father's 10 concubines. This was predicted by Nathan as a coming punishment for David's sin with Bathsheba.

When David is finally forced to battle Absalom, he instructs his men that Absalom is not to be killed. But David's commander Joab yet again goes against the king's will. As Absalom rides away in retreat, his long hair catches on a tree limb and he is stuck, dangling from a branch. Joab and his armor-bearers find him helpless and go for the easy kill. David's son Absalom is dead.

To the amazement of Joab, David is wild with grief over the death of his son. Joab cannot understand why David seems to love those who hate him and ignore those who love him, namely the troops who have just handed David a victory and preserved his throne by putting down Absalom's revolt. But then Joab is nothing like David, the "man after God's own heart." Joab does not love as David loves, which is the way God loves: nothing Absalom could do would ever stop David from loving him.

David is then left to re-unite the kingdom. He replaces Joab with Absalom's commander. David is also forced to put down a Benjamite rebellion. Finally, after re-uniting the kingdom, David avenges the Gibeonites (the Canaanites who had that special protection treaty with Joshua) and battles the Philistines (II Samuel 21).

GIANTS OF THE FAITH: SOLOMON (I King 1-11)

The Bible books I Kings and II Kings were originally one book of Kings, and they cover the period from the reign of Solomon to Israel's exile in Babylon (586 BC).

The End of David's reign and the Beginning of Solomon's (I Kings 1)

As I Kings opens, David is near the end of his life and needs a young girl in bed with him to keep him warm. His men search the country and choose the beautiful young Abishag the Shunammite to attend to David and keep him warm.

Seeing that David is near his end, his son Adonijah decides to set himself up as the next king. He hires horses and chariots, invites family and friends, and offers sacrifices as if he is being crowned. Alarmed, Bathsheba and Nathan the prophet come to David with the news. David has apparently sworn to Bathsheba that Solomon will inherit the throne, and she wants David to keep his promise. David springs into action and anoints Solomon king of Israel immediately, abdicating his own throne in favor of Solomon. Now Adonijah is forced to plead for his life before Solomon, who grants the request on the condition that Adonijah must prove himself worthy of life.

Solomon's revenge (I Kings 2)

David gives Solomon some last-minute spiritual advice about keeping the Lord's commands, then asks him to take care of two men who have harmed their old king: David's military commander Joab (who killed both Abner and Absalom against the king's wishes) and Shimei (who cursed David in public). Then David passes away after 40 years as Israel's greatest king.

With David gone, Adonijah reappears with a request to marry Abishag, the girl who kept David warm near the end of his life. This is an attempt at a crafty move by Adonijah, because if he could claim some part of David's harem, he would still have a claim on the throne. But like many young kings, Solomon was very sensitive to any attempt to weaken his claim to the throne. Solomon saw through Adonijah's ruse and sent his man to kill Adonijah.

Finally Solomon honors his father's requests by killing both Joab and Shimei. Now Solomon's place on the throne of Israel is secure.

THE REIGN OF SOLOMON (I Kings 3-11)

Solomon was Israel's king for forty years. He was known for three w's: wisdom, wealth and wives. He is believed to be the author of much of the Bible's "wisdom literature" in the books of Proverbs and Ecclesiastes. His wealth was enormous, and his wives numbered some 700-- 1000 or more if the concubines are included. He was also known as the builder of the Temple.

The 9 chapters that tell of Solomon's reign form a five-part chiasm. The first section matches the fifth (Solomon's wives), the second section matches the fourth (Solomon's wisdom), and the climactic center section tells of the Temple. The story is written in this style to help the listener remember it.

Solomon's wives (I Kings 3:1 and 11)

Solomon's reign begins and ends on sour notes. He begins with an Egyptian wife (3:1) and ends with seven hundred wives and three hundred concubines, most of them foreigners (11). Most of these marriages are made to form alliances with other nations, but their effect on Solomon's faith is profound. Each wife brings along her household gods, and Solomon allows his wives to continue to worship these gods, providing places for them to worship and make sacrifices. In his last years, Solomon foolishly turns away from God and follows his wives' gods. As a result, the Lord raises up enemies from both inside and outside Solomon's kingdom.

FASCINATING FACTS: Siamun

Solomon most likely married the daughter of Siamun, a pharaoh of Egypt's twenty-first dynasty. It is believed that Siamun captured the city of Gezer and used the city as a dowry for his daughter when she married Solomon. The marriage cemented an alliance between Egypt and Israel.

The Wisdom of Solomon (I Kings 3: 2-28 - 4 and 10)

Soon after Solomon becomes king, the Lord appears to him and asks him what he wants most. Instead of asking for wealth or immortality, Solomon asks for wisdom. The Lord is pleased at this choice, and so he grants Solomon great wisdom and wealth as well. First in chapter 3, then again in chapter 10, Solomon is confronted with women who test his wisdom. In both stories, everyone is awed by his great wisdom and insight.

The Temple (I Kings 4-9)

Back in Deuteronomy 12, the Lord promised the people that when they were settled in the Promised Land and at peace with the nations surrounding them, He would chose a place to dwell with them. When He did, they were to tear down every other place of worship in the land. There would be just one place where they could go to offer sacrifices, and God would choose it.

When David became king, he wanted to build the Lord's temple, but the Lord told David to leave the job for his son. Because David was a man of war, the Lord assigned the job to Solomon, whose name meant "His peace."

Solomon now sets out to fulfill his father's dream using plans David gave him. He orders cedar and pine logs from Hiram, the Phoenician king, and conscripts laborers and artisans to do the work. The picture is an artist's conception of the Temple. What was actually built was probably a fraction of this:

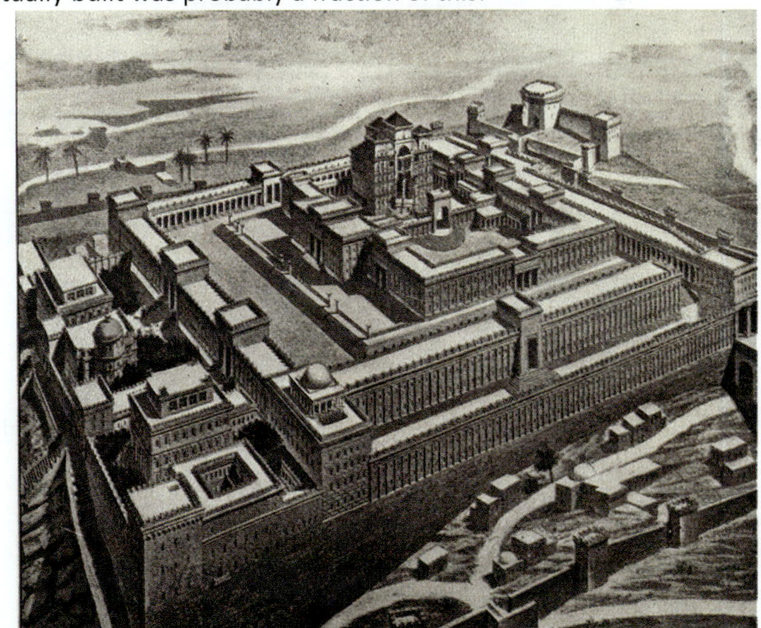

For the temple's site, David selected the threshing floor of Araunah the Jebusite (I Chronicles 21:18-30 and 22:1) because God had spoken to him there. The threshing floor was located on Mount Moriah (II Chronicles 3:1), the same mountain on which Abraham offered Isaac as a sacrifice.

The Temple was about ninety feet long, thirty feet wide and forty five feet high. It had three stories and a full-width front porch. It was actually a fairly small center for worship. Its interior was overlaid with gold, including the floors of both the inner and the outer rooms. Carvings of "cherubim, palm trees and open flowers" covered the walls and doors.

FASCINATING FACTS: Solomon's Palace

Briefly interrupting the description of the Temple's beginnings are twelve verses about Solomon's palace. The contrast between the two building projects is surprising, and it may show the direction in which Solomon's heart was heading.

- The palace took almost twice as long to build as the temple.
- The palace was much larger than the temple and far more costly.
- The palace complex held five buildings: The Palace of the Forest of Lebanon, the Hall of Pillars, the Hall of Justice, Solomon's palace, and a separate palace for Pharaoh's daughter, Solomon's first and most important wife.
- The palace and the Temple had similar courtyards.

SCRIPTURE SPOTLIGHT: I Kings 8

In I Kings 8, the Israelites are assembled at the Temple. While they are sacrificing and praising God, **the Ark of the Covenant is brought into the Temple and the cloud of God's presence fills the Temple**.

Solomon blesses the Israelites and praises God for keeping his promise to David and allowing the Temple to be built.

Solomon then turns, faces the Ark and kneels. He spreads his arms wide and dedicates the Ark and the people to the Lord. Solomon's dedication prayer is profound and prophetic. The seven sections of the prayer are windows into what happens to Israel within a few short years after Solomon's death.

Each section of the prayer contains a pattern with a variation of the following components:

- A sin or sins have been committed
- The Lord sends punishment/judgment
- The sin is confessed by the people
- People cry out to the Lord in His Temple
- The Lord hears from heaven
- The Lord forgives them
- The Lord restores them

After Solomon dedicates the Ark, He blesses the people again and more sacrifices are offered before the Lord.

Chapter 15

The Americas, Elijah and Elisha

GEOGRAPHY FOCUS

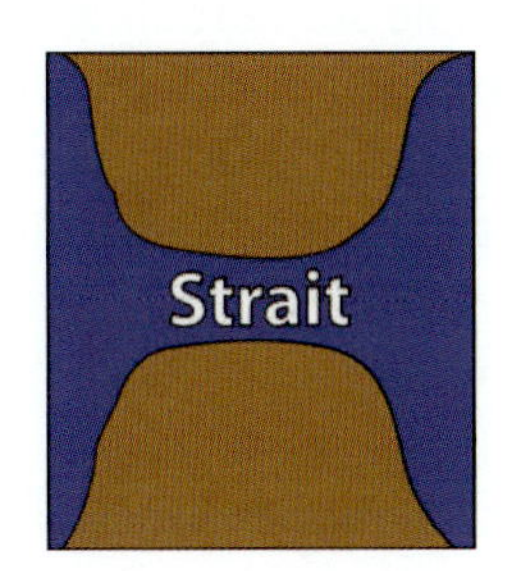

The Straits of the Earth

DID YOU KNOW...

- A strait is a narrow body of water that connects two larger bodies of water.
- Some of world's best-known straits are the Bering Strait (see below), the Strait of Gibraltar (which connects the Mediterranean Sea to the Atlantic Ocean), the Strait of Bosporus (which connects the Black Sea to the Sea of Marmara) and the Strait of Dardanelles (which connects the Sea of Marmara to the Mediterranean Sea).

FASCINATING FACTS: The Bering Strait

The Bering Strait is a narrow sea passage between Asia and North America which connects the Arctic Ocean to the Bering Sea. Today the strait separates the United States (Alaska) and Russia (Siberia) by about 58 miles. The Strait was named for the Russian explorer Vitus Bering, who spotted the Alaskan mainland in 1741 while on an expedition in the area.

Archaeologists believe that during the Ice Age, a natural land bridge connected Asia and North America at the Bering Strait. The theory is that the sea level has risen since then, submerging a ridge of dry land that once connected the two continents.

ANCIENT HISTORY FOCUS

ANCIENT NATIVE AMERICANS

The "New World" of North and South America, unknown to Europeans until 1492, was actually inhabited long ago. Native Americans lived in the Americas around the same time other ancient civilizations were growing up and thriving in Egypt, Babylon, India and China. Relatively little is known about ancient American civilizations because they left no writings behind.

How the Native Americans arrived in the Americas is uncertain. They might have crossed the Pacific by boat, hopping from island to island. They might have crossed on an ice bridge during the Ice Age, perhaps passing across the Bering Strait from Siberia to Alaska. Or they might have crossed a land bridge at the Bering Strait when the sea level was lower.

Ancient North Americans

The first complex civilizations in North America are classified according to periods of time:

Paleo-Indian Period

The Paleo-Indians ("paleo-" means ancient) were the first people to move to the American continent. They used simple stone tools and made spearheads by chipping stones. These same Paleo-Indian tools have also been found in northeastern Siberia, suggesting that the Paleo-Indians came from there. They might have followed their herds across the Bering Strait.

Archaic Period (Before 2000 BC)

After the Paleo-Indian period came the Archaic Period. As the Native Americans spread out, they became less nomadic and began to stay in one place for longer periods of time. Small villages sprang up with mud plastered houses built over shallow pits. As their weapons, tools and skills improved, they hunted smaller game and began to plant crops, including corn, peppers, beans and pumpkins. They began to make pots and weave baskets. Archaic Period villages have been found in the southwestern United States and Mexico.

Formative or Classic Period (?1800 BC - 200 AD)

In the Formative Period, nation-states began to rise in the Southwest and cities developed from the villages along the Gulf of Mexico and south. The use of ceramics became common, and crop farming developed and expanded. In modern-day Guatemala, sculptures called potbellies have been found (see picture) that date from the Formative Period, around 1800 BC. Their purpose is unknown.

Woodland Period (1000 BC - 1000 AD)

The Woodland Period overlaps part of the Formative Period, and describes the eastern part of North America. The Woodland Period Native Americans created sophisticated pottery and had permanent villages. They developed their agriculture and made tools from stone or bone. They also built distinctive burial mounds.

FASCINATING FACTS: Burial Mounds

Burial mounds were flat-topped, conical mounds of earth built over the tombs of the dead. The burial chamber at the base of the mound contained the body plus jewelry, tools and other items associated with the deceased or his family. Later, another body would be buried on top of the mound and more dirt would be added. This would be repeated any number of times, increasing the height of the mound until it became a landmark.

Ancient Central Americans

The Olmecs (1200 - 300 BC)

The Olmec Civilization arose around 1200 BC in Southern Mexico. The Olmec society was divided into two classes, rich and poor. The poor worked the land and lived in rural areas, while the rich lived in urban areas, supported by the labor of the poor.

The oldest Olmec center was San Lorenzo. This city had water and drainage systems and a population numbering in the thousands. It was built on high ground surrounded by an area of lowlands, which suggests that a great deal of earth was hauled in to build up the site, probably in baskets.

The Olmecs are most easily identified by their artwork. They are famous for the building of large stone head sculptures, each as tall as a man. The 17 heads that have been discovered may represent historic Olmec kings.

Olmecs are also considered the originators of the Mesoamerican Ball Game, a deadly court game played with balls made from rubber trees. Rubber balls and ball courts have been discovered at Olmec sites.

The Olmecs may have practiced certain dark religious rituals, including bloodletting (in which blood from body piercing or cutting was collected on paper and burned as a sacrifice) and human sacrifice.

Around 300 BC, the Olmecs simply disappeared. They may have been taken over or destroyed by another culture, or they may have moved to another area.

Ancient South Americans

The Nazca (200 BC)

The Nazca people, who lived on the southern coast of Peru, flourished around 300 BC. They are best known for the "Nazca Lines." These lines were discovered in the 1920s when the first airplanes began to fly over the Peruvian desert. The pilots saw what had been invisible from the ground: a series of huge drawings on the surface of the desert, impossible to distinguish except from the sky. The line figures depict fish, birds, a whale, spiders, a monkey, a little "astronaut" figure and more. Several hundred different characters and shapes can be seen over an area of 190 square miles. Some of the individual figures are as much as 12 miles long.

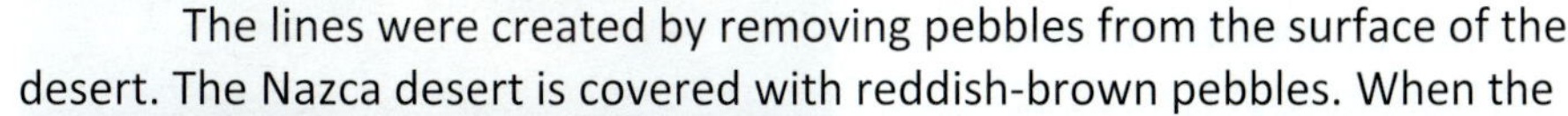

The lines were created by removing pebbles from the surface of the desert. The Nazca desert is covered with reddish-brown pebbles. When the pebbles are removed, the light-colored earth beneath remains, creating distinct lines in the desert. The pebbles had to be raked, sifted and carried off over hundreds of miles of Nazca lines. The climate of this desert is so dry and the rain so scarce that the Nazca lines have been preserved for millennia.

Connected with the lines was the city of Cahuachi, a major ceremonial center for the Nazca culture. Archaeologists believe that Cahuachi and the lines may have been a destination for religious pilgrims. The site of Cahuachi is dominated by an adobe pyramid, and at least 5000 tombs have been discovered around the area.

FASCINATING FACTS: Some theories on the purpose of the Nazca Lines

- They were drainage or irrigation ditches.
- They were a memorial for the Great Flood.
- They were a giant astronomical calendar of stars and planetary events.
- They were intended to be seen by the gods as a tribute to them.
- They were sacred paths used for rites and rituals.
- They were an ancient astronaut landing strip, created for or by aliens.

BIBLE FOCUS

THE KINGDOM DIVIDES (I Kings 11 - 16)

In his last years, Solomon turned away from the Lord and worshipped the gods that his many wives had brought with them into the kingdom.

I Kings 11: 9-13

"The LORD became angry with Solomon because his heart had turned away from the LORD, the God of Israel, who had appeared to him twice. Although he had forbidden Solomon to follow other gods, Solomon did not keep the LORD's command. So the LORD said to Solomon, "Since this is your attitude and you have not kept my covenant and my decrees, which I commanded you, I will most certainly tear the kingdom away from you and give it to one of your subordinates. Nevertheless, for the sake of David your father, I will not do it during your lifetime. I will tear it out of the hand of your son. Yet I will not tear the whole kingdom from him, but will give him one tribe for the sake of David my servant and for the sake of Jerusalem, which I have chosen."

I Kings 11: 26-43

True to His word, God raises up a subordinate against Solomon. Jeroboam the Ephraimite is the head of Solomon's northern labor forces. A prophet approaches Jeroboam to tell him that because Solomon has sinned, Jeroboam will become king of ten of Israel's tribes. He also learns that IF he follows God's commands, then his dynasty will be equal to David's. Upon hearing the news, Jeroboam flees to Egypt for safety. Solomon's old alliance with the Egyptian pharaoh, formed by his marriage to the pharaoh's daughter, is over because there is now a new pharaoh; so Jeroboam is welcomed into the Egyptian courts. He remains in Egypt until Solomon dies. Then he returns to Israel to claim his place as king of the northern tribes.

INTERESTING INDIVIDUALS: Egyptian King Shishak or Sheshonq (935-914 BC)

Sheshonq, a Libyan warrior, was probably the pharaoh who befriended Jeroboam while he was in Egypt. Sheshonq married another of the old pharaoh's daughters, then claimed the throne when the old pharaoh died. This was the beginning of Egypt's 22nd Dynasty.

Sheshonq is best known for his military campaigns against the kingdoms of Judah and Israel. He attacked Jerusalem and stripped the Temple of its treasures, taking even the beautiful gold shields Solomon had made. Later he marched north and attacked Jeroboam's forces at Megiddo, where he erected a stele with his name on it to commemorate his victory.

Kings of the Northern Kingdom, Israel

(The dates listed below are from John Bright's *A History of Israel* and are one of several possible sets of dates. Some scholars date the divided kingdom to 931 BC.)

This week we will look at the kings of Israel from Jeroboam through Ahaziah and learn about the two prophets, Elijah and Elisha.

KINGS OF ISRAEL

Jeroboam - 922-901 BC 	Bad chosen by God reigned 22 years	When Solomon died, the kingdom's loyalties were divided between Rehoboam, Solomon's son and natural successor, and Jeroboam, whom the Lord had chosen. The northern tribes were tired of the hard labor and heavy taxes required to support Solomon's extravagant ways. When they complained to Rehoboam and sought more lenient treatment, he took it as an insult to his kingship and threatened to treat them twice as hard as his father had. This brought on a revolt. The ten northern tribes left the kingdom to follow Jeroboam, and formed a new nation with the same name as the old one, Israel. The two southern tribes, Judah and Benjamin, were left with Rehoboam; this new, smaller nation became known as Judah. Because Jerusalem was located in the land allotted to Benjamin, that land remained with Rehoboam. The great kingdom that had taken David and Solomon 80 years to build was destroyed in a very short time after Solomon's passing. As the new king of Israel, Jeroboam immediately made a fatal mistake. Since the Northern Kingdom did not include Jerusalem, it didn't include the Lord's temple. Israel had no place of worship. To resolve this, Jeroboam created two places of worship with golden calf idols, one in Dan on his northern border and one in Bethel on his southern border. He also appointed non-Levite priests and changed around the God-ordained holidays. When the Lord sent a prophet to warn Jeroboam about these mistakes, he refused to listen. So Jeroboam lost favor with God, and his line was cut off. After Jeroboam died, his son inherited the throne and also did evil in God's sight. From then on, none of Israel's kings followed God (I Kings 12 - 14).
Nadad - 901-900 BC	Bad inherited the throne reigned 2 years **Assassinated**	Nadad did not follow the Lord, but did evil in His sight. Just before Nadad took the throne, Judah captured the southernmost part of Israel's territory. This weakened the kingdom, and the Philistines took advantage of this weakness during Nadad's reign. Nadad had to lead his troops into battle against the Philistines. Baasha, an ambitious Israelite from the tribe of Issachar, took the opportunity to carry out a coup. He killed Nadad and his entire family, then took the throne.
Baasha - 900-877 BC	Bad reigned for 24 years	After this brutal beginning, it is not surprising that Baasha did not follow the Lord, but did evil in His sight. His reign was marked by military losses. A prophet told Baasha that his family line would be wiped out for his sins.

Elah - 877-876 BC	Bad inherited the throne reigned 2 years **Assassinated**	Elah lasted on the throne for just two years. Zimri, one of his army officers, killed Elah while he was drunk. Zimri then proceeded to kill everyone in Elah's line so that he could claim the throne himself.
Zimri - 876 BC	Bad reigned 7 days **Assassinated**	Zimri's murderous brutality didn't serve him well; he lasted on the throne for only seven days. The Israelites refused to acknowledge his kingship. Instead they acclaimed Omri, the commander of the army, as king. When Zimri realized that he had lost all support, he set fire to the palace and died in the fire.
Omri - 876-869 BC	VERY BAD chosen by army reigned 12 years	Omri did not follow the Lord, and was considered even more evil than the other kings before him. His greatest accomplishment was acquiring Samaria and building his capital there. The Scriptures tell little about Omri, but his reign is mentioned in other ancient documents from surrounding countries. These documents refer to the kingdom of Israel as the "house of Omri."
Ahab - 869-850 BC	THE WORST inherited throne reigned 22 years	Ahab did not follow the Lord and was considered the worst in a bad group of Israelite kings. He married the Phoenician Jezebel in order to form an alliance with the king of Tyre. But Jezebel was a devoted Baal worshiper who brought with her hundreds of Baal prophets. Ahab not only tolerated their presence, but also foolishly took part in their ceremonies (I Kings 16:32). The people of Israel were still the Lord's people, so the Lord raised up the great prophet Elijah to confront King Ahab.

GIANTS OF THE FAITH: ELIJAH (I Kings 17 - 22 and II Kings 1)

Elijah ("My God is Jehovah") is the Old Testament's greatest prophet. His many miracles from God include the defeat of the prophets of Baal, raising a boy from the dead, correctly predicting the fates of Ahab and Jezebel, and finally ascending into heaven on a chariot when his time came. Elijah went out with more style than any other character in Scripture.

The stories of Elijah are found in the book of Kings (I and II). He appears again in Malachi in a reference to the "day of the Lord":

"See, I will send you the prophet Elijah before that great and dreadful day of the LORD comes. He will turn the hearts of the fathers to their children, and the hearts of the children to their fathers; or else I will come and strike the land with a curse." (Malachi 4: 5-6)

In the New Testament, Elijah appears again along with Moses at the Transfiguration of Jesus (Matthew 17). Also, the disciples question Jesus about Elijah, wondering about the Malachi passage. Jesus tells them that Elijah has already come in the form of John the Baptist. Some people draw parallels between Elijah (the fiery prophet who rained down fire from heaven) and Elisha (the gentle prophet who cared for the individual) on one hand to John the Baptist and Jesus on the other.

Elijah's ministry begins abruptly when the Lord sends him to Ahab. Elijah approaches Ahab and tells him that there will be no rain in Israel until the Lord says so, and then immediately disappears.

While he waits for the drought to have its effect, Elijah camps out beside a brook, where ravens bring him bread. When the drought dries up the brook, God sends Elijah to the house of a widow in Sidon, a Phoenician city. This is Baal worship territory.

Elijah's first miracle: The poor widow is down to her last bits of food. She plans to feed herself and her son one last time, then lie down to die. When Elijah arrives, he asks her to share this last meal with him. He even has the gall to ask her to feed him first, reassuring her that God will provide. She trusts Elijah and does as he asks, and miraculously, God does provide. Each day their little supply of flour and oil is replenished just enough to make what they need. Even in territory supposedly claimed by Baal, God has power over the forces of nature.

Elijah's second miracle: The widow's son suddenly becomes ill and dies. The widow cries out to Elijah, believing that this has come to pass because of her past sin. Elijah takes the child and cries out to the Lord. He stretches himself out over the body three times, each time asking the Lord to restore the boy. Miraculously, the boy revives, and Elijah carries him back to his mother. After this, she places her faith in Elijah's God. Even in territory supposedly claimed by Baal, God has power over life and death.

Elijah's third miracle: After three years of drought, the Lord directs Elijah to return to Ahab. By now Ahab is in a rage, searching everywhere for the prophet so that he can end the drought. Elijah challenges Ahab to a "duel of the deities." He proposes that Ahab bring all of Baal's 450 prophets to Mount Carmel to represent Baal. Elijah will represent the Lord all by himself. Each side will prepare a bull for a burnt offering and lay it on an altar, but will not light the fire. Whichever god lights the fire for his side will prove that he is the true God.

FASCINATING FACTS: Baal Worship

The Israelites learned Baal worship from the Canaanites and from Phoenicians like Jezebel. Baal worship centered around fertility and the cycles of nature: growing crops, raising livestock and having children. Baal worshippers believed that their storm god Baal brought the life-giving rain. Since rain came at only one time of the year, during the rainy season, the story developed that Baal had to struggle each year with Mot, the god of death, to break the drought and bring rain. The rituals of the Baal worshipers-- body cutting, frenzied dancing, human sacrifice and acts of prostitution in the temple-- encouraged fertility and gave Baal the energy he needed to defeat Mot.

The Israelites were continually drawn into Baal worship. They wanted both gods: the God of their fathers who brought them out of slavery in Egypt, and Baal who supposedly brought life to their crops, their livestock and themselves. Their prosperity depended on their crops and livestock, so many of them were hard pressed to give up Baal.

Ahab agrees to the challenge. Baal's priests build their altar and begin to call on the name of their false god. When nothing happens, they begin to dance. Elijah taunts them, asking if Baal is sleeping or traveling, or perhaps too busy. Frantic, they start to cut themselves, offering their blood in an effort to attract Baal's attention. Absolutely nothing happens. By evening it is apparent that their altar will remain unlit.

When it is finally Elijah's turn, he uses 12 stones to rebuild the altar that the priests have destroyed in their frenzy. He digs a trench around it and fills the trench with water three times, until the altar is surrounded by a moat. Then he prays, and the Lord answers decisively:

"O LORD, God of Abraham, Isaac and Israel, let it be known today that you are God in Israel and that I am your servant and have done all these things at your command. Answer me, O LORD, answer me, so these people will know that you, O LORD, are God, and that you are turning their hearts back again." Then the fire of the LORD fell and burned up the sacrifice, the wood, the stones and the soil, and also licked up the water in the trench.

When all the people saw this, they fell prostrate and cried, "The LORD -he is God! The LORD -he is God!" (I Kings 18: 36-37)

Elijah kills all of Baal's prophets. As he runs back to Ahab's capital, the rain begins. The drought is over. Elijah has proved that God alone has power over fire and rain.

But his great demonstration has only angered the Baal-worshiping Jezebel further against Elijah. She sends a message to Elijah promising that she WILL kill him, and he runs for his life. Once again, God provides for him: an angel appears twice, bringing him bread and water. Nourished but deeply depressed, Elijah travels to Mount Horeb/Sinai. He had hoped that God's demonstration of power would win him the support of some brave Israelites, but no one helps him. Elijah is convinced that he is alone, that in all of Israel, no one else serves God.

Alone in a cave, Elijah waits to hear from the Lord. A windy storm arises, but **God is not in the storm**. An earthquake shakes the cave, but **God is not in the earthquake**. A fire passes by, but **God is not in the fire**. Finally, Elijah hears a still, small voice, and only then does he go out of the cave to hear God speak. **The lesson is clear: God is not Baal**. God is the creator of all of the earth's elements, but **He is not the elements themselves**. **He is a personal God who desires a relationship with His creation**. He comes in the form of a still small voice with encouraging words and a reminder that **He alone is Sovereign**.

Elisha's Call (I Kings 19: 19-21)

Elijah leaves the mountain and finds Elisha, who is plowing the fields with his oxen. Elijah throws his cloak over Elisha, indicating that Elisha is to take up Elijah's ministry. In an agrarian society, oxen are a prized possession; so when Elisha takes his oxen and slaughters them, it indicates a full break from his past. He is ready and willing to leave everything and follow Elijah.

Naboth's Vineyard (I Kings 21)

Elijah has one last encounter with Ahab and Jezebel. Ahab falls in love with a piece of property that sits next to his palace. He offers to buy it from its owner, Naboth, but Naboth refuses. Then Jezebel launches a scheme to get Naboth killed. When it works, Ahab takes possession of the property he wants so badly. Because of this crime, Elijah confronts Ahab to tell him that his line will be destroyed and his wife's dead body will be consumed by dogs.

Ahab attacked by Aramaean king (I Kings 20 and 22)

Ben-Hadad, king of Aram (Damascus, in modern day Syria) gathers his forces and sets out to attack Ahab in Samaria. With the Lord's help, Ahab is able to defeat Ben-Hadad's army twice, and the two nations make a treaty.

Three years later Ahab and Jehoshaphat, king of Judah, consider joining forces to defeat Ben-Hadad's army. Ahab consults his Baal prophets, who predict a victory; but Jehoshaphat wants a Hebrew prophet. When the Hebrew prophet arrives, he predicts defeat for Israel and Judah and death for Ahab. Ahab refuses to believe this prophecy.

The two kings battle against the king of Aram and lose. Ahab is sufficiently worried about the prophecy to disguise himself in battle; but his disguise does not protect him, and he dies in battle.

Ahaziah - 850-849 BC  	Bad inherited the throne reigned 2 years	Ahaziah worshipped Baal as his father did and angered the Lord. Ahaziah injured himself when he fell through the lattice of an upstairs room. Worried that he might not recover, he sent messengers to the shrine of Baal to find out if he would live or die. Elijah met the messengers on the way and told them to tell Ahaziah that he would not leave his bed. Ahaziah responded in fury. He sent fifty soldiers to capture Elijah, but Elijah called fire from heaven to burn up the soldiers. A second group of soldiers met the same fate. When the third group arrived, the soldiers begged Elijah to spare their lives. Elijah then went to the Ahaziah and told him that he would die in bed, which he did (II Kings 1).
Jehoram - 849-843 BC  	Bad inherited the throne reigned 8 year **Assassinated**	Jehoram (Joram) reigned for eight years. Although he did evil, he was not as wicked as his father, because he discouraged some of his father's Baal worship. Jehoram's reign coincides with the ministry of Elisha the prophet, and the two have many encounters. Jehoram witnesses Elisha providing water in the desert; Elisha warns Jehoram each time the king of Aram tries to move against Israel; Elisha delivers the Aramaeans into Jehoram's hands (but doesn't allow him to kill them); and Elisha predicts when the Aramean siege will be broken (the Aramaeans flee when they believe they hear chariots). While Jehoram is in the midst of a battle against the Aramaeans, Elisha anoints his army commander Jehu king of Israel and gives him the mission of wiping out Jehoram and his family, because Jehoram comes from Ahab's doomed line. Wounded in the battle, Jehoram returns to his palace. Jehu chases him in a chariot. He kills Jehoram on the property Ahab stole from Naboth, just as Elijah predicted. Then Jehu hunts down and kills everyone from Ahab's line, including all of his seventy children. Jezebel's eunuchs threw her out of her own palace window; her broken body is eaten by dogs, again as Elijah predicted. Jehu also kills all of Baal's prophets.

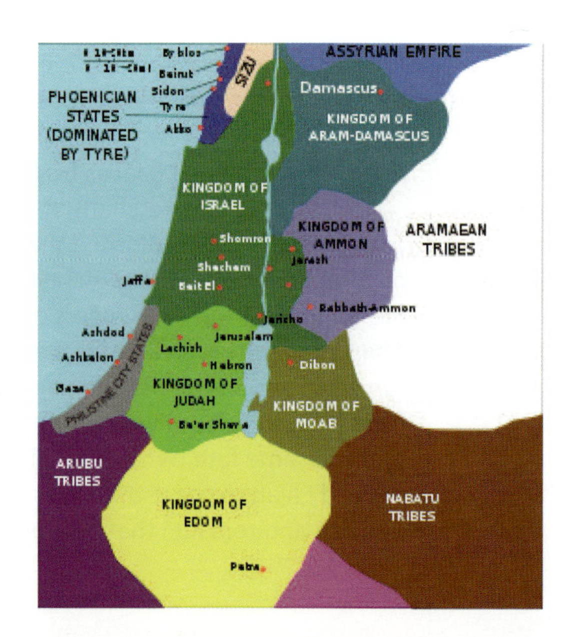

GIANTS OF THE FAITH: ELISHA (II Kings 2 - 6)

Elisha ("God saves") was God's prophet for fifty years through the reigns of Israelite Kings Jehoram, Jehu, Jehoahaz and Jehoash. A servant named Gehazi accompanied Elisha as Elisha had accompanied Elijah. Elisha lived in Samaria when he wasn't traveling.

Elijah is taken up into heaven (II Kings 2: 1-18)

When the time comes for Elijah to be taken up into heaven, Elijah gives Elisha three opportunities to turn away from the ministry that he will inherit. Each time Elisha affirms that he will not turn away. When they reach the Jordan River, Elijah parts the waters and the two of them cross on dry land.

Elijah asks Elisha if he has any requests before Elijah goes. Out of all of the things that one might ask of Israel's greatest prophet, Elisha asks for a "double portion of your spirit." This request mirrors the double portion of the inheritance given to the firstborn son. It means that Elisha wants to carry on the Lord's work in Elijah's place, just as the firstborn son carries on for the father. Elijah tells Elisha that he will know this request has been granted if he sees Elijah being taken up into heaven.

Then Elisha is treated to what must have been one of the greatest sights in all of the Bible: Elijah is taken up into heaven in a whirlwind, riding on a fiery chariot. When it is over and Elijah is gone, Elisha mourns, even though he knows that Elijah is not dead and has gone to heaven with God. Elisha picks up Elijah's mantle (symbolic of his task as God's prophet), returns to the Jordan River and parts the waters, crossing over on dry land. Just as this miracle mirrors Elijah's, many of Elisha's miracles recall Elijah's, and some were even more impressive.

ELISHA'S MIRACLES:

- **II Kings 2: 19-22** - Elisha heals the water using salt.
- **II Kings 2: 23-25** - A group of boys are mocking Elisha and his "bald head." **To mock God's prophet was to mock God himself; it was an act of supreme sacrilege.** Elisha curses the boys in the name of the Lord, and 2 bears appear and tear apart forty-two of the boys. This is one of the more gruesome Elisha stories!

- **II Kings 4: 1-7** - A widow who owes money begs Elisha for help. He tells her to gather empty jars, and then he miraculously fills them with oil. She has enough to pay all of her debt and provide for her family. This story is reminiscent of Elijah's widow story.

- **II Kings 3** - The Moabites who were living in modern-day Jordan (see map above) rebelled against the Israelites. Years before, David had subdued them and forced them to pay a yearly tribute (II Samuel 8). Now Israel was in decline, and they no longer wanted to pay the tribute. Jehoram, the king of Israel, united with Jehoshaphat of Judah and the king of Edom to fight the Moabites. They marched south through Judah and into the Desert of Edom, so that they could access Moab from the south. After seven days in the desert, the three armies had used up all of their water. In desperation, they called for Elisha. The great prophet told them to dig ditches to hold all of the water that the Lord was about to send into the valley. When it miraculously came, it served two purposes: it watered the armies, and it confused the Moabites. It appeared to them as blood, and they believed that the blood came from the united armies attacking each other. The Moabites came out to attack, thinking to find opposing armies at war with one another. Instead, the united armies defeated the Moabites.

- **II Kings 4: 8-37** - Elisha meets a Shunammite woman who gives him food and shelter whenever he comes to her town in Northern Israel. In response, Elisha grants her the desire of her heart, which is to have a child. She becomes pregnant and has a son. Some years later, while the boy is still young, he dies. The Shunammite woman calls for Elisha, and he brings the child back to life. This miracle also recalls Elijah's earlier one.

- **II Kings 4: 38-41** - Elisha cleanses poisonous food that has accidentally been placed in the stew.

- **II Kings 4: 42-46** - Elisha multiplies food to feed 100 men.

ELISHA HEALS NAAMAN

- **II Kings 5** - (Notice how involved the servants are in this story) The commander of the Aramaean king's army, Naaman, develops leprosy. His wife's **Hebrew servant girl** tells him that Israel's great prophet Elisha might heal him. The way in which a servant girl figures in this story is a bit surprising. The little girl has no reason to tell Naaman anything; she is a captive in a foreign land, separated from her family and of no consequence to anyone. But she is still an Israelite, **one of God's chosen people**, and her faith in the one God is evident. She risks much in sending Naaman to Elisha.

Naaman goes to the Aramaean king with the news that a prophet in Israel has the power to heal him. The king sends gifts and letters to the king of Israel, who immediately becomes upset and afraid that trouble will come if Elisha fails to heal Naaman. The king of Israel lacks the faith of the poor Hebrew servant girl.

When Elisha hears of this, he tells the king to send Naaman to him. Instead of going out to meet Naaman, Elisha sends his servant to tell Naaman to wash in the Jordan River seven times. Naaman is disgusted at the request-- he has rivers at home, too, in which he could wash-- and he refuses at first. **His servants** convince him to reconsider-- notice the servants again-- and Naaman washes in the Jordan seven times. His health is restored, and so is his faith in Elisha's God. Naaman tries to give Elisha gifts, but Elisha refuses them all. Then Naaman swears allegiance to the Lord, and takes home some Israelite earth so that he can build an altar to God in his own homeland (a common practice in those days). Finally, Naaman asks forgiveness for a future act he will be forced to commit: when he escorts his king into the temple of Rimmon (another name for Baal), he will have to bow to Rimmon as the king bows. He wants Elisha to know that he will do this out of duty, not belief. Elisha gives him his blessing and Naaman leaves.

Gehazi, Elisha's servant, can't believe that Elisha has turned down the rich gifts Naaman offered. He runs after Naaman and tells him that his master has reconsidered, and Naaman gladly turns over the gifts. When

Elisha confronts him, Gehazi lies again. As his punishment, Gehazi is afflicted with leprosy.

This story begins with a faithful servant without leprosy and ends with a faithless servant with leprosy.

- **II Kings 6: 1-7** - Elisha causes an ax head that has accidentally fallen into the water to float so that it can be found (ax heads were valuable).

- **II Kings 6: 1-23** - When the Aramaean army comes against Israel, Elisha's servant is afraid. Elisha prays that the Lord will open the servant's eyes, and suddenly the servant is able to see an angelic army with horses and chariots of fire surrounding Elisha (one wonders if Elisha saw such things constantly). Elisha then blinds the enemy and leads them into Samaria; but instead of killing them, he feeds them and lets them go home.

FASCINATING FACTS: Leprosy

Leprosy is a mysterious disease characterized by skin sores, nerve damage and progressive debilitation. It deadens the nerves, especially in the feet and hands, so that the leper has no feeling and cannot easily tell when he has injured himself. It also makes the leper prone to infection and gangrene. Indications of leprosy include skin lesions that do not heal after weeks or months and numbness in the hands, feet and legs. If the infections go untreated, gangrene can set in and force amputations of toes, fingers, or even feet, legs and arms. Blindness, caused by infection of the eyes, is also common. Even today there is no cure for leprosy, although there are treatments that can keep infection under control and limit nerve damage. With care and caution, a modern leper can live for years without suffering the disease's worst effects.

In the Bible, "leprosy" covered a wide assortment of skin diseases. Any who suffered from true malignant leprosy were forced out of the towns and into leper colonies. Lepers were required to wear torn clothes, to grow their hair long and keep it unkempt, to cover the lower part of their faces and to warn away all who came near them: "Leper! Outcast! Unclean!" Leprosy was sometimes considered a mark of God's judgment or punishment; and, as we saw with Elisha's servant, it sometimes was.

SPOTLIGHT ON SCRIPTURE: Obadiah

Obadiah is the shortest book in the Old Testament. It has only one chapter of twenty-one verses. The date of Obadiah's ministry is uncertain. It may date to the reign of King Jehoram of Israel. It may also date to the time of Judah's fall, when the Babylonians destroyed Jerusalem.

The book is a condemnation of the Edomites (see map), Esau's descendants, who mocked God's chosen people during their time of distress. It is also a promise of hope to God's people. The little book ends with these words: "...the kingdom will be the Lord's" (Obadiah 21b).

We will cover the remaining kings of Israel and all of the kings of Judah in later weeks

Chapter 16

Assyria and Israel's Prophets

ANCIENT HISTORY AND BIBLE HISTORY

(This week the Ancient and Bible history are woven together)

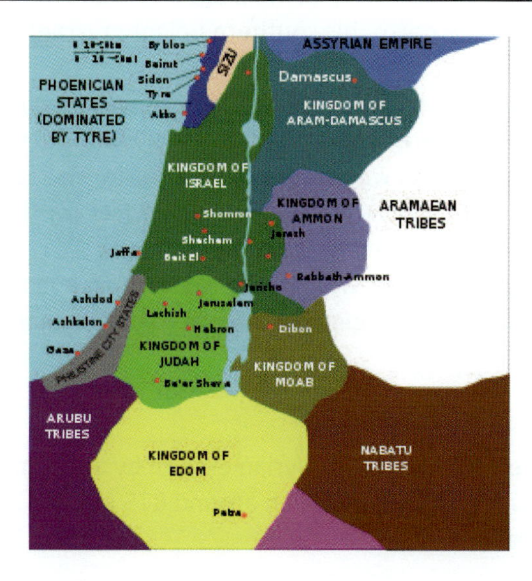

This week we are covering the Kings of Israel from Jehoahaz to Hoshea and Assyria. The Bible history of the kings of Israel and the prophets will be interwoven into the Assyrian history.

ASSYRIA

Simple Timeline of Ancient Assyria

- 2334-2279 BC: Sargon of Akkad rises to power. Sargon establishes the first Assyrian kingdom in Southern Mesopotamia.

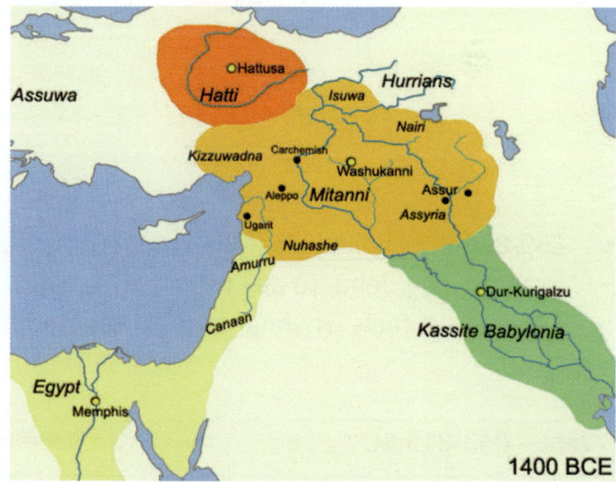

Old Assyrian Period (1900-1300 BC)

- 1813-1781 BC: Shamshi-Adad rules the cities of Ashur, Mari and Nineveh and calls his empire Assyria.
- 1760 BC: Hammurabi of Babylon conquers the cities of Ashur and Mari, and Assyria's short-lived empire ends.
- 1500 BC: The Mittanian king annexes Assyria (Mitanni was in modern-day Syria).

Middle Assyrian Period (1300-900 BC)

- 1365 BC: Ashur-Uballit revolts against Mittanian rule and lays the foundation for the new Assyrian Empire
- 1307-1275 BC: Adad-narari establishes the new Assyrian empire
- 1273 BC: Shalmeneser conquers Mitanni
- 1275 - 1114 BC: Assyria weakens and becomes a tributary to Babylon
- 1114-1076 BC: Tiglath-Pileser I of Assyria reigns

TERRIBLE TYRANTS: Tiglath-Pileser I

Tiglath-Pileser was a king of ancient Assyria. During his reign he invaded Asia Minor, Syria, Armenia and Babylonia. Inscriptions left behind make it obvious that his conquests were brutal and savage, leaving little behind but fire and ruin. He was the first Assyrian king to march to the Mediterranean Sea. He also built temples and palaces, and he created several zoos.

Tiglath-Pileser reigned during the time of Israelite kings David and Solomon. Because Tiglath-Pileser focused his attention on conquests to the north, his southern neighbor Israel was able to flourish in relative peace.

The Assyrian law code written during Tiglath-Pileser's reign was much more brutal than the Sumerian and Babylonian law codes. Punishments were cruel and often involved the severing of body parts such as ears, noses, hands and eyes. Multiple punishments were often meted out for the same crime. Women had no protection under Assyrian law. Men were allowed to divorce their wives for no reason, and could choose to leave them destitute. They could also beat their wives without penalty.

Near the end of his reign, Tiglath-Pileser was unable to fight off repeated attacks from the Aramaeans. Assyria went into decline after Tiglath-Pileser's reign because of the Aramaean problem.

Neo-Assyrian Period (900-612 BC)

- 885-860 BC: Ashurnasirpal II reestablished the Assyrian empire by attacking the Aramaeans and regaining lost territory. He moved the Assyrian capital to Calah around 875 BC. The capital had zoos, irrigation works, botanical gardens and a royal palace.

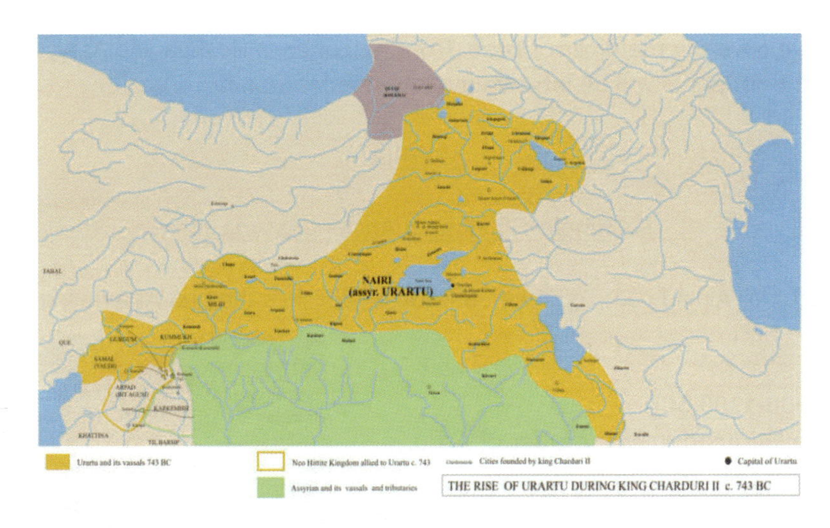

THE RISE OF URARTU DURING KING CHARDURI II c. 743 BC

- 859-824 BC: Shalmaneser III extended Assyrian rule to the Persian Gulf and into Palestine, forcing the Israelite king, Jehu, to pay tribute. This event is not recorded in the Old Testament, but it is depicted on Assyrian artifacts. Shalmaneser III defeated the King of Urartu in 856 BC (Urartu is depicted in yellow on the map).

Jehu - 843-815 BC	Decent - chosen by God - reigned for 28 years

- 824-811 BC: Shamsi-Adad battled with his brother, Assur-danin-apli, who had risen up against their father. Shalmaneser III died before he could quell his son's rebellion, but he named Shamsi-Adad V as his heir in Assur-danin-apli's place. Shamsi-Adad V first had to defeat his brother (with help from Babylon) before he could take the throne himself.

- 810-783: Adadnirari III began incursions into Phoenicia.

Jehoahaz - 815-802 BC 	Bad inherited the throne reigned 17 years	Jehoahaz did evil in the eyes of the Lord, so the Lord allowed Aram to hold Israel under its power. Jehoahaz cried out to the Lord for relief. Relief came when the Assyrians attacked the Aramaeans, and Aram was forced to withdraw from Israel in order to protect its northern boundaries. **"Then Jehoahaz sought the LORD's favor, and the LORD listened to him, for he saw how severely the king of Aram was oppressing Israel. The LORD provided a deliverer for Israel, and they escaped from the power of Aram. So the Israelites lived in their own homes as they had before" (II Kings 13: 4-5).**
Jehoash - 802-786 BC 	Bad inherited the throne reigned 16 years	Jehoash (Joash) did not follow the Lord and did evil in His sight. Despite this, the Lord did not allow Aram to conquer Israel. Before Elisha died, Jehoash visited Elisha on his deathbed. Elisha told him to shoot an arrow out the window in the direction of Aram (Syria). After he did, Elisha told him that he would have victory over Aram. Then Elisha told him to strike the ground with the remaining arrows. Jehoash struck the ground three times. When he was finished, Elisha told him that if he had struck the ground six times instead of three, it would have indicated that he would destroy Aram. Because he struck the ground only three times, Elisha predicted that Jehoash would defeat Aram three times but would not destroy it.

SCRIPTURE SPOTLIGHT: Elisha's bones (II Kings 13:20-21)

Elisha's last miracle took place after he died. While some Israelites were burying a dead man, they were surprised by Moabite raiders. In a hurry to escape, they hastily threw the man's body into Elisha's tomb. When the body touched Elisha's bones, the dead man came to life and stood up!

Jeroboam II - 786-746 BC 	Bad inherited the throne reigned 41 years	Although Jeroboam did not follow the Lord and did evil in His sight, the Lord still blessed the people of Israel during his reign. Israel's territory was as large as it was under Solomon, and the nation was prosperous and at peace. Two prophets named Amos and Hosea rose up to call Israel back to its roots. While Israel prospered, its people grew selfish and turned away from God.

GIANTS OF THE FAITH: Amos

Amos was an unlikely prophet. He was from Judah, not Israel, and he was neither a prophet nor the son of a prophet, but rather a shepherd and a pruner of trees (Amos 7:14). Amos prophesied during the reign of Jeroboam II, at a time when Israel was wealthy and powerful. He spoke against the Israelites for their lack of concern for the poor and helpless and for turning away from the Lord. He also spoke against the nations surrounding Israel, including Tyre, Edom, Ammon, Moab and

Damascus. His message of social justice and judgment did not sit well with the Israelites, who sadly chose to ignore his words. His message of doom was at odds with the prosperity and peace of those times.

GIANTS OF THE FAITH: Hosea

Hosea was called to prophesy to Israel in the latter years of the reign of Jeroboam II. Israel was still at the height of its prosperity when he began his ministry. After Jeroboam II died, Hosea ministered on through the chaotic reigns of the next six kings until finally Israel fell at the hands of the Assyrians.

Hosea's story is quite odd. The Lord tells Hosea to marry a woman who would be unfaithful to him. She gives birth to three children, each of whom receives a horrible name commemorating Israel's unfaithfulness. The wife's unfaithfulness means that the children do not really belong to Hosea. The prophet divorces his wife, but then remarries her in chapter three.

The relationship between faithful, loving Hosea and his unfaithful wife illustrates the relationship between faithful, loving God and faithless Israel. Even when Israel rejects God repeatedly, God honors his covenant with Israel and forgives his children's sins again and again.

Hosea 11 contains a beautiful picture of God's constant love for wayward Israel:

"When Israel was a child, I loved him, and out of Egypt I called my son. But the more I called Israel, the further they went from me. They sacrificed to the Baals and they burned incense to images. It was I who taught Ephraim to walk, taking them by the arms; but they did not realize it was I who healed them. I led them with cords of human kindness, with ties of love; I lifted the yoke from their neck and bent down to feed them."

Zechariah - 746-745 BC	Bad inherited the throne reigned 6 months **Assassinated**	Zechariah reigned for only six months after his father died. He was assassinated by Shallum, the son of Jabesh. With his death the dynasty of Jehu ended.
Shallum - 745 BC	Bad reigned one month **Assassinated**	Shallum reigned for one month after he killed Zechariah. Then Shallum himself was killed by Menahem, son of Gadi.

- 745-727 BC: Tiglath-Pileser III rebuilt the Assyrian empire, which was in decline after the reigns of Adadnirari III's sons. Tiglath-Pileser III invaded Phoenicia, conquered Tyre and reasserted control over Syria and Urartu. When the kings of Aram and Israel joined forces against Judah, Judah's King Ahaz appealed to Tiglath-Pileser III for help. In response, Tiglath-Pileser III marched into Canaan and took over part of Israel. Israel's King Pekah was then assassinated by Hoshea, who took the throne in Pekah's place; but Hoshea was under Assyrian control.

Menahem - 745-737 BC	Bad reigned 10 years	Menahem did not follow the Lord and did evil in His sight. After he killed Shallum, he also brutally massacred anyone who resisted his authority. He was able to keep Assyria at bay during his reign by paying Tiglath-Pileser III an annual tribute of one thousand talents of silver.
Pekahiah - 737-736 BC	Bad inherited the throne reigned 2 years **Assassinated**	Pekahiah followed in his father's footsteps and did evil in the Lord's sight. He was assassinated by Pekah, his chief officer.
Pekah - 736-732 BC	Bad reigned 20 years (?) **Assassinated**	Pekah took the throne after he assassinated Pekahiah. Pekah and the King of Syria joined forces against Tiglath-Pileser III. They tried to draw Judah into the battle, but Judah appealed to Assyria for help. Tiglath-Pileser III gladly obliged by attacking Israel and ravaging the northern region, hauling great numbers of Israelites off to Assyria. All that remained of Israel was the city of Samaria and Ephraim's lands. Pekah was assassinated by Hoshea.

Note: Although II Kings says that Pekah reigned for 20 years, the dates make his reign much shorter. One suggested solution to the problem is that Pekah had been exercising kinglike authority since Menahem assassinated Shallum for the throne. According to this theory, the northern kingdom was split and Pekah had a rival rule along with Menahem and Pekahiah as a sort of military co-regent. Hosea seems to allude to a northern split in his writing (Hosea 5:5). In Assyrian documents, Tiglath-Pileser III also seems to recognize a divided northern kingdom.

- 727-722 BC: Shalmaneser V's reign.

- King Hoshea of Israel refused to pay tribute to Assyria, and instead tried to form an alliance with Egypt. So Shalmaneser V invaded Israel, captured Hoshea and carried him off into captivity (724 BC). Some scholars believe that it was Shalmaneser V who captured Samaria (Israel's capital) and took the rest of the Israelites into captivity. According to surviving Assyrian documents, however, it was Sargon II who captured Samaria. The Biblical text (II Kings 17:1-6) is not clear: Shalmaneser did attack and imprison Hoshea, but it could have been another Assyrian king who captured Samaria.

Hoshea - 732-724 BC	Bad reigned 9 years **Conquered by Assyria**	Hoshea was the last king of Israel. He Shalmaneser V promptly seized Hoshea and put him in prison, leaving Israel leaderless. Shalmaneser V was not as evil as the kings who came before him, but the damage was done, and Israel's fate was sealed. At first Hoshea paid tribute to Shalmaneser V of Assyria, but then he made the fatal mistake of withholding the tribute. Shalmaneser V laid siege to Samaria. Within three years, Israel fell to Assyria.

• 722-705 BC: Sargon II's reign.

SARGON II

Sargon II may have been a son of Tiglath-Pileser III, or he may have been a high-ranking army commander. He may have seized the throne in a coup, or he may have succeeded to it peacefully-- it is unknown. However he got there, Sargon spent his reign embroiled in one battle after another. The kingdom was vast, and he was forced to deal with revolts on all fronts.

THE FALL OF ISRAEL - 721 BC

In 722 or 721 BC, it is believed, Sargon captured Samaria, the capital of Israel. He deported about 28,000 Israelites, who together became known as the "Ten Lost Tribes of Israel" (see *Ten Lost Tribes* section below). He rebuilt Samaria, making it one of the 70 Assyrian provinces. Then Sargon moved Assyrians into Samaria to occupy it (See *The Samaritans* section below).

During his reign, Sargon was so successful that he was able to demand tribute from giants Egypt and Babylon. He died in battle in 705 BC.

FASCINATING FACTS: The Samaritans

When Sargon II captured Samaria, he deported 28,000 Israelites and replaced them with loyal Assyrian subjects, but some Israelites remained in the city. These two different people groups merged into one. Together, they worshipped the gods of Assyria until wild beasts (lions) attacked them. Fearing that they had angered God, they cried out to the Assyrian king for help. He responded by sending Israelite priests to teach them how to worship God as the Israelites used to. Unfortunately, they did not worship God alone, but blended Assyrian customs into Yahweh worship.

The surviving Samaritans claimed to be descendants of the tribes of Ephraim and Manasseh. They built their temple at Mount Gerizim during the reign of Alexander the Great, believing that God had chosen Gerizim instead of Mount Moriah for his temple (Mount Moriah was the site of Solomon's temple). Their temple was destroyed in 128 BC, but the mountain remains the most sacred Samaritan holy place even today. They referred to God as "El" (similar to Islamic Allah) and revered and adored Moses.

Faithful Jews rejected the Samaritans, at first politically and later on religious terms. The first recorded rejection appears in Ezra 4: 1-5. When some Jews returned to Jerusalem from Babylonian captivity, the Samaritans wanted to take part in the rebuilding of the temple. The Jews refused to allow them to participate, so the Samaritans harassed them (Nehemiah 4:2). This began a long tradition of Jews treating Samaritans as second class citizens.

By New Testament times, open hostility between the Samaritans and the Jews was evident. But Jesus, who so often did the opposite of what everyone expected, reached out to the Samaritans, confronting the prejudice and making it clear that the gospel message was also for them (John 4). In the *Parable of the Good Samaritan*, Jesus surprised his Jewish audience by creating a Samaritan hero, and Jewish listeners were chastened at the thought that a Samaritan might behave better than they. In Acts 8, Samaria was one of the first places where the gospel was preached.

FASCINATING FACTS: The Ten Lost Tribes of Israel

The 28,000 Israelites who were taken into Assyrian captivity were never seen again. Speculation abounds about where they went and what might have happened to them.

Some believe that the lost tribes were simply scattered throughout Assyria's kingdom and the people assimilated into Assyrian culture. There are towns in northern Iraq and Iran today where family names are similar to Israelite names; these people could be the lost tribes' descendants.

Others believe that the 10 tribes migrated to different part of the world, including Europe, Africa, Australia and North America. There are people groups in India, Ethiopia, Persia and Japan who claim Jewish descent. They trace their ancestry back to the 10 tribes of Israel. Some also believe that the people of Ireland, Japan and other countries are actually descendants of the ten lost tribes.

- 705-681 BC: Sennacherib's reign. Sennacherib was the son of Sargon and served as his military advisor on his northern campaigns. One of Sennacherib's first duties as king was to put down a rebellion by the King of Babylon. Babylon made more trouble for Sennacherib later (See Chapter 18).

- 701 BC: The King of Judah, Hezekiah, also rebelled against Sennacherib (See Chapter 18).

- 681-669 BC: Esarhaddon's reign. Esarhaddon was forced into hiding after his older brothers killed his father, possibly because he had passed over them when he named Esarhaddon as his heir. When Esarhaddon came out of hiding, he became king of Assyria. He immediately set out to restore Babylon, which pleased the Babylonians. After fighting in the north, Esarhaddon turned his forces toward Egypt. In 671 BC, Esarhaddon pushed deep into Egyptian territory and conquered Egypt for Assyria. He had hardly returned home when Egypt rebelled against Assyrian rule. He tried to return to Egypt, but died before he arrived.

ASHURBANIPAL

- 669-627 BC: Ashurbanipal's reign.

Esarhaddon chose his son Ashurbanipal as his successor and his son Shamash-shum-ukin as crown prince of Babylon. When he became king, Ashurbanipal went to Egypt and quelled the rebellion there in a brutal campaign that included dashing infants to pieces in the streets (Nahum 3:8-10). Egypt remained under Assyrian rule for 20 years. When the Elamites attempted a rebellion, Ashurbanipal quelled that one as well, taking the head of the Elamite king back to Nineveh and putting it on display.

- 652-648 BC: Ashurbanipal's brother Shamash-shum-ukin led a Babylonian revolt against Ashurbanipal and Assyria. Assyria attacked Babylon, and Shamash-shum-ukin committed suicide when it became clear that Babylon would fall. The Assyrians massacred many Babylonians.

- 646 BC: Ashurbanipal turned his armies toward Elam again, sacking the capital city of Susa. Little is known of Elamite history from this point on.

- 627 -609 BC: After Ashurbanipal, Assyria fell into chaos. By 609, Assyria had been swallowed up by the Persian, Seleucid and Parthian empires.

FASCINATING FACTS: Ashurbanipal's library

While much is made of the long-reigning Ashurbanipal's military success, his longest-lived achievement was actually the library he built in the city of Nineveh. Although it was not the first known library in history, it was by far the largest of its time, and it left behind many artifacts that survive to this day. The library contained some 30,000 tablets comprising about 1200 separate texts.

The library was organized somewhat like a modern library, with different rooms and sections for each subject. Each room in Ashurbanipal's library held a tablet near the door that listed the tablets in that particular room-- a cuneiform card catalog.

Ashurbanipal was keenly interested in gathering ancient texts from every culture. He sent out scholars to acquire historical material from civilizations throughout the Ancient Near Eastern world. The great store of knowledge he collected has helped archaeologists immeasurably in understanding the Ancient world.

When Nineveh was destroyed in 612 BC, a fire ravaged the library, baking the clay tablets. Phoenician books of papyrus would have been destroyed by this fire, but the clay tablets were actually better preserved because of it.

SCRIPTURE SPOTLIGHT: JONAH, A BOOK OF CONTRASTS

The story of Jonah is a children's favorite. Jonah is a prophet chosen by God to minister to the people of Nineveh, which of course is the Assyrian capital, packed with enemies of Israel. Jonah would rather not help his enemies, so he deliberately boards a ship headed in the opposite direction. But the ship is beset by storms, and the sailors, looking for a reason for the persistent storms, find out that Jonah is deliberately avoiding God's call. They cast him overboard, where he is promptly swallowed by a whale. In the belly of the whale, Jonah finally humbles himself enough to pray. The whale spits him out, and Jonah reluctantly proceeds to Nineveh. When they hear Jonah's message, the Ninevites repent, which is exactly what Jonah wanted to avoid. An angry Jonah treks out into the desert to pout.

The Book of Jonah is designed to enlighten the listener by highlighting contrasts (differences). The writer draws more than 20 contrasts to teach the listener about God and His ways. Here are some of them:

1. The overarching contrast is between God and Jonah. Jonah is a pitiful, whiny, hate-filled runaway prophet from beginning to end. God, by contrast, is loving, patient, kind and merciful, not only to Jonah but also to the Assyrians.
2. Both God and Jonah see the wickedness of the Assyrians. God is saddened by their sin and sends a prophet to warn them. Jonah, by contrast, hates the Assyrians for their sin and hopes that it will lead to their destruction.
3. When God tells Jonah to warn the Assyrians, Jonah flees. But God does not flee from Jonah. He remains with him, even in the belly of a whale.
4. When the storm hits, the sailors all pray to their many gods. But Jonah doesn't pray to his God.
5. When the sailors draw lots and discover that Jonah is the cause of the storm, they grieve at the thought of throwing him overboard. But Jonah shows no concern for them at all. The Godless sailors are more merciful than Jonah.
6. In their distress, the sailors pray to Jonah's God. Jonah still doesn't pray.
7. When the storm grows bad, the sailors begin to throw things overboard like sacrifices to appease their gods. But when they throw Jonah overboard to appease the one true God, the storm stops.
8. The sailors pray as soon as they realize that Jonah's God is real. Jonah sits on the ship for three days refusing to pray to God, whom He knows is real all along.

9. The sailors offers humble prayers, making vows to God along with their sacrifices. Jonah's prayer is whiny and defensive. He blames God for hurling him into the waters, and even after God saves him, he still doesn't want to carry out God's mission in Nineveh.
10. Jonah doesn't want the salvation he receives from God to be extended to those who worship idols, such as the sailors and the Assyrians. His heart has not changed even in the belly of the whale.
11. The Assyrians repent immediately after hearing Jonah's message for only one day. Jonah sits in the belly of the whale for three days before he reluctantly prays.
12. God hears the cries of the Assyrians for forgiveness and responds with compassion. Jonah responds with anger, telling God he would rather die than see the Assyrians experience God's love.
13. Jonah runs away into the desert. In the hot, barren desert, God provides a vine for shade.
14. Then a little worm eats the vine so that the shade is gone. Both a big fish and a little worm have great impact on Jonah's well-being.
15. Jonah's anger over the loss of the vine is like his anger over Nineveh. God reminds him of some more contrasts: Jonah cares about a plant, but God cares about a people; and while he vine lasted for one day, the people last for generations.
16. Jonah considers God's mercy to be a WEAKNESS! Jonah wants judgment and punishment for the Assyrians, and is angry throughout the story that God wants to offer forgiveness instead. To this day, many Jews like Jonah reject Jesus because Jesus offers forgiveness to their enemies when they want Him to defeat their enemies.

FASCINATING FACTS: Nahum

During the time of Jonah, Nineveh repented and the Lord in His mercy spared them for a time. But the Assyrians of Nineveh eventually returned to their evil ways. The Book of Nahum was written as a prophecy against Nineveh. It foretells the fall of Nineveh, which really came in 612 BC. The book of Zephaniah also foretells Nineveh's fall (Zephaniah 2: 13-15).

FASCINATING FACTS: The Assyrian Battering Ram

A battering ram is a type of siege engine. When armies attacked walled cities, the defenders would often seal themselves inside the walls. In a "siege," the attackers would surround the city and wait for the defenders' food to run out. A siege might require a great deal of time, but it could be sped along if the attackers could break through the city walls. The weakest point in the walls was usually the gates, so the attackers devised battering rams to break down the gates.

The earliest rams were simply long timbers, sometimes tipped with a heavy head or large spear blades, carried by many soldiers. The soldiers would rush the gates with the heavy ram, working together to break through the gate. This type of battering ram dates to around 2500 BC. The drawback to this design was that the soldiers carrying the ram were vulnerable to attack from the defenders atop the walls, who would fire arrows at them or pour boiling oil down on them.

The Assyrians were the first to create a battering ram that provided protection for the soldiers who powered it. In this design, a cart with a steeply pitched roof housed the heavy ram and the soldiers who moved it. The soldiers pushed the cart up to the gates, protected by the roof. The ram was hung from the roof by ropes or chains so that it could be drawn back and swung against the gates repeatedly. Protected siege towers on the top of the structure allowed the soldiers to exchange shots with the defenders on the wall. The soldiers could cover the roof with fresh animal hides to protect it from fire. These rams first appeared around 800-900 BC.

Chapter 17

Crete

GEOGRAPHY FOCUS

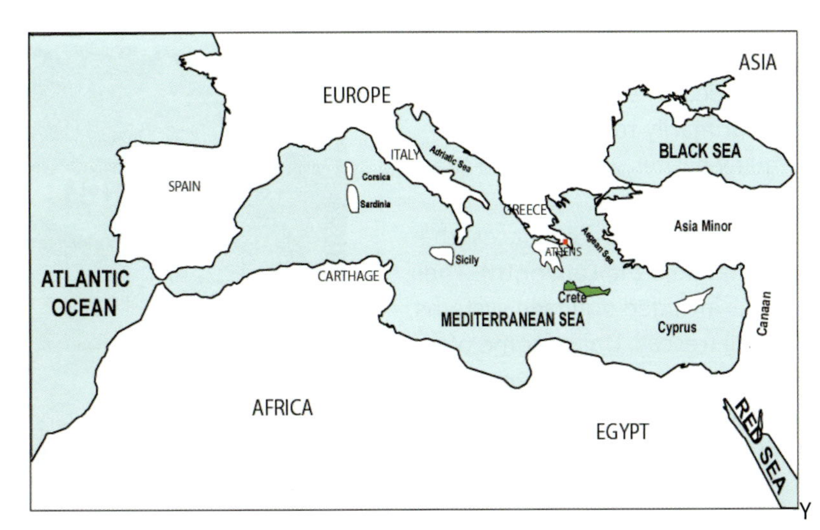

Crete is the fifth largest island in the Mediterranean Sea. It was home to the earliest known European civilization, the Minoans (1720-1400 BC). A British archaeologist named Sir Arthur Evans was the first to discover remnants of this ancient civilization on Crete in the early 1900s. Evans named the people group "Minoans" after their mythical King Minos.

ANCIENT HISTORY FOCUS

CRETE AND THE MINOANS

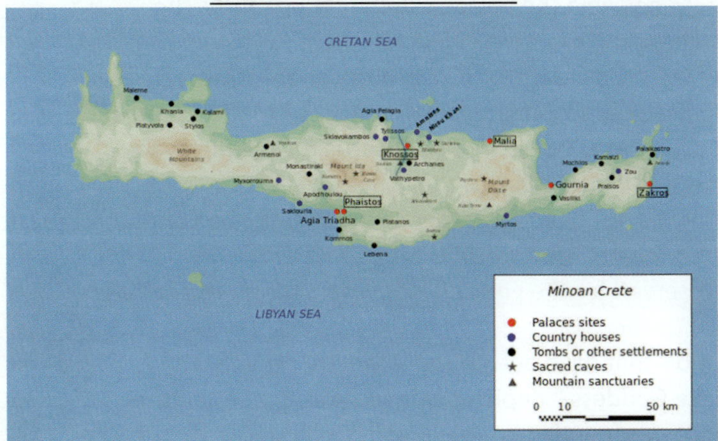

FASCINATING FACTS: King Minos

In Greek mythology, the legendary King Minos struggled with his brothers for the right to rule Crete. Looking for a sign of approval from the gods, Minos prayed that Poseidon would send him a snow-white bull, promising that he would sacrifice that bull to Poseidon as an offering. So Poseidon sent Minos just such a bull. But when Minos saw the bull, he felt that it was too beautiful to kill. Assuming Poseidon would not mind, he kept the bull for himself and sacrificed another bull in its place. When Poseidon found out, he took his revenge by causing Minos' wife Pasipha to fall in love with

There Minos stands. Canto V., line 4.

the bull. Through devious means, she became pregnant and bore a son that had the head and tail of a bull and the body of a man-- the monstrous "Minotaur."

The Minotaur was kept hidden in a maze of confusing passages known as a "labyrinth" at the palace of Knossos. Once a year, fourteen young boys and girls from Athens were taken to the labyrinth and abandoned to the Minotaur as a sacrifice. The people lived in terror of the monster until the Greek hero Theseus slew him using some helpful instructions from King Minos' daughter.

The Minoans were traders, buying and selling goods all around the Mediterranean Sea. They developed the first powerful navy in the world, primarily to protect their merchant ships from the many pirates who roamed the seas.

The Minoans built several elaborate palaces, the largest at Knossos (the one that held the Labyrinth). Their multi-level stonework palaces included drainage systems, flush toilets and beautiful wall frescos. Unlike some other ancient cultures, the Minoans did not hide their palaces behind city walls. After an earthquake shook Crete, destroying the palaces, the Minoans rebuilt on an even grander scale.

FASCINATING FACTS: Daedalus and Icarus

The palace at Knossos, home of the Labyrinth, was probably the political and religious capital of the Minoan Civilization. According to Greek mythology, the palace contained a maze so complex that no unsuspecting person who entered could ever hope to find his way out again. King Minos built the palace as a hiding place for his wife's monstrous son, the Minotaur. So that the ways of the maze would remain secret, Minos held the palace's architect prisoner. The architect's name was Daedalus.

Daedalus, however, was too clever to remain a prisoner forever. He built two sets of wings, one for himself and one for his son Icarus, so that the two of them could fly away to freedom. As Daedalus trained Icarus for the flight, he warned his son that he must not fly too close to the sun, as the wings were held together with wax that would melt in the sun's heat. Icarus did not heed his father's warning. Thrilled with the experience of the godlike power of flight, Icarus soared too near the sun and melted his wings. He fell into the sea and was lost. The lesson of this tale is that powers reserved for the gods are too much for mere mortals.

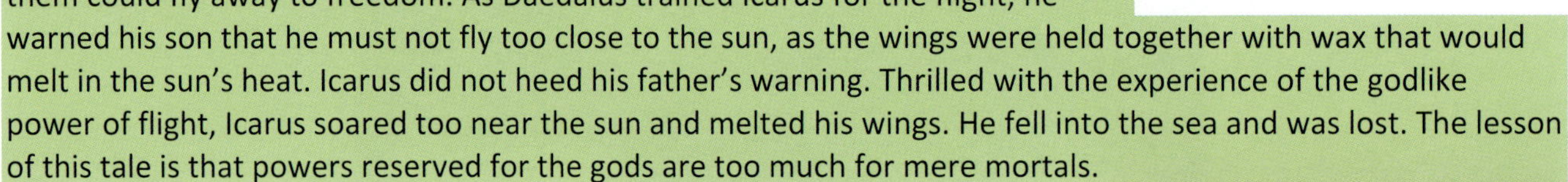

All of the Minoan idols that have been discovered are female. The most popular was the "Snake Goddess," depicted with snakes in her hands or entwining her body. This idol was found in houses and in small shrines in the palaces. She may have been the goddess of the house, a kind of guardian angel. The Minoan priesthood also seems to have been composed entirely of females. There is some evidence that the Minoans practiced ritual human sacrifice.

The Minoans enjoyed two sports, boxing and bull-jumping. A famous wall fresco from Ancient Crete depicts two boys fist fighting with gloves. This is the earliest known example of boxing gloves.

Bull-jumping was a test of the participants' courage and agility. The Minoans would send a bull running at the jumper, and just as it came close enough, in an instant the jumper would grab the bull's horns and either vault over the bull in a somersault or vault onto the bull's back. The purpose of bull-jumping is unknown. The bull was apparently sacred to the Minoans; its image has been found on pottery, drinking vessels, sculptures and frescoes. Bull-jumping may have been part of a religious ceremony to venerate the bull or the gods, or it may have been a form of human sacrifice. Or it may have been simply a very dangerous and challenging sport.

The End of the Minoans

Around 1628 BC, a massive volcanic eruption destroyed the nearby island of Thera. A terrific explosion, perhaps equivalent to a hundred or even several hundred nuclear bombs, obliterated Thera, and the sea swallowed the island. This was not the first eruption on Thera. Earlier eruptions forewarned of the coming disaster, and the people of Crete apparently recognized their danger and decided to evacuate their island. The evacuation and the eruption spelled the end of the Minoan Civilization.

FASCINATING FACTS: Myths surrounding Theras

An eruption as powerful as the one that destroyed Theras could have had effects around the world. Several myths and theories have grown up around the eruption of Theras:

- The lost island of Theras might have been home to the lost city of Atlantis mentioned by the Greek philosopher Plato over a thousand years after the eruption.
- In China, the eruption may have coincided with the collapse of the Xia dynasty. According to Chinese records, "yellow fog, dim sun, three suns, frost in July, famine and the withering of all five cereals" all happened around the same time as the eruption of Theras. The eruption could have sent aloft a lingering cloud of dust and ash that blocked out the sun long enough to cause these effects far away in China.
- The Biblical story of Moses and the Exodus has been linked to Theras. Some of the ten plagues, such as the three days of darkness, hail and the pollution of the Nile, could have been effects of the eruption.

BIBLE FOCUS

THE KINGDOM OF JUDAH, PART I

Over the last two weeks we have covered the kings of the northern kingdom of Israel and their prophets. This week we are going to study the kings and prophets of the southern kingdom of Judah from the division of the kingdoms through Israel's fall to Assyria.

(See the synchronized chart of the two kingdoms in the back as a reference)

Kings of the Southern Kingdom - Judah

Rehoboam - 922-915 BC	Bad - inherited the throne - reigned 17 years

REHOBOAM

Rehoboam took the throne after his father Solomon died, but he angered the northern tribes by continuing Solomon's harsh policies. He was unable to hold together the fragile union created by David and maintained by Solomon, and the kingdom split in two. Rehoboam was left with the lands allotted to the tribes of Judah and Benjamin, including Jerusalem and the Temple. The other ten tribes went with Jeroboam and the northern kingdom.

Rehoboam did not follow God, but worshipped other gods. Even though he held Jerusalem and the Temple, he followed the northern king Jeroboam's lead and created other places of worship. Much evil took place in these new temples, such as temple prostitution and human mutilation and sacrifice. In the fifth year of Rehoboam's reign, the king of Egypt attacked Jerusalem, stripped the Temple of its treasures hauled them off to Egypt.

Abijah - 915-913 BC	Bad - inherited the throne - reigned 3 years

ABIJAH

Abijah did not follow God, but worshipped other gods. During his short reign, Abijah was able to regain some of Judah's lost territory from Israel.

Asa - 913-873 BC	Good - inherited the throne - reigned 41 years

ASA

Unlike Israel, Judah had some good kings after Solomon. Asa was one of these. Asa was so committed to Yahweh worship that he even removed his grandmother from a position of authority because she worshipped Ashtoreth, a Phoenician god. He eliminated the idols and tore down their "high places" of worship. Asa was also a good military commander. He formed an alliance with the king of Aram against Israel, fortified the towns around Jerusalem and fended off an invasion by the Cushites.

Jehoshaphat - 873-849 BC	Good - inherited the throne - reigned 25 years

JEHOSHAPHAT

Jehoshaphat followed in his father Asa's footsteps, fully committed to God and His ways. During his reign, Jehoshaphat sent judges, priests and Levites throughout Judah to teach his people the Law of Moses. The kingdom prospered during his reign, and the surrounding kingdoms left Judah alone.

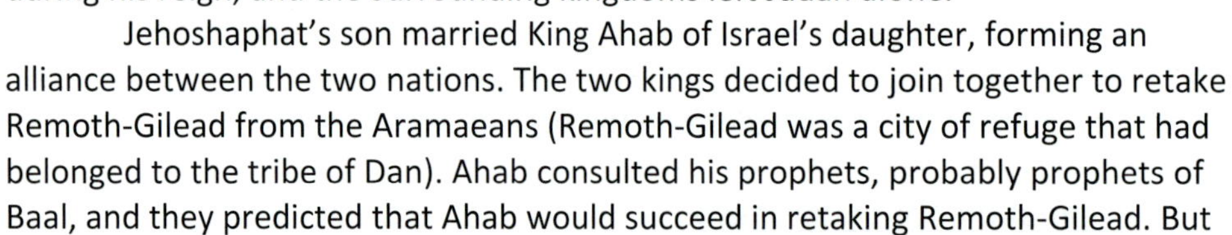

Jehoshaphat's son married King Ahab of Israel's daughter, forming an alliance between the two nations. The two kings decided to join together to retake Remoth-Gilead from the Aramaeans (Remoth-Gilead was a city of refuge that had belonged to the tribe of Dan). Ahab consulted his prophets, probably prophets of Baal, and they predicted that Ahab would succeed in retaking Remoth-Gilead. But Jehoshaphat was not impressed with Ahab's prophets; he wanted prophets of the Lord. When they consulted Micaiah, a prophet of the Lord, he prophesied that Ahab would die in the battle. Ahab shrugged this off, but Micaiah was quite right-- Ahab did indeed die in the battle. The battle was lost, but Jehoshaphat was able to return to Jerusalem safely (I Kings 22).

Jehoshaphat also joined with Israel against the Moabites, and was able to defeat them with the help of Elisha the prophet (II Kings 3).

Jehoram - 849-843 BC	Bad - inherited the throne - reigned 8 years

JEHORAM

Jehoram of Judah was the son of Jehoshaphat whose marriage to Ahab and Jezebel's daughter Athaliah cemented the alliance with Israel. Jehoram foolishly followed his wife's gods and ignored the Lord. As soon as Jehoram took the throne, he had all of his brothers killed.

During his reign, Jehoram lost a major battle to the Edomites. Because of this, he was unable to access the trade routes down to Arabia, and this took away much of the kingdom's prosperity. When the Philistines attacked Jerusalem, they killed all of Jehoram's wives and all of his sons except the youngest. Jehoram became sick with a painful bowel disease, and his death was "to no one's regret" (II Kings 21:20).

Ahaziah - 843 BC	Bad - inherited the throne - reigned 1 year Killed

AHAZIAH

Ahaziah was the youngest and only surviving son of Jehoram. He reigned for one year and, with his mother's encouragement, did evil in God's sight (remember that his mother Athaliah was the wicked Jezebel's daughter). Ahaziah aligned himself with King Jehoram of Israel, Ahab's son. They joined forces against the king of Aram, and during the battle Jehoram was wounded. Ahaziah accompanied Jehoram to his palace. On the way they met Jehu, who had been anointed Israel's king in Jehoram's place by Elisha the prophet. Jehu proceeded to kill both of them.

Note: Yes, there were two King Jehorams, one of Israel, one of Judah. Their reigns overlapped, which makes reading their stories in the Bible confusing at times. However, it is no more confusing than having two presidents named John Adams or George Bush.

Athaliah - 842-837 BC	Bad - (mother of Ahaziah) -reigned 6 years Killed

ATHALIAH

Athaliah was Jehoram of Judah's wife and the daughter of Ahab and Jezebel. She was also Ahaziah's mother. When Athaliah learned that her son was dead, she launched a purge to kill everyone else in the royal family so that she could have the throne for herself and lead Judah into exclusive Baal worship. But Ahaziah had one infant child, Joash, who was saved from the purge. His aunt, the wife of high priest Jehoiada, took Joash to the temple and hid him from his grandmother for seven years.

Athaliah reigned for six years and did not follow God, but did evil in His sight.

Then Jehoiada, the high priest of the temple, led a revolt against the queen. When Joash was seven years old, Jehoiada declared him king. Athaliah was put to death.

Joash - 837-800 BC	Good/Bad - inherited the throne - reigned 40 years Assassinated

JOASH

Joash was seven when he became king. As a youth he was guided by Jehoiada the high priest, and throughout the priest's lifetime, Joash led Judah well according to the priest's wisdom. He was able to raise enough money to repair the temple, which was damaged during Athaliah's reign.

When High Priest Jehoiada died, his son Zechariah took his place. Joash did not respect Zechariah as he had respected Jehoiada. When Zechariah tried to rebuke Joash, Joash had the priest stoned to death in the Temple courtyard. Because of this

vile act, the Lord raised up the Aramaeans against Joash. They invaded Judah and Jerusalem and defeated Joash and his army. Joash was wounded in battle and then killed in his own bed by his own officials.

SCRIPTURE SPOTLIGHT: Joel

Joel is one of those prophets who has Bible scholars stumped. No one knows when to date the Book of Joel.

Joel prophesies that a locust plague that will hit the land of Judah. He calls for repentance and ends with a message of hope and promise. The book is often dated around the reign of King Joash, but it has also been placed after the Babylonian invasion and the fall of Jerusalem. Some date it even later, during the return from Babylonian exile and the re-building of Jerusalem's walls in the time of Nehemiah.

Amaziah - 800-783 BC	Decent - inherited the throne - reigned 29 years Assassinated

AMAZIAH

Amaziah took the throne at age twenty-five after his father Joash was assassinated by two of his officials. He put the assassins to death, but spared their families according to the Law of Moses.

Amaziah followed the Lord half-heartedly. Amaziah took a census in order to build up his military for a battle against the Edomites. Although his army was large, he hired an additional hundred thousand Israelite mercenaries to fight alongside his men. A prophet advised him to get rid of these Israelites, or he would not win; so Amaziah sent them away. He then led his forces against the Edomites and defeated them, but he foolishly brought back Edomite idols and set them up in Judah. This victory reopened the trade routes that Judah had lost during Jehoram's reign, enabling Judah to prosper again.

Emboldened by his victory, Amaziah challenged the King Jehoash of Israel to battle and lost. Amaziah was later assassinated by his own men.

Uzziah - 783-742 BC	Good - inherited the throne - reigned 52 years

UZZIAH

Uzziah (Azariah) became king at the age of sixteen. He was a good king who sought after God. Much of his reign coincided with that of Jeroboam II of Israel. This was a period of great prosperity for both Judah and Israel and there was peace between the two kingdoms. Uzziah was able to expand his kingdom both politically and economically.

Unfortunately, success made Uzziah proud, and he made the mistake of entering the holy place in the Temple and burning incense on the altar. God gave this job to the Levite priests and no one else. The priests followed him in to warn him of his sin, but he grew angry with them. As he raged at them, they saw that leprous spots were appearing on his forehead, and hustled him out. The King of Judah had leprosy for the rest of his life and had to allow his son Jotham to lead in his place.

GIANTS OF THE FAITH: Isaiah

Of all the Bible's prophetic books, the Book of Isaiah is first and greatest. Isaiah's writing has no equal. Filled with brilliant imagery, metaphors, and parables, the Book of Isaiah points the hearer to a God of judgment, grace and salvation. Interlaced with Isaiah's pronouncements on the events of his own time are beautiful allusions to the coming Messiah, Israel's hope.

Chapter 6 describes Isaiah's call to prophetic ministry. Isaiah receives a vision of the Holy Lord on His throne, and he is dismayed because he is unclean and unworthy to be in the Lord's presence. An angel flies to Isaiah and touches his lips with a coal from the altar in the vision, and he is cleansed. The Lord has a message for the people of Judah, and He asks, "Whom shall I send?" Isaiah famously responds, "Here am I. Send me!"

Isaiah's ministry began at the death of Uzziah and spanned the reigns of Jotham, Ahaz, Hezekiah and part of Manasseh. He witnessed the fall of Israel and predicted the captivity and exile of Judah. Isaiah lived all of his life around Jerusalem, calling on the people of Judah to return to God and to trust Him to protect them against the threat of the hostile nations that surrounded them, especially Assyria.

There is a tradition that Isaiah died a martyr's death at the hands of King Manasseh. According to apocryphal sources (sources not officially recognized by any church), Isaiah was accused of heresy for saying that he had seen God (Isaiah 6), when even the great Moses saw only God's back (Exodus 33:18-23). But of course Isaiah's vision was not the same as Moses' encounter, so this was a trumped-up and cynical excuse for the murder of a great prophet. In any event, according to the story, Isaiah was sawn in two with a wood saw.

Jotham - 742-735 BC	Good - inherited the throne - reigned 16 years

JOTHAM

Jotham was Uzziah's eldest son. When Uzziah was stricken with leprosy, Jotham became his father's co-regent, because his father's disease meant that he had to be kept in seclusion. After his father died, Jotham ruled in his own right and followed the Lord, but he failed to tear down the high places where the people offered sacrifices to their idols. Jotham repaired the Temple gate and built up the city walls. He defeated the Ammonites and received tribute from them.

SCRIPTURE SPOTLIGHT: Micah

Micah was a contemporary of Isaiah, prophesying through the reigns of Jotham, Ahaz and Hezekiah. Micah was a spokesman for the poor. He believed that the Lord desired for his people to have a faith that came from the heart and not from religious ritual. His best-known message appears in Micah 6:6-8:

"With what shall I come before the LORD and bow down before the exalted God? Shall I come before him with burnt offerings, with calves a year old? Will the LORD be pleased with thousands of rams, with ten thousand rivers of oil? Shall I offer my firstborn for my transgression, the fruit of my body for the sin of my soul?

He has showed you, O man, what is good. And what does the LORD require of you? To act justly and to love mercy and to walk humbly with your God."

Ahaz - 735-715 BC	VERY BAD - inherited the throne - reigned 16 years

AHAZ

Ahaz did not follow the Lord as his father and grandfather did. He aggressively practiced the dark rites of Baal worship, including child sacrifice. Ahaz turned away from the Lord entirely, placing his trust in the gods of his enemies. Because of this, he suffered defeats at the hands of the Aramaeans, Israelites, Edomites and Philistines.

SCRIPTURE SPOTLIGHT: II Kings 16

When the kings of Aram and Israel banded together against Judah, Ahaz was so desperate that he sacrificed his own son or sons to the idol Molech. Isaiah told Ahaz to trust in God for deliverance because both Aram and Israel would soon be shattered. Ahaz refuses to trust in God, and Isaiah responds with a foretelling of the Messiah:

"The virgin will be with child and will give birth to a son, and will call him Immanuel" (Isaiah 7:14).

Even though Ahaz has attacked his own lineage by killing his own son, Isaiah foretells that God will bring forth Immanuel from Ahaz's line. Like much of prophecy, this passage has more than one meaning and is difficult to understand.

Isaiah also predicted that Assyria would soon take over the Judah. Despite these warnings, Ahaz appealed to the Assyrian king, Tiglath-Pileser III, for help against his enemies. Judah had been paying tribute to Assyria, and with the tribute came protection. Assyria was more than happy to oblige. Tiglath-Pileser III marched into Canaan, captured Damascus (the capital of Aram) and conquered part of Israel (II Kings 15:29). Ahaz gratefully committed himself to Assyria's gods, replacing the Lord's altar with an Assyrian one.

FASCINATING FACTS: Jesus' Ancestors up to this point

Abraham - Isaac - Jacob - Judah and Tamar - Perez - Hezron - Ram - Amminadab - Nahshon - Salmon and Rahab - Boaz and Ruth - Obed - Jesse - King David and Bathsheba - Solomon - Rehoboam - Abijah - Asa - Jehoshaphat - Jehoram - Uzziah - Jotham - Ahaz

FASCINATING FACTS: Ancient Seals

Ancient kings used royal seals to establish a document's authenticity or authority. A seal had a raised design that left a distinctive impression when pressed into wax or soft clay. The earliest seals were engraved on cylinders, which left their mark when they were rolled on the document. Later, kings had signet rings with their seals engraved in them.

In the Bible, Queen Jezebel used a seal in I Kings 21, and the Levites and leaders who returned from Babylonian exile used a seal in Nehemiah 9:38. In Esther 8:8, King Xerxes remarks on the power of his signet ring:

"Now write another decree in the king's name in behalf of the Jews as seems best to you, and seal it with the king's signet ring—for no document written in the king's name and sealed with his ring can be revoked."

Chapter 18

Greek Beginnings

ANCIENT HISTORY FOCUS

THE MYCENAEANS

The Mycenaeans took their name from their capital city of Mycenae. They were the first great culture on the Greek peninsula, where they lived during the late Bronze Age from about 1600 to 1200 BC. While the Minoans of Crete were interested in trade, the Mycenaeans were warlike, advancing their civilization through conquest.

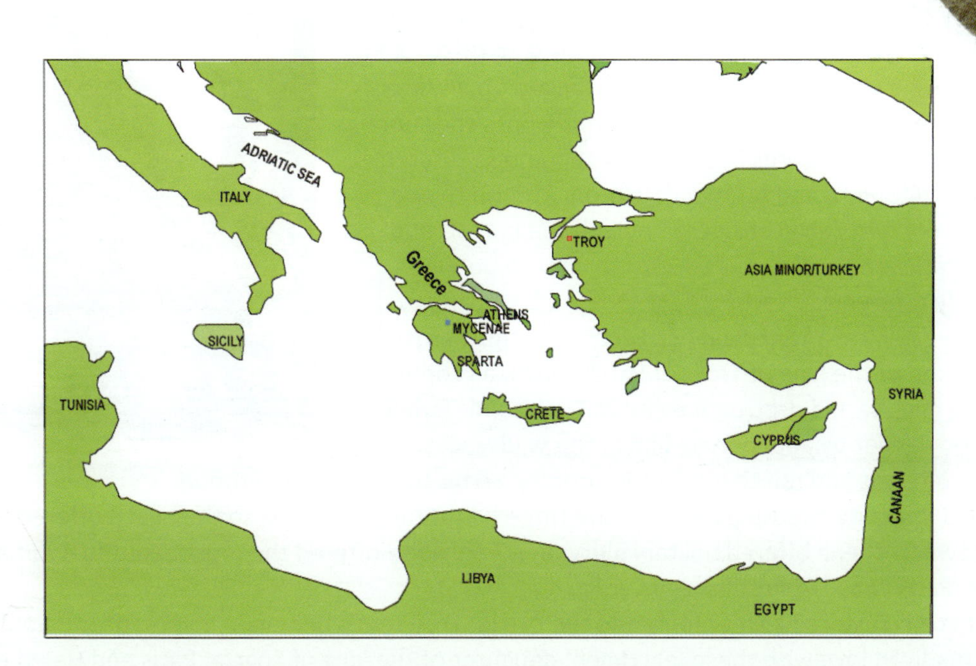

FASCINATING FACTS: From Stone Age to Bronze Age to Iron Age

The standard time-line that most archaeologists use for the Ancient Near East:

Stone Age (Neolithic and Chalcolithic)	8500 - 3300 BC
Early Bronze Age	3300 - 2000 BC
Middle Bronze Age	2000 - 1550 BC
Late Bronze Age	1550 - 1200 BC
Iron Age	1200 - 586 BC
Persian Period	586 - 330 BC
Hellenistic (Greek) Period	330 - 63 BC
Roman Period	63 BC - 330 AD
Byzantine Period	330 AD - 640 AD

People of the Stone Age used stone tools-- stone knives, stone arrowheads, stone mallets, etc. Later, the ancients discovered their first metal: copper. Copper was abundant in the Middle East, and people all over the region learned to mine and craft it. It was a suitable material for simple tools and ornaments, but it was too soft for most weapons. Knives, swords or spear points made of unalloyed copper dented easily and didn't hold their edge.

Around 3300 BC, someone discovered that one could make copper much harder by melting it together with tin. Tin is rather brittle by itself, but when tin is mixed with soft copper, the resulting alloy is hard but not brittle. This useful alloy is called bronze, and its discovery ushered in the Bronze Age. Bronze was useful for both tools and weapons. A warrior equipped with bronze weapons was far superior to one equipped with only stone.

Around 1200 BC, iron was discovered in Asia Minor (modern-day Turkey). Iron metallurgy produced tools and weapons far harder, stronger, lighter, and more durable than even bronze. As the Bronze Age warrior outstripped the Stone Age warrior, so the Iron Age warrior outstripped the Bronze Age warrior. The Israelites suffered this disadvantage against the Philistines around the time of David and Goliath.

The Mycenaeans conquered the island of Crete around 1400 BC. They are also sometimes credited with conquering Troy, a city on the western edge of Asia Minor (see map above). However, the stories of Troy read more like myth than history, and no one knows how much truth is in them.

FASCINATING FACTS: The Trojan War

The story of the Trojan War begins with the gods. All of them were gathered for a wedding except Eris, the goddess of Discord. Eris was not invited to the wedding, and when she showed up anyway, Hermes stopped her at the door. In anger, she threw into the room an apple inscribed with the words "To the Fairest." And so discord was sown: Zeus's wife Hera and his two daughters Aphrodite and Athena were all very fair. Each considered herself the fairest, and each laid claim to the apple. They asked Zeus to choose between them. Zeus wisely refused to choose.

The choice fell to Paris, a plain herdsman. But this herdsman was actually the son of the king of Troy: At Paris's birth, a prophet foretold that the child would destroy the city of Troy, so his family tried to avoid the danger by abandoning him in the wilderness. Shepherds rescued Paris and raised him in the country, so he survived to adulthood.

Paris had difficulty choosing between the three beautiful goddesses, so they each offered him a bribe. Hera offered power, Athena offered military glory, and Aphrodite offered the most beautiful woman in the world as a wife. Paris chose Aphrodite's gift.

Later, Paris is restored to his family and the castle. Troy sends him on a diplomatic mission to Sparta, where he falls madly in love with the lovely Helen, daughter of the king of Sparta. Paris and Helen elope and set sail for Troy, taking with them treasures from Sparta. They travel around the Mediterranean and finally return to Troy.

The Greeks send a delegation including the king of Ithaca, the king of Sparta and the hero Odysseus to demand the return of both Helen and the treasures. When the Trojans refuse, the Greeks assemble an army to invade Troy. Thus Helen's becomes the "face that launched a thousand ships."

After another attempt at diplomacy fails, the Greeks settle down for a siege. The battle for Troy lasts for over nine years. In the tenth year, Odysseus conceives a plan: The Greeks build a giant, hollow, wooden horse and secretly fill it with troops. Then they offer it to Troy as a gift, with the following inscription: "The Greeks dedicate this offering as thanks to Athena for their return back home." They abandon their siege and appear to turn for home. Rejoicing that the Greek army had finally given up, the Trojans roll the gift horse into their city. They celebrate and debate whether to burn it or dedicate it to their gods.

At midnight, the troops inside the horse come out and attack the Trojans. They also open the city gates for the returning Greek army, which had only seemed to depart. The unprepared Trojans are no match for the Greeks, and they are massacred. The Greeks burn Troy to the ground and return to Greece victorious. Thus the prophecy at Paris's birth comes true, and Paris's deeds destroy his city.

Little is known of the Mycenaeans. They left behind a style of writing that became known as early Greek, different from that of the Minoans. Their distinctive style of pottery has been found throughout the Mediterranean area. They buried their nobles in beehive style tombs and used chariots in battle. The Minoan culture had great influence on the Mycenaeans, and much of their art is similar in style.

Around 1200 BC, the Mycenaeans were invaded by the Sea People (sea-faring raiders) and the Dorians.

FASCINATING FACTS: The Dorians

The Dorians seem to have come from northern Greece. Beginning around 1200 BC, they swept into central and southern Greece with their iron swords, conquering everything in their path. They held sway throughout Greece for the next 200 years. Exactly how or why they were able to overcome the Mycenaeans is unclear. They may have arrived around the time of some natural disaster or epidemic that had already weakened the Mycenaeans. Or they may simply have overwhelmed the Mycenaeans with superior numbers and weaponry. The Dorian invasion marks the end of the Bronze Age and the beginning of the Dark Age of Greece, which lasted until around 750 BC.

Despite their advanced weaponry, the Dorians were a primitive, pastoral people. They did not read or write, so little is known about their culture. They scattered throughout the region except for Athens. They finally settled in large numbers in the far south, where Sparta became their main city.

Eventually, the Dorians merged with the Hellenistic Greeks. The high culture of the Mycenaeans disappeared, except in the region of Athens.

After the Sea People and the Dorians had lived in Greece for hundreds of years, they began to put down roots and merge into a single people group known as the Greeks. At the end of the Dark Ages, a Greek writer of mythology named Homer emerged. Homer's poetic tales told of times before the Dark Age, but their influence helped to unify the different Greek peoples into one Greek culture.

AMAZING ANCIENTS: Homer

Homer was a blind Greek poet who lived around 800 BC. His two epic poems *The Iliad* and *The Odyssey* are the best known surviving literature of the Greek Dark Age. *The Iliad* tells of the siege of Troy, and *The Odyssey* tells of the wanderings of the hero Ulysses. Although the poems are credited to Homer, some have questioned whether such a person really lived. Some believe that the two poems are actually collections of work by different authors, gathered over a period of years by a group of poets.

FASCINATING FACTS: Greek Writing

Unlike the Mycenaeans, the Dorians and the Sea People did not read and write; they were illiterate. This is one reason why their coming brought on the Greek Dark Age. All that is known about their period in history comes from excavations and from texts written about them later. Coming at the end of the Dark Age, Homer helped to illuminate early Greek history.

It was the Phoenicians who introduced writing back into the Greek culture. The later Greeks adapted the Phoenician alphabet, creating the first truly alphabetic writing system. The Greek alphabet spread quickly through the Mediterranean and was adapted for other languages.

Fun Facts about the Olympic Games

- The Olympic games began in 776 BC in Olympia, Greece
- An "Olympiad" is a period of four years, and the games were held once each Olympiad.
- The Olympic games were for men only. Beginning around 500-600 BC, women competed in a separate competition called the Heraea Games, a set of footraces. Heraea games winners won an olive crown and

meat.

- Only free men were allowed to compete in the Olympic games.
- The athletes wore no clothes during the competition.
- Women were not allowed to watch the Olympic games under penalty of death.
- Winners received a crown of olive leaves (no medals) and hero status for the rest of their lives. The next Olympiad carried the winner's name.
- The *stadion* foot race was the only event in the first 13 Olympic games.
- When wrestling became an Olympic event, the referee was allowed to beat a wrestler with a whip if he made a wrong move.
- Ancient Olympic boxing matches were not divided into rounds. The boxers simply fought until one was beaten senseless.
- *Pankration*, another fighting event, was a cross between wrestling and boxing. Every means of attack was permitted except biting and eye gouging. The fight did not stop until one of the combatants was unconscious or dead.
- During the Olympic games, a truce was observed between all participating cities. Wars were suspended, and athletes were allowed to travel safely to the Games without hindrance.
- Roman Emperor Theodosius I banned the Olympic games in 393 AD. They were not revived until 1896.

FASCINATING FACTS: Greek Vases

The Greeks are famous for their black on red and red on black painted pottery. In early Greek pottery, the silhouette figures were painted black on a background of red-orange. Later the colors were reversed: the figures appear in red on a black background.

The drawings found on ancient Greek vases include scenes from mythology, events from everyday life and exquisite patterns.

GEOGRAPHY FOCUS

Geography's Beginnings

Did you know…

- An Ancient Greek named Eratosthenes invented the science of geography.
- Eratosthenes believed that the Earth was as a sphere, not flat as some believed.
- In 250 BC, Eratosthenes measured the circumference of the Earth by measuring the angle to the sun at two different locations a known distance apart. The circumference he calculated was within 76 miles of the Earth's true circumference.
- Eratosthenes also charted the course of the Nile River and created a map of the known world.

BIBLE FOCUS

THE KINGDOM OF JUDAH, PART II

Last week we covered the Kingdom of Judah from its beginnings with King Rehoboam through the reign of Ahaz. This week we will cover the reigns of Hezekiah, Manasseh and Amon.

Kings of the Southern Kingdom, Judah

Hezekiah - 715-687 BC	THE BEST - inherited the throne - reigned 25 years

HEZEKIAH

During the reign of Hezekiah, the Assyrians were at the height of their power. Sargon II ruled Assyria until he died in 705 BC. His son Sennacherib took the throne and ruled from 705-681 BC.

In 701 BC, King Hezekiah of Judah rebelled against paying tribute to the Assyrian king.

SCRIPTURE SPOTLIGHT: Hezekiah and Sennacherib (II Kings 18-20)

Hezekiah was a good king who desired to please God in all he did. His rebellion against Assyrian rule was probably due to the devastating effect that it had on the religious life of his people. One could hardly claim that God was all powerful and still pay tribute to a tyrant like Sennacherib. But like most tyrants, Sennacherib did not allow rebellion to go unpunished.

Sennacherib gathers his forces and invades Judah, heading for Jerusalem. Realizing that he is no match for Sennacherib, Hezekiah strips the royal palace of its treasures and sends an envoy to offer them to Sennacherib. Sennacherib accepts the tribute but continues to march toward Jerusalem. Sennacherib's commander tells Hezekiah's officials that they do not stand a chance against the Assyrian army. The Judeans are outmanned, and the Egyptians are too weak to provide support. Speaking in Hebrew, the commander tells all Judeans who can hear that Hezekiah has been misleading them when he tells them to trust in the Lord. Hezekiah's God, the commander says, is no more able to deliver them than the gods of all the other lands that Sennacherib has conquered.

Hezekiah's reaction is to tear his robes and cry out to the Lord. Still believing that only the Lord can save Judah, he sends messengers to Isaiah. Isaiah condemns Sennacherib's arrogance and prophesies that he will never enter Jerusalem. That night the angel of the Lord kills 185,000 Assyrian soldiers in one night. Sennacherib withdraws to Nineveh.

After Sennacherib leaves, Hezekiah becomes ill. Isaiah tells him that he will die, but Hezekiah prays for more time and God grants it to him. Then the king of Babylon seeks out Hezekiah, perhaps to form an alliance with him. Hezekiah is friendly to the Babylonians, perhaps too friendly. Isaiah prophesies that all of Judah's treasures will one day be carted off to Babylon, and that descendants of David will one day become eunuchs in the palace of the Babylonian king. Both of these prophecies come true in Daniel 1.

In 681 BC, Sennacherib was killed by two of his sons while worshipping in the temple of one of his gods. In 1813 AD, Lord Byron wrote *The Destruction of Sennacherib*. The poem became so popular that British schoolchildren were required to memorize it.

THE DESTRUCTION OF SENNACHERIB

The Assyrian came down like the wolf on the fold,
And his cohorts were gleaming in purple and gold;
And the sheen of their spears was like stars on the sea,
When the blue wave rolls nightly on deep Galilee.
Like the leaves of the forest when Summer is green,
That host with their banners at sunset were seen:
Like the leaves of the forest when Autumn hath blown,
That host on the morrow lay withered and strown.
For the Angel of Death spread his wings on the blast,
And breathed in the face of the foe as he passed;
And the eyes of the sleepers waxed deadly and chill,
And their hearts but once heaved, and for ever grew still!
And there lay the steed with his nostril all wide,
But through it there rolled not the breath of his pride;
And the foam of his gasping lay white on the turf,
And cold as the spray of the rock-beating surf.
And there lay the rider distorted and pale,
With the dew on his brow, and the rust on his mail:
And the tents were all silent, the banners alone,
The lances unlifted, the trumpet unblown.
And the widows of Ashur are loud in their wail,
And the idols are broke in the temple of Baal;
And the might of the Gentile, unsmote by the sword,
Hath melted like snow in the glance of the Lord!
By: George Gordon (Lord) Byron (1788-1824)

(Lord Byron is one of the greatest British poets. *The Destruction of Sennacherib* was first published in 1815).

FASCINATING FACTS: Hezekiah's Tunnel

When Sennacherib marched on Jerusalem, Hezekiah realized that if Sennacherib laid siege to Jerusalem as the Assyrians did to Samaria, Jerusalem would be lost for lack of water. In preparation for the possibility of a siege, Hezekiah built a new water storage pool and a new tunnel to fill it with water from the Gihon Spring east of the city. The pool was called the Pool of Siloam, and the tunnel was called the Siloam Tunnel.

At 1749 feet (533 meters) long, the Siloam Tunnel is considered one of the greatest works of water engineering of its time. The tunnel did not follow a straight line, probably because it followed a natural fault in the rock. In addition to providing water for Jerusalem, the tunnel limited enemies' access to water by diverting other outside springs to the Pool of Siloam.

From II Chronicles 32:2-4 and 30:

"When Hezekiah saw that Sennacherib had come and that he intended to make war on Jerusalem, he consulted with his officials and military staff about blocking off the water from the springs outside the city, and they helped him. A large force of men assembled, and they blocked all the springs and the stream that flowed through the land. "Why should the kings of Assyria come and find plenty of water?" they said.

It was Hezekiah who blocked the upper outlet of the Gihon spring and channeled the water down to the west side of the City of David. He succeeded in everything he undertook."

From II Kings 20:20

"As for the other events of Hezekiah's reign, all his achievements and how he made the pool and the tunnel by which he brought water into the city, are they not written in the book of the annals of the kings of Judah?"

Inside the tunnel is an inscription in Ancient Hebrew script that explains how the tunnel was built. The script corresponds to other Ancient scripts from Hezekiah's time, providing confirmation from outside the Bible that Hezekiah built the tunnel.

Manasseh - 687-642 BC	THE WORST - inherited the throne - reigned 55 years

MANASSEH

After Hezekiah died, his son Manasseh took the throne. Manasseh served as co-regent with his father before Hezekiah's death, then inherited the throne around the age of twenty-two. Manasseh's reign was the longest of all the kings in the Davidic line. Unfortunately, he did not share his father's faith. Manasseh plunged Judah into idol worship on a scale that rivaled Israel's idol worship under Ahab and Jezebel. Manasseh offended the Lord in many ways:

- He embraced the idols of the nations Israel had expelled from Canaan
- He rebuilt the high places his father had torn down
- He erected altars to the Baal and made Asherah poles
- He bowed down to the starry hosts (Astral worship)
- He built altars to false gods inside the Temple of the Lord
- He practiced child sacrifice, even with his own sons
- He practiced sorcery and witchcraft

Manasseh led the Judeans so far into sin that they were no better than the Canaanites whom they drove out of the Promised Land. Through prophets, the Lord tried to call Manasseh back, but he would not listen. II Kings 21:16 says:

"Moreover, Manasseh also shed so much innocent blood that he filled Jerusalem from end to end—besides the sin that he had caused Judah to commit, so that they did evil in the eyes of the LORD.

Some interpret this verse to mean that Manasseh murdered the Lord's prophets, which is why they are not mentioned by name. According to legend, Isaiah was sawn in two at the hands of Manasseh. The verse could also refer to child sacrifice.

According to II Chronicles 33:10-11, the Lord allowed the king of Assyria to kidnap Manasseh and take him back to Babylon:

The LORD spoke to Manasseh and his people, but they paid no attention. So the LORD brought against them the army commanders of the king of Assyria, who took Manasseh prisoner, put a hook in his nose, bound him with bronze shackles and took him to Babylon.

This Assyrian king was most likely Esarhaddon, the son and successor of Sennacherib. Assyrian documents indicate that Manasseh was one of the kings who was compelled to visit Nineveh during Esarhaddon's reign. The hook through the nose, reminiscent of the treatment of livestock, was one of many cruel tricks the Assyrians used.

Once in Babylon, Manasseh was forced to deal with his sin. In utter despair he prayed to the Lord, and the Lord listened. Manasseh returned to Judah as king and tried to undo the evil he had previously done. According to II Chronicles 33: 15-17:

"He got rid of the foreign gods and removed the image from the temple of the LORD, as well as all the altars he had built on the temple hill and in Jerusalem; and he threw them out of the city. Then he restored the altar of the LORD and sacrificed fellowship offerings and thank offerings on it, and told Judah to serve the LORD, the God of Israel. The people, however, continued to sacrifice at the high places, but only to the LORD their God."

Amon - 642-640 BC	VERY BAD - inherited the throne -reigned 2 years Assassinated

AMON

Manasseh's son Amon took the throne after his father died. During his short, evil reign, he repeated the sins of his father and led Judah back into idolatry. Amon's officials rose up against him and killed him. Then another group killed Amon's officials and placed Josiah, Amon's eight year old son, on the throne of Judah.

(Continued in Chapter 19)

Chapter 19

India

GEOGRAPHY FOCUS

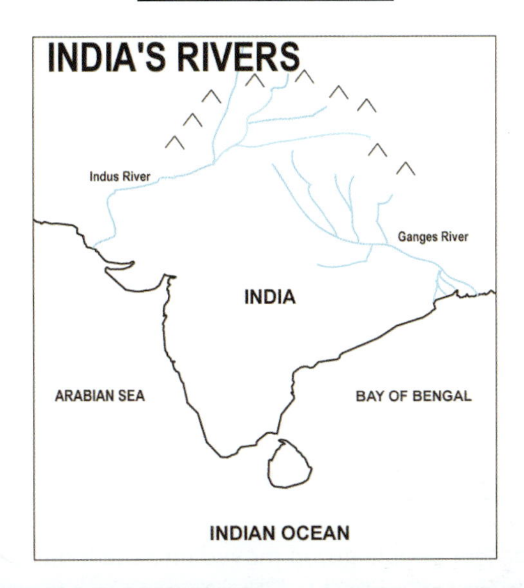

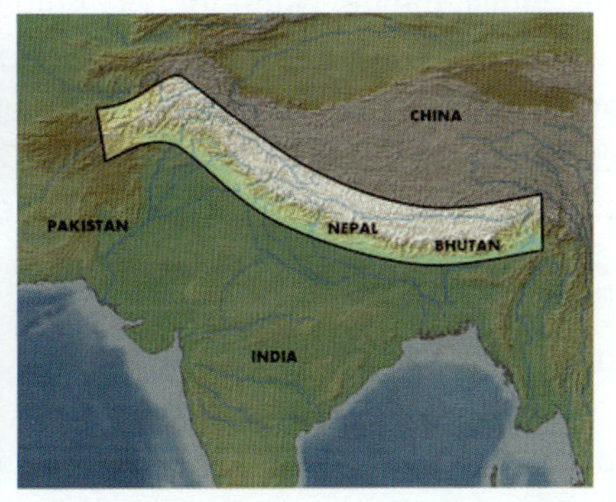

The Himalayas

Did you know…

- Asia's Himalaya Mountain Range is the world's highest mountain range.
- The Himalayas form the borderland between modern-day Pakistan, India, Nepal, Bhutan and Burma (to the south and west) and China (to the north and east).
- "Himalaya" means "home of snow."
- Mount Everest, the tallest mountain the world (over 29,000 feet above sea level), is part of the Himalayas.
- The sources of the Indus, Ganges and Yangtze Rivers all lie in the Himalayas.

FASCINATING FACTS: The Ganges River

The Ganges River rises in the Himalayas, then runs for more than 1500 miles before it finally drains into the Bay of Bengal. To Indian believers of the Hindu faith, however, the Ganges is more than just flowing water: It is sacred. Washing in the waters of the Ganges can cleanse one from sin, and scattering the ashes of a dead loved one in the waters of the Ganges can send that loved one along toward heaven.

Every morning, thousands of Hindus wade out into the Ganges to face the rising sun, murmur prayers and give thank offerings of flowers or food to the river goddess Ganga. Worshippers drink from the Ganges, then take a bottle of its water home with them. At night, they float candles on the Ganges' surface to represent their wishes.

ANCIENT HISTORY FOCUS

ANCIENT INDIA

2500-1750 BC: The Harappan Civilization flourishes along the Indus Valley

Around 1750 BC the Harappan civilization, which had thrived along the Indus river valley in India, simply disappeared (see Chapter 12). The reason for its disappearance is unknown: It might have been a natural disaster, an epidemic of disease or an invasion.

1600-1500 BC: The Aryans invade the Indus Valley

Between 1600-1500 BC, another people group moved into the Indus Valley. These people called themselves *Aryans,* which means "superior" or "noble." The Aryans were tough nomads with a conquering mentality. Armed with war chariots and other superior weaponry, they swept in from the north and claimed the Indus Valley from the Harappans, or whoever else might have been living there. Eventually they moved southeast, concentrating their population along the Ganges floodplain.

Centuries later, an Austrian named Adolf Hitler would claim kinship with this "superior, noble" race, the Aryans.

870 BC: The Hindus invent the zero.

600 BC: The Hindus write the Rig Veda. The priestly caste known as the *Brahmin* appears.

The Aryans (Vedic civilization) spoke and wrote in a language called Sanskrit. The earliest known writings in India were a collection of sacred poems and hymns called the *Rig Veda*.

ANCIENT TEXTS: The Rig Veda

The Rig Veda is a book of hymns and verses that explain the mythology of the Hindu gods. These hymns include praises, blessings, curses and sacrifices. The Rig Veda contains more than 1,000 sacred hymns, and is the earliest and holiest of all Hindu scriptures.

The hymns of the Rig Veda were written for chanting. Its repetitive chants are believed to create a mood in which the chanter is elevated to a higher state of mind. The chants of the Rig Veda show meditation and yoga in its earliest forms.

The religion that sprang from the Rig Veda helped shape India's culture and society for centuries to come, including India's distinctive caste system (see below).

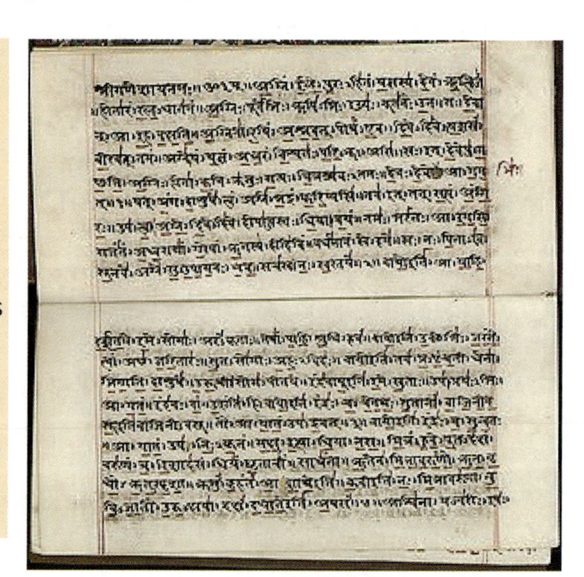

HINDUISM

The Hindu religion is difficult to define. Unlike Christianity, Judaism or Islam, Hinduism has no single founder or central figure, no central organization or standardized teachings. Instead, Hinduism has evolved in different ways in different parts of India. Over the centuries since the Aryan invasion, Hindus have formed thousands of different religious groups.

INTERESTING INDIAN RELIGIONS: Hinduism

Photo shows the Akshardham Temple, the world's largest Hindu temple (New Delhi, India)

Hinduism is India's most ancient religion. Hinduism's oldest scriptures, a collection of religious writings known as the *Rig Veda*, were first written down around 600 BC; but Hinduism itself is far older. There are several different branches of Hinduism, each with its own favorite scriptures and beliefs; but nearly all Hindus agree on the following:

1. **Brahma:** Brahma, the Hindu god, is three gods in one. He consists of Brahma the creator, Vishnu the preserver, and Shiva the destroyer.
2. **Castes:** All people are not born alike. Instead, there are categories or *castes* of people, some higher and superior, some lower and inferior. India has thousands of castes, and they vary from place to place; but the most common castes are these: (1) *Brahmins* (scholars and priests); (2) *Ksatriyas* (warriors and nobles); (3) *Vaisyas* (merchants, farmers, herders and artisans); and (4) *Sudras*, slaves. There are also people so lowly that they have no caste at all; these are considered "out-castes."

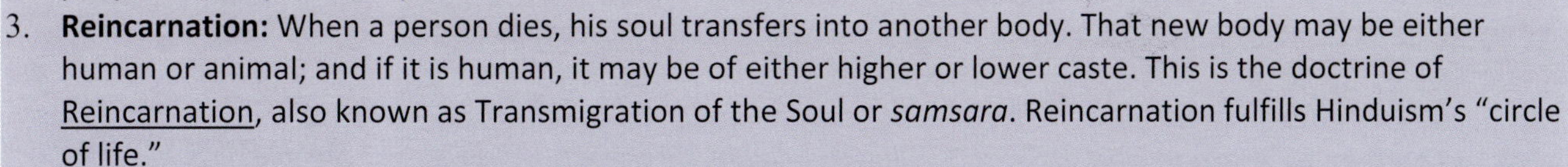

3. **Reincarnation:** When a person dies, his soul transfers into another body. That new body may be either human or animal; and if it is human, it may be of either higher or lower caste. This is the doctrine of Reincarnation, also known as Transmigration of the Soul or *samsara*. Reincarnation fulfills Hinduism's "circle of life."
4. **Karma:** *Karma* is the accumulated sum of the good and bad deeds that each person does in his or her life. A person's placement in his next, reincarnated life depends upon his karma in his current life: when good deeds outweigh bad, one may be reborn into a higher caste; but bad deeds may send one into a lower caste.
5. **Nirvana:** *Nirvana*, also known as *Moksha*, is the goal of every Hindu. The person who achieves nirvana is released from the endless stresses of life, the cycle of reincarnation and the circle of life. He transcends the mundane cares of daily life, becomes one with Brahma, and is at peace.
6. **Good Karma leads to Nirvana:** Good deeds create good karma, and good karma allows the Hindu be reincarnated into higher and higher castes. With enough good karma, the Hindu can finally achieve nirvana and be released from the circle of life. Chants and meditation also aid the Hindu in this quest: they lead to a heightened state of consciousness in which a person is able to realize his or her identity with Brahma. Prayer and devotion to the many Hindu gods through temple rituals, worship, pilgrimages, offerings and sacrifices also help toward the same goal.

The foundation of Hinduism is India's caste system, which divides all of India's people into separate classes or castes, each with a different set of privileges and duties.

FASCINATING FACTS: India's Caste System

The Rig Veda describes a cosmic giant named Purusha, a huge god with a thousand heads and a thousand feet who was somehow at one with the universe. The Hindus believe that when Purusha sacrificed himself (or was sacrificed by other gods), the world and its people all sprang from different parts of his body and spirit. The moon came from Purusha's mind, the sun from his eyes, and the wind from his breath.

The different Hindu castes also came from different parts of Purusha's sacrificed body:

- From Purusha's mouth came the highest caste, the *Brahmins*. Brahmins were scholars and priests.
- From Purusha's arms came the *Ksatriyas*, who were warriors and nobles.
- From Purusha's thighs came the *Vaisyas*, who were merchants, farmers, herders and artisans.
- From Purusha's feet came the *Sudras*, who were slaves.

These four castes – Brahmin, Ksatriyas, Vaisyas and Sudras – were the basic castes, but there were also thousands of sub-castes that varied by region. These castes' names, duties and privileges shifted over the years.

One final group, the Untouchables (now known as Dalits), had no caste at all, and became "outcastes." The higher castes considered the Untouchables ritually impure, so they segregated (separated) them from the rest of Indian society. The higher castes forced the Untouchables to live outside of their villages; they excluded them from Hindu worship, and kept them as unschooled and poor as possible. The Untouchables did the work that no one else would do: they cleaned toilets and sewers, collected garbage, butchered animals and so on.

The caste system could also be racist, because one's caste could be based partly on skin color. Lighter-skinned Indians filled the upper castes, while darker-skinned Indians (possibly the descendants of the surviving Harappans) filled the lower castes.

Because the caste system was based on birth alone, no Hindu could ever win his way into a higher caste by doing well in school, achieving great things or earning more wealth. A Hindu could enter a higher caste through death and reincarnation.

FASCINATING FACTS: Indian Jewelry

Distinctive Indian jewelry dates all of the way back to Harappan times. Indian people created jewelry out of seeds, feathers, leaves, berries, fruits, animal bones, tAkseeth and other things found in nature. Both men and women wore jewelry handcrafted of gold, silver, copper, ivory and precious stones. The Indian people adorned their temple idols with earrings, nose rings, anklets, bracelets and necklaces.

Indians wore abundant jewelry for special occasions, such as weddings and religious ceremonies. Married women wore a full array of bridal jewelry, including toe rings, bangles, bracelets, nose rings and a special ornament called a *mangalsutra* (see picture). Symbolically comparable to a Western wedding ring, the mangalsutra consists of a gold ornament fastened to a yellow thread tied around the woman's neck. The husband ties the mangalsutra around his new wife's neck on their wedding day, and she wears it until her husband dies.

599 (?) BC: Mahavira, the founder of **Jainism**, is born (see below).

563 (?) BC: Siddhartha (Buddha), the founder of **Buddhism**, is born.

BUDDHISM

Siddhartha Gautama, born around 563 BC, was the first Buddhist.

Siddhartha began his life as a privileged prince in a part of ancient India that now lies in Nepal. However, Siddhartha was one of those rare princes who couldn't seem to forget the suffering of his poor and elderly subjects. The terrible suffering of India's poor made Siddhartha ashamed of his privileged life. The problem of suffering haunted Siddhartha so much that, at the age of 29, he traded luxury for poverty: Siddhartha became a wandering ascetic, living a life of self-denial while he searched for solutions to the problems of suffering, old age and death.

Among India's early Hindus and Jainists, self-denial was a common way of seeking spiritual fulfillment. Under different Hindu and Jainist teachers, Siddhartha practiced extreme forms of self-denial – starving himself, going without sleep, abandoning all forms of material comfort – until he nearly died. Unlike his teachers, however, Siddhartha eventually decided that mere self-denial could never answer his deepest questions.

Since self-denial couldn't solve his problems, Siddhartha decided to seek a new solution of his own. He sat down under a tree and began to meditate, determined to remain there until he finally discovered a perfect solution to the problem of suffering.

After spending 49 days deep in thought, Siddhartha finally discovered an enlightened truth: That there was a "middle way" between the self-indulgence of the rich and the extreme self-denial that earlier Hindus and Jainists had practiced. From that time on, as the *Buddha* (or "enlightened one"), Siddhartha Gautama Buddha set out to teach others the enlightened truth that he had discovered under his tree of meditation.

INTERESTING INDIAN RELIGIONS: Buddhism

The basic concepts of Buddhism involve the Four Noble Truths and the Noble Eightfold Path:

- Noble Truth # 1: Life is suffering.
- Noble Truth #2: Suffering is caused by craving and desire for worldly pleasures.
- Noble Truth #3: One can overcome suffering and obtain happiness by freeing oneself from cravings and desire.
- Noble Truth #4: The Noble Eightfold path laid out by the Buddha leads to the end of cravings and desire, and therefore to the end of suffering.

These are the steps along the Noble Eightfold path:

Right view	Right intention	Right speech	Right action
Right livelihood	Right effort	Right mindfulness	Right concentration

Followers of the 8-fold path must (1) revere the life in everyone, (2) never steal, (3) abstain from immoral relationships, (4) always tell the truth and (5) always remain sober. According to Buddhism, when one has reached an enlightened state, he becomes a Buddha and reaches "nirvana."

Although nirvana is common to Buddhism, Hinduism and Jainism, it does not mean the same thing to each. Buddhist nirvana is not the release from rebirth and the circle of life that is found in Hinduism. Instead, it is an enlightened state of bliss, selflessness and freedom from suffering.

By the time Buddha died at the age of eighty, his followers had established communities of Buddhist monks across northern India.

537 BC: Cyrus of Persia campaigns into the Indus River Valley.

525-509 BC: Darius the Persian conquers the Indus River Valley region.

327 BC: Alexander the Great invades the Indus River Valley and installs Greek officials in the area.

The Nanda Empire (424 - 321 BC)

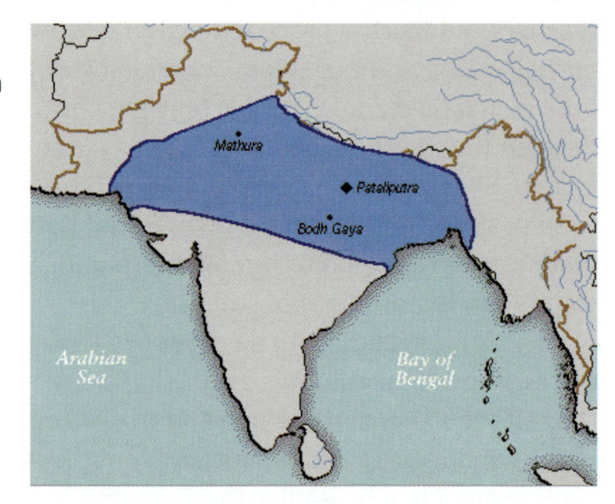

The Indo-Europeans who replaced the Harappans spread out all across northern India, settling in the Ganges River Valley in the east as well as the Indus River Valley in the west. From about 700 - 300 BC, northern India lay divided among 16 large city-states known as *maha janapandas* ("Great countries").

Mahapadma Nanda (450 - 362 BC), a warrior king from the *maha janapanda* of Magadha, built an enormous army, then used it to defeat most of the other 15 *maha janapandas*. Nanda united his conquered territories into northern India's first major empire, the Nanda Empire. The vast Nanda Empire stretched all the way across northern India, from the Bengal region in the east to the Punjab region in the west.

It was the Nanda Empire that put a stop to the Macedonian Greek emperor Alexander the Great's conquest of India in 326 BC (see chapter 24). When Alexander's men heard how large the Nanda army was, they mutinied, refusing to march any farther into India. Alexander had to content himself with Persia, Afghanistan and part of the Indus River Valley; he would never add the rest of India to his empire.

The Nanda Empire was also India's first Hindu empire.

Mahapadma Nanda's sons proved unable to hold all that their father had conquered for them, so the Nanda Dynasty gave way to the Mauryan Dynasty.

The Maurya Empire (321 - 185 BC)

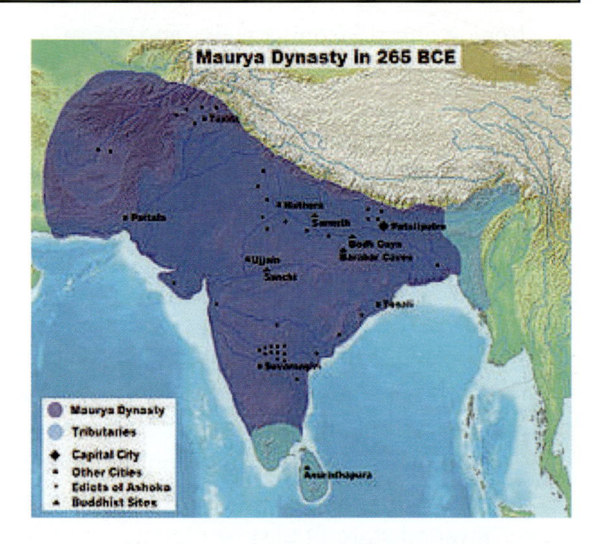

The Maurya Empire was the first empire that united northern and southern India, bringing almost all of India under a single emperor. The horrible violence that was required to accomplish this unity caused both of the Mauryan Dynasty's great emperors, Chandragupta and Asoka, to reconsider their warlike ways later in life.

Chandragupta Maurya (~ 340 - 298 BC)

The Mauryans' empire-building hunger was a response to Alexander the Great's invasion of India: Chandragupta and his mentor, Chanakya, believed that the people of India would have to unite if they were to defend themselves against future invaders from the west. Chandragupta's conquests proceeded in stages:

1. First, he defeated the Nanda Dynasty, took over its territory and united its armies with his own.
2. Next, he reclaimed the Indus River Valley from Alexander the Great's successor in Persia, General Seleucus. When their battles were over, Chandragupta and Seleucus sealed the peace treaty between them with an exchange of gifts: Chandragupta received a Macedonian princess as a wife, while Seleucus received 500 war elephants in payment for his part of the Indus River Valley.
3. Finally, Chandragupta fought his way into southern India as well.

For most of his life, Chandragupta was a faithful Hindu, like most of his Indian subjects. Around 301 BC, however, Chandragupta turned his nearly-finished empire over to his son so that he could pursue his newfound faith, Jainism.

INTERESTING INDIAN RELIGIONS: Jainism

Jainism is an ancient Indian religion that is almost as old as Hinduism. The last of Jainism's 24 founders, Mahavira, was born around 599 BC. Jainism shares some ideas with Hinduism and Buddhism, but there are important differences. Jainists do not believe in a creator god, but they do believe in the divine, and their goal is to break free of the material world in order to achieve a divine consciousness.

The Jainist religious philosophy centers on five great vows:

1. A vow of nonviolence, promising to commit no violence against either humans or animals (which means that Jainists must live as strict vegans, touching no meat)
2. A vow of honesty, promising to speak only the truth and to avoid all falsehood
3. A vow of non-theft, promising never to steal
4. A vow of chastity, one husband promising to remain bonded to one wife for life
5. A vow of non-possession, promising not to grow attached to material possessions

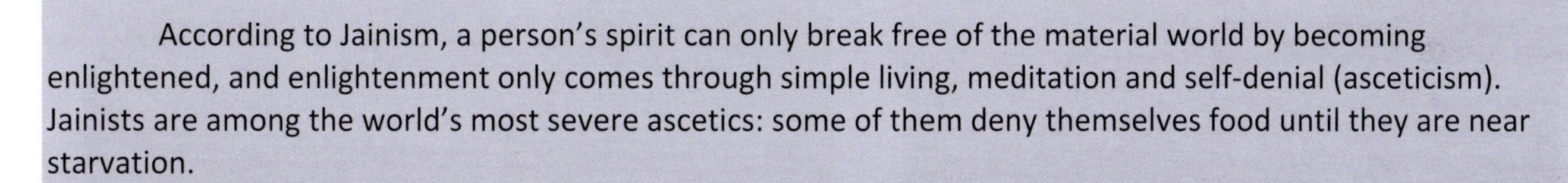

According to Jainism, a person's spirit can only break free of the material world by becoming enlightened, and enlightenment only comes through simple living, meditation and self-denial (asceticism). Jainists are among the world's most severe ascetics: some of them deny themselves food until they are near starvation.

The Jainists' symbol was the swastika, a cross with its arms bent at right angles. Buddhists and Hindus also used the swastika. The National Socialist Party (Nazi Party) of Germany adopted the swastika as its symbol in 1920. In the 1930s and 1940s, it became the symbol of Nazi Germany.

FASCINATING FACTS: *Santhara* and the Death of Chandragupta

Some Jainists take their vow of non-violence so seriously that they become unwilling to eat even plants. Plants, after all, have life, and to eat them is to take away that life. In order to avoid the negative karma that might come from killing even plant life, some Jainists are willing to starve themselves to death in a ritual known as *Santhara* or *Sallekhana*.

As a military general who had fought bloody wars all over India, killing men and beasts by the thousands and trampling countless plants, Chandragupta might not seem like a very good candidate for *Santhara*. Yet that is apparently how he died: Around 298 BC, in a quest to avoid bad karma, the former warrior emperor Chandragupta starved himself to death in the Jainist ritual of *Santhara*.

268 BC: Asoka, grandson of Chandragupta Maurya, becomes ruler of the Maurya dynasty. He is considered the greatest Mauryan ruler.

Asoka (~ 304 - 232 BC)

Asoka, Chandragupta's grandson, began his career as violently as Chandragupta had begun his. Reportedly, Asoka won the Mauryan Dynasty's throne by defeating and killing as many as 99 of his own brothers and half-brothers. These killings within his own family, however, seem not to have bothered him. What changed Asoka's heart was the Kalinga War.

Kalinga was one of the last places in India that was not yet ruled by the Mauryan Dynasty: A prosperous, proud and independent nation on India's east coast that had somehow managed to resist all of Chandragupta's efforts to conquer it. Asoka succeeded where his grandfather had failed: in the bloody Kalinga War of 265 - 264 BC, Asoka finally conquered Kalinga and folded it into the Maurya Empire. The costs of that victory were terribly high: As many as 100,000 people on each side of the battle died, and a nearby river ran red with blood.

When the Kalinga War was over, Asoka was stricken with horror at its awful costs:

> "What have I done.... Is this a victory or a defeat .... Is it gallantry or a rout? Is it valor to kill innocent children and women? Do I do it to widen the empire and for prosperity or to destroy the other's kingdom and splendor?"

The horrors of the Kalinga War changed Asoka's mind about warfare. From 264 BC on, Asoka was a man of peace, not of war. Asoka's change of heart about war changed his religion as well: He converted from Hinduism to the more peaceful religion of Buddhism.

After Asoka converted to Buddhism, he encouraged his people to convert as well. As the leader of the greatest empire in the East, Asoka became Buddhism's biggest supporter. He carved Buddhist teachings into stone pillars (see picture at left) and on cliff faces all over his empire. He built thousands of *stupas*, mounded Buddhist religious monuments that often began as burial sites (see picture at right).

Asoka also sent Buddhist missionaries throughout his empire and beyond. Over the next several centuries, through the efforts of Asoka and his heirs, Buddhism spread all over Asia. Later, as India returned to Hinduism, Buddhism became far more important in other parts of Asia than it was in India.

FASCINATING FACTS: The Spread of Buddhism

Because of the influence of Asoka, Buddhism spread throughout India. By 500 AD, Buddhism had spread beyond India and into other parts of Asia. As Buddhism flourished outside of India, it began to die out within India as most Indians returned to Hinduism and other religions. Buddha was still revered in India, but he was placed on the same level with all of the other Hindu gods.

The two major branches of Buddhism are *Theravada* and *Mahayana*. Theravada is the more conservative branch, faithfully following the Buddha's original teachings. Theravada is common today in Sri Lanka, Cambodia, Laos and Thailand.

Mahayana Buddhism began as a movement to bring more common people into the Buddhist faith. While Theravada Buddhists focus on meditation and concentration, Mahayana Buddhists believe that enlightenment is achieved through a virtuous daily life. The Mahayana's highest virtue is compassion, and his highest goal is to help all Buddhists reach Nirvana. For this reason, Mahayana Buddhists believe that those who have attained Nirvana can choose to "come back" to life on earth so that they can help others achieve Nirvana as well. Mahayana is common today in China, Korea, Japan and Tibet.

184 BC: The Maurya dynasty ends when its last ruler is assassinated.

FASCINATING FACTS: Diwali

Diwali is the Hindu New Year. Before Diwali comes, Hindus must clean their homes so that their goddess of wealth can enter. Because the goddess will not enter a home that is poorly lit, Hindu households burn clay lamps known as diyas for Diwali.

ANCIENT TEXTS: The Bhagavad Gita

The *Bhagavad Gita* ("Song of the Divine One") is an ancient, 700-line-long Hindu poem that relates a young Indian prince's conversation with Lord Krishna. The *Gita* is part of a far longer epic poem called the *Mahabharata*, a Hindu scripture that tells stories from ancient Indian history and explains the Hindu faith.

As the *Gita* begins, young Prince Arjuna is dismayed because a dispute within his family is forcing him to go to war against his own cousins. Arjuna's teacher Lord Krishna, it turns out, embodies the Hindu creator god Brahma himself. Lord Krishna tells Arjuna that he must not fear death, because while his body may die in battle, his soul never can. According to Lord Krishna's Hindu doctrine of reincarnation, two things are true: everyone who lives must die, and everyone who dies must live again:

"For certain is death for the born/ And certain is birth for the dead;
Therefore over the inevitable/ Thou shouldst not grieve."

BIBLE FOCUS

JUDAH'S KINGS, CONTINUED

Kings of the Southern Kingdom, Judah

This week we will cover the reigns of Josiah and Jehoahaz and the prophets Nahum and Zephaniah.

Josiah - 640-609 BC	THE BEST - inherited the throne - reigned 31 years	Killed

GIANTS OF THE FAITH: JOSIAH

II Kings 22-23 and II Chronicles 34-35

Josiah became king of Judah at the age of eight after the assassination of his father Amon. Josiah was the last great king of Judah. Unlike his father and grandfather, Josiah followed the Lord in everything that he did.

Josiah took the throne of Judah during the reign of the Assyrian king Ashurbanipal. His reign ended just as Assyria's power declined and Babylon's power grew. Coming as it did between the peaks of these two giants' power, Josiah's reign was a time of relative peace and prosperity for Judah.

Assyria's Timeline during the reign of Josiah

- King Esarhaddon of Assyria chose his son Ashurbanipal as his successor and his son Shamash-shum-ukin as crown prince of Babylon, which was then under Assyrian control. Ashurbanipal reigned from 669-627 BC.
- Josiah became king of Judah in 640 BC. Assyria had bigger problems than Josiah, and his reforms went largely unnoticed.

- After Ashurbanipal's death in 627, his Assyrian empire disintegrated rapidly. The Assyrians had to fight off the Scythians, Medes and Cimmerians from the north and the east. The Scythians marched all the way to Egypt (bypassing Josiah).
- Ashurbanipal's son Sin-shum-ishkin succeeded him on the Assyrian throne. Another son took the throne of Babylon, which was still part of the Assyrian empire. The two brothers began to fight. Into the struggle came another contender, Nabopolassar, who wanted to make himself king of an independent Babylon freed from Assyrian domination.
- Nabopolassar united with the first king of the Medes and Persians, Cyaxares, to attack the Assyrian capital of Nineveh. Together they destroyed Nineveh in 612 BC.
- Assyrian general Ashur-uballit II tried to keep the Assyrian empire alive in the wake of this disaster. He allied with Egyptian King Necho II.
- Necho II's archers killed Josiah in 609 BC on their way to attack Babylon and help Assyria regain its footing. Weeks later, the Babylonians crushed the Assyrian-Egyptian alliance.
- The Assyrian Empire, which stood in one form or another for 1200 years, was eliminated by Babylon by 605 BC.

SCRIPTURE SPOTLIGHT: Nahum

During the time of Jonah, Nineveh repented and the Lord in His mercy spared the Ninevites for a time. But the Assyrians of Nineveh eventually returned to their evil ways. The Book of Nahum was written as a prophecy against Nineveh. It foretells the fall of Nineveh, which really came in 612 BC. The book of Zephaniah also foretells Nineveh's fall (Zephaniah 2: 13-15).

"The LORD is good, a refuge in times of trouble. He cares for those who trust in him, but with an overwhelming flood He will make an end of Nineveh; He will pursue his foes into darkness" (Nahum 1: 7-8).

The date of Nahum's prophecy is uncertain; the most likely date seems to be around the time of Ashurbanipal's death. Nahum might have witnessed Assyria's repression of Egypt and prophesied that the same thing would happen to Assyria.

"Cush and Egypt were her boundless strength; Put and Libya were among her allies. Yet she was taken captive and went into exile. Her infants were dashed to pieces at the head of every street. Lots were cast for her nobles, and all her great men were put in chains. You too will become drunk; you will go into hiding and seek refuge from the enemy" (Nahum 3: 8-11).

Nahum's message to Judah during the reign of Josiah is one of hope. Nahum wants his people to know that although Assyria has oppressed them, God has not forgotten them. Nahum's book is a reminder that God is in control of their destiny. He forgives the contrite, but does not leave the guilty unpunished. Judah does not need to fear, because God will punish Assyria for its sins against His people.

Josiah's Reform

When Josiah was eighteen years old, the High Priest found the book of the Law in the Temple and read it to Josiah (it had apparently been abandoned for many years). Upon hearing God's words, Josiah suddenly realized how far Judah had strayed from God's way. Josiah tore his robe in mourning. Then he set out to restore the kingdom of Judah to its spiritual roots, even though he knew from the prophetess Huldah that Judah would one day be punished for the wickedness of his grandfather Manasseh.

FASCINATING FACTS: Female Prophets in the Bible

The Old Testament mentions five female prophets, or prophetesses: Miriam (sister of Moses), Deborah (one of the Judges), the prophet Isaiah's wife (mentioned in Isaiah 8:3), Huldah (mentioned in II Kings 22) and Noadiah (a false prophetess mentioned in Nehemiah 6:14).

In the New Testament, the prophetess Anna proclaims the baby Jesus as the Messiah when Mary and Joseph bring him to the temple (Luke 2:36-38). The other prophetesses mentioned in the New Testament are the four unmarried daughters of Philip the evangelist (Acts 21:9).

The prophet Joel foresaw a day when both men and women would prophesy (Joel 28-32):

"And afterward, I will pour out my Spirit on all people. Your sons and daughters will prophesy, your old men will dream dreams, your young men will see visions. Even on my servants, both men and women, I will pour out my Spirit in those days."

SCRIPTURE SPOTLIGHT: Zephaniah

Zephaniah prophesied during Josiah's reign (Zephaniah 1:1). According to his genealogy, he might have been a great grandson of King Hezekiah and a close relative of King Josiah.

Zephaniah's message begins with an announcement that the Lord would soon bring judgment on Judah and on the nations, and ends with words of hope that God will restore those who seek him. In the center of the book is a beautiful call for repentance (Zephaniah 2:3):

"Seek the LORD, all you humble of the land, you who do what he commands. Seek righteousness, seek humility; perhaps you will be sheltered on the day of the LORD's anger."

Josiah read the Law to the people and led them in renewing their covenant with the Lord. He purged idols and altars from the Temple and all of Judah, and he removed the pagan priests. He destroyed the apartments of the temple prostitutes and the altar used for child sacrifice. He traveled throughout Judah tearing down high places and destroying altars. He even traveled north and purged Samaria, killing all of the Baal prophets. He rid the land of mediums and sorcerers. Josiah did more to rid the land of evil than any king before him.

In the middle of all of this, Josiah called all of Judah to participate in a national celebration of Passover. Thousands of lambs and bulls were slaughtered for the occasion.

"And there was no Passover like to that kept in Israel from the days of Samuel the prophet; neither did all the kings of Israel keep such a Passover as Josiah kept, and the priests, and the Levites, and all Judah and Israel that were present, and the inhabitants of Jerusalem" (II Chronicles 35:18).

Josiah had little time to enjoy the fruits of his cleansing labor. In 609 BC, the king of Egypt and the king of a much-weakened Assyria united together in a final attack on Babylon. Josiah had just finished wiping out centuries of sinful Assyrian influence on his beloved country, and the last thing he wanted was another Assyrian victory. So when Assyria's ally Necho II of Egypt marched through Judah, Josiah confronted him.

Necho II sent ambassadors to warn Josiah away, but Josiah was undeterred. He died at the Battle of Megiddo (II Chronicles 35: 21-25):

"But Necho sent messengers to him, saying, "What quarrel is there between you and me, O king of Judah? It is not you I am attacking at this time, but the house with which I am at war. God has told me to hurry; so stop opposing God, who is with me, or he will destroy you."

Josiah, however, would not turn away from him, but disguised himself to engage him in battle. He would not listen to what Necho had said at God's command but went to fight him on the plain of Megiddo.

Archers shot King Josiah, and he told his officers, "Take me away; I am badly wounded." So they took him out of his chariot, put him in the other chariot he had and brought him to Jerusalem, where he died. He was buried in the tombs of his fathers, and all Judah and Jerusalem mourned for him.

Jeremiah composed laments for Josiah, and to this day all the men and women singers commemorate Josiah in the laments. These became a tradition in Israel and are written in the Laments."

Note: The prophet Jeremiah, who also prophesied during the time of Josiah, is covered in Chapter 20.

Jehoahaz - 609 BC	BAD - inherited the throne - reigned 3 months Kidnapped/died

Jehoahaz would turn out to be a very poor successor to Josiah, Judah's most faithful king. Almost as soon as he became king, Jehoahaz turned away from his father's reform and went back to the wicked ways of his grandfather Amon and his great-grandfather Manasseh.

Jehoahaz reigned for just three months before Necho II of Egypt, whose archers had killed Josiah, returned from Babylon. Necho II took Jehoahaz captive and made Jehoahaz's brother Eliakim king in his place. Necho also demanded tribute payments from Judah, making Judah a vassal state of Egypt. Jehoahaz died a captive in Egypt.

"Jehoahaz was twenty-three years old when he became king, and he reigned in Jerusalem three months. His mother's name was Hamutal daughter of Jeremiah; she was from Libnah. He did evil in the eyes of the LORD, just as his fathers had done. Pharaoh Necho put him in chains at Riblah in the land of Hamath so that he might not reign in Jerusalem, and he imposed on Judah a levy of a hundred talents of silver and a talent of gold. Pharaoh Necho made Eliakim son of Josiah king in place of his father Josiah and changed Eliakim's name to Jehoiakim. But he took Jehoahaz and carried him off to Egypt, and there he died. Jehoiakim paid Pharaoh Necho the silver and gold he demanded. In order to do so, he taxed the land and exacted the silver and gold from the people of the land according to their assessments" (II Kings 23: 31-37).

Chapter 20

The Babylonians

ANCIENT HISTORY AND BIBLE FOCUS

(This week the Ancient and Bible history are woven together)

THE RISE OF BABYLON

Kings of the Southern Kingdom, Judah

This week we are going to cover the last three kings of Judah and the prophets Jeremiah, Zephaniah and Habakkuk. Since these Judean kings overlap the reign of King Nebuchadnezzar of Babylon, we will discuss them when we reach Nebuchadnezzar.

FASCINATING FACTS: Babylonia

Babylonia was an ancient empire that first appeared in the long, narrow region between the Tigris and Euphrates rivers around 1894 BC. Babylonia's first great king was Hammurabi, author of the well-known Code of Hammurabi (see Chapter 5).

For much of Babylonia's history, it was bordered in the north by Assyria, on the west by the Arabian Desert, on the south by the Persian Gulf and on the east by Elam. Because of its location, Babylon spent most of its history in conflict with the giant of the area, Assyria.

The Babylonians were farmers, and they developed a complex irrigation system to water their crops in the hot, dry region where they lived. They were also experts at making sun-dried clay bricks for building. By mixing dye with their clay, the Babylonians were able to create colorful, beautiful temples and palaces.

Simple Timeline of Babylonia

- 2334 BC: Sargon unifies the city-states of southern Mesopotamia to create the first Assyrian Empire.
- 1792 BC: Hammurabi inherits the city of Babylon from his father.
- 1760 BC: Hammurabi conquers northern Mesopotamia, thus ending the first Assyrian Empire.
- 689 BC: Sargon II of the second Assyrian empire, a.k.a. the neo-Assyrian Empire, captures Babylon.
- 652-648 BC: The Babylonians rebel against their neo-Assyrian rulers.
- 627 BC: Ashurbanipal of Assyria dies, leaving his neo-Assyrian Empire in chaos.
- 625 BC: Nabopolassar of Babylon leads a successful rebellion against neo-Assyrian rule, becoming the first king of the newly independent neo-Babylonian Empire.

NABOPOLASSAR

Nabopolassar was a Babylonian who served as a general in the Assyrian army. After Ashurbanipal of Assyria died, Nabopolassar led a Babylonian rebellion against the neo-Assyrian Empire, thus becoming the first King of a newly-independent Babylon in 625 BC. This was the beginning of an 80-year dynasty that was to become the most powerful in Babylonian history.

Nabopolassar allied his Babylonians with the Medes, who had recently conquered northern Mesopotamia. Together the two nations set out to conquer Assyria. Beginning with the empire's outskirts, they pushed through one city and territory after another until 612 BC, when they conquered Assyria's capital city of Nineveh.

Assyria was almost finished, but not quite. A surviving general named Ashur-uballit II managed to preserve some of Assyria's strength and call on Assyria's ally, Egypt. Around 609 BC, King Necho II of Egypt joined what remained of Assyria to attack Nabopolassar and Babylon. On his way north, Necho met and killed King Josiah of Judah in the battle of Megiddo, and Josiah's son Jehoahaz assumed the throne of Judah (see Chapter 19). Necho II proceeded north and joined forces with the Assyrians against Nabopolassar. But Nabopolassar was too strong for them, and Necho II retreated to Egypt in defeat. Along the way he kidnapped King Jehoahaz of Judah and placed his brother Jehoiakim on the throne as a puppet king (see Jehoiakim below).

In 605 BC, Egypt and what remained of Assyria again allied against Nabopolassar. Nabopolassar died before the outcome of this battle was determined. His son Nebuchadnezzar II defeated the Egyptian/Assyrian alliance at the Battle of Carchemish. The Assyrian Empire came to its final end, and Judah, Syria and Phoenicia came under Babylonian control. Egypt was driven back within its borders and no longer interfered in Babylonian territory.

During his reign, Nabopolassar's empire extended from the border of Egypt to the Persian Gulf.

Jehoiakim - 609-598 BC	BAD - inherited the throne - reigned 11 years

JEHOIAKIM

Jehoiakim, a son of Josiah, was originally named Eliakim. The Egyptian king Necho II changed Eliakim's name to Jehoiakim when he installed him on the Judean throne after kidnapping his brother Jehoahaz. As a puppet king, Jehoiakim was forced to pay a steep tribute to Necho II, and he did this by placing heavy taxes on the Judean people. Jehoiakim did not follow the Lord as his father Josiah did, and Jeremiah the prophet spoke out against him (Jeremiah 22: 18-23); but Jehoiakim rejected Jeremiah's criticism, even going so far as to burn the scroll containing the words the Lord had spoken to Jeremiah (Jeremiah 36).

In 605 BC, the Egyptians were defeated at the Battle of Carchemish and driven out of the region. Now Judah fell under the control of the Babylonian King Nebuchadnezzar, and Jehoiakim's tribute went to Babylon. Around this time some of the Judean royal family was carried off to Babylon, including Daniel and his friends (Daniel 1:1-- see below).

Around 601 BC, Nebuchadnezzar tried to expand his empire into Egypt, but was turned back. With Babylon's defeat, Jehoiakim of Judah thought he saw a chance to break free from Babylonian rule. Against the advice of the prophet Jeremiah, he withheld Judah's tribute payments.

In response, Nebuchadnezzar ordered Judah's neighboring vassal states to raid Judah. Jehoiakim probably died in one of these raids (598 BC), although the exact circumstances of his death are unknown. Jeremiah predicted a gruesome death for Jehoiakim (Jeremiah 22:18-19 and 36: 30).

SCRIPTURE SPOTLIGHT: Habakkuk

Habakkuk prophesied during the kingdom of Judah's last days, around the time of Jeremiah. He wrote his book around the time of the Battle of Carchemish (605 BC), when Nebuchadnezzar II of Babylon defeated the Egyptian/Assyrian alliance.

As the book opens, Habakkuk asks God when He will respond to Judah's oppression of its poor. The Law of Moses, with its many protections for the poor, is no longer in operation, so Habakkuk cries out:

"How long, O LORD, must I call for help, but you do not listen? Or cry out to you, "Violence!" but you do not save? Why do you make me look at injustice? Why do you tolerate wrong? Destruction and violence are before me; there is strife, and conflict abounds. Therefore the law is paralyzed, and justice never prevails. The wicked hem in the righteous, so that justice is perverted" (Habakkuk 1: 1-3).

The Lord responds that he is raising up the Babylonians:

"I am raising up the Babylonians, that ruthless and impetuous people, who sweep across the whole earth to seize dwelling places not their own. They are a feared and dreaded people; they are a law to themselves and promote their own honor" (Habakkuk 1: 6-7).

Habakkuk is a bit shocked by this, because no matter how bad Judah has become, Babylon is certainly far worse. God responds that in His time, justice will prevail for the wicked of both Judah and Babylon, but the righteous who live by faith will prevail:

"Has not the LORD Almighty determined that the people's labor is only fuel for the fire, that the nations exhaust themselves for nothing? For the earth will be filled with the knowledge of the glory of the LORD, as the waters cover the sea" (Habakkuk 2: 13-14).

605 BC: Nebuchadnezzar II becomes king of Babylon

NEBUCHADNEZZAR II

Upon the death of his father Nabopolassar, Nebuchadnezzar became king of Babylon and reigned for 44 years. Just before his father's death, Nebuchadnezzar led his army to victory at the Battle of Carchemish, putting a final end to the Assyrian Empire.

Nebuchadnezzar's marriage to Amytis, the daughter of the Persian king, created an alliance between Babylon and the Persian Empire to his north and east. This allowed him to focus his attention to the west, including Syria, Judah and Egypt. In 601 BC he confronted Necho II and the Egyptians at the Egyptian border, but neither side gained ground. This display of weakness encouraged several vassal states, including Judah, to rebel. In response, Nebuchadnezzar captured Jerusalem in 597 BC and carried Judah's King Jehoiachin off to exile, along with thousands of Judean nobles, officers and craftsmen. Nebuchadnezzar also carried off vast amounts of treasure from the Temple and the royal palace. This fulfilled the prophecy of II Kings 20: 16-18:

"Then Isaiah said to Hezekiah, "Hear the word of the LORD : The time will surely come when everything in your palace, and all that your fathers have stored up until this day, will be carried off to Babylon. Nothing will be left, says the LORD. And some of your descendants, your own flesh and blood, that will be born to you, will be taken away, and they will become eunuchs in the palace of the king of Babylon."

Jehoiachin - 598 BC	BAD - inherited the throne - reigned 3 months Taken into exile

JEHOIACHIN

Jehoiachin reigned for only three months after his father Jehoiakim died. Just after he assumed the throne, Nebuchadnezzar arrived with his vast army and laid siege to Jerusalem in order to put down the rebellion Jehoiakim had started. Realizing that the rebellion was hopeless, Jehoiachin surrendered. The Babylonians carried him away into exile, along with his mother and a great number of officials, nobles and others, including the prophet Ezekiel. Only the poor remained in Judah, leaderless.

Jehoiachin did not fare poorly in Babylon. Even though he was a prisoner, he was apparently allowed to live with his family in Babylon. He was known as the "King of Judah" even in exile.

After Nebuchadnezzar died, Jehoiachin was released from prison and given a place of honor at the king's table:

"In the thirty-seventh year of the exile of Jehoiachin king of Judah, in the year Evil-Merodach became king of Babylon, he released Jehoiachin from prison on the twenty-seventh day of the twelfth month. He spoke kindly to him and gave him a seat of honor higher than those of the other kings who were with him in Babylon. So Jehoiachin put aside his prison clothes and for the rest of his life ate regularly at the king's table. Day by day the king gave Jehoiachin a regular allowance as long as he lived" (II Kings 25: 27-30).

After removing Jehoiachin, Nebuchadnezzar installed Jehoiachin's uncle Mattaniah on the Judean throne and changed his name to Zedekiah.

Zedekiah - 598-587	BAD - inherited the throne - reigned 11 years Taken into exile

ZEDEKIAH

Zedekiah was the last king of Judah. Nebuchadnezzar installed Zedekiah on the throne of Judah when he conquered Jerusalem and carried Jehoiachin into Babylonian exile.

Like his nephew, Zedekiah did not follow the Lord, but did evil in His sight. Most of what is known about Zedekiah comes from the prophets Jeremiah and Ezekiel. He was forced to listen to the prophets' counsel because Nebuchadnezzar had carried away all of the former kings' advisors.

Unfortunately, Zedekiah did not follow the prophets' advice. Against their wise counsel, he openly rebelled against Nebuchadnezzar in 589 BC. Zedekiah hoped that Babylon would be distracted by its conflict with Egypt, but instead Nebuchadnezzar marched his army into Judah and laid siege to Jerusalem.

Zedekiah appealed to Jeremiah for God's intervention in Jeremiah 21:

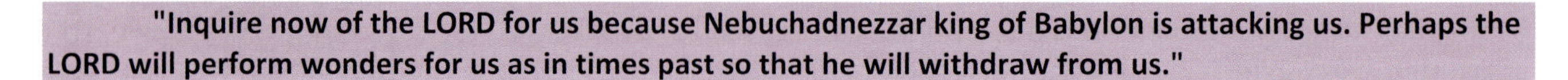

"Inquire now of the LORD for us because Nebuchadnezzar king of Babylon is attacking us. Perhaps the LORD will perform wonders for us as in times past so that he will withdraw from us."

Jeremiah responded that, far from rescuing Judah, God would send plague and famine to the besieged city. Then even worse would happen:

"After that, declares the LORD, I will hand over Zedekiah king of Judah, his officials and the people in this city who survive the plague, sword and famine, to Nebuchadnezzar king of Babylon and to their enemies who seek their lives. He will put them to the sword; he will show them no mercy or pity or compassion" (Jeremiah 21:7).

Jeremiah told the people of Jerusalem that Babylon would spare only those who chose to surrender. Those who chose to fight would burn with the city. Zedekiah refused to listen, and when Nebuchadnezzar's army broke through Jerusalem's walls, Zedekiah was captured. His captors killed Zedekiah's sons before his eyes, then put his eyes out. They bound and shackled him and carried him off to Babylon, where he died in prison.

THE FALL OF JERUSALEM (587 BC)

In 587 BC, King Zedekiah of Judah rebelled against Babylonian rule. In response, Nebuchadnezzar laid siege to Jerusalem. After a siege of two years, he recaptured Jerusalem just as he had in Jehoiachin's time. Once again he carried many Judeans into exile, including members of the royal family. This was a second fulfillment of Isaiah's prophecy in II Kings 20:16-18 (see "Jehoiachin" above).

This time, however, Nebuchadnezzar decided to put a final end to Judah's troublesome rebellions. He sent a commander to destroy what was left of Jerusalem. The city of David was plundered, razed to the ground and utterly destroyed. The Temple, which had stood from its dedication by Solomon in 953 BC, was leveled. The Kingdom of Judah, which had stood in one form or another from the time of Joshua around 1400 BC, was no more.

After he destroyed Jerusalem, Nebuchadnezzar subdued Tyre and conducted further campaigns against Egypt. In addition to his military campaigns, Nebuchadnezzar carried on tremendous construction campaigns. He rebuilt the city of Babylon, adding numerous temples, canals and aqueducts and beautifying the city. He also built the famous Hanging Gardens of Babylon, one of the seven wonders of the ancient world, probably for the sake of his Persian wife Amytis. Another great project was the construction of the Median Wall.

FASCINATING FACTS: The Median Wall

The Median Wall was a defensive wall that stretched from the Tigris River to the Euphrates River north of the city of Babylon. Its facings were built of baked brick and tar, and its center was filled with rammed earth. It may have stood as much as 100 feet high.

The Median wall takes its name from the Medes of northern Persia; the wall protected Babylon from northern invasion by the Medes. Nebuchadnezzar's alliance with the Persians and Medes, formed by his marriage to the Persian Princess Amytis, did not last forever. Trouble with the Persians was coming.

Although Nebuchadnezzar was a successful ruler, he was not at peace with himself. For a number of years of his reign, Nebuchadnezzar suffered from mental illness. He apparently went quite mad.

GIANTS OF THE FAITH: DANIEL, PART I

SCRIPTURE SPOTLIGHT: Nebuchadnezzar II and Daniel

After the battle of Carchemish in the time of Judah's King Jehoiakim, Nebuchadnezzar carried members of the Judean royal family back to Babylon. One of them was a Jewish boy named Daniel, who became one of the Bible's major prophets.

Daniel 1:1-7:

In the third year of the reign of Jehoiakim king of Judah, Nebuchadnezzar king of Babylon came to Jerusalem and besieged it. And the Lord delivered Jehoiakim king of Judah into his hand, along with some of the articles from the temple of God. These he carried off to the temple of his god in Babylonia and put in the treasure house of his god.

Then the king ordered Ashpenaz, chief of his court officials, to bring in some of the Israelites from the royal family and the nobility- young men without any physical defect, handsome, showing aptitude for every kind of learning, well informed, quick to understand, and qualified to serve in the king's palace. He was to teach them the language and literature of the Babylonians. The king assigned them a daily amount of food and wine from the king's table. They were to be trained for three years, and after that they were to enter the king's service.

Among these were some from Judah: Daniel, Hananiah, Mishael and Azariah. The chief official gave them new names: to Daniel, the name Belteshazzar; to Hananiah, Shadrach; to Mishael, Meshach; and to Azariah, Abednego."

Daniel and his friends, not wanting to partake of food that had been offered to idols, refused what was offered. Instead they asked to be brought vegetable and water. In the first instance of six times in Daniel, God blesses and cares for Daniel and his friends. The guards and the king are forced to acknowledge that beside these four young men, no one was equal. Although they were foreigners and captives in his court, Nebuchadnezzar came to trust them because of their integrity, wisdom and virtue. The book of Daniel relates three stories about Nebuchadnezzar:

- **Nebuchadnezzar's dream (Daniel 2):** Nebuchadnezzar has a dream that troubles him. He wants someone to interpret the dream, but he doesn't want to reveal the dream to his counselors because he doesn't trust them. He insists that they must tell him both the contents of the dream and its interpretation. None of the counselors dares to attempt the task, saying:

"What the king asks is too difficult. No one can reveal it to the king except the gods, and they do not live among men" (Daniel 2:11).

Furious, Nebuchadnezzar orders the executions of all of his counselors, including Daniel and his friends, who have not even heard of the King's request. When Daniel hears of it, he and his friends pray to God for guidance, and God reveals the dream to Daniel.

Daniel approaches Nebuchadnezzar and is able to tell him not only the contents of the dream, which tells of a great statue with "feet of clay" (Daniel 2, most interesting reading), but also its interpretation. Nebuchadnezzar is forced to acknowledge that:

"Surely your God is the God of gods and the Lord of kings and a revealer of mysteries, for you were able to reveal this mystery" (Daniel 2:47).

Daniel's great success as an exile in a foreign land is similar to Joseph's. Nebuchadnezzar makes him a ruler of the province of Babylon.

- **The Fiery Furnace (Daniel 3:1-30 - 4:1-3):** Nebuchadnezzar builds an idol in his own image and places it in a temple so that the people could revere him as a god. His counselors, who hate Daniel and his friends, take the dedication of the statue as a golden opportunity to rid themselves of these Hebrews.

  Knowing that the Hebrews will refuse to bow down to any idol, the counselors flatter the king into making a decree that everyone must bow down to his new idol. Nebuchadnezzar readily agrees, not realizing that his decree will place his favorite foreigners in deadly danger. When they refuse to bow to the idol, they are thrown into a fiery furnace. But the fire doesn't burn them. The king sees the three of them walking around in the furnace unharmed, accompanied by what appears to be a "son of the gods." When he calls them out of the furnace, they are unharmed--even their clothes are not singed--and Nebuchadnezzar is again forced to acknowledge:

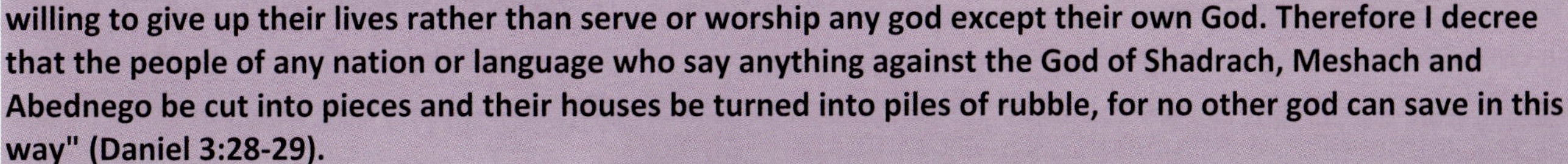

"Praise be to the God of Shadrach, Meshach and Abednego, who has sent his angel and rescued his servants! They trusted in him and defied the king's command and were willing to give up their lives rather than serve or worship any god except their own God. Therefore I decree that the people of any nation or language who say anything against the God of Shadrach, Meshach and Abednego be cut into pieces and their houses be turned into piles of rubble, for no other god can save in this way" (Daniel 3:28-29).

- **Nebuchadnezzar's dream and subsequent madness (Daniel 4: 4-37):** Nebuchadnezzar has another dream, and again his counselors are confounded by his dream. Once again, only Daniel is able to interpret the dream. Daniel tells the king that he will lose his sanity for a time, and that only when he acknowledges God will his sanity be restored. Daniel's words come true, and for seven years, Nebuchadnezzar lives like a wild animal. When he finally acknowledges God, his sanity is restored:

"At the end of that time, I, Nebuchadnezzar, raised my eyes toward heaven, and my sanity was restored. Then I praised the Most High; I honored and glorified him who lives forever. His dominion is an eternal dominion; his kingdom endures from generation to generation" (Daniel 4:34).

Nebuchadnezzar's period of insanity has been verified by sources outside the Bible, first by a clay tablet describing his bizarre behavior and then by the absence of any recorded deeds from 582 to 575 BC.

GIANTS OF THE FAITH: Jeremiah

Jeremiah is one of the major prophets of the Old Testament. He prophesied during the latter part of

King Josiah's reign and through the reigns of Kings Jehoahaz, Jehoiakim, Jehoiachin and Zedekiah-- right through to the very end of the kingdom of Judah. Of all of these last kings of Judah, only Josiah followed God, so Jeremiah was at odds with all of the other kings. All through his ministry to the kings and people of Judah he was attacked by his brothers, beaten and put in stocks, imprisoned, threatened, thrown down a well and left to die, accused falsely and opposed by a false prophet. Despite all of this, Jeremiah never faltered from speaking the truth and calling God's people to repentance.

Because his message was so often one of doom, Jeremiah's message was rarely well received. According to Jeremiah, Judah was headed for certain doom because of its past sins. Recognizing that nothing could stop the inevitable, Jeremiah called for Judah to surrender to Babylon when the time came. Judah rejected his call, and he was viewed as a traitor and an outlaw. During Zedekiah's reign, Jeremiah was imprisoned, and he was only freed when Nebuchadnezzar conquered Jerusalem for the last time.

"Therefore the LORD Almighty says this: "Because you have not listened to my words, I will summon all the peoples of the north and my servant Nebuchadnezzar king of Babylon," declares the LORD, "and I will bring them against this land and its inhabitants and against all the surrounding nations. I will completely destroy them and make them an object of horror and scorn, and an everlasting ruin. I will banish from them the sounds of joy and gladness, the voices of bride and bridegroom, the sound of millstones and the light of the lamp. This whole country will become a desolate wasteland, and these nations will serve the king of Babylon seventy years. "But when the seventy years are fulfilled, I will punish the king of Babylon and his nation, the land of the Babylonians, for their guilt," declares the LORD, "and will make it desolate forever. I will bring upon that land all the things I have spoken against it, all that are written in this book and prophesied by Jeremiah against all the nations. They themselves will be enslaved by many nations and great kings; I will repay them according to their deeds and the work of their hands" (Jeremiah 25: 8-14).

Jeremiah's message of doom for the people of Judah was interlaced with a message of hope.

"This is what the LORD says: "When seventy years are completed for Babylon, I will come to you and fulfill my gracious promise to bring you back to this place. For I know the plans I have for you," declares the LORD, "plans to prosper you and not to harm you, plans to give you hope and a future. Then you will call upon me and come and pray to me, and I will listen to you. You will seek me and find me when you seek me with all your heart. I will be found by you," declares the LORD, "and will bring you back from captivity. I will gather you from all the nations and places where I have banished you," declares the LORD, "and will bring you back to the place from which I carried you into exile" (Jeremiah 29:10-14).

FASCINATING FACTS: The Hanging Gardens of Babylon

The Hanging Gardens of Babylon, built by Nebuchadnezzar, are one of the Seven Wonders of the Ancient World. Nothing remains of the gardens, and very little is known of them. No one can say with any certainty where they were or what they looked like. From the name, it has been theorized that they were built with a number of terraces, with plants overhanging the railings at many levels.

The popular theory is that Nebuchadnezzar built the Hanging Gardens for his Persian wife Amytis, to soothe her homesickness for her beloved Persia. Amytis was native to the mountains of northern Persia, or Media (modern Iran). Since Babylon was built on the low, flat land between the Tigris and Euphrates, Nebuchadnezzar may have tried to imitate a mountain landscape for her.

FASCINATING FACTS: The Ishtar Gate

The Ishtar Gate, one of the eight gates in the walls that surrounded the inner city of Babylon, was built during the reign of Nebuchadnezzar II.

As the main gate into the inner city, it was lavishly decorated with reliefs of different animals, including dragons, bulls and lions. The gate was named for the Babylonian goddess Ishtar, whose symbol was the lion.

GEOGRAPHY FOCUS

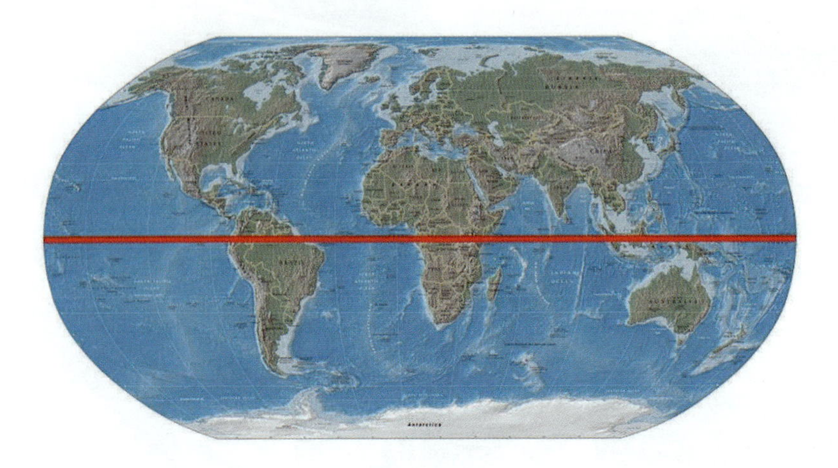

The Equator

Did you know…

- The Equator is an imaginary line around the Earth, halfway between the north and south poles.
- It divides the earth into two hemispheres, the Northern Hemisphere and the Southern Hemisphere.
- It is the line of 0° latitude. All other latitude lines, which measure a location's angle on the globe north or south, are measured from the Equator.
- Because the Equator encircles the Earth at its widest diameter, it is the longest latitude line.
- The sun passes directly over the Equator twice each year, at the equinoxes in March and September.
- Locations along the Equator have nearly equal hours of day and night throughout the year
- Locations along the Equator have the fastest sunrises and sunsets on Earth. The transition from day to night takes just minutes.
- The Earth is not perfectly spherical; it bulges at the Equator (or is flattened at the poles).
- Locations along the Equator have high temperatures all year long.
- The majority of the Earth's rainforests are located on or near the Equator.

Chapter 21

The Rise of the Persians

BIBLE AND ANCIENT HISTORY FOCUS

NOTE: THIS LESSON CONTAINS A SECTION ON A TOPIC YOU MAY WISH TO AVOID IF YOUR CHILD IS TOO YOUNG. READ THE "NOTE TO PARENTS" SECTION BEFORE YOU GIVE THIS LESSON TO YOUR CHILD!

BABYLON

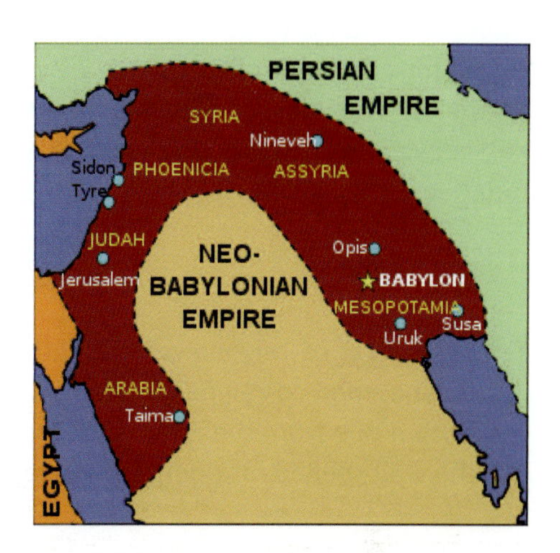

The Neo-Babylonian Empire

- **Nabopolassar** reigned for 21 years, from 626-605 BC. His son Nebuchadnezzar II conquered Assyria at the Battle of Carchemish in 605 BC, making Babylon the dominant empire in the region for the next 80 years. Nebuchadnezzar's marriage to the daughter of the king of Media united the Medes and the Babylonians.
- **Nebuchadnezzar II** reigned for 44 years, from 605-562 BC. He conquered Judah and Jerusalem, rebuilt the city of Babylon, and built the famous Hanging Gardens of Babylon. Nebuchadnezzar figures prominently in the Bible Book of Daniel.

GIANTS OF THE FAITH: Ezekiel

(Picture to the left is Ezekiel by Michelangelo)

Ezekiel was called to be a prophet after he was carried into Babylonian exile along with thousands of other Jews during Nebuchadnezzar's reign. His messages center around three major events in Judah's history:

- The lead-up to the final siege of Jerusalem (Ezekiel 1-24)
- The final siege of Jerusalem (Ezekiel 25-31)
- The aftermath of the destruction of Jerusalem (Ezekiel 32-48)

Unlike his contemporary Jeremiah, who prophesied in Jerusalem, Ezekiel ministered to Jewish exiles in Babylon. Ezekiel's prophecies centered around visions such as his well-known "wheel in the middle of a wheel," and his message was for the people to turn from their sin and acknowledge God. The phrase "know that I am God" appears over and over throughout the book.

- **Evil-Marduk** reigned for 2 years, from 562-560 BC. He released King Jehoiachin of Judah from prison, giving him a seat of honor in his palace (II Kings 25: 27-30). Evil-Marduk was assassinated by his brother-in-law.
- **Nergal-sharezer** reigned for four years, from 560-556 BC, after assassinating Evil-Marduk. He married a daughter of Nebuchadnezzar. He spent his time beautifying Babylon and working on one of its major canals. Nergal-sharezer died in his prime, and his son succeeded him.
- **Labasi-Marduk** reigned for nine months in 556 BC. He was murdered in a palace coup by Belshazzar, son of Nabonidus.
- **Nabonidus** was the last king of the Neo-Babylonian Empire, reigning from 556-539 BC. He reigned alone for two years, and then co-reigned with his son Belshazzar (the one who dethroned Labasi-Marduk).

INTERESTING INDIVIDUALS: Nabonidus

Nabonidus was a Babylonian army officer of ordinary birth. In the place of the primary Babylonian god, Marduk, Nabonidus worshipped the ancient Mesopotamian moon god Sin. This caused tension in Babylon. He restored Sin's temple in Haran and ignored the New Year festival of Marduk celebrated by past Babylonian kings. Nabonidus' absence from the festival upset the priests of Marduk. Nabonidus avoided this conflict by spending at least ten years in Arabia, leaving his son Belshazzar to rule Babylon in his place. He returned to Babylon in 540 BC to defend his kingdom from the Persians. Leaving Belshazzar to protect the city, Nabonidus led his troops north to face Cyrus. But his troops were no match for the might of Cyrus, and he was forced to surrender. His son Belshazzar still held the throne in Babylon, but two days later, Cyrus of Persia overtook the city. This was the end of the Babylonian Empire founded by Nabopolassar and Nebuchadnezzar.

BELSHAZZAR

- **Belshazzar** co-reigned with his father Nabonidus from 553-539 BC. Belshazzar helped his father gain the throne, then co-reigned with his father after three years. Little is known of Belshazzar except for one well-known tale from the Bible: the story of the fateful night when the kingdom was lost and the handwriting on the wall spelled his doom (see below).

GIANTS OF THE FAITH: DANIEL, PART II

SCRIPTURE SPOTLIGHT: Belshazzar, Daniel, and the Handwriting on the Wall (Daniel 5)

This story is arranged as a 7-part chiasm. The first portion corresponds to the seventh, the second to the sixth, and the third to the fifth. The fourth section stands alone at the center.

Belshazzar's pride (Daniel 5: 1-4): Belshazzar acts as his father's regent while his father is away confronting Cyrus of Persia. On the night the sign appears, he is feasting and drinking with his nobles. It is customary for the king to receive the food offered to the idols, and this is probably what Belshazzar and his nobles are eating. In his arrogance, Belshazzar calls for the gold and silver goblets from the Temple of Jerusalem so that he can drink offerings to Marduk from them. Acts like this are both arrogant and extremely profane. Belshazzar and his nobles continue to taunt the Hebrew God by toasting their own gods with the Temple goblets.

"MENE, MENE, TEKEL, PARSIN"

Handwriting on the wall appears (Daniel 5: 5-6): In the midst of the party, a disembodied hand appears in mid-air and writes the words "Mene, mene, tekel, parsin" on the wall. The eerie scene causes a terrified Belshazzar to fall into a faint.

Wise men summoned/kingdom offered (Daniel 5:7-9): Belshazzar issues an urgent call for anyone who can interpret the meaning of the words on the wall. He offers the interpreter the third highest position in the kingdom, behind only his father and himself. None of the wise men can interpret the words, and terror fills the hall.

Daniel is remembered (Daniel 5: 10-12): Belshazzar's mother the queen comes in and tells him about Daniel, whom she believes might be able to interpret the dream. She refers to Nebuchadnezzar as Belshazzar's father, when he is in fact his grandfather; but her word can also mean "ancestor."

Daniel summoned/kingdom offered (Daniel 5: 10-16): Belshazzar summons Daniel and offers him the third highest position in the kingdom if he can do what all of the other wise men are unable to do: interpret the writing on the wall.

Handwriting on the wall explained (Daniel 5:17-28): Daniel turns down the offer of high position, possibly because he understands how briefly he would hold it, possibly because he is disgusted with Belshazzar's behavior. First, Daniel tells Belshazzar that he will be judged for mocking God. Then he explains the meaning of the words:

"This is what these words mean:
Mene: God has numbered the days of your reign and brought it to an end.
Tekel: You have been weighed on the scales and found wanting.
Parsin: Your kingdom is divided and given to the Medes and Persians."

Belshazzar's downfall (Daniel 5:29-31): Belshazzar's attempt to buy off Daniel and Daniel's God fails. Cyrus and the Persian army flood into the city of Babylon that very night, and Belshazzar is killed.

AMAZING ANCIENTS: CYRUS THE GREAT

SCRIPTURE SPOTLIGHT: Daniel in the Lion's Den (Daniel 6)

With Nabonidus and Belshazzar defeated, Babylon fell under the Persian Empire. Babylon's new conqueror was Cyrus the Great of Persia. Cyrus apparently installed a governor over Babylon named Darius the Mede. There is some confusion over Darius's identity. He may have been a military commander, a relative of Cyrus, or even Cyrus himself. Whoever he was, Darius functioned as Babylon's king, and hence Daniel's king.

Darius was so impressed with Daniel that he placed him in a high position in the court. Daniel seemed likely to rise above all others, and his success caused some jealousy among the other advisers in the court. These enemies sought a way to bring Daniel down.

Daniel's enemies flattered Darius much as they had flattered Nebuchadnezzar, and they convinced him to decree that he must be worshipped as a god for thirty days. The punishment for any who refused to worship Darius as a god was to be thrown into a lions' den. Darius sealed the decree (probably with a seal on his ring) so that it could not be rescinded.

As a good Hebrew, Daniel of course refused to worship Darius, instead praying and trusting that God would keep him safe. His enemies were watching for his refusal, and they dragged him before Darius. Darius had no wish to see Daniel thrown to the lions, but even he could not rescind the sealed decree.

As Daniel was tossed into the lions' den, Darius wondered if Daniel's God was really powerful enough to save him. When Daniel left the den unharmed after a night among the lions, the king rejoiced and then promptly tossed Daniel's accusers into the den along with their families.

Darius then decreed that everyone in the kingdom must acknowledge Daniel's God:

"I issue a decree that in every part of my kingdom people must fear and reverence the God of Daniel. For He is the living God and He endures forever; His kingdom will not be destroyed, His dominion will never end. He rescues and He saves; He performs signs and wonders in the heavens and on the earth. He has rescued Daniel from the power of the lions" (Daniel 6:26-27).

FASCINATING FACTS: Daniel 1-6

The Book of Daniel contains six stories. Each of the six features a Hebrew character, either Daniel or his friends, and a foreign king. Five of these stories end with the foreign king acknowledging the power of Daniel's God. The sixth story, which tells of Belshazzar and the writing on the wall, ends with the death of the unbelieving king.

Daniel's great success in a foreign court carries on the tradition begun by Joseph. The polytheistic foreign kings learn to respect the one God by watching the way He cares for Daniel and Joseph.

PERSIA

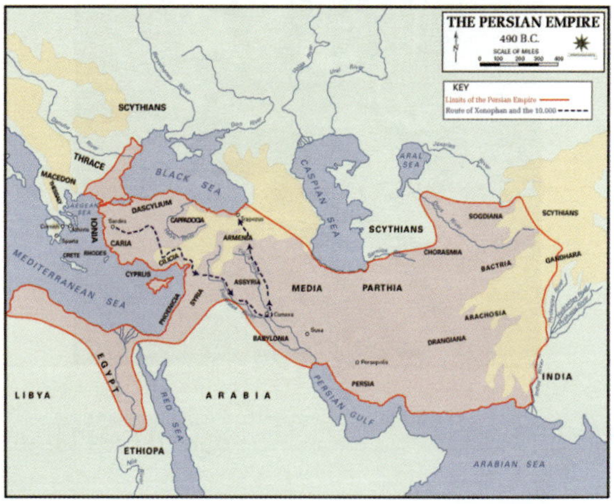

Ancient Persia lay between the Persian Gulf and the Caspian Sea (present day Iran). Around the **800-900 BC**, two people groups called the Medes and the Persians settled in the area, the Medes in the north, the Persians in the south. Both were Indo-European people, probably related to the Hittites, Greeks and Romans. Another Indo-European group that migrated with them continued down into the Indus Valley of India, where it became the forerunner of the Brahmin caste.

In **612 BC**, the Medes united with the Babylonians and attacked the Assyrian capital of Nineveh, causing the eventual fall of the Assyrian empire.

In **550 BC**, a Persian named Cyrus the Great seized the throne of the Median king Astyages, who happened to be his grandfather. Persia absorbed the Median Empire.

Cyrus was the grandson of the Median king Astyages and the son of a noble from the house of Persia. Astyages tried to eliminate Cyrus when he was only a baby because his dreams indicated that Cyrus would overthrow him. These dreams were interpreted for Astyages by the Magi.

<u>FASCINATING FACTS: The Magi</u>

The Magi were Persian priests, probably followers of the prophet Zoroaster. They were known for their ability to read the stars. The best known Magi are the three "wise men" who followed a special star to find the Christ child, bringing Him gifts of gold, frankincense and myrrh. They also had the wisdom to deceive Herod, who wanted to kill the child (Matthew 2:12).

Astyages ordered his trusted servant Harpagus to take the infant Cyrus out and kill him. Instead, Harpagus gave the child to a shepherd to kill; but the shepherd and his wife kept the child and raised him as their own. Years later, when Astyages discovered that Cyrus was still alive, he was outraged. He ordered the execution of Harpagus' son. This cruel and pointless punishment turned his servant's heart against him.

Cyrus took his father's place as king of Persia in **<u>559 BC</u>**. Harpagus allied himself with Cyrus, and together the two of them gathered a group of men disenchanted with the leadership of Astyages. When Astyages met Cyrus in battle, Cyrus defeated his grandfather easily, but he did not allow his troops to kill Astyages. Instead, he took him into his court and cared for him. This was a brilliant stroke: by keeping Astyages alive and in his court, Cyrus was able to unite Persia and Media into a single large empire that worked as a unit. This was far better than conquering Media and then stationing troops there to guard against rebellion.

Standard of Cyrus the Great

After the conquest of Media, Cyrus had to face conflict on three fronts: against the Lydians in Asia Minor, the Egyptians and the Babylonians. He attacked the Lydians first. Harpagus wisely recommended the use of camels. Cyrus' camels frightened the Lydian horses, which bolted and forced the Lydian cavalry to retreat. Cyrus then laid siege to the Lydian capital, eventually breaching the walls and taking the city. After capturing Asia Minor, Cyrus marched through India to the Indus River and laid claim to a vast territory in the east.

Cyrus waited eight years before he decided to try himself against Babylon. The city was well-fortified, and its outer wall seemed impenetrable. But Cyrus was crafty: in 539 BC, instead of attacking the walls, Cyrus dug trenches to reroute the mighty Tigris River, which flowed under the city. This was no small feat, but when it was done, Cyrus marched his men along the dry riverbed into the city. Belshazzar, who saw the writing on the wall, was killed. His father Nabonidus was captured and treated with dignity until his death a year later.

The prophet Isaiah wrote of Cyrus:

"Who says to the watery deep, 'Be dry, and I will dry up your streams; who says of Cyrus, 'He is my shepherd and will accomplish all that I please…'" (Isaiah 44: 27-28b)

Isaiah wrote these words about 200 years before Cyrus conquered Babylon. How did he know?

After he conquered Babylon, Cyrus declared himself king of the universe. He extended his control throughout the Arabian Peninsula and all the area east of the Mediterranean. He conquered all of the territory up to the Egyptian border, but he never conquered Egypt.

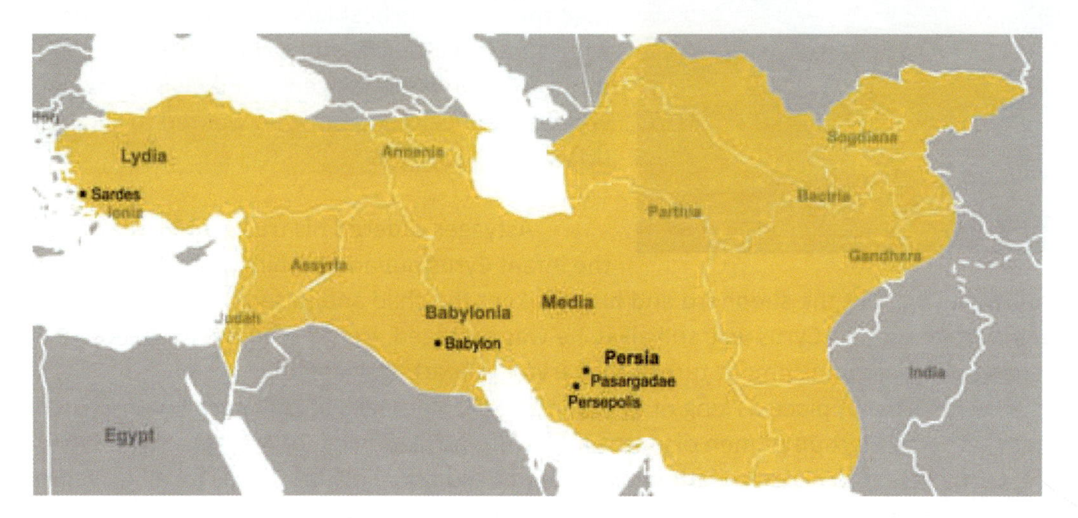

Babylon had tried to control its vast empire by capturing a conquered kingdom's nobles and carrying them into exile. Cyrus is credited with creating a new and better way to control his empire. His way was to divide his empire into districts, each under its *satrap*, and allow each district a measure of independence. Cyrus respected the religions of the people he conquered and allowed them to continue their customs. He sent the exiles who had been captured by the Babylonians home to their lands and temples. He adopted Aramaic as the common language of his empire.

When Cyrus died in battle in 530 BC, his son Cambyses became king. Cambyses assassinated his brother to protect his throne. During his short reign, the new king succeeded where his father had failed, conquering Egypt and adding it to the Persian Empire. Cambyses was either murdered or committed suicide in 522 BC, and Darius I, a distant cousin, seized the throne.

THE JEWS RETURN TO JERUSALEM

Timeline of Persian and Biblical History

CYRUS	559- 530 BC	Ezra 1-6: First wave of Hebrew exiles return, work begins on rebuilding the Temple
DARIUS I	522-486 BC	Haggai and Zechariah: Temple rebuilding is finished
XERXES	486-464 BC	Esther
ARATAXERXES I	464-424 BC	Ezra 7-10, Nehemiah 1-13: Second and third waves of Hebrew exiles return, work begins on the walls of Jerusalem

God's prophets foretold the return of His people to Judah. Jeremiah predicted that Judah's people would be exiled in Babylon, but for a limited time: In Jeremiah 25, the prophet foretells that their exile would last for 70 years. After that, they would return. Long before Judah fell to Babylon, Isaiah predicted that a shepherd named Cyrus would conquer Babylon and allow the exiles to return to Jerusalem and rebuild it:

"Who says of Cyrus, 'He is my shepherd
and will accomplish all that I please;
he will say of Jerusalem, "Let it be rebuilt,"
and of the temple, "Let its foundations be laid."
"This is what the LORD says to his anointed,
to Cyrus, whose right hand I take hold of
to subdue nations before him
and to strip kings of their armor,
to open doors before him
so that gates will not be shut:
I will go before you
and will level the mountains;
I will break down gates of bronze
and cut through bars of iron.
I will give you the treasures of darkness,
riches stored in secret places,
so that you may know that I am the LORD,
the God of Israel, who summons you by name.
For the sake of Jacob my servant,
of Israel my chosen,
I summon you by name
and bestow on you a title of honor,
though you do not acknowledge me" (Isaiah 44:28, 45: 1-4).

Cyrus the Great did in fact allow the Jews to return to Jerusalem in 538 BC. He also gave them permission to rebuild their temple:

"In the first year of Cyrus king of Persia, in order to fulfill the word of the LORD spoken by Jeremiah, the LORD moved the heart of Cyrus king of Persia to make a proclamation throughout his realm and to put it in writing:

"This is what Cyrus king of Persia says:

" 'The LORD, the God of heaven, has given me all the kingdoms of the earth and he has appointed me to build a temple for him at Jerusalem in Judah. Anyone of his people among you—may his God be with him, and let him go up to Jerusalem in Judah and build the temple of the LORD, the God of Israel, the God who is in Jerusalem. And the people of any place where survivors may now be living are to provide him with silver and gold, with goods and livestock, and with freewill offerings for the temple of God in Jerusalem'" (Ezra 1:1-4).

FASCINATING FACTS: Cyrus and the Exiles

Cyrus allowed the Jews to return to Jerusalem and rebuild the Temple, but they were not the only exiles he set free. Cyrus released exiles and allowed them to rebuild their local temples for a number of reasons. Although he was probably a Zoroastrian (see below), he was very sensitive to the gods of other cultures and wanted to cover all of his bases. By allowing the temples to be rebuilt, he probably felt that he appeased the gods, gaining the favor of these small local deities just in case they were real. In returning exiles to their homes, Cyrus also created grateful and loyal subjects who would be a buffer against enemies from beyond the empire.

As a result of Cyrus' decree, a group of about 50,000 exiles returned to Jerusalem led by Zerubbabel (a descendent of David and a grandson of King Jehoiachin) and others. The empire allowed them to take back their temple treasures and provided them with money, food and provisions to rebuild the temple.

The Jews began rebuilding the Temple with the help of some skilled Phoenicians. They soon fell into conflict with the Samaritans (descendants of northern kingdom Jews who intermarried with their Assyrian conquerors), who wanted to take part in the rebuilding. The Samaritans felt that they, too, were followers of the God of Abraham, Isaac and Jacob. The returning Judeans felt that the Samaritans were second class citizens, their ancestry and worship blended with that of Assyria (see Chapter 16). The conflict brought work on the Temple to a halt. From that point on, the Samaritans wrought havoc with all of the Jews' rebuilding projects. Because of the Samaritan conflict, the temple lay desolate from 536 to 520 BC, and the Jews grew complacent about finishing the rebuilding work.

When Darius I became King of Persia in 522 BC, he adopted a policy of religious tolerance that should have encouraged the Jews to resume their rebuilding, but they were unmoved. It took the preaching of the prophets Haggai and Zechariah to shake them out of their complacency. They finally completed the second Temple in 516 BC.

GIANTS OF THE FAITH: Haggai and Zechariah

Humble-born Haggai did not begin his ministry until he was eighty years old. He was old enough to have lived in Jerusalem as child, and he remembered the first Temple before Nebuchadnezzar's men destroyed it.

Zechariah was the son of a priest. He began his ministry soon after Haggai began his, but he continued long after Haggai had finished. The mission of both Haggai and Zechariah was to rouse the returned Jews from their lethargy and inspire them to finish the temple. The Jews responded well to Haggai and Zechariah. Their hearts were so stirred that they completed the second Temple within a few years.

FASCINATING FACTS: The Second Temple

When the second temple was completed in 516 BC, twenty years after the exiles returned from Babylon, the Jews dedicated it with great rejoicing:

"Then the people of Israel—the priests, the Levites and the rest of the exiles—celebrated the dedication of the house of God with joy. For the dedication of this house of God they offered a hundred bulls, two hundred rams, four hundred male lambs and, as a sin offering for all Israel, twelve male goats, one for each of the tribes of Israel. And they installed the priests in their divisions and the Levites in their groups for the service of God at Jerusalem, according to what is written in the Book of Moses" (Ezra 6: 16-18).

Unlike Solomon's first Temple, the second temple did not hold the Ark of the Covenant, the Ten Commandments, the pot of manna or Aaron's rod. All of these were lost over the centuries. Like the first Temple, the second Temple was razed-- this time by the Romans in 70 AD.

FASCINATING FACTS: Zoroastrianism

Founded by the prophet Zoroaster around 1500 BC, Zoroastrianism is one of the world's oldest religions. The most famous Zoroastrian of his day was probably Cyrus the Great. The Magi or Wise Men of the Christmas story were also probably Zoroastrians.

Unlike the many polytheists who surrounded them, the Zoroastrians were monotheists. They believed in one creator god named Ahura Mazda. Fire and water formed the basis of their ritual life, and they worshipped at a fire temple (see picture). Their holy book is the *Avesta*. Zoroastrians pray several times a day, and they believe that in order to keep chaos at bay and attain happiness, one must participate actively in a daily life of good thoughts, good words and good deeds.

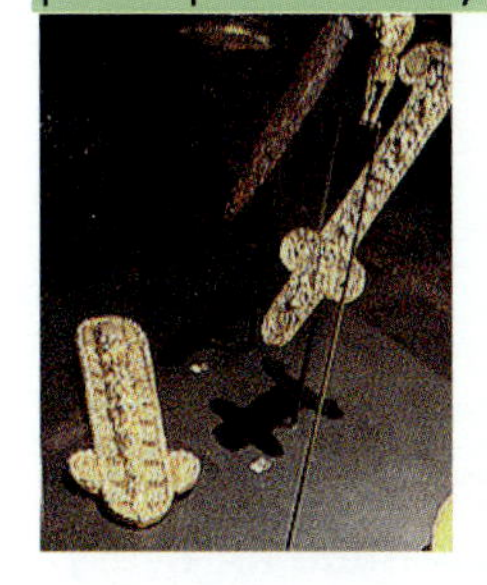

FASCINATING FACTS: Akinakes

The akinakes was a short dagger used first by the Persians and later by the Greeks. It had a short, straight double-edged blade about 16" in length. Kings sometimes gave the akinakes as a gift. Ornate versions of the akinakes are depicted in Ancient Persian art carried by king's bodyguards and important nobles.

GEOGRAPHY FOCUS

The Prime Meridian

Did you know...

- The Prime Meridian (and its opposite, the 180th Meridian) form the imaginary line from north to south around the globe that divides the earth into two hemispheres, the Eastern Hemisphere and the Western Hemisphere (just as the Equator divides the earth into the Northern and Southern Hemispheres).
- The Prime Meridian is the line of 0° longitude, just as the Equator is the line of 0° latitude.
- The equator was defined centuries ago, but the Prime Meridian didn't receive its name until 1884. At the International Meridian Conference, scientists chose a line through Greenwich, England as the Prime Meridian.

NOTE TO PARENTS: If you do not wish to discuss the topic of eunuchs with your child, avoid this section!

FASCINATING FACTS: Eunuchs in Kings' Courts

Although many Jews eventually returned to Jerusalem after their Babylonian exile, there is no indication that Daniel ever returned. If he didn't, then it might have been because he was a eunuch.

Eunuchs were young males rendered physically incapable of fathering children. Such young men were highly useful in royal courts, for these reasons:

- Because only eunuchs could protect and attend to the king's wives and concubines without any danger of fathering children with them.
- Because eunuch high officials produced no sons to compete with the king's sons for the throne.

- Because eunuchs had neither families nor futures of their own, and thus were more likely to invest their hopes in the king, his family and his future.

Outside the royal court, average citizens regarded a eunuch as something less than a man— for a man with no children had no future, and thus was more a king's man than a real man. Being a eunuch carried a social stigma that was difficult to ignore. Once a man was made a eunuch, he had little place outside the court for the rest of his life.

Because Daniel was forcibly removed to Babylon as a young man, it is quite possible that he was made a eunuch like so many court slaves of his time. If he was, then he had little reason to leave the king's court ever again. Isaiah predicted that some of Judah's young men would become eunuchs:

"Then Isaiah said to Hezekiah, "Hear the word of the LORD Almighty: The time will surely come when everything in your palace, and all that your fathers have stored up until this day, will be carried off to Babylon. Nothing will be left, says the LORD. And some of your descendants, your own flesh and blood who will be born to you, will be taken away, and they will become eunuchs in the palace of the king of Babylon" (Isaiah 39:5-7).

This prophecy was fulfilled in Daniel 1:

"Then the king ordered Ashpenaz, chief of his court officials, to bring in some of the Israelites from the royal family and the nobility --young men without any physical defect, handsome, showing aptitude for every kind of learning, well informed, quick to understand, and qualified to serve in the king's palace..." (Daniel 1:3-4).

The practice of creating eunuchs shows how little regard the ancient kings had for the natural rights of their subjects. Such a king might make dozens or hundreds of eunuchs, ruining the lives and hopes of all of them, solely to keep peace in the depraved world of his royal harem and to keep his throne safe from challenge.

The Lord offers hope to the eunuch in Isaiah 56:

"For this is what the LORD says: "To the eunuchs who keep my Sabbaths, who choose what pleases me and hold fast to my covenant- to them I will give within my temple and its walls a memorial and a name better than sons and daughters; I will give them an everlasting name that will not be cut off."

Chapter 22

Athens, Sparta and Esther

ANCIENT HISTORY FOCUS

THE GREEKS

We first met the Greeks in Chapters 17 and 18. In Chapter 17 we read about the Minoans, who lived on the island of Crete from around 1720-1600 BC. When a tremendous volcanic eruption on a nearby island forced the Minoans to move, the Mycenaeans (chapter 18) emerged and lived on the Greek peninsula from around 1600-1200 BC. The Mycenaeans were the first great culture to live in the land that became Greece. They were overcome and displaced by the Sea People and the Dorians from the north.

Because the Sea People and the Dorians left no writings behind, the next period is known as the Greek Dark Age, from 1200-750 BC. During this time, Greece moved into the Iron Age (see Chapter 18).

By the end of the Greek Dark Age, the different peoples of the Greek peninsula had blended into a single group, although they were not ruled by a single king. The Greeks considered themselves citizens of the city-states in which they lived. Each city-state had its own laws, customs and government. Some had kings, while some were governed by the aristocracy (the wealthy). Still others experimented with early forms of democracy. These city-states sometimes banded together to defend against outside enemies, and at other times fought among themselves. The largest and most powerful city-states were Athens, Sparta, Corinth, Megara and Argos.

This period of Greek history, which lasted from 750-490 BC, is called the Archaic Period. During this time the Greeks began to outgrow their peninsula, and began to spread out around the Mediterranean and Black Seas.

SPARTA

One of the largest city-states of Ancient Greece was Sparta. Sparta was unusual in that it was co-ruled by two kings, each descended from one of a set of twin brothers.

In the early Archaic Period, the people of Sparta conquered a nearby group of people called the Messenians. In the First Messenian War, from 743-724 BC, the Spartans defeated and enslaved the Messenians. The Spartans referred to the enslaved Messenians as "helots," and they used them cruelly. The helots were beaten, starved and forced to give the produce of their own land to the Spartans.

The Messenians outnumbered the Spartans ten to one. In order to keep such a large group of people under control, the Spartans had to maintain constant vigilance. A long Messenian revolt, from 685-668 BC, eventually collapsed. The Messenians remained under Spartan control.

The continuing subjugation of the Messenians required a strong military and harsh discipline. To this end, the Spartans developed a specialized military class and special schools. The purpose of education in Sparta was not to enlighten the mind, but to produce strong warriors. Each child was inspected by the city elders. If he or she showed any sign of weakness or birth defect, he was thrown from a cliff or left to die. Children who were deemed fit were raised by their parents until they reached the age of seven. After that, the Spartans enrolled each young boy in an *agoge*.

FASCINATING FACTS: The Agoge

When a Spartan boy reached the age of seven, he left his parents' home and went to live a military life in a military style barracks. There he went through a rigorous training regime called the *agoge*. Over the next five years he underwent mental and physical conditioning in the harshest of environments. Brutal punishments taught severe discipline and increased tolerance for pain. Boys were not allowed the luxury of crying during their whippings. They received little food, little clothing, little bedding and no nurturing. They were encouraged to steal to satisfy their hunger, but they were punished severely if they were caught.

At the age of twelve the boys moved to the next level, in which they were forced to live in the open for a year with only one garment and no shoes. At thirteen they began to participate in war games. These brutal "games" left many Spartan boys dead or seriously injured. At the age of 20, if they survived, the boys were given a test. Those who passed became soldiers. Those who failed were doomed to join a lower caste sometimes called the *Tremblers*.

For the next ten years, the young soldier lived in the barracks as part of the Spartan army, even if he was married. When he was thirty, he could finally live at home with his family, but he could only leave the army when he was sixty.

Although Spartan women did not participate in the agoge, they too learned toughness through physical and gymnastic training. Spartan women generally had more freedom than their contemporaries from other cultures, and were even allowed to own and operate their own businesses.

Other facts about Sparta:

- In Sparta, life centered around the state, not the family. Children belonged to the state, and marital relationships were less important than affairs of state.
- A Spartan male's grave was marked with a headstone only if he died in combat; a Spartan woman received a headstone only if she died in childbirth.
- Only those who completed the agoge and became soldiers were true citizens of Sparta.
- Sparta's high officials consisted of the two kings, a group of five officials called *ephors* and a council of 28 elders called the *Gerousia*. Plato called the ephors "tyrants" because they wielded the most power.

WORD ORIGIN: *Spartan*

The Spartans' well-known stern discipline gave rise to the English adjective *Spartan,* which describes much of what the Spartans were: disciplined, frugal, austere, and self-denying. It can also mean brave.

ATHENS

Before the Dark Age of Greece, Athens was part of the Mycenaean empire. Its people were known as Ionians. When the Dorians swept into Greece, they did not conquer Athens, and the people of Athens remained Ionians. Athens was the largest city in Greece, ruling over a large area of mountains and fertile valleys-- a region called Attica, which jutted into the Aegean Sea. Attica's valuable resources included silver, marble, lead and cash crops of wine and olive oil. Athens boasted the largest navy in Greece.

FASCINATING FACTS: Life in Athens

While the Spartans were famous for their military, Athenians were famous for their study of the arts and sciences. Named for Athena, the goddess of wisdom (see below), Athens placed much emphasis on its wisdom and education. When an Athenian boy reached the age of 7, he began to attend a formal school. He studied reading, writing, science and mathematics. He also studied public speaking, government and drama. He learned to play a musical instrument, and he memorized the works of Homer. After completing this course of study at the age of eighteen, he attended two years of military school.

A man's military rank was determined by his social class. The wealthiest became commanders, the second class became cavalry and the third class became infantry (foot soldiers). The lowest class, the poor, served as navy oarsmen or as army archers.

Athenian girls learned homemaking from their mothers. They learned how to sew, cook and run a home, and they learned to be good and obedient wives. They received no formal education and passed directly from the control of their fathers to that of their husbands when they married. Teaching a woman to read and write was considered both dangerous and a waste of time. Except during festivals, Athenian women did not go out in public. Fortunately, Athens had numerous festivals.

FASCINATING FACTS: The Naming of Athens

Athens lies on a beautiful piece of land in Greece. Its site was so beautiful that the gods of Olympus argued over whose name the city would bear. The two top rivals were Poseidon, god of the sea, and Athena, goddess of wisdom.

The highest god, Zeus, instructed each of them to present the city's king with a gift for the city. The king would choose his favorite gift, and then name the city for the god who gave it.

Poseidon's gift was first: He struck a rock and caused a spring of water to flow from it. This was quite a gift for a city, because it promised that its citizens would never thirst, even in the face of drought. It also symbolized that the city would have a mighty navy. Unfortunately, Poseidon's water tasted salty and did not impress the king.

When Athena's turn came, she planted a seed in the ground, which grew into an olive tree. This gift provided the city with food, oil and firewood, all necessary items for survival. Her gift also symbolized peace and prosperity. The king chose Athena's gift over Poseidon's, so the city received the name "Athens."

At first Athens was ruled by kings, but by 700-600 BC, monarchy had given way to a land-owning aristocracy or oligarchy (an oligarchy is a small group of rulers who hold power together). A group of wealthy landowners controlled the city-state.

Around 600 BC, a man named Draco established a legal code for Athens. This became Athens' first written constitution, and it was written on steles (large carved stones) for all to see. Draco's famously brutal code specified the death penalty for nearly all infractions, both major and minor. Even the smallest of crimes meant death under Draco's law.

WORD ORIGIN: *Draconian*

The severity of Draco's laws grew so well known that it became the origin of the English adjective *Draconian.* Rules or laws which are exceedingly harsh, very severe, rigorous or cruel are known as Draconian.

Not surprisingly, Draco's laws favored the wealthy. When a rich man failed to pay a debt to a poor man, his punishment was much lighter than that of a poor man who owed money to a rich one. In certain cases, the laws forced the poor to pay exorbitant taxes and then forced them into slavery when they could not pay.

In protest of Draco's severe laws, the Athenian oligarchy chose another man to create a fairer legal code. Under Solon's new laws, only murder was punishable by death. Solon allowed the rich to keep their land and their power, but he also allowed the cancellation of debts, which freed many Athenians from slavery. He banned the practice of enslaving those who could not repay their loans. He declared that every male in Athens had the right to vote, and this became the foundation for democracy in Athens. Unfortunately, Solon's reforms did not last, and the poor continued to suffer severely.

Around 560 BC, a man named Peisistratus came to power promising that he would help the poor if they supported him. Peisistratus had several false starts before he became firmly established as Athens' "kind dictator." Athens prospered under his leadership. He instituted a fairer tax system and used the tax money to build roads, temples and public water fountains. He also made laws governing borrowing that protected the poor.

Peisistratus' son Hippias took over when Peisistratus died in 527 BC. Hippias was not a benevolent dictator like his father, and the Athenians enlisted the help of Sparta to oust him in 510 BC.

In 508 BC, an aristocrat named Cleisthenes became the ruler of Athens. Cleisthenes reorganized the city-state's entire political structure to allow all citizens a voice. His reforms established democracy as Athens' permanent form of government-- until Alexander the Great conquered Athens in 338 BC.

FASCINATING FACTS: Athenian Democracy

In Athenian Democracy, each male citizen had a vote and a voice. The aristocracy no longer held power; instead, ordinary people participated in important decisions. A new law could only pass with a quorum of 6000 men. Each month, the citizens met at an Assembly to decide important issues, and each man had an equal vote.

Lesser matters were decided by a council of five hundred men chosen by lottery. The council managed such things as building projects, road construction and temple repair. Nine men known as *archons*, also chosen by lottery, handled religious affairs. Ten generals, all elected by the Assembly, commanded the army and the navy.

The Athenian democratic system also applied to the courts. Each day, five hundred men serving as jurors heard legal cases. The majority ruled, and the decision of the court could not be appealed. If the accused was convicted, the jury also voted on his sentence.

Timeline of Persian and Greek History

Persian King	Bible	Greek Event
Darius I - 522-486 BC	Haggai/Zechariah Temple completed	490 BC Battle of Marathon (Persians defeated)
Xerxes - 486-464 BC	Esther	480 BC Battle of Thermopylae (Spartans defeated) 479 BC Battle of Salamis (Persians defeated)
Artaxerxes I - 464-423 BC	Ezra/Nehemiah Malachi	461-431 BC Age of Pericles Athens rules 431-404 BC Peloponnesian Wars
Darius II - 423-404 BC	Biblical Silence	Peloponnesian Wars continue Sparta rules
Artaxerxes II - 404-359 BC		
Artaxerxes III - 359-338 BC		338 BC Battle of Chaeronea (Philip II defeats Greeks)
Arses 338-335 BC		
Darius III - 335 - 331 BC		336-323 BC Persian Empire overthrown by Alexander the Great

INTERESTING INDIVIDUALS: Herodotus

"These are the researches of Herodotus of Halicarnassus, which he publishes, in the hope of thereby preserving from decay the remembrance of what men have done, and of preventing the great and wonderful actions of the Greeks and the Barbarians from losing their due meed of glory; and withal to put on record what were their grounds of feuds."

This quote is the opening sentence from *The Histories,* a nine-volume history text written by Herodotus. Herodotus is considered the "Father of History" because he was the first author to set down history in a systematic and logical style. Herodotus did his own research and wrote his own words in an attempt to offer an unbiased perspective of the history, myths, poetry and legends of his time. *The Histories* relates Herodotus' story of the Persians' rise to power and their invasion of ancient Greece (490-479 BC). Herodotus was a child at the end of the Persian and Greek wars, so his records of the battles of Marathon, Thermopylae and Salamis were based on interviews of his elders.

Herodotus was born around 484 BC to a wealthy family in Halicarnassus, a Greek city that lies in what is now Turkey. When Herodotus was born, Halicarnassus was under Persian rule, but all of his city's people considered themselves Greeks.

Herodotus was quite well traveled for a man of his time. In addition to the Persian wars, *The Histories* recounts his journeys around the Mediterranean and Black Seas and into Egypt, Phoenicia and Mesopotamia.

THE GRECO-PERSIAN WARS

In Chapter 21 we read about the rise of Persia under Cyrus the Great. Cyrus was succeeded by his son Cambyses, who extended the empire into parts of Egypt. Darius I seized the throne when Cambyses died in 522 BC. Persia was at its peak in size and power, and Darius was able to maintain his vast kingdom through several rebellions.

DARIUS I

INTERESTING INDIVIDUALS: Darius I

Darius I's rise to the Persian throne is filled with intrigue. Darius's own version of events differs greatly from that of other Greek historians. Rulers of his day often resorted to fratricide (the murder of a brother) and worse to secure thrones for themselves. However he gained the Persian throne, Darius was considered a strong and wise ruler, known by some as Darius the Great.

Darius was forced to suppress numerous rebellions throughout his empire during his reign. He reorganized his empire into provinces and established a new monetary system. He also built a road from Persia to Asia Minor, made Aramaic the official language of the empire, reorganized his military and initiated numerous building projects.

Darius also extended the empire into India and pushed north into Europe. His foray into Europe ended when he was unable to defeat the Scythians and had to turn back. He also met defeat at the hands of the Athenians in the Battle of Marathon (see below). After that battle, he was forced to attend to a revolt in Egypt. He died in 486 BC before he could avenge his loss at Marathon. Xerxes I succeeded him on the Persian throne.

Around 500 BC, Darius I was forced to suppress a rebellion among the Greek city-states of Asia Minor, beginning with Miletus. Athens contributed ships to aid in the rebellion. After a number of years, Persia was able to defeat the rebels. Darius punished the city of Miletus by killing its entire male population and enslaving its women and children. Then he turned his attention to Athens, seeking to punish the city for aiding the rebellion.

In 490 BC, Darius launched an expedition against Athens, only to meet defeat at the Battle of Marathon.

FASCINATING FACTS: The Battle of Marathon

The Battle of Marathon was a classic David/Goliath tale. Persia sent 25,000 troops against 10,000 Athenians. When the Persian army arrived, Athens sent a messenger to Sparta asking for reinforcements. The foot messenger ran to Sparta and back in three days (the first "marathon"). He returned with the news that the Spartans would be glad to help, but because they were in the middle of a religious holiday, their law forbade them to engage in any military operation until the next full moon, which would come in six days.

Forced to get by on their own, the Athenians decided to make a daring move. On the Plain of Marathon, they moved their small army into position opposite the larger Persian army, stretching their line until it was as wide as the Persian line. Then the Greek hoplites attacked the Persian line at a dead run. Their brave "suicide run" worked. The Greeks killed 6400 Persians, but lost only 192 of their own troops.

The Persians fled to their ships and tried to attack Athens by sea, but again the Athenians turned them back.

The Battle of Marathon remains one of the most important battles in Greek history, because if the Greeks had lost, the entire Greek peninsula would probably have fallen under Persian control. This would have had a tremendous effect on Greek culture, to which the modern world owes much of its thought. The Athenians considered their victory at the Battle of Marathon their greatest achievement.

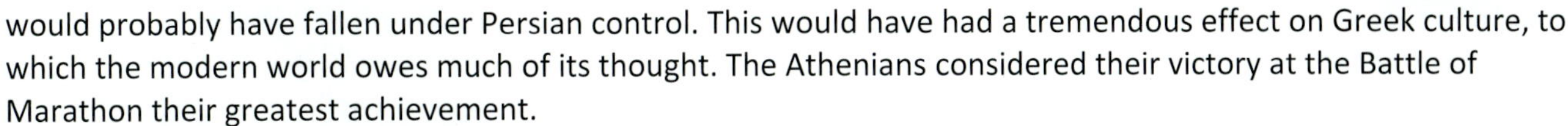

FASCINATING FACTS: Hoplites

Hoplites were the heavily armed infantry citizen-soldiers of the Ancient Greek city-states. Hoplites were trained to fight in lines standing shoulder to shoulder in what was called a "hoplite phalanx." Each man was protected by the shield of the man standing next to him. When the phalanx marched forward as a unit, enemy spears and arrows could not penetrate the shields. The phalanx was only effective if the entire unit moved together in step. If even one hoplite broke formation, the whole line could fall apart.

In addition to his neighbor's shield, each hoplite was also protected by a breastplate, a helmet and greaves (shin/leg armor).

After Darius I died, his son Xerxes I took the throne. His first task was to suppress the Egyptian revolt that had occupied his father before his death. Then in 481 BC, Xerxes set out with a force of two hundred thousand men and 600 ships on a quest to conquer Greece.

INTERESTING INDIVIDUALS: Xerxes

Xerxes I was the son of Darius. His mother was Atossa, a daughter of Cyrus the Great. Although Xerxes wasn't Darius' eldest son, his pedigree as a grandson of Cyrus gave him an extra claim to the throne. Xerxes is best remembered as the Persian king who married Esther, the beautiful Hebrew girl whose story is told in the Bible Book of Esther.

Xerxes' invasion of Greece was an effort to avenge his father's defeat at Marathon. But Xerxes, too, found the conquest of Greece to be beyond him. After one victory at Thermopylae, he was eventually defeated and forced to retreat.

Xerxes returned home and concentrated on building projects, including a massive palace for himself. Xerxes was murdered, and his son Artaxerxes succeeded him on the throne.

To begin his attack on Greece, Xerxes built two bridges across the strait at Hellespont (now known as the Dardanelles, see map above) so that his army could cross. According to the *Histories* of Herodotus, a storm destroyed Xerxes' new bridges before he could use them. In a petulant fit, Xerxes beheaded his bridge builders (the anger of kings has life and death consequences for their subjects). Then he had his soldiers give the strait three hundred lashings with the whip, brand the strait with red-hot irons and curse at the strait. The soldiers must have wondered if their king had thoroughly lost his mind. As for the strait, it took its punishment like a Spartan agoge boy, with no crying at all.

Xerxes finally built his bridge by lashing his anchored ships together with their bows turned into the current. The Persian soldiers crossed by moving from ship to ship.

In 492 BC, a Persian fleet had been destroyed by the wild Aegean Sea. To avoid the area where this had happened, Xerxes dug a canal across the isthmus of Mount Athos and sailed his ships through it.

When the mighty Persian army began advancing along the coast, many of the Greek city-states yielded without a fight. But Sparta, Athens and a number of other city-states refused to yield.

In 480 BC, the Spartans and other Greek warriors met Xerxes and his Persian troops at Thermopylae.

FASCINATING FACTS: The Battle of Thermopylae

Thermopylae sat in a narrow mountain pass that controlled the only road into central Greece. The Spartans were hoping that if Xerxes could be delayed at Thermopylae, his provisions would run out and he would be forced to retreat. Delaying Xerxes would also allow the Athenians more time to build up their navy.

Although the Spartan army was greatly outnumbered, only a small part of Xerxes' larger army could enter the pass at one time, so the odds in battle were evened a bit. For days the two armies fought fiercely as the Spartans held the pass against the Persians.

Unfortunately, the Spartans had a traitor in their midst who gave Xerxes information about an alternate route around the pass. This information soon would have allowed Xerxes to attack the Spartans from behind and destroy them entirely. When the Spartan king learned of this betrayal, he decided to retreat and abandon the pass, leaving behind three hundred soldiers to give battle to the Persians and cover the retreat. The famous "300" sacrificed themselves so that the rest of the army could live to fight on. The Battle of Thermopylae ended when all 300 were dead. The rest of the Greeks safely completed their retreat into southern Greece.

After his victory at Thermopylae, Xerxes headed for Athens. Anticipating his arrival, the Athenians had abandoned the city; so all that remained for Xerxes to do was to burn it to the ground. Next, a lack of provisions forced Xerxes to move against the Greek fleet at the Strait of Salamis near Athens.

FASCINATING FACTS: The Battle of Salamis

It is often said that an army moves on its stomach. Invasions of distant lands require the constant care and feeding of tens of thousands of men far from home. The amount of provisions required is staggering. The supply of the army was one of the functions of the Persian fleet. If they could control the sea, the Persians could keep their army supplied. If they could not, the vulnerable supply ships would be subject to enemy attack and plunder.

After the Battle of Marathon, the Athenians had wisely spent their time building up their navy. By the time Xerxes moved against Greece in 480 BC, Athens had two hundred ships in the water. To defeat Persia's larger navy, Athens had to use its ships wisely.

Instead of meeting the Persian navy head on, the Athenians held their ships in harbor. Xerxes' boats were forced to maneuver through the Aegean Sea in order to attack. The Aegean Sea can be a violent ship-killer, with dangerous winds and fast-rising storms. Before the Persian navy could even reach the Strait of Salamis, many of its ships were lost at sea.

According to Herodotus, an Athenian admiral pretending to be Xerxes' friend told him that the Greek navy was preparing to abandon its position at Salamis. Xerxes immediately sent his navy into the strait, but he soon discovered that it was a trap. The lighter Greek triremes (see picture) rammed the flanks of the larger Persian vessels. By evening, two hundred Persian ships were sunk, and Xerxes recalled his navy.

Within a year after their victory at Salamis, the Greeks again beat back the Persians at the Battle of Plataea, and the Persians finally abandoned their desire to conquer Greece. The Greeks had won their independence.

BIBLE FOCUS

GIANTS OF THE FAITH: ESTHER

The Book of Esther is filled with contrasts and ironies. It begins with despair and ends with hope. It begins with a feast in celebration of a man and ends with a feast in celebration of God's deliverance. Its characters include a selfish king, an evil noble, a vulnerable girl and her Godly uncle. It is the only book of the Bible that never mentions God, yet God's hand is evident throughout the book.

The story begins with a seven day feast in honor of King Xerxes of Persia, who wanted to show off his wealth. The entire party was designed to display Xerxes' greatness. After a week of partying in both the Queen's and the King's banquet halls, Xerxes was quite drunk. He had shown off his entire kingdom, and he had nothing left to display except his beautiful wife Vashti. He called for her to come and dance for his drunken nobles. It is uncertain exactly what he wanted her to do, but whatever it was, Queen Vashti wanted no part of it. She refused King Xerxes' command. Her refusal was unthinkable, and it raised a ruckus among the nobles. If the queen could deny the king's request, what might their own wives do? After much discussion, Xerxes banished Vashti from his presence and proclaimed in an edict that women were to be subject to their husbands' rule.

When Xerxes was no longer drunk, he realized that he missed his beautiful wife. But his nobles didn't want him to change his mind about the edict, so they proposed that he find another beautiful girl and make her queen. They sent out a call for beautiful girls from all over the kingdom to become prospective brides for the king.

One of the girls they chose was Esther, a Hebrew girl from the tribe of Benjamin (and therefore the kingdom of Judah). Esther was an orphan who had been raised by her uncle Mordecai. Before she left for the palace, Mordecai made Esther swear not to tell anyone there that she was a Hebrew.

For one year, Xerxes' prospective brides received "beauty treatments" and lessons on how to behave in the king's harem. When the year was up, each girl appeared before the king. If the king liked a girl, she would be called back to see him again; if not, she joined the harem as a concubine. Out of all of these most beautiful girls in the world's largest empire, Xerxes chose Esther to become Queen in Vashti's place.

Among the king's advisers was a wicked man named Haman. Like many who dwell in the halls of power, Haman lived only to increase his own authority, honor and wealth. Such people hated the Jews, because faithful Jews refused to bow down to any but God alone. Esther's uncle Mordecai was a faithful Jew, and he never bowed to Haman as everyone else did. Xerxes honored Haman above all of his other nobles, but Haman's enjoyment of all of these honors was marred each time Mordecai refused to bow to him.

Because he was a powerful man, Haman was not content to take his revenge against Mordecai alone. Instead, he sought to eliminate all Jews everywhere in the kingdom for their impudent refusal to bow down to royalty. Haman's behavior was an early example of *anti-Semitism*, or Jew-hating. The general hatred of Jews for their beliefs and practices became common over the centuries, giving rise to a long and sad history of mistreatment and violence against Jews that culminated in the Holocaust of World War II.

Haman flattered Xerxes into putting his seal on an edict that condemned all of the Jews in the empire. By casting lots, or *pur*, Haman chose the date for this massive slaughter: the thirteenth day of the month of Adar on the Jewish calendar. When Mordecai learned of the edict, he went into mourning and wore sackcloth and ashes to represent his deep sorrow. When Esther learned of the state he was in, she sent him some clothes, perhaps hoping that he would stop embarrassing her. In reply, Mordecai sent her a copy of the edict against her people, the Jews. Mordecai wanted Esther to use her position to intervene with Xerxes.

Esther's intervention was not a simple matter. Even though Esther was a queen, she did not speak often with the king, and when Mordecai made his request, she had not seen the king for thirty days. Without a summons, it was unlawful for her to appear before the king. There was one exception: she could approach the king uninvited in the hope that he would extend his scepter to her. If he did, then her interruption would be forgiven. Esther was naturally reluctant to risk her life on the whim of a petulant king (remember how Xerxes tried to punish a body of water?). But Mordecai insisted that Haman's edict was a matter of life or death for all of Esther's people, well worth the risk to her. Mordecai's faith in God's promises shines through in his appeal to her:

"Do not think that because you are in the king's house you alone of all the Jews will escape. For if you remain silent at this time, relief and deliverance for the Jews will arise from another place, but you and your father's family will perish. And who knows but that you have come to royal position for such a time as this?" (Esther 4: 13-14)

Mordecai knew that God would not abandon the Jews— that even if his people were unfaithful, God would save them somehow. He did not claim the role of a prophet, but he simply suggested that all of the events of Esther's life, her great beauty and her selection as queen, might possibly have been focused on this one event. If she could find the faith to act, she could be the instrument of God's salvation. Esther agreed to try.

Esther and her women fasted for three days and asked that all of her people do likewise. Then she held her breath and approached the king. Pleased at her appearance, Xerxes extended his scepter to her. But instead of simply making her request outright, which would have involved her in political arguments in the presence of many men, Esther invited the king and Haman to a private banquet she had prepared. At the banquet, the king asked Esther what she wanted of him. Her response was to invite him to a second banquet, at which she would finally make her request.

Haman left the banquet feeling quite pleased with himself, but his high spirits were spoiled when he saw faithful Mordecai unbowing and uncowed at the gate. That night he built a tall gallows, on which he hoped to hang Mordecai for his insolence. But that night, the king was reminded that Mordecai had never been honored for once saving the king's life by exposing a plot among the palace guards. The next day, Haman was humiliated when the king asked him to honor Mordecai dramatically in public.

Haman's bad day only got worse at Esther's banquet that evening. After delighting the king with two lovely banquets, she finally revealed her request: She wanted the king to save her people from an evil man who wanted to destroy them. Bewildered, the king asked who that man might be. "This vile Haman," she replied. That night, in a gruesome irony, Haman hung by the neck on the gallows he built for Mordecai.

The Jews of Persia were still in danger. The king could not rescind his first sealed edict calling for the Jews' destruction, so instead he issued a second empowering the Jews to fight back. The Jews destroyed their enemies. Esther received Haman's large estate, and Mordecai received Haman's honored position at the king's court. In celebration of their deliverance, the Jews began an annual remembrance known as *Purim* (after the lots Haman had cast).

FASCINATING FACTS: Purim

Purim is celebrated every year on the 14th of the Jewish month of Adar. The day before Purim is a day of fasting. On Purim day, the rabbis read Book of Esther publicly. Each time Haman's name is mentioned (54 times), the listeners boo, hiss, rattle their graggers and stamp their feet. Some even write Haman's name on the soles of their shoes so that they can stamp on him.

After the reading, the celebrants distribute gifts to the poor and everyone enjoys a feast with abundant wine. Since Esther hid her Jewish identity from the king, dressing up in costumes has become a part of modern Purim celebrations. Some dress as characters from Esther, while some choose other Bible characters. Puppet shows and plays retell the Esther story for the children.

Hamantash cookies

Hamantash cookies are a popular Purim food. They are triangular cookies baked of dough filled with sweetened poppy seeds. They are often referred to as "Haman's ears" or "Haman's hat." The name "Hamantash" seems to refer to Haman, but origins and meanings of the cookies are uncertain. According to one tradition, Haman wore a three cornered hat. If he did, then eating an image of Haman's hat might be a symbol of the Jews' victory over him.

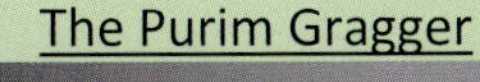

The Purim Gragger

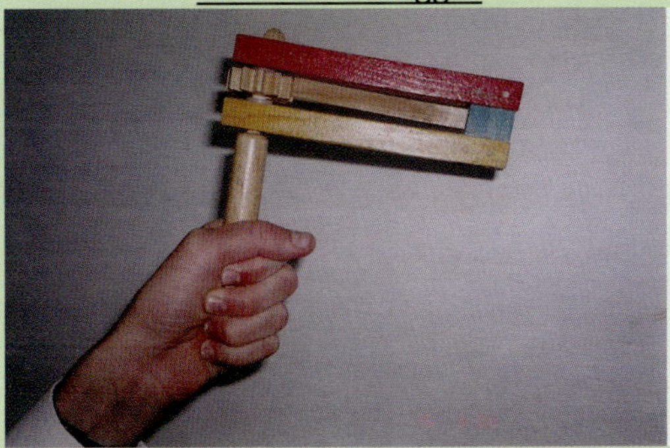

A Purim gragger is a noisemaker used during the annual reading of the story of Esther at Purim. Each time Haman's is mentioned, the Purim celebrants boo, hiss and swirl their graggers to display their low opinion of one of history's great villains.

The traditional Purim gragger has a fixed gear on an axle, its teeth meshed with a stiff board that swings around the axle. When the celebrants swing their axles, the board clacks against the gear teeth, making a loud racket that Haman no doubt hears from his place in deepest hell.

GEOGRAPHY FOCUS

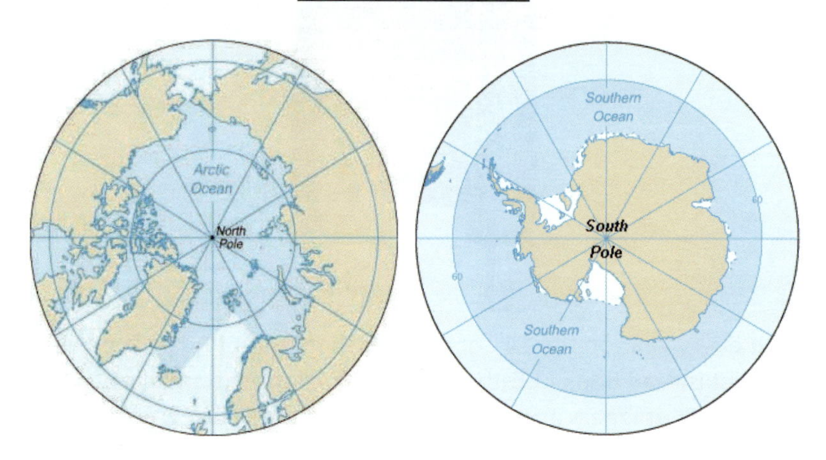

The Poles of the Earth

Did you know...

- The axis on which the earth rotates passes through the North and South Poles.
- The North Pole is the northernmost point on the globe. Its latitude is 90° north.
- The South Pole is the southernmost point on the globe. Its latitude is 90° south.
- The South Pole is dark 24 hours each day from April through September. From September through April, it is light 24 hours each day. The North Pole is light while the South Pole is dark, and vice versa.
- The climate at both poles is extremely cold.
- There is no land at the North Pole, but it is almost always covered with ice.
- The South Pole is located on the continent of Antarctica.
- The first humans to reach the North Pole were Robert Peary and Matthew Henson. The reached it in April 1909.
- The first human to reach the South Pole was Norwegian Roald Amundsen. He reached it in December 1911.

Chapter 23

Greek Gods and Greek Wars

ANCIENT HISTORY FOCUS

GREEK GODS AND GODDESSES

The principle gods of Greek mythology were the twelve Olympians who lived atop Mount Olympus. According to myth, these twelve gained supremacy among the gods after the strongest of them, Zeus, led his brothers and sisters to victory over their forebears, the Titans, in the Battle of the Titans.

FASCINATING FACTS: The Battle of the Titans

The Titans were 12 elder gods who ruled during the mythical Golden Age. They were the first children of Mother Earth, or Gaia. Mother Earth also bore three Cyclops (one-eyed) children and three monstrous sons. Her husband Uranus, the father of all Titans, was disgusted with these last six offspring, so he cast them into Tartarus, the lowest part of the underworld. Mother Earth was angry at this, so she gave her youngest son, Cronus, a sickle so that he could destroy her husband for his cruelty. Cronus did overcome his father, just as his mother wished; but then he refused to release his brothers from Tartarus.

This left Cronus as the chief Titan. His wife Rhea bore him five children, but he swallowed each of them in turn because a prophecy had warned him that his child would be his downfall. When his sixth child was born, Rhea hid the child and instead gave Cronus a stone to swallow. Her ploy succeeded: Cronus was fooled, and the sixth child, Zeus, lived and grew strong.

Seeking to free his three sisters and two brothers, Zeus fed Cronus a potion to make him vomit. Being immortal, they were all still alive in there; so when Cronus vomited, up they came. Then, wearing his aegis (breastplate) for protection, Zeus led his freed brothers and sisters against their father and cast him down into Tartarus. The victorious Zeus became the chief god.

The rest of the Titans rose up against Zeus and his siblings, and the Battle of the Titans began. Looking for more help, Zeus released the three Cyclops and the three monstrous brothers from Tartarus. After a long struggle, Zeus and his allies cast most of the Titans down into Tartarus, and Zeus and his siblings were set free to rule from Mount Olympus.

Although the Olympians always numbered twelve, fourteen different gods were recognized as Olympians at different times. The primary Olympians were Zeus and his wife Hera, Poseidon, Ares, Hermes, Hephaestus, Aphrodite, Athena, Apollo and Artemis. Hestia, Demeter, Dionysus and Hades were also known as Olympians at different times.

ZEUS (Roman name Jupiter)		Zeus, god of sky and rain, was the most powerful god. Zeus carried a thunderbolt, which he threw at anyone who displeased him. He was married to Hera, but he had other women as well. His symbols were the eagle and the thunderbolt.

HERA (Roman name Juno)		Hera was both wife and sister to Zeus, but they were not a happy couple. Zeus tricked Hera into marrying him by appearing to her as a hurt bird. When she held the bird to her breast in order to warm it, Zeus returned to his usual form. They married with much fanfare. Hera was jealous of Zeus's other women. She tried tying him up to keep him home, but he broke free and punished her. She never rebelled again, but she was always trying to outsmart him. Hera was the queen of the gods and the goddess of women, motherhood and marriage. Her symbols were the peacock and the cow.
POSEIDON (Roman name Neptune)		Mighty Poseidon, god of the sea and earthquakes, was second in power only to his brother Zeus. He carried a three-pronged spear known as a trident which shook the very earth when he used it (hence the earthquakes). Despite all of these advantages, Poseidon was moody, greedy and quarrelsome. Poseidon was considered the creator of horses. His symbols were the horse, the dolphin and the trident.
ARES (Roman name Mars)		Ares, the god of war, was a son of Zeus and Hera. Neither of his parents liked him, nor in fact did anyone else. Ares was a typical bully, cruel and cowardly. He often carried a bloody spear. He was such an unpopular god that no Greek city wanted him as its patron. His symbols were the vulture and the dog.
HERMES (Roman name Mercury)		Hermes, the messenger god, was a son of Zeus but not of Hera. As the fastest of the gods, he served as Zeus' messenger. He wore wings on his sandals and on his hat, and he carried a winged staff. Hermes was the only god who visited Heaven, Earth and the Underworld. He had a weakness for stealing, so he was also the god of thieves and commerce (apparently commerce cannot always be distinguished from theft).

HEPHAESTUS (Roman name Vulcan)		Hephaestus was considered a son of Zeus and Hera, but some myths say that Hera produced him alone. According to some, Hera was so disgusted with Hephaestus' ugliness that she threw him off of Mount Olympus, breaking his legs and rendering him permanently lame. Hephaestus was the god of fire and of iron, and he was often busy at his forge. Kind and peace loving, he was married to the beautiful Aphrodite. His symbols were fire, the axe and the hammer.
APHRODITE (Roman name Venus)		Aphrodite, the goddess of love, desire, beauty and fertility, was the most beautiful of the goddesses. Her origins were uncertain: She was either the daughter of Zeus and Dione (a Titan), or she was formed from the foam of the sea and rose out of the water on a shell. She was married to Hephaestus, but she also had a secret love affair with Ares. She became the mother of Eros (Roman name Cupid), who struck love into the hearts of humans with his arrows. Aphrodite was also the protector of sailors. Her symbols were the myrtle tree, the girdle and the dove.
APOLLO (Roman name Apollo)		The sun god Apollo was a son of Zeus, but not of Hera. Apollo had a twin sister named Artemis. Apollo's daily task was to harness his chariot with four horses and drive the sun across the sky. He was always depicted as handsome, youthful and strong. In addition to the sun, Apollo was also the god of music, healing, light, prophecy, poetry and truth. His symbols included the lyre, the crow and the laurel tree.
ATHENA (Roman name Minerva)		Athena, the goddess of wisdom, arts and strategy, was a daughter of Zeus but not of Hera. As Zeus' favorite, she was occasionally allowed to use his thunderbolt. Athena was the patron goddess of the city of Athens, named in her honor. The Athenians also built the famous Parthenon to honor her. Her symbols were the owl and the *aegis*, or warrior's breastplate.

ARTEMIS (Roman name Diana)		Artemis was the twin sister of Apollo, another daughter of Zeus but not of Hera. She was the goddess of the hunt, maidens and the moon. As a hunter, Artemis both killed and protected wild animals. She was also the protector of women in childbirth, but she herself was ever a virgin. Artemis was always depicted armed with her bow and silver arrows. Her symbols were the bow, the cypress and the deer.
HESTIA (Roman name Vesta)		Hestia was Zeus' sister. She was the goddess of home and hearth. The hearth had a special significance to the Greeks. In Greek homes, the hearth fire was never allowed to go out unless it was ritually extinguished. When any newborn child was born, it was presented to the hearth fire before it was received into the family. This gave Hestia a special place in the hearts of the Greeks. Hestia loved mortals so much that she gave up her place on Olympus to live among them. Dionysus took her place on Olympus. Hestia's symbol was fire.
DEMETER (Roman name Ceres)		Demeter was another sister of Zeus. She was the goddess of the harvest, fertility, nature and seasons. Demeter was considered the source of life and growth. She taught mortals how to cultivate the earth and grow food. Demeter usually wore a dark cloak. Her symbol was wheat.
DIONYSUS (Roman name Bacchus)		Dionysus, the god of wine and celebration, was the son of Zeus and a mortal princess named Semele. He did not live at Mount Olympus, but traveled around the world. He was a joyful god, willing to help whomever had need. He wore a wreath of ivy around his head and held a staff in his hand. His symbols were ivy, the snake and grapes.

HADES (Roman name Pluto)		Hades was the brother of Zeus. Despite his powerful pedigree, Hades did not live on Olympus. As god of the dead, Hades ruled the Underworld, where he lived with his helper Charon, the angel of death. It was Charon's job to ferry dead souls across the river Acheron (or the Styx in some stories) in his boat, from the land of the living to the land of the dead. Hades also had a three-headed dog named Cerberus, who guarded the entrance to the Underworld. Hades' symbol was his helmet, which rendered him invisible when he wore it.

FASCINATING FACTS: The Parthenon

The most famous surviving building of Ancient Greece is the Parthenon, which was built in Athens between 447 and 432 BC. The Parthenon was a temple built as a tribute to Athena, whom the Athenians credited with protecting their city throughout the Persian Wars. It was designed to house a 40-foot tall statue of the goddess. For almost one thousand years, the Parthenon stood as the most important temple of ancient Greek religion.

The Parthenon stands as an example of the very advanced thought of the Greeks. In the field of architecture, the Greeks considered every detail. The height and taper of the Parthenon's columns, the proportion and detail of their bases and capitals, the ratio of column height to the height of the beam (or *architrave*) above-- all of these were chosen for the most eye-catching effect possible. Greek architecture remains the standard to which all that follows must be compared.

INTERESTING INDIVIDUALS: Aesop's Fables

Little is known of Aesop, the author of the well-known collection of moral tales called *Aesop's Fables*. He was born a slave in Ancient Greece around 620 BC. His second master recognized his exceptional talent and set him free. He became well known and traveled extensively.

Aesop's high moral standards shortened his life. In his post as an ambassador, he was dispatched to distribute money to the citizens of Delphi. But he was appalled at their greedy behavior, and refused to give it to them. The good people of Delphi promptly executed him.

Aesop is credited with writing over 600 fables, but admiring imitators might have written some of these. Each fable was a simple story with a surprising ending and a one- or two-sentence "moral," or lesson, at the end. Aesop's best-known fables include "The Tortoise and the Hare," "Androcles and the Lion," "The Ants and the Grasshopper" and "The North Wind and the Sun."

AMAZING ANCIENTS: Three Greek Philosophers

The years between 470 and 320 BC were the heyday of three great Greek philosophers: Socrates, Plato and Aristotle.

Socrates lived during the Peloponnesian War and fought with the Athenians. Socrates' method of teaching was to ask difficult questions in order make his students think. These tough questions became known as "Socratic questions," and his question-and-answer teaching style became known as the "Socratic method." Socrates' students were the wealthy young sons of Athens.

But Socrates angered the Athenian authorities when his questions began to challenge Athenian democratic law, ritual and religion. Suspected of corrupting young minds, Socrates was accused of treason against the gods and found guilty. His sentence was death. In 399 BC he was ordered to drink a cup of poisonous hemlock in front of his students, which he calmly and bravely did.

Although he wasn't present for Socrates' suicide, **Plato** related the tale in his writings. Born into a wealthy and powerful family in Athens, Plato became Socrates' most famous student. Like Socrates, Plato questioned the idea of pure democracy on the basis that most people were not wise or educated enough to cast an intelligent vote.

Another Platonic notion, outlined in his well-known analogy called The Cave, was that everything humans see is only an imperfect representation of a perfect spiritual ideal. Trapped in imperfect material bodies, humans are unable to see the perfect ideal. Only the enlightened philosopher begins to understand the perfect ideal, and the unenlightened hate the philosopher because they only see the imperfect.

Plato established a school of philosophy called *The Academy*. It was one of the world's first universities, and surprisingly, it was open to both men and women.

Plato's best-known student at The Academy was **Aristotle**. The son of a doctor, Aristotle began attending the Academy around 350 BC. He was chosen to be the tutor of the royal prince Alexander, who later became known as Alexander the Great. As Alexander traveled throughout western Asia on his mission of conquest, he sent home samples of exotic plants for his former tutor to study.

Aristotle was a scientist as well as a philosopher, and he is considered the father of the modern scientific method. Aristotle established his own school of philosophy called *The Lyceum*. Like his two predecessors, Aristotle challenged Athenian democracy and advocated constitutional government. When Alexander died, Aristotle lost some of his protection. Like Socrates, he was accused of a lack of reverence for the gods. He had to leave Athens, and he died a year later.

Timeline of Persian and Greek History

Persian King	Bible Events	Greek Events
Darius I - 522-486 BC	Haggai/Zechariah Temple completed	490 BC Battle of Marathon (Persians defeated)
Xerxes - 486-464 BC	Esther	480 BC Battle of Thermopylae (Spartans defeated) 479 BC Battle of Salamis (Persians defeated)
Artaxerxes I - 464-423 BC	Ezra/Nehemiah Malachi	461-431 BC Age of Pericles Athens rules 431-404 BC Peloponnesian Wars
Darius II - 423-404 BC	Biblical Silence	Peloponnesian Wars continue Sparta rules
Artaxerxes II - 404-359 BC		

Artaxerxes III - 359-338 BC		338 BC Battle of Chaeronea (Philip II defeats Greeks)
Arses 338-335 BC		
Darius III - 335 - 331 BC		336-323 BC Persian Empire overthrown by Alexander the Great

THE PELOPONNESIAN WARS

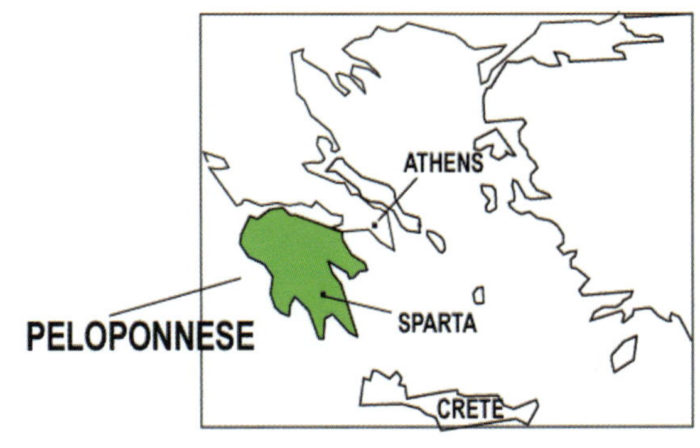

After the Persian Wars, Greek city-states Sparta and Athens parted ways. The Athenians rebuilt their burned-out city and formed an alliance with several smaller city-states called the Delian League. Because of its naval superiority, Athens was the natural head of the Delian League. Later, under the commander Pericles, Athens began to dominate the Delian League. Sparta chose to join a different league, the Peloponnesian League.

INTERESTING INDIVIDUALS: Pericles

Pericles commanded Athens for almost forty years, from 461 to 429 BC. Under his leadership, Athens reached its pinnacle. The Delian League, which had been a cooperative alliance of Greek city-states, became an Athenian empire under Pericles. The smaller city-states paid tribute to Athens, which used the funds to bolster its own wealth and prosperity. Pericles's time in power became known as a Greek golden age, the "Age of Pericles."

Under Pericles, Athens became the cultural and educational center of the Greek world. Pericles used tribute money from the other city-states to build the Acropolis, a fortified city center that lay on Athens' highest hill. The Parthenon, Athena's famous temple, dominated the city from its high place in the Acropolis. Pericles also fortified the city walls. When the league's smaller city-states tried to rebel, Athens was able to keep them in check.

Pericles was a great advocate of democracy and a great speechmaker. His inspired speeches kept him close to the hearts of Athens' people.

The *Peloponnese* is the name of a large peninsula in southern Greece (green area), of which Sparta was part. As Athens grew more powerful, the smaller city-states began to feel bullied. Sparta watched from a distance as Athens prospered and built up its walls of defense. Sparta suffered worse luck: a devastating earthquake in 464 BC brought the city to the ground and killed thousands. This was followed by a revolt of the Helots (conquered peoples enslaved by the Spartans). When Athens offered military assistance against the revolt, Sparta refused. Soon after this, in 460 BC, war broke out between the Delian League (led by Athens) and the Peloponnesian League (led by Sparta). This First Peloponnesian War carried on until 447, when Sparta and Athens signed a peace treaty.

Fifteen years later, Sparta accused Athens of violating that treaty. A smaller city-state named Corcyra was trying to break free of another city-state, Corinth. Since Corcyra was not a part of either league, Athens felt free to answer Corcyra's call for aid. But Sparta considered Corinth an ally, so Athens' interference was regarded as an act of war. This new war was called the Peloponnesian War, and it dragged on for 28 years, from 431-404 BC. This was the most important of the Peloponnesian Wars.

Although Athens had the stronger navy, Sparta had superior land forces. Pericles' strategy was to fight a defensive war against Sparta. Since Sparta was ceaselessly paranoid about maintaining control of its conquered slaves, the Helots, Pericles believed that Sparta would not be able to manage an extended siege. If Athens could keep the Spartans outside its walls, he thought, Sparta would give up and retreat. Pericles therefore holed his people up inside his city walls and prepared to wait the Spartans out. Despite the Spartans' provocations, including the burning of Athenian farms and forests, the Athenians listened to Pericles and remained within their walls.

Pericles' strategy was a good one, but it failed to consider one possibility: infectious disease. In the second year of the siege, 429 BC, a plague swept through the confined population of Athens. One-fourth of its people died, including Athens' brilliant commander, Pericles.

The Peloponnesian War dragged on for years with little movement either way, as each side tried to wear the other down. Around 421 BC, Athens and Sparta negotiated a peace treaty called the Peace of Nicias. This peace lasted until 413 BC, when Athens attacked Sicily. This disastrous move cost Athens most of its naval fleet. Sparta took advantage of Athens' loss and attacked. By 405 BC, Sparta had eliminated the rest of the Athenian fleet and defeated Athens. Athens surrendered in 404 BC, and Sparta ruled Greece.

FASCINATING FACTS: Greek Mosaics

A *mosaic* is any work of art built up of small tiles. The Greeks created mosaics out of *tessera* (small pieces of stone, glass or pebbles), combining them in patterns. The earliest mosaics were cone mosaics (see Chapter 6), in which early builders created patterns by pushing colored stone cones into wet plaster. By 700 BC, builders paved floors and streets in mosaic patterns by pushing colored pebbles into pavements.

Around 400 BC, the Greeks raised the art of the mosaic to a new level. They covered their floors with elaborate mosaic patterns and framed the entire pattern with tiny black pebbles. They used tesserae to create complex scenes of animals and people, as well as precise geometric patterns.

By 300 BC, the Greeks were manufacturing glass mosaic tiles in a wide range of colors. This enabled them to create intricate wall mosaics that resembled paintings.

BIBLE FOCUS

PERSIA

While the Peloponnesian Wars raged in Greece, Persia had two different kings. After Xerxes I was assassinated (see Chapter 22), his son Artaxerxes I killed both of his brothers to cement his claim and seized the throne in 464 BC.

AMAZING ANCIENTS: Artaxerxes I (ruled Persia from 464-423 BC)

Artaxerxes I was also known as *Longimanus*, Latin for *long hand*, apparently because his right hand was much longer than his left. Artaxerxes' first tasks were to contain two rebellions against Persia, the 460 BC revolt of Egypt (which coincided with the First Peloponnesian War and was encouraged by Athens) and the 448 BC revolt of Syria.

Artaxerxes I kept alive the old flame of malice against Athens lit by his father Xerxes and his grandfather Darius I. Seeking to dethrone Athens from its position of power, he used his wealth to fund Athens' enemies in Greece. His meddling helped to weaken Athens and contributed to the general unrest that sparked the Peloponnesian Wars.

Artaxerxes I is best known, though, for his Biblical role of allowing the return of the exiled Jews of Judah. When Persia absorbed the Babylonian Empire, it inherited exiles from many of Babylon's conquered realms, but Persia's attitude toward the exiles was different. Persia allowed Judah's Jews to return home and rebuild the Temple and the walls of Jerusalem. Artaxerxes I's name appears numerous times in the Bible books of Ezra and Nehemiah.

After Ezra, Nehemiah and Artaxerxes, the Bible falls silent for the next four hundred years. It resumes its tale in the New Testament with the main event of all time: the birth, life, death and resurrection of Jesus Christ.

SCRIPTURE SPOTLIGHT: EZRA, NEHEMIAH AND THE WALLS OF JERUSALEM

Although the Bible books of Ezra and Nehemiah are separate in English versions, in Hebrew Bibles they appear as one. Together, these books tell the story of the return of Judah's exiles, the rebuilding of the Temple and the restoring of Jerusalem's city walls. Ezra and Nehemiah's stories stretch through the reigns of four Persian kings: Cyrus the Great, Darius I, Xerxes (story of Esther) and Artaxerxes I. The Jews rebuild their Temple during the reigns of Cyrus and Darius I (see Chapter 21, Ezra 1-6). It is during Artaxerxes' reign that both Ezra and Nehemiah return to Jerusalem and restore the city walls.

In 458 BC, Artaxerxes allowed Ezra to return to Jerusalem so that he could teach and lead the Jewish nation. Ezra carried with him a group of Jewish exiles, a letter from Artaxerxes granting him safe passage and a claim on the royal treasury to fund his endeavors. In his letter, Artaxerxes wrote:

"And you, Ezra, in accordance with the wisdom of your God, which you possess, appoint magistrates and judges to administer justice to all the people of Trans-Euphrates—all who know the laws of your God. And you are to teach any who do not know them. Whoever does not obey the law of your God and the law of the king must surely be punished by death, banishment, confiscation of property, or imprisonment" (Ezra 7: 25-27).

When Ezra arrived back in Jerusalem, he immediately faced the problem of the intermarriage of Jews with all sorts of foreigners. The chaste and law-abiding Ezra was shocked to find that many returned exiles had married foreign wives:

"O my God, I am too ashamed and disgraced to lift up my face to you, my God, because our sins are higher than our heads and our guilt has reached to the heavens. From the days of our forefathers until now,

our guilt has been great. Because of our sins, we and our kings and our priests have been subjected to the sword and captivity, to pillage and humiliation at the hand of foreign kings, as it is today.

"But now, for a brief moment, the LORD our God has been gracious in leaving us a remnant and giving us a firm place in his sanctuary, and so our God gives light to our eyes and a little relief in our bondage. Though we are slaves, our God has not deserted us in our bondage. He has shown us kindness in the sight of the kings of Persia: He has granted us new life to rebuild the house of our God and repair its ruins, and he has given us a wall of protection in Judah and Jerusalem" (Ezra 9:6-9).

When the men of Judah saw Ezra's distress, they realized their sin. They had failed to remain a people set apart for God. Together, they decided to divorce their foreign wives and send away the children of these sinful unions.

"While Ezra was praying and confessing, weeping and throwing himself down before the house of God, a large crowd of Israelites—men, women and children—gathered around him. They too wept bitterly. Then Shecaniah son of Jehiel, one of the descendants of Elam, said to Ezra, "We have been unfaithful to our God by marrying foreign women from the peoples around us. But in spite of this, there is still hope for Israel. Now let us make a covenant before our God to send away all these women and their children, in accordance with the counsel of my lord and of those who fear the commands of our God. Let it be done according to the Law. Rise up; this matter is in your hands. We will support you, so take courage and do it" (Ezra 10: 2-4).

Back in Persia, Artaxerxes I had a Jewish cupbearer named Nehemiah. Nehemiah was faithful to Artaxerxes, but he was also faithful to the God of Judah. In a letter from one of his brothers, Nehemiah learned that Jerusalem was unprotected because her walls were broken down. He was deeply concerned, and couldn't hide his distress when he went in to serve the king.

Artaxerxes I noticed Nehemiah's downcast face and asked him what troubled him. Nehemiah told him about the situation in Jerusalem, and Artaxerxes immediately agreed to send Nehemiah to Jerusalem so that he could oversee the rebuilding of Jerusalem's walls. Nehemiah promised to return when the work was complete.

After he arrived in Jerusalem, Nehemiah spent three days studying the problem of the walls before he revealed his mission to the city leaders. These leaders gladly approved his desire to rebuild the city walls.

Once the rebuilding began, though, opposition arose from the Samaritans, the Edomites and even some Jews. In order to protect his wall builders, Nehemiah had to place half of his men on guard duty while the other half rebuilt the walls. After fifty-two days, Jerusalem's city walls were once again in decent repair.

With the walls finished, Ezra read the Book of the Law of Moses to the returned exiles:

"Ezra opened the book. All the people could see him because he was standing above them; and as he opened it, the people all stood up. Ezra praised the LORD, the great God; and all the people lifted their hands and responded, "Amen! Amen!" Then they bowed down and worshiped the LORD with their faces to the ground.

"The Levites...instructed the people in the Law while the people were standing there. They read from the Book of the Law of God, making it clear and giving the meaning so that the people could understand what was being read.

"Then Nehemiah the governor, Ezra the priest and scribe, and the Levites who were instructing the people said to them all, "This day is sacred to the LORD your God. Do not mourn or weep." For all the people had been weeping as they listened to the words of the Law.

"Nehemiah said, "Go and enjoy choice food and sweet drinks, and send some to those who have nothing prepared. This day is sacred to our Lord. Do not grieve, for the joy of the LORD is your strength" (Nehemiah 8: 5-10).

After Artaxerxes I died in 423 BC, his son Xerxes II took the throne, but he only held it for a month, and then his brother assassinated him (If you were shocked when Artaxerxes I killed his two brothers, now you know why!). Then Xerxes II's murderous brother was himself murdered by another brother, Darius II, who proceeded to purge the Persian kingdom of any who could challenge his right to the throne.

Darius II continued his father's policy of support for Sparta in the Peloponnesian War. He also regained some of the cities that Persia had lost to the enemy Athens. Darius II died in 404 BC and was succeeded by his son Artaxerxes II, just as Sparta was dealing Athens its final defeat.

SCRIPTURE SPOTLIGHT: Malachl

Malachl, wrote his book of prophecy, the last book in the Old Testament, after the returning Jewish exiles rebuilt the Temple. His preaching addressed the Jews' indifference about spiritual matters and called them to repentance. If God's people would return to Him, Malachi said, God would bless them:

"Bring the whole tithe into the storehouse, that there may be food in my house. Test me in this," says the LORD Almighty, "and see if I will not throw open the floodgates of heaven and pour out so much blessing that you will not have room enough for it. I will prevent pests from devouring your crops, and the vines in your fields will not cast their fruit," says the LORD Almighty. "Then all the nations will call you blessed, for yours will be a delightful land," says the LORD Almighty" (Malachi 3: 10-12).

GEOGRAPHY FOCUS

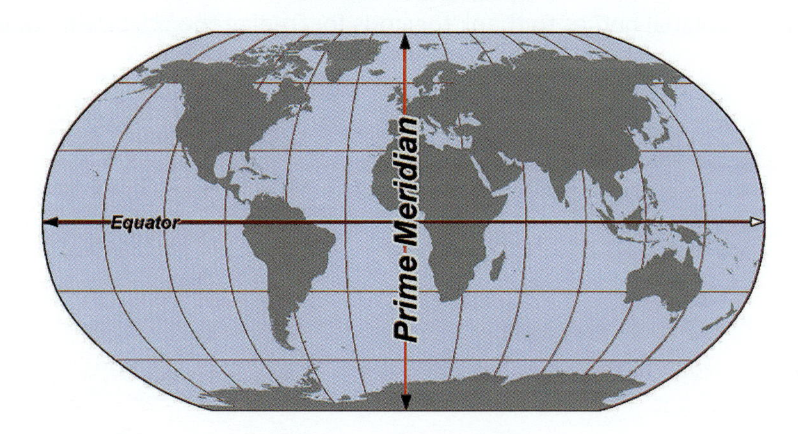

Longitude and Latitude

Did you know...
- Any point on the globe can be located precisely by its latitude and longitude.

Longitude:
- Longitude lines, or meridians, run from north to south.
- Longitude is always measured east or west of the prime meridian, which marks 0° longitude.

- There are 180 longitude lines east of the prime meridian and 180 longitude lines west of the prime meridian.
- All meridians run from the North Pole to the South Pole. Unlike latitude lines, which never intersect, longitude lines all intersect at the North and South Poles.

Latitude:

- Latitude lines, or parallels, run east to west.
- Latitude is always measured north or south of the equator, which marks 0° latitude.
- There are 90 latitude lines north of the equator and 90 latitude lines south of the equator. The North Pole is at 90 degrees north latitude, and the South Pole is at 90 degrees south latitude.
- Latitude lines are parallel; they never intersect.

FASCINATING FACTS: Mount Olympus

Mount Olympus is the highest mountain range in Greece. It has 52 peaks. In Greek mythology, Mount Olympus was the home of the twelve Olympians. The entrance to the gods' hidden home on Olympus was said to be guarded by a gate of clouds. According to legend, the Cyclops children of Gaia and Uranus built the gods' beautiful city and its twelve palatial homes to thank the gods for freeing them from the underworld, Tartarus.

Chapter 24

Alexander the Great's Reign

ANCIENT HISTORY FOCUS

Timeline of Persian and Greek History

Persian King	Bible Events	Greek Events
Darius I - 522-486 BC	Haggai/Zechariah Temple completed	490 BC Battle of Marathon (Persians defeated)
Xerxes - 486-464 BC	Esther	480 BC Battle of Thermopylae (Spartans defeated) 479 BC Battle of Salamis (Persians defeated)
Artaxerxes I - 464-423 BC	Ezra/Nehemiah Malachi	461-431 BC Age of Pericles Athens rules 431-404 BC Peloponnesian Wars
Darius II - 423-404 BC	Biblical Silence	Peloponnesian Wars continue Sparta rules
Artaxerxes II - 404-359 BC		
Artaxerxes III - 359-338 BC		338 BC Battle of Chaeronea (Philip II defeats Greeks)
Arses 338-335 BC		
Darius III - 335 - 331 BC		336-323 BC Persian Empire overthrown by Alexander the Great

THE CONQUEST OF GREECE

After its victory over Greece in the Peloponnesian Wars, Sparta emerged as the dominant military power in Greece. But military power is not the same as political power. The strict discipline of Sparta was not popular elsewhere in Greece. The long Peloponnesian Wars had left all of Greece weakened and ripe for conquest.

In Macedonia, a northern region of Greece, a man named King Philip II dreamed of uniting all of Greece under one flag and then moving against Persia. He began by bringing the surrounding Greek city-states under his power.

AMAZING ANCIENTS: Philip II of Macedonia

Philip II came to power in Macedonia in 359 BC. When Prince Philip was born, Macedonia was a struggling country, surviving by paying tribute to the Illyrians (who lived northwest of Macedonia). Philip's father the king died when Philip was very young, and his older brother Alexander II took the throne. Soon after this, Alexander II was assassinated by his mother's lover, a man named Ptolemy. The second son, Perdikkas, who was also very young, assumed the throne with Ptolemy as his regent. When Perdikkas was old enough to rule independently, he killed his regent Ptolemy (perhaps he remembered what Ptolemy had done to his brother).

During all of this time, poor Philip was held hostage in the city-states to which Macedon paid tribute, first in Illyrium, then in Thebes. But even though he was a captive, he was still treated like royalty. He had great opportunity to learn about warfare, politics and foreign cultures. Finally, Perdikkas was able to negotiate Philip's release, and Philip returned to Macedonia.

When Perdikkas died, his young son Amyntas inherited the throne of Macedonia, and Philip II served as his regent. Soon, however, Philip was reigning in his own right. When Philip's son Alexander III was born, Philip had the heir he needed to proclaim his own dynasty. Philip hired the great Greek philosopher Aristotle as a tutor for Alexander (see picture).

Philip II expanded his kingdom with a combination of military power and political maneuvering. He created alliances and purchased loyalty through his many marriages. By 336 BC, when he had been in power for 23 years, Philip II felt ready to begin his campaign against Persia. Ironically, he was assassinated at his own going-away party just as he planned to depart for Asia.

Philip II's successor was his son Alexander III, who became known as Alexander the Great.

ALEXANDER THE GREAT

Phillip II's assassination came when Alexander was twenty years old. Although he was still quite young, he already had experience as a military commander, and he had already gained the respect of his soldiers for his bravery. Upon ascending his father's throne, he set out to purge the kingdom of potential enemies and rivals for the throne. The assassination of his father had cast the kingdom into chaos, and Alexander had to work quickly to restore order.

His next task was to fulfill his father's dream of conquering Persia. His success was absolutely remarkable. Against overwhelming odds, Alexander led his armies into Asia Minor (modern-day Turkey), Syria and Egypt. By the age of 25, he had conquered all of these countries. This son of an exiled prince was now the king of Persia and the pharaoh of Egypt.

Alexander used his military genius to pursue his quest to control the world's largest empire. His territory expanded on three continents: north into Europe as far as the Danube (the map shows the Danube river), south into Egypt and east into Asia as far as India.

Unfortunately, Alexander's constant warring and conquest left him little time for anything else. In 323 BC, at Nebuchadnezzar's former palace in Babylon, Alexander died-- perhaps from an illness such as malaria, perhaps from poison-- at the age of thirty-two. His son Alexander IV had not yet been born, and he had no obvious heir; so his generals began to fight among themselves. Generals Ptolemy, Seleucus and Lysimachus (among others) fought the *Wars of the Diadochi* (*successors*) to decide who would control Alexander's empire. These wars were long and complex, carrying on in various forms for around 50 years after Alexander's death. Territory changed hands again and again. In the end, Ptolemy controlled Egypt, Lysimachus controlled Greece and Macedonia, and Seleucus controlled modern Israel, Syria, Iran, Iraq and Afghanistan.

This period of history, the time immediately following the death of Alexander the Great, is called the Hellenistic Period (*Hellenistic* means *Greek* or *Greek-influenced*). After Alexander unified most of the known world under the control of the Greeks, Greek culture and influence began to spread freely throughout Asia, Africa and Europe. Greek became the official language throughout the empire, and the entire region was united through trade and commerce.

HISTORIC HORSES: Bucephalus

Bucephalus was Alexander the Great's war horse. He was a huge black horse of tremendous strength, and he apparently had an overly large head (his name means "ox-head"). He may have had a white star on his forehead.

Alexander was around ten years old when he first rode Bucephalus, and from that time on the two were inseparable. Alexander rode the great horse into countless victories throughout most of the known world. Bucephalus finally died at Alexander's last battle in 326 BC, just three years before Alexander himself died. To honor his great horse, Alexander founded a new city in modern Pakistan and named it Bucephalus.

FASCINATING FACTS: The Gordian Knot

Once upon a time, according to an ancient Greek legend, a poor peasant named Gordius drove his ox cart into the public square of the city-state of Phrygia. At the time, Phrygia had recently lost its king. An oracle told the Phrygians that they must make the first person who rode into their city square in a wagon their new king. So when the Phrygians saw Gordius arriving in his cart, they obediently made him their king.

King Gordius gratefully dedicated his ox cart to Zeus and made it into a shrine. To secure his shrine in place, he tied the cart to a pole using a highly intricate knot that somehow left no rope ends exposed. Hundreds of interwoven thongs made the knot a centerpiece for the shrine. Over time, the weather hardened the knot until it became impossible to untie. A legend grew around the Gordian Knot, saying that whoever finally untied the Gordian Knot would become king over all of Asia.

Alexander the Great heard the legend of the Gordian Knot, and he very much wanted to be king over all of Asia. In 333 BC, Alexander the Great went to Phrygia and cut the knot with his sword. The fact that he cheated rather badly seems not to have mattered. Alexander did in fact became king over the known part of Asia.

Nowadays, the term *Gordian Knot* refers to any impossibly complicated situation or conundrum.

AMAZING ANCIENTS: Hippocrates

The ancient Greek Hippocrates is revered as the founder of medical science. Born in 460 BC in Greece, he may have learned medicine from his father. Hippocrates was the first physician to keep records of patients' symptoms and the progressions of their illnesses. In this way he was able to determine which symptoms went with which ailments and to prescribe treatments based on the observed symptoms. Like any good doctor, his prescriptions included rest, good food, fresh air and strategies for pain relief. He also believed in cleanliness and in allowing the body to heal itself.

In Hippocrates' day, people commonly believed that illness came because one had angered the gods or was demon possessed. When someone grew ill, his or her family took him to the temple and offered prayers and sacrifices for his healing. Hippocrates' method was different. After his close observation of many cases, he came to believe that most illness came from natural causes rather than heavenly ones.

Hippocrates also developed a code of ethics for doctors, embodied in what became known as the *Hippocratic Oath*. Doctors still pledge a form of this oath today before they begin medical practice. Much of Hippocrates' original oath has been removed, but medical doctors still pledge to "do no harm."

The Hippocratic Oath

I swear by Apollo, the healer, Asclepius, Hygieia, and Panacea, and I take to witness all the gods, all the goddesses, to keep according to my ability and my judgment, the following Oath and agreement:

To consider dear to me, as my parents, him who taught me this art; to live in common with him and, if necessary, to share my goods with him;

To look upon his children as my own brothers, to teach them this art.

I will prescribe regimens for the good of my patients according to my ability and my judgment and **never do harm to anyone**.

I will not give a lethal drug to anyone if I am asked, nor will I advise such a plan; and similarly I will not give a woman a pessary to cause an abortion.

But I will preserve the purity of my life and my arts.

I will not cut for stone, even for patients in whom the disease is manifest; I will leave this operation to be performed by practitioners, specialists in this art.

In every house where I come I will enter only for the good of my patients, keeping myself far from all intentional ill-doing and all seduction and especially from the pleasures of love with women or with men, be they free or slaves.

All that may come to my knowledge in the exercise of my profession or in daily commerce with men, which ought not to be spread abroad, I will keep secret and will never reveal.

If I keep this oath faithfully, may I enjoy my life and practice my art, respected by all men and in all times; but if I swerve from it or violate it, may the reverse be my lot.

AMAZING ANCIENTS: Archimedes

Archimedes is considered the greatest mathematician in an age of great mathematicians. He was also a physicist, scientist, engineer, astronomer (like his father) and inventor. He was born in 287 BC in Syracuse, Sicily, which was an independent Greek city-state at the time.

Archimedes' power of concentration was legendary. He had the ability to shut out the world's distractions and bring his entire considerable mind to bear on whatever problem he was studying. But this power, enviable as it was, had its drawbacks. After Syracuse was overrun by the Romans, soldiers were turned loose in the streets to pillage. Archimedes was also in the streets, working on some problem by drawing figures in the sand. When a soldier asked him who he was, he worried that the soldier might trample his figures and ruin them, so he replied, "I beg you, don't disturb this." The soldier did not consider this an adequate response, so he killed Archimedes.

These are some of Archimedes' accomplishments:

- Derived the formula for the volume of a sphere (4/3 Pi times the radius cubed)
- Developed the principle of buoyancy, Archimedes' Principle (Buoyant force is equal to the weight of the volume of the fluid displaced)
- Invented the Archimedean screw, a type of water pump
- Invented the compound pulley system
- Designed war machines used in the defense of Syracuse
- Discovered the laws of levers and pulleys
- Devised mirrors to focus sunlight on the sails of enemy ships in order to set them ablaze (although some doubt that this ever really worked)

FASCINATING FACTS: THE SEVEN WONDERS OF THE ANCIENT WORLD

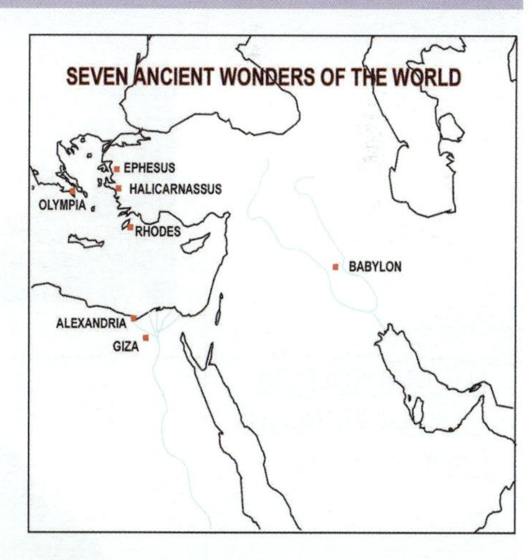

Since ancient times, there has been a list of seven "wonders," manmade objects so grand that they inspire wonder in all who see them. The items on the list have changed over the years as people argued over which items should make the cut.

The original list of seven ancient wonders was compiled by historians of ancient Greece. It included the seven most magnificent structures known to the ancient Greeks. Of these original seven, only the Great Pyramid of Giza survives, and even it is much diminished in appearance (though not in size). These are the Seven Wonders of the Ancient World:

GREAT PYRAMID OF GIZA (Giza):		See Chapter 8

THE HANGING GARDENS OF BABYLON (Babylon):		See Chapter 20
THE STATUE OF ZEUS (Olympia):		Built at the city of Olympia to honor the Olympic Games and Zeus, the Greeks' mightiest god, the Statue of Zeus was an immense likeness made of ivory and gold-plated bronze, inlaid with precious gems. It is believed to have been about 40 feet high and 22 feet wide. In Zeus's right hand was the figure of Nike, goddess of victory; and in his left was a scepter with an eagle on top. The throne upon which Zeus sat was carved with images of Greek gods and mystical animals. The means of its destruction are uncertain, but it may have been beheaded by the Roman emperor Caligula so that he could replace Zeus's head with a likeness of his own.
THE TEMPLE OF ARTEMIS (Ephesus):		Built at the city of Ephesus to honor Artemis, the virginal huntress and sister of Apollo, the Temple of Artemis was a large and lofty edifice supposedly crafted entirely of marble. It was destroyed several times, but it was always rebuilt on the same site. During the time of Alexander the Great the temple was 425 feet long, 225 feet wide and 60 feet high. The ravaging Goths finally destroyed it for the last time around 200 BC.
THE MAUSOLEUM OF HALICARNASSUS (Halicarnassus):		Halicarnassus was a city in Asia Minor. The Mausoleum of Halicarnassus was the grand tomb of King Mausolus, a king of Halicarnassus who died in 353 BC. His wife, Queen Artemisia, was broken-hearted when he died, so she decided to commemorate him with the most extravagant tomb imaginable. It was eventually destroyed by earthquakes. The tomb took the name *Mausoleum* from its inhabitant, King Mausolus. It was so grand that it became the standard for all such tombs, and now many tombs and monuments are known as *mausoleums*.

THE COLOSSUS OF RHODES (Rhodes):		Rhodes is an island in the Aegean Sea. Alexander the Great conquered Rhodes in 332 BC, but when he died, the generals who divided Alexander's kingdom fought over the island. The people of Rhodes supported General Ptolemy, but another general attacked the island. Ptolemy came to Rhodes' aid and drove the invaders off. To commemorate this victory, the people of Rhodes decided to use the enormous amount of weaponry left behind by the invaders to create a statue of their patron god, Helios. Built astride their harbor in a forbidding pose as if to ward off invaders, the statue stood over 100 feet high, and was covered with bronze plates. An earthquake destroyed the Colossus 56 years after its completion.
THE PHAROS OF ALEXANDRIA (Alexandria):		Alexandria is a city on the Mediterranean coast of Egypt. The terrain around the port is flat, without landmarks visible from the sea; so on the island of Pharos, just off the coast, Ptolemy built a huge lighthouse to guide ships into port. Built around 300 BC, the Lighthouse of Alexandria stood about 400 feet tall, which made it the ancient world's third tallest structure (behind two great pyramids). Supposedly, its light was visible from distances up to 35 miles. It has also been suggested that its light could be focused to burn enemy ships, although this seems doubtful. An earthquake severely damaged the lighthouse around 1300 AD, and its ruins were incorporated into another structure.

FASCINATING FACTS: Greek Masks

The ancient Greeks loved drama and theatrical plays, and actors in their productions commonly used masks made of wood, cloth or leather. Although the masks themselves have not survived the ages, pictures of such masks appear on Greek pottery and mosaics.

Stage actors wore masks for several reasons:

- Greek women were not allowed to appear on stage, so men had to play any female roles.
- With multiple masks, a single actor could play many roles.
- Masks could give a grand appearance to any god characters, who figured prominently in Greek drama.
- The masks conveyed emotion. The mask faces wore exaggerated grins or scowls so that distant audience members could understand a character's feelings.

FASCINATING FACTS: The Greek Aspis

The Greek Aspis was the large round wooden shield used by the hoplites (Greek infantry). The aspis was also known as a *hoplon*. The shield was made of wood covered with leather or, later, bronze. The cover was decorated with art that honored the gods or the warrior's city-state. The hoplites held their aspis using an armband at the center and a handle at the edge. The aspis was an excellent defensive weapon.

GEOGRAPHY FOCUS

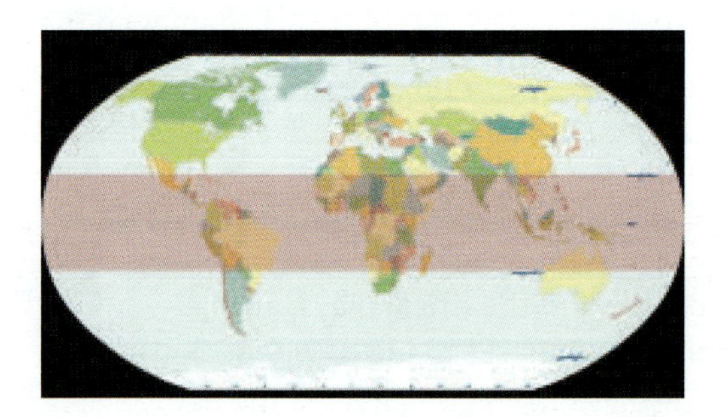

The Tropics

Did you know...

- The warm region near the equator is called the Tropics. The Tropics lie between the Tropic of Cancer and the Tropic of Capricorn.
- The Tropic of Cancer's latitude is a little over 23° N (This angle equals the angle of the earth's tilt on its axis of rotation). During the Northern Hemisphere's summer solstice (June 20-21), the sun is directly over the Tropic of Cancer. This is the northernmost point the sun reaches.
- The Tropic of Capricorn's latitude is a little over 23° south. During the Southern Hemisphere's summer solstice (December 20-21), the sun is directly over the Tropic of Capricorn. This is the southernmost point the sun reaches.

Chapter 25

China

ANCIENT HISTORY FOCUS

CHINA

The Xia Dynasty (reigned 2205 - 1766 BC, dates are disputed)

The Xia Dynasty was the first Chinese dynasty, and it reigned from 2205-1766 BC (see Chapter 12).

The Shang Dynasty (reigned 1766 - 1122 BC, dates are disputed)

The Shang Dynasty was the second Chinese dynasty, and it reigned from 1766-1122 BC (see Chapter 12).

The Zhou Dynasty (reigned 1122 - 221 BC, dates are disputed)

The Zhou Dynasty conquered the Shang Dynasty and took its place.

The Zhou Dynasty was the longest-lived Chinese dynasty (1122-221 BC). The Zhou created a new system of governance, their own version of the feudal system. The immense size of their territory forced the Zhou to divide their holdings into hundreds of smaller territories, each with its own leader or feudal lord. After the lords in the feudal hierarchy came the soldiers, then the peasants and finally the slaves. As the Chinese civilization continued to expand, these feudal lords began to break away and seek independence.

In coming to power, the Zhou taught their subjects a doctrine called the *Mandate of Heaven*. According to this doctrine, the Zhou had a right to replace the kings of the Shang Dynasty because this was the will of heaven.

FASCINATING FACTS: The Mandate of Heaven

The doctrine of the Mandate of Heaven says that Heaven places its mandate to rule, or official approval, on a family that is morally worthy of the responsibility. In other words, as long as the Zhou acted as good and moral rulers, they had the Mandate of Heaven. If, however, they became immoral and self-seeking, then the Zhou would lose the throne and another family would receive heaven's mandate to rule China. The reason the Zhou were able to conquer the Shang dynasty, according to this doctrine, was that the Shang had become morally degenerate.

Historians have divided the time of the Zhou Dynasty into two periods, Western Zhou and Eastern Zhou. Western Zhou, when the Zhou ruled primarily in western China, lasted from 1122 to 771 BC.

Around 771 BC, barbarians (Mongols) from the north attacked and killed the Zhou king. His surviving son moved the entire capital east, and this began the period known as the Eastern Zhou. During the Eastern Zhou period, the Chinese began to formulate new doctrines and philosophies. Three main schools of thought arose during Eastern Zhou: Confucianism, Taoism and Legalism (see below).

The Eastern Zhou period is further divided into two sub-periods, the Spring and Autumn Period and the Warring States Period.

The Spring and Autumn Period (771-476 BC): This was a period of political upheaval, but also a time of prosperity. The beginning of the Iron Age fell during the Spring and Autumn Period. The use of iron tools boosted agriculture, improving the food supply and therefore the population. Communication improved through the use of horses, and the Zhou built palaces and encouraged the arts.

Later, the various feudal lords squabbled with one another, seeking dominance. Larger lords took over the territories of smaller lords, so there were fewer territories and fewer lords. By the close of the Spring and Autumn Period, the territories had virtually disappeared. Only a handful of lords remained, and a few of their states declared independence from China and the Zhou Dynasty. The Zhou kings lost most of their power.

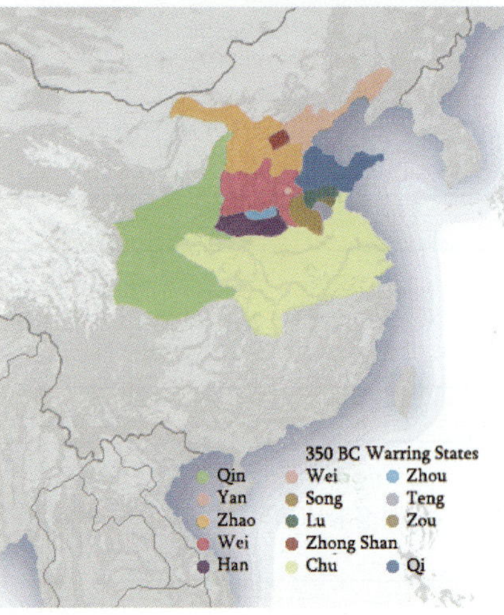

The Warring States Period (475-221 BC): During the Warring States Period, chaos reigned in China as the six remaining territorial lords warred with one another. Massive armies moved against one another in lengthy, vicious battles. The Warring States Period lasted for over 200 years. By 221 BC, the Qin Kingdom was the last kingdom standing, and the Qin Dynasty begun.

Chinese Philosophy

Between 403-221 BC, an intellectual movement swept across China. The three prominent philosophies that emerged from this movement were Confucianism, Taoism and Legalism.

Confucianism

Confucius (551-479 BC) was a Chinese philosopher who lived about five hundred years before Christ. His father died when he was a toddler, but he was still able to obtain an education. After his mother died, he began his career as a teacher. In those days, Chinese teachers Like Confucius were *itinerant*, traveling around and teaching their beliefs to groups of disciples who followed them.

Confucius' time was the Warring States Period of the Eastern Zhou Period (see below), a time when China was in chaos. Confucius was dismayed by the warring leaders' total disregard for human life, and he came to believe that China should revert to the ideals of the Mandate of Heaven taught by the early Zhou Dynasty. According to Confucius, good morals and virtues made good leaders and good men. He believed that men are basically good, and he taught that anyone could attain virtue through well-defined patterns of right behavior.

For more on Confucius, see Companion year 3 Chapter 25.

Some Confucian quotes to ponder:

- "Forget injuries, never forget kindnesses."
- "It does not matter how slowly you go as long as you don't stop."
- "Respect yourself and others will respect you."

- "To see what is right and not to do it is want of courage."
- "Whosesoever you go, go with all your heart."
- "The superior man is modest in his speech, but exceeds in his action."
- "Don't do unto others what you would not have them do to you" (known as the Confucian Golden Rule).

Taoism

Taoism (pronounced "dowism") was supposedly founded by Lao-Tzu, but historians disagree over exactly how much of Lao-Tzu's story is real. Lao-Tzu was a contemporary of Confucius, so he lived through the same time of raging conflict. Like Confucius, he sought to encourage peace and harmony instead of conflict.

Lao-Tzu invented the doctrine of the Tao, a sort of force that flows through all living things. According to Lao-Tzu, each person must harmonize himself with the Tao. Time progresses in a circle, not a line; and Taoists must let nature take its course, moving with life instead of struggling against it.

Lao-Tzu's Tao had two sides, the *yin* and the *yang*. The yin is the dark side, and it is associated with women, the moon and death. The yang is the light side, and it is associated with men, the sun, creation and birth. To remain healthy, the Taoist must maintain a balance between the yin and yang that exists inside him. To maintain this balance, one must live in harmony with others and with nature and eat healthy foods. One must also adhere to a simple life and seek inner peace, following the three basic commandments of Taoism: be charitable, be thrifty and do not push ahead of others.

Legalism

Legalism began with a disciple of Confucius named Xun-Zi. Xun-Zi disagreed with Confucius on a fundamental point: He believed that man was basically evil, not good, and so he needed strict laws to keep him under control. Every aspect of life should be governed by a set of strict rules and regulations. In this way, China could rein in the chaos of the time and bring order.

Like Confucius, the Legalists wanted to return to a unified and orderly China, but they wanted China's leaders to rule with an iron fist. The philosophy of Legalism emphasized the power of the state over the rights of the individual. Under Legalism, an individual had no civil rights; but if he performed well in the system, he could advance. In a Legalist society, the state rules using tactics of fear and terror. Neighbors are encouraged to inform the authorities on one another. Speaking out against the government is not allowed, and the punishment for any who oppose the government is execution.

When Qin Zheng (Shi Huangdi) became the first emperor of China, he embraced the Legalist philosophy. In more modern times, Mao Zedong also embraced Legalism. Modern Chinese Communism is highly legalistic.

CRITICAL CONCEPTS: None of these newer religions-- not Confucianism, not Taoism, and not the Buddhism that later arrived from India-- replaced Chinese Folk Religion. Instead, they blended with it. The rules of Confucianism and Taoism reinforced the old Chinese Folk Religion rules of filial piety and ancestor veneration.

The Qin Dynasty (reigned 221 - 206 BC)

THE QIN DYNASTY

The Qin Dynasty ruled for only a short time, from 221-206 BC, and had only two emperors, yet it had a profound influence on the Chinese. The name *China* originated with the Qin name. The Qin Dynasty's first and most powerful emperor was Qin Zheng, who led his mighty army against all of the other Chinese territories and defeated them all in order to establish his dynasty.

After he became emperor, Qin Zheng changed his name to Shi Huangdi and settled down to become China's first Legalist tyrant.

TERRIBLE TYRANTS: Shi Huangdi (reigned 221-210 BC)

After Qin Zheng defeated the other kingdoms and brought all of China under his rule, he changed his name to Shi Huangdi and became the first emperor of China. He adopted the philosophy of the Legalists and ruled with an iron fist.

In order to keep his subjects under control, Shi Huangdi did away with the feudal system and established counties that were ruled directly by the emperor. He used military might to control his subjects. He executed all who spoke out against him. He even sought to control his subjects' thoughts by burning books he considered subversive and burying alive as many as 500 scholars.

Shi Huangdi was also famous for his many massive building projects. The Great Wall of China was one of his projects, although he did not live to see it finished. He also built a mausoleum for himself that included the Terracotta Warriors (see below).

Shi Huangdi died in 210 BC at the age of fifty. His son inherited his throne, but the empire collapsed in rebellion after only four years. The Han Dynasty rose up to replace the Qin.

FASCINATING FACTS: A Japanese Myth

One of Shi Huangdi's ambitions was to find an elixir that would give him eternal life. Legend has it that he sent one of his most trusted men, Xu Fu, on a quest to search for the rare plant from which the elixir was derived.

Xu Fu knew that if he did not find the elixir plant, Shi Huangdi would execute him. So Xu Fu told Shi Huangdi that he would have to travel to an island in the South Sea where, he had learned, the mysterious elixir plant grew. For this trip he requested a crew of 500 men, women and children (different versions of the tale give different numbers). Shi Huangdi agreed to his terms, and Xu Fu set out on his quest. But instead of seeking the elixir, he took his 500 companions and traveled across the East China Sea to the islands of Japan. He and his crew settled in Japan, and Xu Fu became the first Japanese emperor.

FASCINATING FACTS: The Terracotta Army

Shi Huangdi, the first emperor of the Qin Dynasty, had a sense of his own importance to equal that of any Egyptian pharaoh. Beginning when he was just 13, long before he became emperor, he built for himself what may turn out to be the world's largest and most expensive mausoleum. Archaeologists are still excavating and studying the mausoleum, but even the small part revealed so far is grand beyond belief.

Chinese farmers discovered the first part of Shi's mausoleum in 1974, when they were digging a well. Their discovery was perhaps the greatest archaeological find of modern times. Inside the mausoleum they found an army of thousands of life-sized clay soldiers, apparently created to be Shi's army in the afterlife. According to an ancient account, the tomb itself resides in a city-sized replica of Shi's earthly kingdom, complete with rivers of quicksilver (liquid mercury). This part of the mausoleum has never been excavated, partly because of concerns about preserving it, partly out of respect for those who built it. According to that same ancient account, Shi left none of the mausoleum's 700,000 laborers alive to carry its story back to the world of the living.

Ancient sources suggest that Shi went mad near the end of his life because of the many odd potions he drank in his search for the elixir of life. The stories of the elixir and the Terracotta Army suggest that Shi suffered from an unhealthy obsession with his own death, although the deaths of others seem to have bothered him not at all.

Some facts about the Terracotta Army and Shi Huangdi's mausoleum:

- The makers used only eight different face molds to create the soldiers, but no two soldiers look alike. After casting the faces, the workers added clay to create unique facial features.
- The soldiers are life-sized, but like real soldiers, they are of differing heights. Interestingly, although the Chinese are generally short-statured, the tallest figures are the generals.
- The soldiers were placed in pits and aligned in military formation according to rank and duty.
- 700,000 workers built the mausoleum and the Terracotta Army over a period of 36 years.
- Archaeologists have found 6,000 terracotta soldiers so far, but only part of the mausoleum has been excavated.
- The terracotta soldiers were originally armed with real weapons and armor, but these were apparently stolen by grave robbers.

<u>FASCINATING FACTS: The Diamond Sutra</u>

The Diamond Sutra is the world's oldest known dated, printed book. It is a Buddhist text consisting of seven strips of paper, each of which were printed from carved wooden printing blocks. The pages were pasted together to make a scroll.

The Diamond Sutra was printed in 868 AD. It was hidden in a cave in northwest China, then re-discovered in the early 1900s.

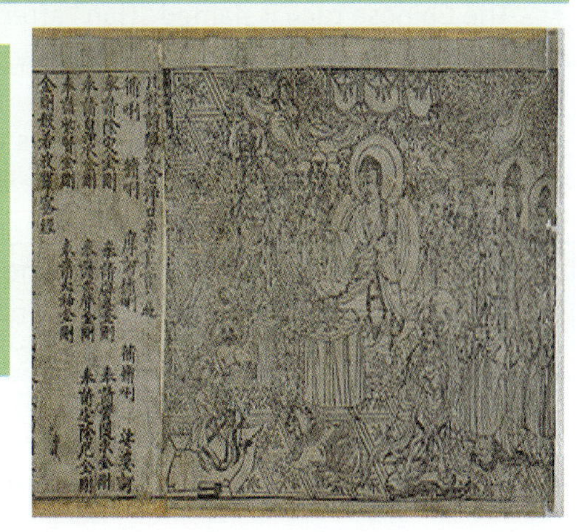

The Han Dynasty (reigned 206 BC - 220 AD)

THE HAN DYNASTY

(Picture shows the ruins of an ancient Chinese watchtower from the Han Dynasty)

The Han Dynasty replaced the Qin in 206 BC and ruled for the next 400 years. After Shi Huangdi died, China's warring provinces nearly broke apart again. The Han Dynasty began when Liu Bang, a military general from a peasant background, defeated both the last Qin Dynasty emperor and the king of the Chu Province to become China's first Han emperor.

The Han Dynasty would rule China for the next 400 years. Like the Qin, the Han Dynasty had a large and lasting influence on China. Most modern Chinese people still refer to themselves as Han Chinese. The Han Dynasty did not discard the Qin government, but it did incorporate Confucian ideals, so it was less Legalistic and iron-fisted than the Qin.

The reign of the Han Dynasty was a time of progress and change.

- Under the Han, traders established the Silk Road, an overland trade route through central Asia that connected China to the Mediterranean world for the first time.
- Missionaries from India (sent by Asoka and his descendants, see Chapter 16) brought Buddhist beliefs into China during the Han era. Buddhism would fade in India, but in China it would grow and prosper.
- China added modern Tibet, North Korea and North Vietnam to its territory.
- Education and the arts thrived under the Han Dynasty.

These last two ancient dynasties, the Qin and the Han, brought order to the chaos of China's Warring States Period and built China into a united, enduring empire. The lasting importance of these two empires is clear in the words "China" and "Han":

- The word "China" probably comes from the word "Qin." If so, then China is named for the dynasty that gave the nation its first strong central government.
- The Chinese race is named "Han" after the Han Dynasty, the dynasty that unified China and gave the Chinese people their national identity.

In its later years, political rivalries weakened the Han Dynasty. In 220 AD, the Han Dynasty disintegrated as China split into three kingdoms.

The Three Kingdoms (220 - 280 AD)
The First Jin Dynasty (reigned 265 - 420 AD)
The Sixteen Kingdoms (304 - 439 AD)

Near the end of the Han Dynasty era, the Chinese Empire divided into the Three Kingdoms of Cao Wei, Shu Han and Dong Wu. Each of these Three Kingdoms believed that its king was the rightful successor to the Han

Dynasty, and they all fought constantly. The incessant warring of the Three Kingdoms era made life in China so unbearable that, when the era was over, large areas of China lay entirely empty of people. Some areas had been ravaged by war and famine, and some had simply been abandoned by people who fled to seek peace elsewhere.

When the First Jin Dynasty took control of China in 165, it tried to repopulate some of these empty areas by bringing in non-Chinese settlers known as the Wu Hu from the far north. This idea backfired in 304 AD, when the Wu Hu rebelled against the First Jin Dynasty. The Wu Hu Uprising of 304 - 316 AD forced the Jin emperors to move their capital south of the Huai River. For the remainder of the First Jin Dynasty era, the Jin emperors ruled only in the south, while a collection of Sixteen Kingdoms ruled in the north.

FASCINATING FACTS: Chinese Calligraphy

Calligraphy means *beautiful writing,* and has been an art form since ancient times. Chinese calligraphers combined their art with communication. Chinese calligraphy began during the reign of the Yellow Emperor, but the ideograms were only standardized during the Qin Dynasty, when Shi Huangdi required all writers to conform to one early standard. Calligraphy blossomed during the Han Dynasty. Calligraphers were free to mix art with their writing, and they created many beautiful works, although most were unsigned.

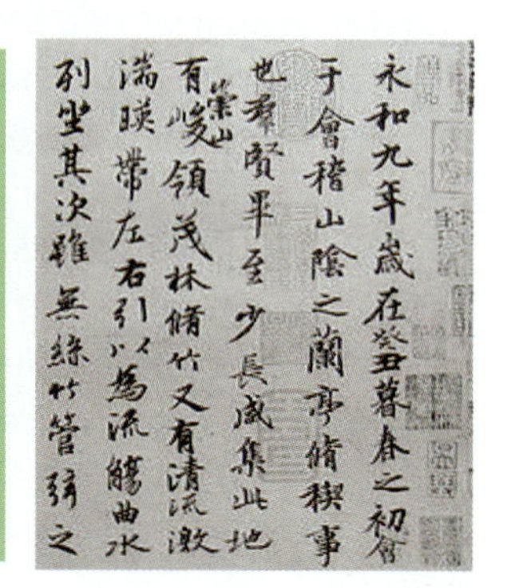

GEOGRAPHY FOCUS

ASIA

Did you know…

- Asia is the world's largest continent
- Asia is often divided into four regions: east (includes Hong Kong, Japan, North and South Korea, China, Taiwan and Mongolia), southeast (Burma, Thailand, Laos, Cambodia, Vietnam, Malaysia, Brunei, Philippines, Singapore, Indonesia), south (Afghanistan, Pakistan, India, Sri Lanka, Nepal, Bhutan and Bangladesh) and west (Anatolia, Middle East, Arabian Peninsula, part of Russia, Georgia, Armenia and Azerbaijan Iran).
- China lies in East Asia.
- China is the most populous country in the world. India is the second most populous.
- Asia's vast Gobi desert covers about 500,000 square miles
- The locations with the highest and lowest dry land elevations on earth both lie in Asia. Mount Everest is the highest, and the shores of the Dead Sea are the lowest.

FASCINATING FACTS: The Great Wall of China

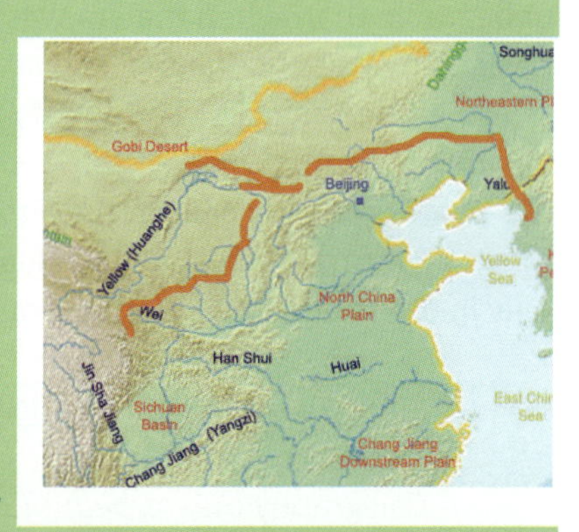

During China's Warring States Period, several of China's territories built walls at their borders for protection against their neighbors. When Shi Huangdi unified all of China under his rule, he tore down the walls between the former territories. But some of these walls were on China's northern border. These he began to strengthen and interconnect. Over the next nine years, Chinese laborers completed the first Great Wall of China as a first line of defense against raiding northern tribes.

Little of that first Great Wall survives. Built primarily of local stone or gravel and rammed earth, it could not withstand the ravages of time. No one knows its exact length or location. One thing is certain, however: many, many Chinese died to build it. Some jokingly referred to the Great Wall as the world's longest cemetery because the harsh building conditions cost so many lives.

Over the centuries, trouble with the northern tribes continued, so building and maintenance of the Great Wall was a perennial project through the Han and later dynasties. Some of these later builders used stone, bricks and mortar to build a stronger, more permanent wall complete with guardhouses and watchtowers.

Together with its trenches, cliffs, rivers and other natural barriers, the entire Great Wall stretches about 5500 miles. It is the world's longest manmade structure, and it is said to be the only manmade structure visible from earth orbit with the naked eye. Because China was mostly unknown to the Greeks, the Great Wall was never on their list of seven Ancient Wonders; but it is on a list of seven Medieval Wonders.

FASCINATING FACTS: The Silk Road

During the Han Dynasty, merchants forged trade routes between China and the trading posts of middle and western Asia. The Greco-Roman world desired China's exotic goods-- silk, tea and chinaware, among other things. For their part, the Chinese purchased gold, cotton, slaves and more from the West. As trade increased, traders convinced governments to build and improve trails, roads and bridges to make the journey easier. As always, governments benefited by taxing trade.

The trade route that developed was not a single long road, but a series of interconnected smaller roads and pathways. The route stretched across Asia's vast reaches, more than 4,000 miles over desert and river, plain and mountain. Because the people of the west prized Chinese silk, a German geographer dubbed the trade route the "Silk Road" in 1877. Traveling the Silk Road was not without its dangers. The terrain was often rough, and the trail passed through areas full of wild animals or controlled by bandits. Nevertheless, traders braved the Silk Road for centuries, slowly forging bonds between West and East.

Chapter 26

Rome's Rise

ANCIENT HISTORY FOCUS

EARLY ROMAN HISTORY

The history of the earliest Italians is shrouded in tales and myths. The city of Rome began as a collection of settlements representing several ethnic groups, among them Latins, Sabines and Umbrians. These settlements sat on seven hills near the Tiber River, and were separated by marshland. Separately, they were all vulnerable to attack, so as the years went by, they began to unite and work together.

According to one well known legend, Rome was founded on April 21, 753 BC by Romulus, a son of a Latin King. Supposedly, Romulus and Remus were twins raised by a she-wolf. Romulus killed Remus in a fight over the city's throne, and then named the city "Rome" after himself. The Sabines joined the Latins, and together they began to conquer the other nearby settlements. From this point on, we will call these people the *Romans*.

North of Rome lived a tribe called the Etruscans.

FASCINATING FACTS: The Etruscans

The Etruscans lived in northern Italy long before the founding of Rome. Etruscan merchants traded extensively with Greek and Phoenician merchants, and the Etruscans absorbed a great deal of Greek culture over the years. They used stone in their buildings, dug canals, built roads, engineered water and sewage systems and installed aqueducts. They also used the Greek alphabet and incorporated the Greek gods into their own religious practice.

Although the Romans and the Etruscans often fought, Rome absorbed Greek culture through its contact with the Etruscans. The fledgling Roman culture was subject to the powerful influence of the advanced Greek culture. Soon the Romans had much in common with both the Etruscans and the Greeks.

The Kingdom of Rome Timeline

753-715 BC: Romulus, first king of Rome
715-673 BC: Numa Pompilius, second king

After Romulus died, the Latins and the Sabines held an election to choose Rome's next king. To make matters fair, the Latins were supposed to vote for a king from among the Sabines, and the Sabines were supposed to vote for a king from among the Latins. But after the Latins elected a Sabine named Numa Pompilius, the Sabines agreed to his election without even selecting a Latin. Somehow they got away with this, and the Sabine Numa Pompilius took the throne.

673-642 BC: Tullus Hostilius, third king, a warrior king of the Sabine tribe
642-612 BC: Ancus Marcius, fourth king, the grandson of Numus Pompilius
616-578 BC: Lucius Tarquinius Priscus, fifth king, an Etruscan King
578-534 BC: Servius Tullius, sixth king, another Etruscan King

FASCINATING FACTS: Servius Tullius

(Picture shows part of the Servian wall that may have originally been built under Servius Tullius)

There are numerous legends surrounding Servius Tullius. According to one, he was born a slave boy in the palace of Lucius Tarquinius Priscus, the first Etruscan king of Rome. One day at the palace, while Servius was sleeping, his hair caught fire. Somehow the child did not awake, and when the king's wife saw, she refused to allow anyone to douse the flames. When Servius finally awakened on his own, the flames went out. After this episode, the king and his wife believed that Servius was special and decided to raise him as their own. They gave him their daughter in marriage and made him their heir, so when King Lucius died, Servius Tullius became the next king of Rome.

534-509 BC: Lucius Tarqunius Superbus, seventh king, another Etruscan King. Lucius was the last Roman king. He assassinated Servius Tullius and stole the throne, and he was a cruel dictator. He was finally ousted by members of the senate led by Lucius Junius Brutus, who went on to found the Roman Republic.

FASCINATING FACTS: The Roman Fasces

The Roman Fasces symbol dates to the time of the Etruscans. The fasces consisted of a number of bundled and bound birch rods, which symbolized power, strength and unity. Bound with the birch rod was an ax with its blade protruding from the bundle, which symbolized power-- the power of life or death. The Fasces was a symbol of the Roman Republic, and the Romans revered the Fasces in the same way that Americans revere their flag.

THE ROMAN REPUBLIC

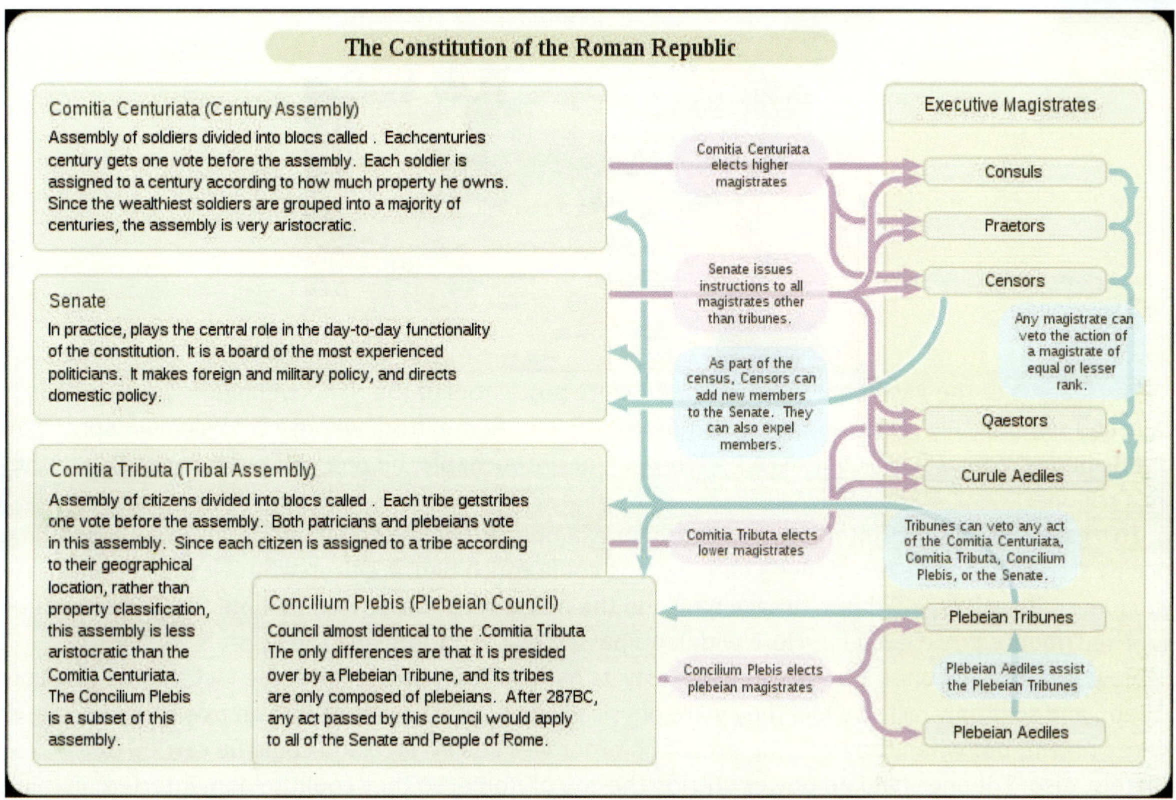

In 509 BC, the Romans did away with their monarchy and established the Roman Republic. In a republic, the power of government is held by the people's representatives rather than a king or a dictator. In the Roman Republic, the government was divided into three main branches: the Senate, the consuls and the Assemblies.

The Senate: Rome had a senate from the days of the early kings, but the early senate had little power. Its members were the city's wealthy landowners and nobles (patricians). The Senate could advise the king, but the king could take or leave the Senate's advice.

After the overthrow of the last king, Lucius Tarquinius Superbus, the Senate assumed greater power under the new republic. Its number was set at 300 men (later 900), all elected by other high ranking officials. **All senators were elected for life**. The Senate's jobs included:

- Budget matters (taxing and spending)
- Holding debates over proposed legislation
- Advising the Consuls and the Assemblies
- Foreign affairs (treaties, trade agreements)
- Electing the consuls

The Assemblies: Rome also had Assemblies of common people, or plebes, from its earliest days. Under the monarchy, the Assemblies elected Rome's kings. The king presided over the Assemblies, and the Assemblies "ratified," or simply approved without question, whatever the king decided. The early Assemblies' power was largely symbolic.

Under the Republic, the Assemblies' main power was the election of Consuls (highest officials), Praetors (army commanders or magistrates) and Censors (census-takers and moral guides). The Assemblies could also vote on legislation debated in the Senate and vote to declare war, but the Senate and the Consuls could overrule the Assemblies.

The leaders of the Assemblies were the *Tribunes*.

FASCINATING FACTS: Roman Tribunes

The leaders of the Assemblies, the *Tribunes*, were protectors of the rights of plebes. The Tribunes physically and symbolically represented the common people of Rome, from whom Rome's power sprang. As such, the Tribunes' bodies were considered *sacrosanct*, or untouchable; no one, not even a consul, had the right to harm a tribune.

This gave the Tribunes interesting powers. For example, a Tribune could temporarily halt a death sentence by standing in the executioner's path; no one could touch him. A citizen who felt that a magistrate had wronged him could call on a Tribune to save him, and the magistrate was powerless until the Tribune got out of his way. The Tribunes could even interfere with laws passed by the Senate and the Consuls.

However, the Tribunes' power was limited by its nature. Their power lay in the fact that no one could touch them, and so it only lasted while they were physically present. They could halt an execution as long as they were present, but when they left, the execution order was still in force and could be carried out immediately. Also, Tribunes held no power outside the city of Rome, so they could seldom interfere in military matters.

Modern newspapers often bear the name *Tribune* because they speak for the people and consider themselves protectors of the common people.

The Consuls: The two Consuls, or highest government officials, were elected by the Assemblies from the ranks of the Senate. Consuls served one-year terms and were responsible for all government operations, both military and civilian. They were Rome's highest military commanders and its highest civil magistrates and judges. They also presided over the Senate and conducted its meetings. Their power was very great, but each consul's power was held in check by the other consul's power to veto.

FASCINATING FACTS: The Meaning of *Veto*

Veto is Latin for *"I forbid."* The power of the veto began with the Roman consuls as a limit on their power. Both consuls had to agree on any major decision. If one consul disagreed with the decision, he had the power to *veto* or forbid it. The veto meant that no single man could make an important decision such as a declaration of war without the approval of at least one other.

The President of the United States has veto power today. If the President disagrees with a bill approved for his signature by both the Senate and the House of Representatives, he may stamp it with a veto, and the bill does not become law. However, after his veto, if both the House and the Senate pass the bill again with a two thirds majority vote, then they "override" the President's veto. The bill becomes law without the President's agreement.

Life in the Roman Republic

Religion:

The Romans were polytheists, worshipping any number of gods (or spirits). Romans believed that the gods were everywhere and in everything, controlling the lives and fates of mortals. Their religious lives centered around making offerings to the gods so that the gods would be pleased with them and grant them good fortune. For that purpose, the Romans built beautiful temples all over the Roman Empire.

Each Roman god had a specific, limited function. For example, the sun god Apollo had no power over the sea, which had its own god, Neptune. If a Roman wanted successful hunting, he prayed to Diana, goddess of the hunt. Each Roman household had a shrine for the household spirits with Vesta, the goddess of hearth and home, at its center. Roman commanders never undertook military campaigns without seeking *auguries*, or pre-visions of the battle's outcome.

As Rome grew, it absorbed more gods from surrounding cultures. The Romans borrowed gods from everyone, including the Greeks, the Egyptians and the Celts, but they often changed the gods' names and forms. The Romans adopted all of the Greek gods, but changed their names and made their personalities more formal and godlike, less human.

FASCINATING FACTS: Roman Gods and Goddesses

Jupiter (Greek god Zeus)		Jupiter was the king of the gods, the god of rain, thunder and lightning. His symbols were the thunderbolt and the breastplate, and his animal was the eagle. Jupiter was the patron deity of Ancient Rome.
Cupid (Greek god Eros)		Cupid was the god of love and beauty. His symbols were the bow and a quiver of arrows.
Neptune (Greek god Poseidon)		Neptune was the god of water and the sea. His symbol was the trident, and his animal was the horse.
Pluto (Greek god Hades)		Pluto was the god of the dead. According to Roman mythology, borrowed from the Greeks, all mortals who died had to travel to the Underworld by crossing the river of the dead. As with the Greeks, the dead had to pay a ferryman and pass the three-headed dog Cerberus.

Apollo (Greek god Apollo)		Apollo was the god of the sun and music. His symbol was the lyre.
Mercury (Greek god Hermes)		Mercury was the messenger god and the god of trade and thieves. His symbols were winged shoes, a winged cap and his special wand entwined with snakes (the *caduceus*).
Vulcan (Greek god Hephaestus)		Vulcan was the god of the forge. He provided the gods with armor, weapons and other creations.
Mars (Greek god Ares)		Mars was the god of war. His symbols were the crested helmet, the shield and the lance. His animals were the vulture and the dog.
Minerva (Greek goddess Athena)		Minerva was the goddess of wisdom. Her symbols were the helmet and armor, and her animal was the owl.
Venus (Greek goddess Aphrodite)		Venus was the goddess of love and beauty. She was associated with gardens.
Juno (Greek goddess Hera)		Juno was queen of the gods and the goddess of women and childbirth. Her symbol was the peacock. She was married to Jupiter.
Vesta (Greek god Hestia)		Vesta was the goddess of the hearth. Her symbol was fire.

Diana (Greek god Artemis) (picture is by Rembrandt)		Diana was the goddess of the moon and hunting. Her symbols were the bow and arrow. Like her Greek counterpart, she appeared as a young maiden and helped women in childbirth.
Ceres (Greek god Demeter)		Ceres was the goddess of the earth and agriculture. Her symbol was the cornucopia, a sort of horn filled with plenty of fruits and vegetables.
Bacchus (Greek god Dionysus)		Bacchus was the god of wine and theater. His symbol was a staff encircled with vines.

Roman Houses:

Rome's wealthiest citizens, the Patricians, lived in large detached homes, often with many relatives under one roof. These homes were usually built of brick with tile roofs. Their many rooms--several bedrooms, an office, a kitchen, a dining area, and a shrine for the family gods--often overlooked a central courtyard with a garden. The complex would also include a bathhouse complete with running water. The floors were often covered with marble or stone laid in a mosaic pattern. The walls were often covered with frescoes or lined with marble.

Rome's poorer citizens, the Plebeians, were more likely to live in apartments. Plebeian apartments usually consisted of one or at most two rooms situated over ground floor shops or inns. Entire families squeezed into these tiny apartments. Plebeian apartments had no running water, so the plebes had to use public bathhouses and facilities. Without water, it was difficult to cook in these city apartments, so most plebeians ate at the nearby inns.

FASCINATING FACTS: Arenas and Roman Gladiators

Photo courtesy of David Iliff: Colosseum in Rome, Italy

The Greeks had their dramas, but the Romans developed a much more distinctive, notorious and savage form of entertainment: watching arena combat. They built great amphitheaters in which they could watch staged arena fights between both professional and amateur combatants. The largest and best known such amphitheater was the Roman Coliseum, part of which still stands in the center of Rome.

At the arena, the Romans could watch any sort of fight: man versus man, man versus bear, man versus bull, man versus lion, or man versus tiger. Condemned criminals might be executed at the arena in any of several brutal fashions for the public's viewing pleasure. Sometimes condemned men were given weapons and allowed to fight to the death against armed and armored soldiers. Interspersed between fighting events were singing, dancing and dramatic acts.

The highlight of the arena entertainment was always gladiator combat. Gladiators were fighters trained specifically for arena combat in established gladiator schools. Some gladiators were trained to fight with sword and shield, others with net and trident. Gladiators armed with different weapons were pitted against one another to add to the variety of events. Gladiators were often kidnapped slaves or prisoners of war forced into arena combat, but some were paid volunteers. An exotic-featured gladiator captured in some far-off land could raise the crowd's interest.

Because gladiators fought with deadly weapons, their combats usually ended in death for one or sometimes both of them; but death was not always necessary. Nevertheless, under the emperors, gladiators began their combats with the traditional hail *"Ave, Caesar, morituri te salutant,"* or "Hail, Caesar, we who are about to die salute you."

ROMAN FAMILIES

Fathers

The Roman father was the unchallenged head of his household, exercising great power over his wife, children, slaves and servants. His power over his sons' affairs continued even after they were married. A son could not become head of his own household until his father was dead.

Roman fathers were harsh and rarely showed affection. They showed little concern for most of their children, and sometimes sold them into slavery. The Roman father could beat his wife and children at will, divorce his wife, and force his daughters into arranged marriages, usually around the age of thirteen.

Mothers

The Roman mother had little power in the home or in the political arena. Some wealthy women had slaves to do their housework, but most were responsible for keeping their own houses and raising their children.

Children

When a child was born in Rome, his or her father had a decision to make: Was the child worth keeping? If he decided the child was worthless to him, he could sell the child into slavery. Because infants often died in their first months, they were not even named until they had survived to a certain age. If they survived, boys received three names (personal, clan and family), while girls received two (personal and family).

Roman children were to be seen and not heard. Boys from wealthy families began their education at the age of seven. They used wax tablets for their lessons or wrote their letters in the sand. They learned Latin, Greek, reading, writing and arithmetic. Along with their formal education, Roman boys learned how to ride and how to swim. Roman girls received no formal education, but learned from their mothers at home. Roman children usually married in their early teens and remained under the control of the boy's father.

FASCINATING FACTS: The Wax Tablet

Wax writing tablets are an ancient technology. The tablets consisted of a wooden frame that was filled with melted wax, then allowed to cool into a smooth writing surface. The user wrote on his wax tablet with his *stylus*, a metal-tipped wooden stick. The flattened reverse end of the stylus was an "eraser" of sorts. It could be heated and then used to melt the wax, restoring its smooth surface.

GEOGRAPHY FOCUS

Roman Roads and Highways:

The saying "all roads lead to Rome" was actually true in Roman times. The Romans were the world's first great road builders. Their huge network of roads was first inspired by the need to move their great armies quickly anywhere in the known world. Later, they recognized the value of good, safe roads for encouraging trade. Governments throughout history have prospered by taxing trade.

The building of the Roman roads was the job of the military. Military engineers surveyed routes, designed roads and bridges and supervised construction. The cost, however, was borne by the nearby cities, towns and villages. The locals had to provide materials and extra labor for road construction. After a road was finished, the locals were also responsible for its maintenance.

Roman engineers understood road building better than any before them. They built their roads with a crown or crest in the center so that rainwater wouldn't puddle in the road. They also provided gutters on both sides, again to carry away water that would damage the road, making it too soft for chariot and wagon wheels. Ancient Roman roads were so well built that some are still in use today.

FASCINATING FACTS: The Appian Way

The *Via Appia*, or Appian Way, was Rome's most famous and important road. Connecting Rome to Brindisi, a port city near the southeast end of the Italian peninsula, the Appian Way stretched over 350 miles. The road took its name from Appius Claudius

Caecus, a Roman censor who began its construction in 312 BC. It became the best route for travel across the Italian peninsula and onward by sea to Greece and beyond.

Over the centuries, much of the old road fell into disrepair. In 1784, Pope Pius VI built a new Appian Way, the "Via Appia Nuova," alongside the track of the ancient road.

FASCINATING FACTS: Roman Aqueducts

As the cities of the Roman Republic grew, their need for clean water also grew. Where large groups of people are gathered together, plentiful, clean water is an absolute necessity for health and sanitation. To provide that water, the Romans developed a highly advanced system of waterways called *aqueducts*. Aqueducts were stone channels that carried water into the cities from nearby hill and mountain springs.

In the absence of modern pump technology, the aqueducts had to rely on gravity alone to move water. This required an uninterrupted downhill path into the city's reservoirs. Any valleys, rivers or roads in the aqueducts' paths had to be crossed with elevated waterways. The Romans built distinctive, arched bridges of stone, brick and volcanic rock to carry water over such obstacles. These arches were often the only visible part of the aqueduct system.

At its peak, the city of Rome received water from no fewer than eleven aqueducts.

BIBLE FOCUS

FASCINATING FACTS: The Septuagint

After Alexander the Great swept through most of the known world, conquering all in his path, Greek became the common language throughout his empire. Because so many people knew Greek, important documents and literature were translated into the Greek language. One such document was the Hebrew Bible.

Jewish scholars translated the Torah (Genesis, Exodus, Leviticus, Numbers and Deuteronomy) into Greek around 300 BC. According to the story, Ptolemy of Alexandria requested the translation and put 72 translators in 72 separate rooms. As they began their work, God placed the same translation in each translator's mind. When they were finished, their translations were all the same!

Other scholars translated the remainder of the Old Testament over the next two centuries. Their translation became known as the *Septuagint*. The word means "seventy" in Latin, and refers to the (roughly) seventy translators in Ptolemy's story. Bible scholars refer to the Septuagint so often that it has its own shorthand: it is abbreviated LXX, the Roman numeral 70. The Septuagint was the authoritative translation of the Hebrew Scriptures for centuries.

Chapter 27

Roman Wars

ANCIENT HISTORY FOCUS

ROMAN WARS

By 265 BC, Rome had conquered the entire Italian peninsula, and the Romans began to set their sights on more distant lands. Their most immediate challenge was the city of Carthage, which lay just across the Mediterranean Sea.

FASCINATING FACTS: Carthage

The city of Carthage lies on the North African coast of modern Tunisia. The Phoenicians founded the city-state of Carthage around 800 BC. Over the next three hundred years, the Carthaginians established coastal colonies all around the western Mediterranean, even into the Iberian Peninsula (modern Spain). They controlled the islands of Corsica and Sardinia, and had colonies on part of the island of Sicily (blue section on map), all of which were close to Rome. In 265 BC, Carthage was the dominant naval power in the Mediterranean.

The Roman word for a native of Carthage was *punicus*, which came from Carthage's Phoenician origins. Thus the wars that raged between Rome and Carthage became known as the *Punic Wars*.

The conflict between Rome and Carthage was cultural as well as political. Carthage lay beyond the area conquered by Alexander the Great and was not part of the *Hellenized*, or Greek-influenced, world. The culture of Carthage was a blend of Phoenician, Egyptian and Berber influences, and was more North African than Greek. The Greek peoples considered the Punics of Carthage savages, and when Carthage threatened Greek cities, some Greeks chose suicide over the prospect of life under the dominion of Carthage.

In 264 BC, trouble on the island of Sicily became the spark that touched off a hundred years of warring between Rome and Carthage. The three wars that followed became known as the Punic Wars.

The First Punic War (264-241 BC)

The stage for the First Punic War was the island of Sicily. At the time, Sicily was divided between the Greeks in the east and the Carthaginians in the west. In 265 BC, some mercenaries captured Messene, a Greek-controlled city. The Messenians asked Carthage for help in expelling the mercenaries. But Carthage's help came with unexpected strings attached: after the Carthaginians had cleaned out the mercenaries, they remained and occupied the city.

Meanwhile, the Messenians had also asked Rome for help with their mercenary problem. When the Romans arrived, they were not at all pleased to find that Carthage had expanded its holdings into Messene. So in 264 BC, Rome invaded Sicily and captured Messene. The First Punic War had begun.

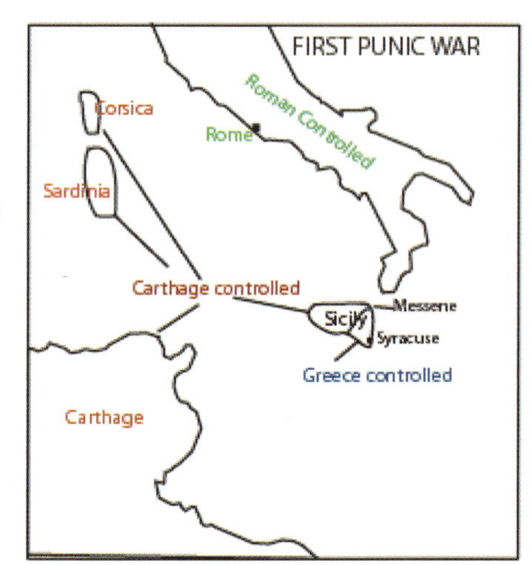

When the war began, the Carthaginians had a clear advantage. The Romans had never really ventured across the water, and their inexperienced navy was outmatched by Carthage's war-hardened sailors. Soon, however, the Romans captured a shipwrecked Carthaginian warship and copied its design for use in their own ships. With their knock-off warships and a new boarding device called a *corvus*, the Romans were able to equalize the war at sea.

FASCINATING FACTS: The Quinquereme and the Corvus

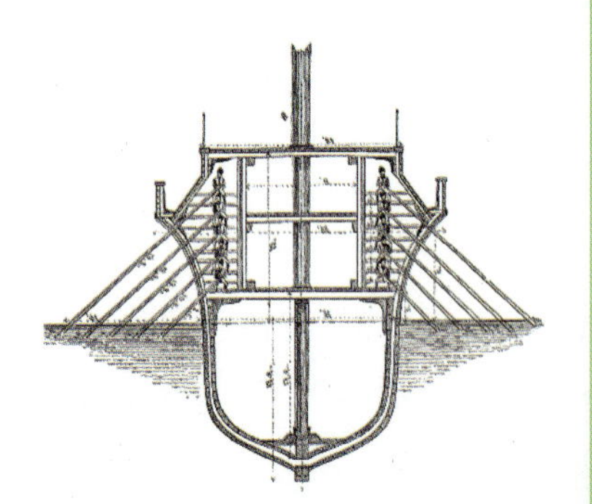

The *quinquereme* was a heavy warship propelled by five separate decks of oarsmen. It was an advanced version of the earlier triremes built by the Phoenicians and the Greeks, but it was larger, heavier and far more fearsome. It was heavy enough to carry catapults, with which it could bombard ports or other ships. A quinquereme could carry as many as 300 oarsmen and 100 marine soldiers. Both Carthage and Rome relied on quinqueremes to fight the Punic Wars.

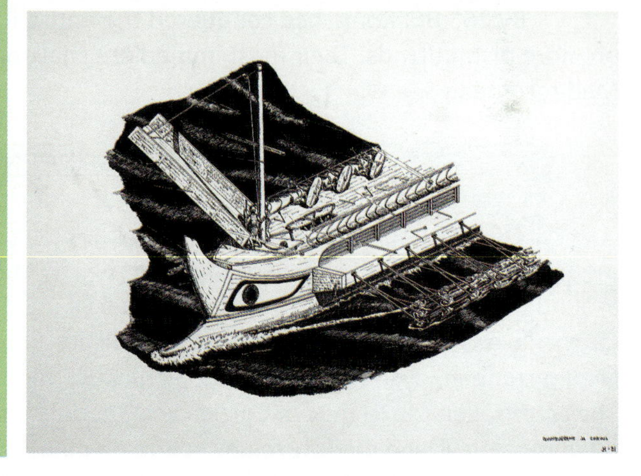

The *corvus* was a Roman innovation. It was a sort of shipboard drawbridge mounted near the ship's side. When the Romans got close enough to an enemy ship, they could lower the corvus onto the ship's deck and send their marine soldiers over it to board and capture her. The Romans excelled in man-to-man fighting, and the corvus helped them use this advantage by turning a naval battle into a man-to-man battle.

After Rome had sorted out its navy problem, it was able to focus its attention on Sicily. Rome's superior land forces began to cut off Carthage's supply lines. By 241 BC, Carthage was forced to sign a treaty that ceded Sicily to Rome. Carthage also had to pay Rome war damages. The First Punic War ended with Rome as the master of Sicily.

Weakened by the terms of the treaty, Carthage was unable to prevent Rome from overtaking the islands of Sardinia and Corsica in 238 BC. Rome was creating a buffer of islands between Carthage and the Italian peninsula, growing well outside its natural borders, and Carthage grew concerned about Rome's growing power.

Seeking to improve their military might to match Rome's, the Carthaginians sent a general named Hamilcar to Iberia, the territory that became Spain. Allying himself with the Iberians, Hamilcar was able to increase Carthaginian power and influence on the Iberian Peninsula. When Hamilcar died in 228 BC, his son-in-law Hasdrubal succeeded him. When Hasdrubal was killed, the generalship fell to Hamilcar's son, a young military commander named Hannibal (see picture).

AMAZING ANCIENTS: Fascinating Facts about Hannibal (247-182 BC)

- Hannibal was born in Carthage in 247 BC. His name meant *mercy of Baal* in the Punic language.
- He was the eldest son of Carthaginian general Hamilcar Barca.
- According to legend, when Hamilcar left for Spain after the First Punic War, his nine year old son Hannibal begged to go with him. Hamilcar agreed on the condition that Hannibal must swear to make the Romans pay with their lives for what they had done to Carthage.
- Hannibal was fond of war elephants. Hannibal's personal elephant was named Cyrus (or Surus).
- Hannibal popularized a battle maneuver called the *pincer movement*. In his pincer movement, Hannibal sent out two columns of troops, one to the left of the enemy position and one to the right. If the columns moved quickly and stealthily, the enemy was unaware of their presence until it was too late. Both columns then turned inward simultaneously to attack the enemy from both sides at once.

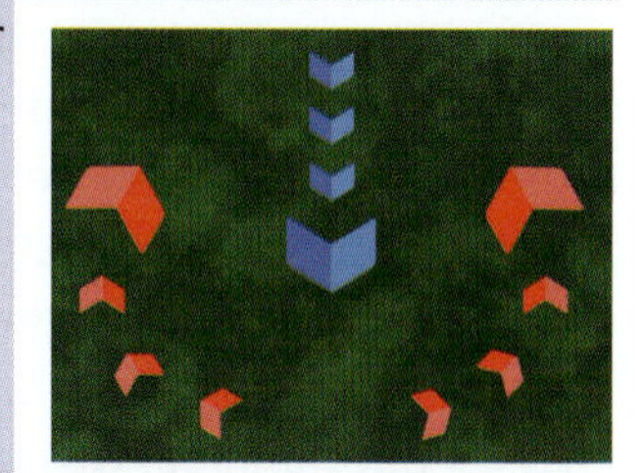

- Hannibal named his son after his brother-in-law, Hasdrubal. Hannibal also had a brother named Hasdrubal. A religious name meaning "help of Baal," Hasdrubal was apparently a family favorite.
- At his final defeat, in order to avoid being captured alive, Hannibal committed suicide by drinking a dose of poison he kept hidden in his ring.

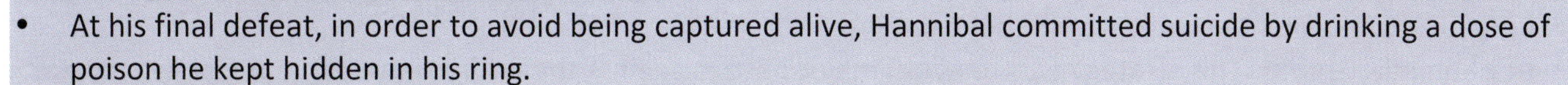

The Second Punic War or the Hannibalic War (218-201 BC)

One of the terms of the treaty with Rome was that Carthage could not advance its territory past the Ebro River on the Iberian Peninsula (modern Spain). Under the treaty, the Ebro was to be the dividing line between the territories of Rome and Carthage. However, Rome saw no reason not to maintain an alliance with Saguntum, a Greek-cultured city south of the Ebro River that wanted nothing to do with Carthage. Hannibal saw matters differently. Saguntum was the gateway to his plans for fulfilling his father's wishes and striking back at Rome. He could not leave a Roman ally unconquered so near his home base.

Rome saw Carthage as a sea power and expected any attack to come by sea, probably back on Sicily. When Hannibal laid siege to Saguntum in 218 BC, the Romans were distracted and sent no aid to their ally. But Hannibal's surprising plan was to lead a huge army overland to strike against Rome itself. With Saguntum under control, he led his army of up to 120,000 troops north out of the Iberian peninsula, through Gaul (modern France), across the Alps and down into the Italian Peninsula. He also led something which he hoped would be a fearsome weapon: a herd of war elephants.

FASCINATING FACTS: Hannibal's Elephants

Hannibal is best remembered for his use of war elephants in the Second Punic War. He had about 37 elephants at the outset of his Roman campaign. He planned to use his elephants to intimidate the Romans and break up their battle formations. The animals were huge and frightening to horses, and seemed unstoppable to cavalry riders. Their thick hides were nearly impenetrable to swords and arrows, and their riders had an excellent view of the battlefield from the elevation of their backs.

Unfortunately for Hannibal, the elephants were only a limited success. Only a few elephants survived the peril-filled crossing of the Alps. Those who survived did indeed terrify the enemy, but they were not immune to terror themselves. After the Romans learned of the elephants, they developed tactics to frighten them with noise and fire. When the elephants did die, they provided a further benefit: a large supply of meat.

There are two types of elephants, African and Asian. Asians are more easily trained and were used by Syrians against Alexander the Great. Hannibal's elephants were probably African, but it is possible that his personal elephant, named Cyrus or Surus, was an Asian with only one tusk.

The Alpine Mountain Range is formidable, high, cold and forbidding. The trip over the Alps was grueling, and Hannibal lost about a third of his men and most of his elephants before it was over. Despite these losses, Hannibal was able to push into northern Italy with a tremendous force. Encouraged by his success, Gauls from the north reinforced him, and together they defeated the Romans in great battles at the Trebbia River and at Lake Trasimene. Hannibal was an excellent strategist, and the Romans were defeated for a time.

But Hannibal was far from home and supply, and so the Romans developed the *Fabian Strategy*, named for the military dictator Fabius Maximus whom they appointed to meet Hannibal's threat. This strategy was to avoid major battles against the crafty Hannibal, but instead to take every opportunity to cut him off from supply. Over time, Fabius knew, the tremendous expense of keeping so many troops in the field would force Hannibal to leave. For years, Hannibal harried the outskirts of Rome, attacking, pillaging and destroying small villages and cities throughout Italy. But Rome itself remained unconquered.

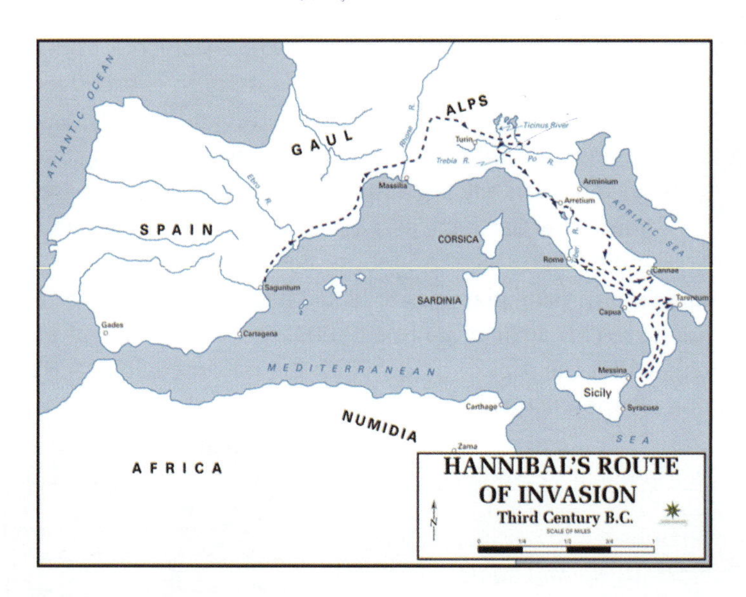

Around 215 BC, Hannibal gained two significant allies: Philip V of Macedon (from the family of Alexander the Great) and the island of Sicily. The Romans were beginning to despair that they would ever rid their land of Hannibal, whose constant attacks began to wear down their morale. But time was against Hannibal, who had his own morale problems as the years wore on without a decisive victory. In 211 BC, Hannibal tried to lay siege to Rome itself. The attempt ended in failure, and many of Hannibal's allies deserted him in frustration.

In the meantime, Rome attempted a new strategy. Unable to defeat Hannibal at home, they decided to attack his allies abroad. They deployed a young Roman officer named Scipio (Publius Cornelius Scipio Africanus), who hated Carthage as much as Hannibal hated Rome. Scipio attacked Hannibal's brother Hasdrubal back on the Iberian Peninsula (modern Spain), where Hannibal had begun his campaign. Scipio defeated Hasdrubal, and Rome took control of Carthage's holdings on the Iberian Peninsula. Hasdrubal and his men fled over the Alps to join Hannibal.

But Hasdrubal never made it to his brother. The Romans managed to intercept a message from Hasdrubal to Hannibal, and they knew Hasdrubal's movements. At the Battle of the Metaurus, Rome defeated Hasdrubal's army and killed Hasdrubal himself. In brutal Roman fashion, they placed Hasdrubal's severed head in a sack, carried it to Hannibal's camp and tossed it in so that Hannibal would know his brother's fate with certainty. This turned out to be a decisive battle of the Second Punic War.

Meanwhile, Scipio returned to Rome and convinced the consuls to attack Carthage as they had Spain. In 203 BC, an alarmed Carthage recalled Hannibal to defend it from Scipio's threat. A temporary peace treaty kept Scipio out of the city, but when Hannibal returned the treaty was thrown out and the battle was on. At the 202 BC Battle of Zama, Scipio defeated Hannibal and finally brought an end to The Second Punic War.

FASCINATING FACTS: The Battle of Zama

The Battle of Zama was Hannibal's first loss in a major battle. His loss meant the end of Carthage as a world power.

The two armies met at Zama, an area in modern Tunisia, in October 202 BC. Each side had 35,000-45,000 troops, and Hannibal also had about 80 war elephants. Hannibal deployed his war elephants at his front and arranged his foot soldiers in three lines behind them, with horse cavalry on his flanks. His most experienced veterans were in the last line.

Scipio also had three lines. The first line held his youngest, weakest and worst equipped soldiers, the *hastate*. The second line held his heavy infantry or *principes*, those with more training and the wealth to purchase better equipment. The third line held his most experienced and best equipped fighters, the *triarii.* Scipio also placed horse cavalry on each flank.

Scipio's greatest concern was Hannibal's war elephants. To counter them, he devised a plan to exploit their weaknesses. As Hannibal pushed his elephants forward, Scipio's cavalry began to blow loud horns to frighten the elephants. Some of them broke ranks, stampeded and wiped out their own cavalry on Hannibal's left wing. The rest pushed forward, but instead of resisting them, Scipio opened his lines to allow them through. They ran to the rear of the Roman army, where Scipio's best troops disposed of them.

With the threat of the elephants gone, Scipio unleashed his cavalry and quickly overwhelmed what remained of Hannibal's cavalry. Then the infantry battle began. Scipio's army charged and defeated Hannibal's first two lines, but his veterans held. Scipio was forced to regroup.

The next attack was a toe-to-toe battle between the best troops from both sides. They fought to a stalemate until the return of Scipio's cavalry, which finally turned the tide in favor of Rome. Hannibal's army was defeated.

The terms of peace that ended the Second Punic War permanently eliminated Carthage as a world power. Never again would Carthage threaten Rome. The Carthaginians were forced to abandon all of their holdings in Iberia and Italy. They were allowed only a small navy, and they were required to pay war damages for the next fifty years.

But even though Carthage stopped fighting Rome, Hannibal never did. He left North Africa and traveled to Asia Minor, where he joined with the Syrians to battle the Romans. Later he battled the Romans in Crete and in northern Asia Minor. His burning hatred for Rome never abated. In his sixties, when the Romans were about to capture him, Hannibal the Great committed suicide by drinking a dose of poison he carried concealed in his ring.

AMAZING ANCIENTS: Scipio (236-183 BC)

Scipio (Publius Cornelius Scipio Africanus) was a Roman general who earned his fame by defeating Hannibal in the Second Punic War. Scipio hated Carthage with all of his heart, and just like Hannibal, Scipio promised his father that he would never give up until Carthage was defeated. Scipio's first battles, fought during his teens, were against Hannibal's forces in Northern Italy. At the age of 18, he saved his father's life in the Battle of Ticinus. After one of Rome's many defeats in the early years of the Second Punic War, Scipio held would-be Roman deserters at sword-point and forced them to swear an oath that they would never give up on Rome.

When Scipio was 25, his father and uncle died in the Battle of the Upper Baetis on the Iberian Peninsula. Scipio took command of the Roman army in Iberia in 211 BC, and within a few years he conquered the territory. Hannibal's brother Hasdrubal was forced to leave Iberia and move across the Alps to regroup with Hannibal. In the attempt, Hasdrubal was defeated and killed by other Roman generals.

Scipio returned to Rome and convinced the Roman consuls to adopt a new strategy: The best way to defeat Hannibal, he argued, was to attack the relatively undefended Carthage. With the consuls' permission, he departed for Africa in 203 BC. A frightened Carthage hastily recalled Hannibal, and in 202 BC the armies of Scipio and Hannibal met near Carthage. Scipio defeated Hannibal in the Battle of Zama (see below), and the Second Punic War was finally over.

With his promise to his father fulfilled and Carthage reduced to a minor power, Scipio retired from the military. He died in 183 BC at the age of 53.

The Third Punic War (149-146 BC)

After the Battle of Zama ended the Second Punic War, Rome departed to fight new battles against Carthage's former allies in Iberia and elsewhere. Carthage returned to the trade that had first made it wealthy. Despite the costly war damages it owed to Rome, Carthage was soon flourishing again. Rome, however, recovered less quickly. The many battles fought on Roman soil had caused great and costly damage, which the war damage payments didn't entirely cover. The Romans grew angry at the rising wealth of the Carthaginians. A respected Roman leader named Cato the Elder traveled to Carthage and became convinced that Carthage's wealth meant that it would arise to challenge Rome again. He promoted the idea that for the safety of Rome, Carthage must be destroyed.

In 149 BC, Carthage took up arms against an African tribe. This provided Rome with the excuse it needed. Rome claimed that Carthage had violated the peace treaty that ended the Second Punic War. Carthage tried to negotiate with Rome, offering up three hundred children and all of their weaponry as hostages. But this did not satisfy the Romans, who were bent on Carthage's destruction. Rome laid siege to Carthage for the next three years. In the end, the Romans breached the city walls and swept through the city, killing every man, woman and child they found. Carthage was destroyed (see picture on previous page), and any Carthaginian captives were sold into slavery.

The Results of the Punic Wars

The Punic Wars began with a dominant Carthage and ended with a supremely dominant Rome. With the end of the Third Punic War, Carthage was laid waste and Rome emerged as the new world power. Rome would become the world's greatest empire and would remain the dominant power in the world for the next six centuries.

FASCINATING FACTS: Roman Gear

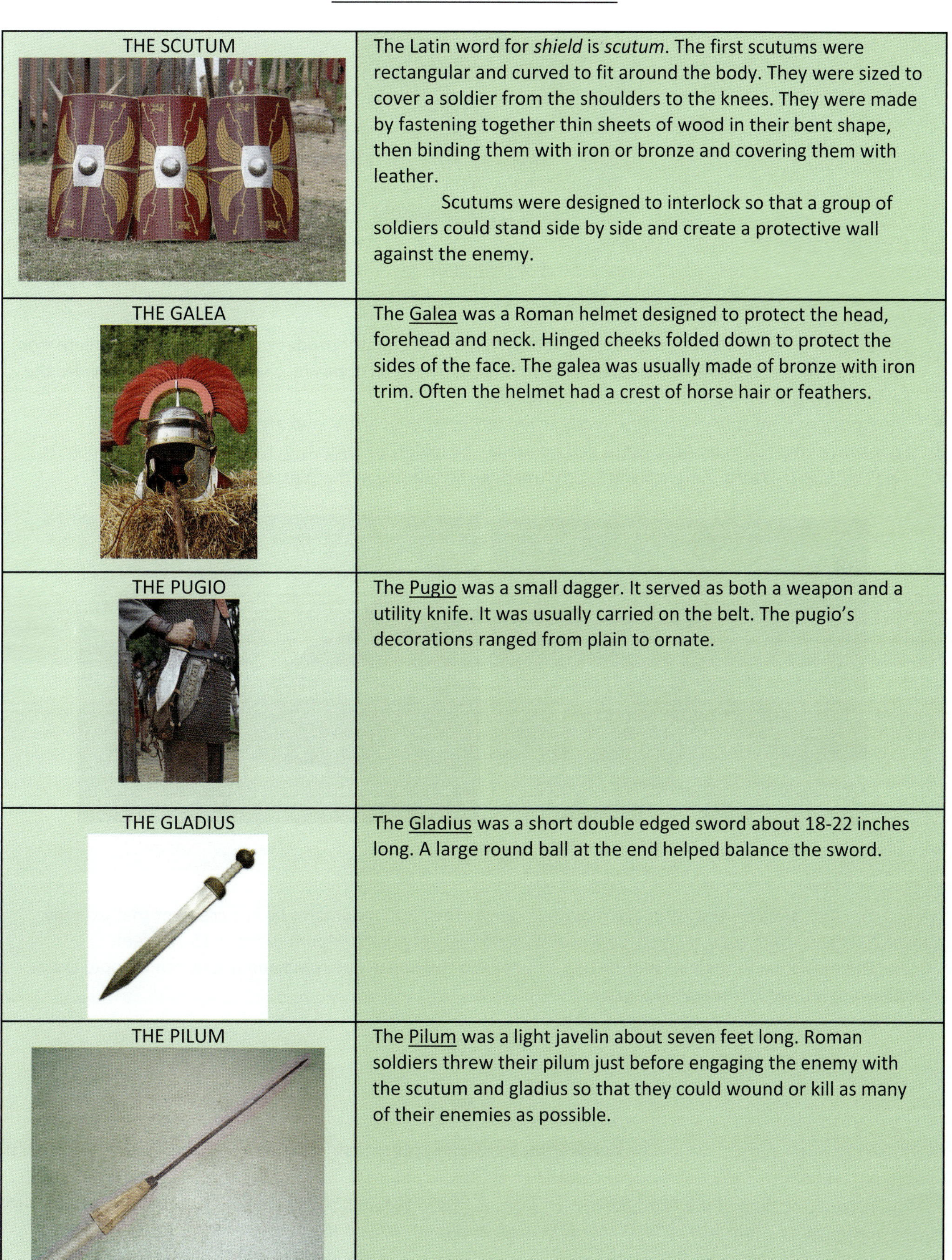

THE SCUTUM	The Latin word for *shield* is *scutum*. The first scutums were rectangular and curved to fit around the body. They were sized to cover a soldier from the shoulders to the knees. They were made by fastening together thin sheets of wood in their bent shape, then binding them with iron or bronze and covering them with leather. Scutums were designed to interlock so that a group of soldiers could stand side by side and create a protective wall against the enemy.
THE GALEA	The Galea was a Roman helmet designed to protect the head, forehead and neck. Hinged cheeks folded down to protect the sides of the face. The galea was usually made of bronze with iron trim. Often the helmet had a crest of horse hair or feathers.
THE PUGIO	The Pugio was a small dagger. It served as both a weapon and a utility knife. It was usually carried on the belt. The pugio's decorations ranged from plain to ornate.
THE GLADIUS	The Gladius was a short double edged sword about 18-22 inches long. A large round ball at the end helped balance the sword.
THE PILUM	The Pilum was a light javelin about seven feet long. Roman soldiers threw their pilum just before engaging the enemy with the scutum and gladius so that they could wound or kill as many of their enemies as possible.

GEOGRAPHY FOCUS

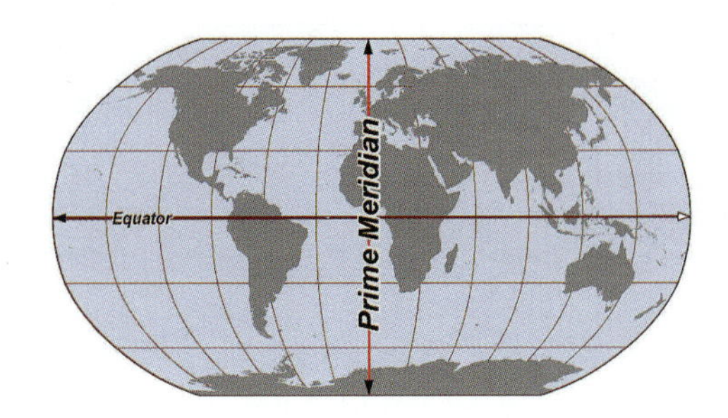

The Hemispheres

Did you know….

- The earth is divided into four overlapping hemispheres. The equator divides the Northern Hemisphere from the Southern Hemisphere. The Prime Meridian (together with its opposite, the 180th Meridian) divides the Eastern Hemisphere from the Western Hemisphere.
- The Northern Hemisphere contains nearly seven tenths of the earth's land area.
- Four continents– Europe, Asia, Africa and Australia– lie mainly or entirely in the Eastern Hemisphere.
- Two continents– North America and South America– lie entirely in the Western Hemisphere.

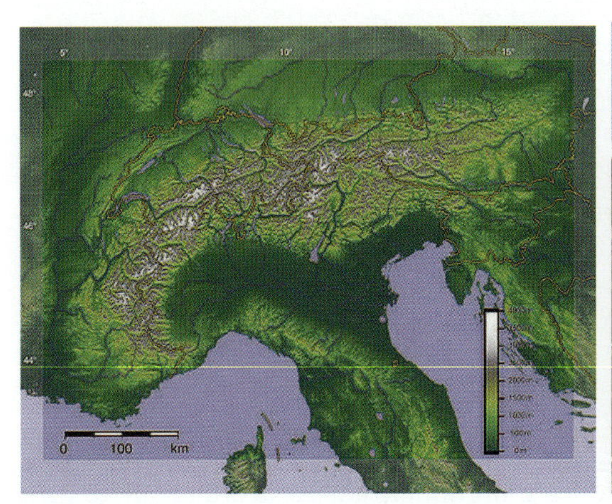

FASCINATING FACTS: The Alps

The Alps are a central European mountain range. Their 180 mountains lie in a crescent that extends almost 700 miles, from coastal France to Slovenia. Their highest peak is Mount Blanc at 15,732 feet.

The Alps are a formidable natural barrier between the Italian Peninsula and the rest of Europe, but as Hannibal proved, not an impenetrable one.

BIBLE FOCUS

Israel

The Maccabean Revolt (168-135 BC)

Around the time of the Third Punic War, Jerusalem's Jews had troubles of their own. Their city was ruled by the Seleucid king Antiochus IV, who hated the Jews and their religion (recall that the Seleucids were the eastern remnant of Alexander the Great's empire). Wherever in the world Jews have gone over the centuries, they have been hated for their strange and exclusive religion that prevents them from bowing down to other gods.

Antiochus IV set out to eliminate every Jew who refused to worship the Greek gods. He ordered that any Jew caught praying or observing the Sabbath must be put to death. Any circumcised child must be killed, along with his mother. Any Jewish scrolls must be burned. In the second Temple, rebuilt in the time of Ezra and Nehemiah, Antiochus IV erected an altar to Zeus and sacrificed a pig on it.

Outraged at the desecration of their Temple, the Jews revolted. The revolt was led by a family known as the Maccabees (the name means *hammerer*). The family's father, an elderly priest named Mattathias, organized a guerilla army and launched raids against Antiochus. Mattathias died soon after the revolt began, but left his son Judas (or Judah) Maccabee in charge.

Even though he was outnumbered, ill-equipped and untrained, Judas Maccabee led his Jewish troops to victory over Antiochus again and again. Within three years, Judas fought his way to Jerusalem and reclaimed the Temple. He cleared out the idols and dismantled the Zeus altar. In 165 BC, three years to the day after Antiochus' defiling pig sacrifice, the victorious Jews rededicated their Temple and relit the menorah to begin eight days of celebration.

According to tradition, they had only enough olive oil to burn the menorah for a single day. Miraculously, however, it burned for the entire eight days of their celebration. This miracle came to be known as the "Feast of Lights," or *Hanukkah.* Jewish people still celebrate Hanukkah every year around Christmastime.

Chapter 28

Julius Caesar

ANCIENT HISTORY FOCUS

END OF THE ROMAN REPUBLIC

The Roman Republic began in 509 BC when members of the Senate overthrew the last Roman king (Chapter 26). The Republic stood for more than 450 years, years in which Rome emerged as the superpower of the known world. These years were not without conflict. The Punic Wars (264-146 BC, see Chapter 27) took a heavy toll on Rome. For many of these same years, Rome was forced to fight four Macedonian Wars (215-148 BC). At the end of the fourth Macedonian War, Rome finally controlled Macedonia.

The last 200 years of the Roman Republic were marked by civil war and slave revolts.

FASCINATING FACTS: Roman Slave Revolts (The Servile Wars)

There were three major slave revolts in Rome between 135-70 BC. These became known as the Servile Wars.

Life as a Slave in Ancient Rome

Slavery was common in Rome. Every time Rome conquered a new land, it sold hundreds or thousands of captured men, women and children into slavery. At the slave market, the prospective purchase stood elevated on an auction block wearing a plaque around his or her neck listing desirable qualities for buyers. Household slaves were inexpensive, so it was common for a home to have ten or more slaves for household tasks. Slaves also worked in mines, on plantations, or as tradesmen. Well-educated slaves could even work as teachers or private tutors. Some also went to the arena as gladiators.

Although slaves were considered the property of their masters, some masters allowed them to earn and save money in order to purchase their freedom eventually. However, these freed slaves could never vote or attain the privileges of Roman citizens.

Slaves who worked on farms or plantations suffered harsher conditions than city slaves. Plantation slaves worked in gangs managed by whip-wielding slave drivers, and were often separated from their families. Any who tried to escape were severely punished, sometimes with death. Slaves who worked in the mines had the hardest lives of all. These harsh conditions led to discontent and unrest among the slaves, and ultimately to revolt.

First Servile War (135-132 BC): The First Servile War took place on the island of Sicily. It began as an uprising led by a former slave named Eunus, who supposedly breathed fire. The rioting slaves massacred their masters and seized a number of towns. Rome sent an army to defeat the slave army and capture Eunus.

Second Servile War (104-100 BC): The Second Servile War also took place on the island of Sicily. A Roman army officer offered some of Sicily's slaves freedom if they would fight for Rome, and many jumped at the chance. When the governor ordered some of them to return to slavery, they revolted under the leadership of a slave named Salvius. The Romans put down the rebellion after four years.

Third Servile War (73 - 71 BC): A well-known gladiator named Spartacus led the Third Servile War. Spartacus was trained in the Roman army before he became a slave and a gladiator. In 73 BC, Spartacus and about seventy other gladiators escaped from their gladiator school at Capua, near Naples. They sought refuge in the mountains and began to gather followers. Thousands of slaves eager to revolt against Rome's cruelty joined Spartacus, until he had amassed a formidable army.

Rome sent a force of 3,000 soldiers to deal with the rebellion, but Spartacus and his followers defeated this force and took all of its supplies. Rome sent a second force, but it too was defeated. Soon Spartacus had about 70,000 slaves fighting at his side, and he trained his army as he himself had been trained. In battle, Spartacus was an excellent tactician. Rome grew alarmed by this large army running loose in the heart of Italy.

Finally, the Romans had to send eight well-trained legions to deal with Spartacus and his slave army. After three years of fighting, the Romans defeated the slaves, killing the vast majority in battle. Rome crucified about 6,000 captured rebels and left their bodies hanging along the Appian Way to demonstrate the punishment for rebel slaves. Spartacus himself probably died in battle, but his body was never recovered.

Modern literature and movies paint Spartacus as a freedom fighter and a defender of the oppressed. This seems fitting, because all of the Servile Wars were a direct result of Rome's harsh oppression of its slaves. However, no records remain of anything that Spartacus said, wrote or thought, so much of the romance that surrounds his name is based on conjecture.

THE SOCIAL WARS (91-88 BC)

Conflict also arose between Rome and the neighboring Italian cities. Between 400-200 BC, Rome either conquered or formed voluntary alliances with all of Italy's other major city-states. All of these cities were subject to Roman taxes and tribute, and all of them offered up their men as soldiers in the Roman army; yet none of their people were Roman citizens, which meant that none of them could vote in Roman elections. When Rome refused to share the spoils of its many wars with these neighbors, the neighbors began to rebel.

In 91 BC, many of these Italian neighbors essentially seceded from Rome and tried to form a new nation in opposition to Rome. The complex set of conflicts that followed became known as the Social Wars (from the Latin *socii*, meaning friend or ally). Rome defeated its former allies and brought them back into the fold, but not without making concessions: Rome conferred a sort of citizenship on the Italian neighbor states, allowing them to participate in Roman elections.

Two generals who emerged victorious from the Social Wars, Marius and Sulla, fought for control of Rome. The victor, Lucius Sulla, became Rome's dictator until he retired in 78 BC.

JULIUS CAESAR

Early Life (100-78 BC)

Julius Caesar (100-44 BC) was born in a time of civil war and unrest in the Republic. When Caesar was a young man, Rome was under the control of Lucius Sulla, who had made himself Dictator. Caesar's family was connected with Sulla's arch nemesis, Gaius Marius.

When Caesar was fifteen years old, his father died and Caesar became a man in the eyes of the law, responsible for his own household. Although he had been betrothed to a wealthy Plebeian girl from childhood, he instead married a Patrician girl whose father was connected to Marius. Sulla was bent on destroying anyone with ties to Marius, and so he tried to ruin Caesar. Sulla relented, but Caesar didn't feel safe in Rome, so he left the city and joined the army.

Early in his military career, Caesar won a high military honor, the Civic Crown.

FASCINATING FACTS: Rome's Civic Crown Award

Rome's second highest military honor was the Civic Crown. The Civic Crown was awarded to Roman citizens who saved the life of another citizen in battle. The honor was the same whether the citizen saved was a plebe or a general; unlike much in Roman life, the Civic Crown did not depend on one's class or wealth.

The crown itself was woven from simple oak leaves, otherwise unadorned. In itself, it was practically worthless. The honors afforded to its wearers, though, were great. When Civic Crown honorees wore their crowns in public, senators stood up to honor them, and they had the right to sit next to the senators. They were exempted from public service duties, along with their fathers and even their paternal grandfathers. Under Sulla, Civic Crown honorees gained automatic entrance into the Senate.

Pirates (78 - 74 BC)

After Sulla's death, Caesar returned to Rome hoping to pursue a career in government. Back in Rome, he enjoyed the privileged life of the wealthy while working as an attorney, and he built a reputation as a great speechmaker. The Romans were proud of their language and admired good oratory, and Caesar was by all accounts one of the best.

In 75 BC, Caesar set out across the Aegean Sea to study in Greece. Before he could arrive there, however, he was kidnapped by pirates and held for ransom. His family paid the ransom-- the captive Caesar chided them for setting it too low, suggesting an increase-- and Caesar was released. But the pirates didn't enjoy their money for long, for they had chosen the wrong victim. Soon after his release, Caesar raised a fleet and hunted down the pirates, imprisoning and later killing them.

FASCINATING FACTS: Pirates in Roman Times

Because the world's seas are so vast and difficult to police, piracy has always been a tempting way of life for those who would rather steal than work. The unrest in Rome in the days of Caesar's youth made piracy even more attractive. Piracy became a form of resistance against harsh Roman rule. Rome could not control, tax or imprison those whom it could not catch, so pirates roamed the Mediterranean Sea in large numbers.

Pirate vessels typically attacked merchant vessels filled with trade goods. Whatever crew the pirates captured would be taken to an island and sold into slavery. If they happened to capture anyone from a wealthy or high-ranking family, they would sometimes demand a ransom payment, as they did with Caesar. The family had little choice but to pay.

Rome got control of its pirate problem a few years later under the consulship of Pompey.

Waiting (74 - 69 BC)

Caesar returned to Rome and in 72 BC was elected a military tribune, the first step on the road to political prominence. In 69 BC he was elected *quaestor*, a financial officer. He was on his way to higher office, but his progress was not fast enough for him. When he saw a statue of Alexander the Great, he sadly noted that when Alexander was Caesar's own age, he had already conquered most of the known world.

In 70 BC, two men were elected as consuls: Crassus and Pompey.

INTERESTING INDIVIDUALS: Crassus and Pompey

Marcus Crassus: Marcus Crassus was born into a wealthy family, and he grew so wealthy that he is still on a list of the top ten richest people of all time. At one time he owned most of the city of Rome.

Crassus' devious method of building wealth revolved around house fires, both accidental and deliberate. He bought large numbers of slaves who were skilled in the building trades, then used them to restore or replace homes damaged or lost in Rome's constant house fires. If fires grew scarce, some said, Crassus was not above using some of his men to set a few. Then he charged rent on his new properties, sometimes to the same people who had lost their homes in the fires. He also took advantage of his political connections: When his friend Dictator Sulla purged Rome of the friends of his enemy Marius, Crassus bought the former homes of these deceased and disgraced citizens.

Crassus used his wealth to support Sulla's rise to power, and he also supported Julius Caesar in his early years. Crassus' money opened doors for him, including the door of the consulship he shared with Pompey.

Gnaeus Pompeius Magnus (Pompey): Pompey was also born into a wealthy family, but he earned fame through his brilliant military career. Pompey fought in Spain and in Africa, and he helped suppress Spartacus in the Third Servile War back in Italy. After his great performance in Africa, his troops bestowed upon him the title *Pompeius Magnus* (*Pompey the Great*).

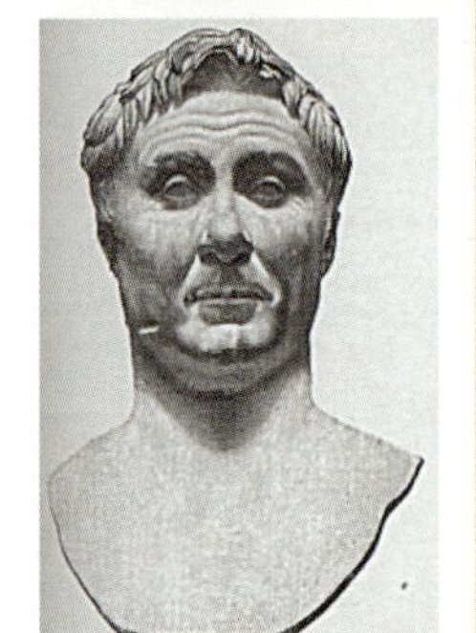

Pompey was elected to the consulship alongside Crassus. Crassus did most of the work of defeating Spartacus, but Pompey managed to steal most of the glory. For his part, Pompey was responsible for controlling the problem of the Mediterranean pirates. His successes made him wildly popular and earned him a reputation as one of Rome's most successful military commanders of all time.

Pompey also campaigned in the east. He conquered part of the Seleucid Empire, the eastern remnant of Alexander's empire, which still held Syria and Canaan. In doing this, Pompey claimed Jerusalem for Rome and brought the former territory of the kingdoms of Israel and Judah into the Roman Republic. This would become important for the Jews who still lived there and for the coming Jesus of Nazareth.

To Spain and Back (69 - 60 BC)

Caesar's quaestorship took him to Spain at the age of 30. He did well in Spain, but he was too ambitious to be happy as the eventual governor of a mere province. So in 65 BC, back in Rome, Caesar was elected to the office of *aedile*, which put him in charge of public buildings, festivals and games. Caesar's popularity grew as he spent himself into tremendous debt organizing fun events for the public. He moved up through the offices of *Pontifex Maximus* (head of the state religion), *praetor* (magistrate and military leader) and governor of part of Spain. He went to Crassus for help with his debts, and this became the beginning of an important political alliance.

Consulship and the First Triumvirate (59 BC)

Caesar knew that he needed help if he was to be elected to the office of consul, Rome's highest office. He wanted the backing of both Crassus and Pompey, but the two had been at odds since their joint consulship ten years before. He already had a relationship with Crassus. In order to woo Pompey, Caesar promised to back legislation that Pompey supported and cemented the deal by offering his own daughter to Pompey in marriage.

In 59 BC, Julius Caesar was elected consul with the support of Pompey and Crassus. Their powerful political alliance became known as the First Triumvirate, or "rule of three" (three leaders). During his year as consul, Caesar dominated his co-consul, a man named Bibulus. He strong-armed his way into the Assembly and pushed for measures that advanced the careers of both Pompey and Crassus. His intimidation tactics overwhelmed the opposition. Some of what he did was questionable and probably illegal, but his government office kept him safe from prosecution.

At the end of his year as consul, Caesar left Rome for a new appointment as proconsul (regional governor) of Gaul, the territory that became France.

The Gallic Wars (58 - 50 BC)

Caesar would not return to Rome for the next nine years. During his time away he conquered most of central Europe and even pushed into Britain, adding to his reputation with every conquest (Caesar did not truly conquer Britain, which did not come under Roman rule until 43 AD). He was careful to report only his victories, never his losses. His clever way with words meant that his reports were widely read back home, boosting his reputation even higher.

Both Crassus and Pompey continued to support Caesar through his time in Gaul, but Pompey began to grow jealous of Caesar's fame. With the 54 BC death of Julia, Caesar's namesake daughter given in marriage to Pompey, the rift between Caesar and Pompey widened.

Crassus and Pompey were again elected co-consuls in 55 BC, so each had another opportunity to add to his military glory. Crassus tried to push Rome's boundaries even farther east, but the attempt was his undoing-- he died in battle. One story tells that his enemies poured molten gold into the wealthy man's dead mouth to symbolize his "thirst" for gold. This was the end of Caesar's strongest ally.

In 52 BC, the popular Pompey was again elected consul. Hoping to remain in Pompey's good graces, Caesar offered his niece to Pompey as a bride. But the great general had soured on Caesar, so he refused. The two were on a path toward confrontation.

In 51 BC, Caesar published his *Commentaries on the Gallic Wars,* which detailed his nine years of campaigning in Britain, Gaul and Germany. His excellent command of language made this work a scholarly standard. Caesar's reports from Gaul are still used today in the teaching of the Latin language.

Caesar and Pompey (52-49 BC)

With both Julia and Crassus gone, the alliance between Pompey and Caesar disintegrated. The members of the Roman Senate feared Caesar's popularity and his ambition, so they continued to support Pompey while they considered how they might rein Caesar in. Finally, in 50 BC, the Senate ordered Caesar to give up his command in Gaul and return to Rome as a private citizen.

Caesar knew that to give up his army and meekly return to Rome would be the end of his political ambitions. Pompey and the Senate had turned against him, and they would eliminate him if they could in order to cement their own hold on power. If he was to gain power in Rome, he would have to do it now, while he still had his army. So he led his army down through Gaul and back toward Italy.

The boundary between Gaul and Italy was the Rubicon River. When Caesar led his army across the Rubicon on January 10, 49 BC, he was launching a civil war in Rome and making his bid to become Rome's supreme ruler. As he crossed, Caesar said in Latin "Alea iacta est," or "The die is cast." There was no turning back from such a bold maneuver. Even today, "crossing the Rubicon" still refers to any irrevocable and life-altering action.

Pompey and most of the Senators fled Rome and sailed across the Adriatic Sea to Greece. Instead of pursuing them, Caesar went to Spain to deal with Pompey's army.

Caesar in Egypt (48 BC)

After Caesar defeated Pompey's army in Spain, he challenged Pompey in Greece. Although his army was smaller than Pompey's, Caesar was still the victor. Pompey had to flee to Egypt. Caesar returned to Rome, where he pardoned his enemies in the Senate and reestablished himself in Rome's leadership. Soon he would be consul again in Rome, then Dictator. For the next six months, he battled enemies in Spain and tried to validate his victories in Gaul by granting Roman citizenship to the peoples he had conquered there.

FASCINATING FACTS: Caesar's Clemency

One of the surprising things about Caesar was his willingness to grant clemency (mercy) to his defeated enemies. The Roman norm was brutality. The Roman way was to make an example of enemies, whether by cutting off the head of Hannibal's brother and tossing it into Hannibal's camp or by crucifying Spartacus's rebels and leaving their bodies hanging all along the Appian Way. Caesar's way was new: he often pardoned his enemies, possibly in the hope that they would one day join him.

The clemency policy was at best a mixed success for Caesar, because more than once he had to fight generals whom he had already defeated and then pardoned. Caesar's 48 BC pardon of the Roman Senate earned him few long-term friends there. In the end, the Senate would turn against him again in a deadly way.

The defeated Pompey found himself unwelcome in Egypt, which had recently lost its king. On the suggestion of his advisers, ten-year-old King Ptolemy XIII of Egypt had Pompey killed and then beheaded. When Caesar found out where Pompey had fled and chased him there, Ptolemy made him a gift of Pompey's head in the hope that this would win Caesar's support. This was a miscalculation: Caesar did not approve of Ptolemy's murder of such a prominent Roman citizen, however great an enemy. So instead of supporting Ptolemy, Caesar threw his considerable weight behind Ptolemy's rival for Egypt's throne: his sister Cleopatra VII.

Caesar defeated Ptolemy's army and installed Cleopatra as Egypt's Queen, under the oversight of Rome. Meanwhile, Caesar and Cleopatra had a famous love affair, and Caesar extended his stay in Egypt so that he wouldn't have to leave his new lover. Cleopatra bore Caesar a son, whom they named Caesarion. Caesar remained with Cleopatra until June of 47 BC (See more on Cleopatra in Chapter 29).

Campaigns (47-45 BC)

- Battle of the Nile (February 47 BC): Caesar defeats King Ptolemy XIII of Egypt
- August 47 BC: Caesar sweeps through Asia Minor and defeats King Pharnaces II. His well-known saying "Veni, vidi, vici" ("I came, I saw, I conquered") comes from this victory.
- 46 BC: Caesar moves into Africa and defeats Pompey's supporters.
- March 45 BC: Caesar follows Pompey's sons to Spain and defeats them.

During this time, Caesar was elected consul again in both 46 and 45 BC. In 45 he served as consul alone, although by law there were supposed to be two consuls.

During brief stints in Rome, Caesar made several changes to Roman law. He extended Roman citizenship and its benefits to all who lived on the Italian peninsula and to all who fought with him. He overhauled the Roman calendar, provided land for his veterans and provided government grain for the poor.

Caesar's style of governance angered many in the Senate, because he often bypassed the Senate entirely. Instead of leading a debate in the Senate and calling for a vote, Caesar would simply announce his own decisions and have them written into the record as Senate decisions. Caesar was making more enemies in the Senate (picture is of Caesar's enemies plotting to kill him).

<u>FASCINATING FACTS: The Roman Calendar</u>

Painting of Roman Calendar before the Julian reforms - about 60 BC

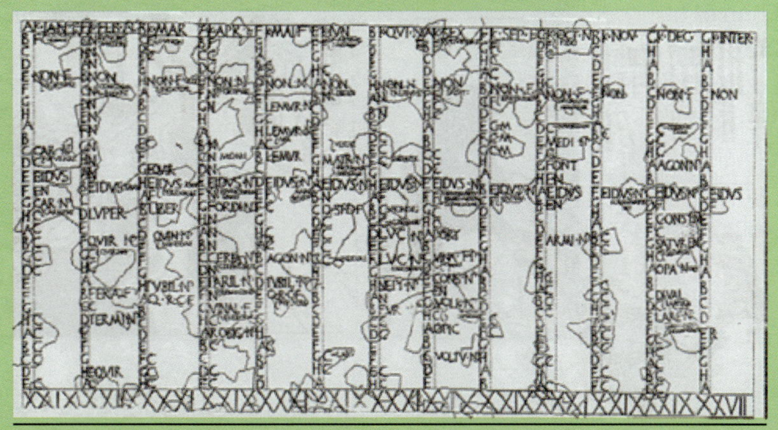

The Roman Calendar dates to the time of Romulus. The original calendar year was divided into ten lunar months, beginning in Spring and ending in December. The winter months were not counted in this first Roman Calendar.

The second king of Rome, Numa Pompilius, added two more months to the calendar, making the Roman year 355 days long. Every other year, he added an extra month to keep the calendar roughly in line with the solar year.

It was under Caesar that the calendar was reformed into one closely resembling the modern calendar. The new Roman calendar was called the Julian Calendar. The science of the day was sufficiently advanced to allow the Romans to arrive at the true length of the solar year, 365 ¼ days. Every four years, they added an extra day to cover the four extra quarter days. To bring the new months into line with the solar year, Caesar added 90 extra days to the end of 46 BC, and then the new Julian calendar took effect in January 45 BC.

Within each month, the Romans had markers. The first day of each month was *Kalends*, from which the English word *calendar* is derived. Kalends was probably originally intended to fall on the new moon, although the lunar calendar had to be abandoned as the solar year took over. The day of the half moon was *Nones*, and the day of the full moon was *Ides*-- although again, after the adoption of the solar calendar, these days were no longer associated with the phases of the moon. Under the Julian Calendar, the Nones fell on the fifth or the seventh of each month, the Ides on the thirteenth or fifteenth. The Ides of any month was a special day, believed to be a day for important deeds or events.

The End (44 BC)

By the end of 45 BC, Caesar had a great number of enemies who resented the amount of power he had taken for himself. He appointed his own selections to government office without consulting the Senate. He issued coins with his picture engraved on them. He commissioned statues of himself in which he was adorned like the gods. He sat in a gilded chair, and he directed the Senate to give him the right to wear a kingly purple and gold toga with a laurel wreath crown.

In February 44 BC, Caesar was named *dictator perpetuus* ("eternal dictator," although he could resign if he so desired). On February 15 (the Ides of February), Caesar appeared in public adorned in his new purple toga. He was offered the crown, but he ostentatiously refused it, to the delight of the crowd. His enemies ground their teeth at the adoration the crowd showed for Caesar.

A month later, on March 15, 44 BC (the famous "Ides of March"), Caesar went to a Senate meeting prior to his planned departure on another military campaign. Members of the Senate had other plans. As the Senate convened, a group of Caesar's enemies attacked him with knives, stabbing him 23 times. As the great man fell, he recognized one of his cousins in the group of attackers and supposedly cried out in disbelief, "Et tu, Brute?" ("You too, Brutus?") Brutus was part of the Senate Caesar had pardoned in 48 BC, and as his cousin, he also stood to inherit some of Caesar's wealth.

After Caesar died, his killers fled and Rome fell into chaos.

Fascinating Facts about Julius Caesar

- Caesar traced his lineage back to Romulus, Rome's legendary founder.
- Caesar's armies were known for their great speed. His armies marched as far as 40 Roman miles per day.
- Caesar and Cleopatra were lovers and had one son together, but they never married. It was illegal for a Roman citizen to marry someone who was not a Roman citizen, and their son was unqualified to be Caesar's heir under Roman law.
- Caesar adopted his nephew, Gaius Julius Caesar Octavianus, as his heir. Octavian became the first Emperor of Rome.

FASCINATING FACTS: Caesar's Coin

The ancient Romans considered it improper to engrave a living person's portrait on a coin. Their coins were adorned with pictures of animals, nature, ancestors or one of the gods. Julius Caesar was the first to put his picture on a coin, and it contributed to his downfall. By placing his likeness on a coin, he was setting himself up as king in the eyes of many, and the Romans were proud of the fact that their representative republic had no king. Only a few weeks after Caesar put his image on coins, Brutus and his republican allies assassinated him for assuming too much power. Thus his coin is sometimes called "the coin that killed Caesar."

Ironically, after he helped his fellow senators assassinate Caesar, Brutus designed a coin to commemorate Caesar's death and Rome's freedom from Caesar's tyranny. This coin became known as the EID MAR (Ides of March) coin. On the heads side was a portrait of Brutus and the title IMP (Emperor), which Brutus wasn't. On the tails side were daggers (murder weapons used against Caesar) and the date of the assassination. For someone who took great offense at Caesar's image on a coin, Brutus was quick to produce his own.

FASCINATING FACTS: The Bulla

A *bulla* was a protective amulet worn by the male children of Ancient Rome. Boys received their bullae when they were nine days old. Each bulla was hollow, and inside were protective charms and symbols intended to ward off harm. When boys achieved Roman citizenship at the age of 16, they could remove their bullae and dress like Roman men. From that time one, they wore their bullae only on special occasions.

The material of the bulla varied with one's station in life. Wealthy boys wore gold bullae, while middle class boys wore leather and poor boys wore cloth.

Chapter 29

Augustus Caesar and the Birth of Jesus

ANCIENT HISTORY FOCUS

CAESAR AUGUSTUS (Gaius Octavian, 63 BC - 14 AD)

After the 44 BC assassination of Julius Caesar, two men arose from the confusion to make their own bids for absolute power in Rome: Marc Antony and Gaius Octavian. Both men were related to Caesar and both had supported him loyally. Gaius Octavian was Caesar's heir, adopted before the assassination; while Marc Antony had served under Caesar as a military commander and advised him during his last term as consul.

INTERESTING INDIVIDUALS: Mark Antony (82 - 30 BC)

M. Antonius.

Mark Antony was born in Rome in 82 BC. His father died when he was young, and Antony spent his early years in rebellion and wild living. In his twenties he left Rome to study rhetoric in Greece. Then he joined the Roman legions, where his officers quickly recognized his natural ability as a military leader. Antony became a commander in Caesar's army in Gaul and a devoted supporter of Caesar.

As Caesar rose in power, Marc Antony rose with him. When Caesar was consul later in his career, Marc Antony reigned in Caesar's place whenever Caesar was away from Rome on a military campaign. Then Antony was elected Caesar's co-consul for the year 44 BC. After Caesar's assassination, Antony took over the treasury and established himself at the top of Rome's political ladder.

He didn't count on Gaius Octavian.

Nineteen year old Gaius Octavian was Caesar's acknowledged heir. After the dust from Caesar's assassination settled, Octavian decided to return to Rome and claim his inheritance from Caesar. He was not without competition for Caesar's estate: Caesar had actually left most of his property to the people of Rome. This act of philanthropy cemented the citizens' love for the departed Caesar, and in many of their minds he was elevated to the status of a god. Octavian's inheritance came more in the form of a share of Caesar's power and political influence. The Romans' good opinion of Caesar extended to Caesar's heir.

Octavian took the name Gaius Julius Caesar Octavianus, but he asked to be addressed as "Caesar." When he arrived back in Rome, he was able to gather his uncle's former troops to his side. Marc Antony tried to hold Octavian off, but Antony's legions refused to fight Caesar's heir. In order to preserve any power for himself at all, Antony was forced to enter into an alliance with Octavian and Marcus Aemilius Lepidus. This alliance became known as the Second Triumvirate.

INTERESTING INDIVIDUALS: Marcus Aemilius Lepidus

Marcus Aemilius Lepidus was one of Julius Caesar's strongest supporters. Caesar trusted Lepidus with positions of authority when he was away from Rome, just as he trusted Marc Antony. Just before Julius Caesar died, Lepidus became Caesar's deputy. The two were so close that some of the Senate conspirators who assassinated Caesar actually considered killing Lepidus and Antony as well. Brutus overruled this idea, so Lepidus and Antony survived to strike back at Caesar's murderers.

Lepidus joined with Marc Antony and Octavian to form an alliance called the Second Triumvirate, which lasted for ten years. Under their agreement, Lepidus became the ruler of the provinces of Spain and Gaul. In 36 BC, Octavian summoned Lepidus to Sicily to help him win a battle. When this was done, instead of leaving, Lepidus assumed control of part of Sicily. Octavian demanded that Lepidus leave, and the two battled. Octavian defeated Lepidus and banished him. He was kept under strict supervision until his death in 12 BC.

The Second Triumvirate

These were the three unlikely allies of the Second Triumvirate: Octavian, Antony and Lepidus. The Second Triumvirate was a much more formal arrangement than the first. It was a legal and binding agreement, and its terms essentially ended the Roman Republic. The power assumed by the Second Triumvirate was greater than that of the consuls, and the Senate and the Assemblies surrendered some of their power. Rome was becoming an Empire, but it was not quite there yet.

The Second Triumvirate held the powers of a dictator, which the three men agreed to use toward the following goals:

- To battle the conspirators who had killed Caesar
- To provide farms for Caesar's war veterans (which they achieved by taking farms from their rightful owners without payment and giving them to Caesar's veteran soldiers, displacing thousands of farmers)
- To give battle to any who opposed them and to execute their enemies (including close relatives)
- To appoint all magistrates themselves, taking over the power of the Senate
- To divide the Roman Empire between them with Lepidus in the west (Spain and Gaul), Octavian in Italy and Marc Antony in the east (Greece).

By 42 BC, the powerful Triumvirate had defeated the ringleaders of the conspiracy to assassinate Caesar, Brutus and Cassius. The Second Triumvirate was reduced to two members after Lepidus' failed attempt to take over part of Sicily in 36 BC. Lepidus was banished and stripped of his power, but the Triumvirate didn't end in the eyes of the law until 33 BC.

Cleopatra and Marc Antony

In 41 BC, Marc Antony met Cleopatra VII of Egypt. He was as taken with her as Caesar before him, and their romance was both well-known and tragic-- so much so that it was depicted in the Shakespeare play *Antony and Cleopatra*.

INTERESTING INDIVIDUALS: Cleopatra VII (69 - 30 BC)

Cleopatra VII of Egypt was a smart, clever and manipulative woman who used her beauty to influence powerful men. She was Egypt's last Pharaoh, because after her defeat and death, Egypt became part of the Roman Empire.

Cleopatra was the daughter of Egypt's King Ptolemy XII, a descendant of the same Ptolemy who served as a general under Alexander the Great. Ever since the division of Alexander's empire, Egypt had remained under the rule of Ptolemy and his heirs. Ptolemy XII died when Cleopatra was eighteen and her brother, Ptolemy XIII, was only ten. Cleopatra and her brother contended for the throne, but their father's advisers supported her brother, and Cleopatra had to flee.

After the Roman General Pompey's defeat at the hands of Julius Caesar, Pompey fled to Egypt seeking shelter and protection. Instead, he met death: Ptolemy XIII killed Pompey in an attempt to gain favor with Caesar. When Caesar arrived in Alexandria, Ptolemy offered him his enemy Pompey's head. But Caesar surprised Ptolemy: he was disgusted by this mistreatment of

Pompey, who was after all a highly honored citizen of Rome. Meanwhile, Cleopatra managed to meet Caesar secretly by smuggling herself into his quarters rolled up inside a carpet. Caesar quickly grew smitten with Cleopatra, and he was already angry with Ptolemy. He used his military might to defeat Ptolemy (who ended up drowning in the Nile) and place Cleopatra on the throne of Egypt-- although in order to please Egypt's priests, she had to marry her younger brother and serve as his queen.

Caesar remained in Egypt for a time so that he could be near Cleopatra. The couple took a romantic trip up the Nile which lasted for several months. During this time Cleopatra became pregnant with Caesar's son, whom they named Caesarion, born in 47 BC. Much to Cleopatra's dismay, Caesar refused to make the boy his heir. As Caesarion was not a Roman citizen, he was not legally qualified to be Caesar's heir; but of course Cleopatra knew that Caesar had broken rules before, and she wanted him to break this one for her son.

After Caesar's return to Rome, Cleopatra moved in with him there, causing quite a stir. But then Caesar was assassinated in 44 BC, so Cleopatra fled back to Egypt. There she disposed of her brother/husband and placed her son Caesarion on the throne. Because he was only three years old, Cleopatra ruled as his regent. All the while she observed events in Rome, hoping that somehow her son could take advantage of his parentage and achieve power there.

In 41 BC, Cleopatra invited the powerful Marc Antony to Egypt, where she wined and dined him despite an ongoing famine in her homeland. Like Caesar before him, Antony was taken in by Cleopatra's beauty, and the two became lovers (see picture). Cleopatra bore Marc Antony twins, a boy and a girl. Despite this, Antony departed Egypt and did not see Cleopatra for the next four years.

Then in 37 BC, Antony returned to visit Cleopatra, and she became pregnant with another son. From this time on, Antony made Alexandria his home, even though he was still married to a sister of Octavian.

In 34 BC, while he was still part of the Second Triumvirate, Marc Antony did something that raised many eyebrows in Rome: he divided up parts of the eastern Roman Empire, which he controlled, between his own children, Cleopatra and Caesarion. Neither Cleopatra nor any of her children were Roman citizens, so in doing this, Antony was ceding the rule of Roman territory to foreigners. To make matters worse, he divorced his wife, Octavian's sister, in 32 BC. With the end of the Second Triumvirate in 33 BC, the link between Octavian and Antony was fully severed. Octavian let it be known that he felt that Cleopatra was trying to overthrow Rome, then declared war on Cleopatra and Egypt. True to his love, Antony sided with Egypt.

But Egypt could not resist the full might of the Roman Empire under Octavian. In August 30 BC, after losing at the Battle of Actium, Marc Antony committed suicide by falling on his own sword. A few days later Cleopatra called for a cobra. She allowed the poisonous snake to bite her, and so she died.

Octavian killed Cleopatra's son Caesarion, ending his rival claim to the throne of Rome. "Two Caesars is one too many," remarked Octavian. Interestingly, the children Cleopatra shared with Marc Antony were raised by Antony's ex-wife Octavia.

FASCINATING FACTS: Cobra bites

According to ancient Egyptian religion, the bite of an Egyptian cobra (asp) guaranteed immortality (you could live forever) for the one bitten. When Cleopatra induced the poisonous snake to bite her, she was trying not only to kill herself, but also to secure immortality and seal her status as a goddess in the afterlife.

After he defeated Cleopatra and Antony, Octavian took for himself the title "Pharaoh of Egypt." The ancient Egyptian Empire, which had survived in one form or another for thousands of years, was no more. Like most of the known world, Egypt was now part of the Roman Empire.

Caesar Augustus

After the Battle of Actium, Octavian spent some time setting up the government of Egypt under Roman control. Then in 29 BC, Octavian returned to Rome, bringing with him a great deal of Egyptian wealth that now belonged to Rome. The victorious heir of Caesar was wildly popular in Rome. With both Lepidus and Antony defeated, Octavian was the only remaining member of the Second Triumvirate and the undisputed master of the entire Roman Empire.

Back in Rome, firmly in control as consul, Octavian made himself still more popular. He used money from his conquest of Egypt to settle thousands of veterans on their own farms, guaranteeing these veterans' undying support. When the Senate tried to honor him, he refused some of these honors as Caesar had done, which made his people love him all the more. The end of the near-constant civil wars also left his people grateful. And he did not seek to increase his personal power or take any special title beyond consul.

On the contrary, in January of 27 BC, Octavian shocked the Senate by voluntarily giving up his position as consul and claiming that he wished to retire to private life. Knowing how the Roman people loved him, the senators begged him to stay, offering him the office of proconsul (regional governor) of Spain, Gaul, Syria and Egypt. These governorships also left him in command of most of Rome's legions, so he remained the most powerful figure in Rome. During this time, the Senate conferred titles on Octavian: *Princeps*, *Augustus* and *Imperator*. Octavian was now Imperator Caesar Augustus, and Caesar Augustus became the title he would carry into history.

WORD ORIGINS:

Princeps: *first head* or *first citizen*. Originally, the title of Princeps was bestowed on the oldest or most distinguished member of the Senate to honor him. The Princeps had the right to speak first on any topic and to lead the debate. The English word "prince" is derived from Princeps.

Augustus: *the revered one* or *majestic*.

Imperator: During the Roman Republic, Imperator was the title of a high military commander. After Caesar Augustus, the title signified the supreme power of the Roman Emperor. The English word "emperor" is derived from Imperator.

Life Under Caesar Augustus

Augustus Caesar ruled for forty years, and his reign was the beginning of a long internal peace for Rome. This period of peace became known as the Pax Romana.

FASCINATING FACTS: The Pax Romana

Pax Romana is Latin for *Roman Peace*, and it refers to a long period of time in which peace reigned within the borders of the Roman Empire. This great peace began with Caesar Augustus and continued for about 200 years, from 27 BC to 180 AD. For most of those years, Rome was free from inner turmoil and therefore able to concentrate its energy on improving itself. Rome was also rich with the wealth it brought back from conquered lands and with tax money from its vast territory. Peace is much easier to achieve when all are well fed and money is plentiful.

The Pax Romana was by no means a complete peace: the Roman Empire continued to expand, and its conquests were not peaceful. The map above illustrates the Roman Empire at its height in 117 AD.

During the reign of Caesar Augustus, Rome reached the peak of its glory. The empire's roads and highways were improved for ease of travel throughout the empire. Rome's tax laws were reformed, and its government grew more efficient, more honest and less corrupt. Rome commissioned huge public building projects including public baths, government buildings, bridges and aqueducts. Rome had fire-fighting and police forces as well as a postal service. Trade was brisk, while literature and the arts flourished. Most of Rome was rebuilt. The last official words of Caesar Augustus in Rome were, "I found Rome a city of brick and left it a city of marble."

Fun Facts about Caesar Augustus (Octavian)

- Octavian made his first public appearance when he delivered the eulogy at his grandmother's funeral at the age of twelve
- Octavian was an adult when he was adopted by his uncle, Julius Caesar.
- Caesar Augustus refused to wear the diadem or the purple robe that Julius Caesar wore. He did place the civic crown above his door, and laurels were draped on his doorposts. These were honors bestowed upon him by the Senate.
- Caesar Augustus was declared a Roman god upon his death.
- Every emperor after Augustus adopted the title of "Caesar."
- Caesar Augustus banished the Druids from Gaul, possibly because they practiced human sacrifice.
- Caesar Augustus died in 14 AD. His step-son Tiberius succeeded him.

FASCINATING FACTS: Druids

The Druids were priests of the Celtic religion practiced in Gaul and Britain. The Celts had no written language, so little is known of the druids or the religion they practiced. They are associated with the worship of trees and nature. They also taught that the human soul did not die, but instead passed from one body to another. Druid priests and priestesses acted as mediums for these souls and summoned them with their secret rituals.

Druids are also associated with Britain's many circles of standing stones, including Stonehenge. Like the druids, the purposes and uses of the standing stones are obscure; but they may have marked burial sites, and they are also associated with astrology and the movements of celestial bodies.

The druids were active in Gaul when Julius Caesar campaigned there. The Romans were tolerant of many local religions, but they did not tolerate anything that disrupted trade or interfered with their rule. When Caesar's nephew and heir Caesar Augustus came to power as proconsul in Gaul, he encountered the druids himself. Somehow, the druids fell afoul of Caesar Augustus. It has been suggested that they practiced human sacrifice, which was against Roman law. Whatever it was, it upset Caesar Augustus so much that he banned all druid practice in Gaul. The druids retreated beyond the Roman Empire or went underground. If they carried on their religious practices, they did so secretly to hide them from the Romans. Little more is known of them.

GEOGRAPHY FOCUS

The Seas around the Mediterranean Sea

Did you know…

- The Mediterranean Sea is bordered by three different continents: Africa, Asia and Europe.
- The Mediterranean Sea is subdivided into several smaller seas. Among them:
    1. the Alboran Sea (between Spain and Morocco)
    2. the Balearic Sea (between Spain and Majorca)
    3. the Ligurian Sea (between northwest Italy and Corsica)
    4. the Tyrrhenian Sea (between Italy and the islands of Sardinia and Sicily)
    5. the Adriatic Sea (between the Italian Peninsula and the Balkan Peninsula)
    6. the Ionian Sea (between southern Italy and Greece)
    7. the Aegean Sea (between Greece and Turkey)

BIBLE FOCUS

ISRAEL

Although the Bible falls silent for the 400 years leading up to the birth of Christ, the Jewish people continued to live out their unique faith in Jerusalem and elsewhere. Their former kingdoms of Israel and Judah had changed hands more than once over the years since Babylon and Persia: their region was conquered by Alexander the Great, then parceled out to General Seleucus and the Seleucid Empire after Alexander's sudden death.

The success of Maccabean Revolt (see Chapter 27) led to a brief comeback for the Jewish nation. In 168 BC, Seleucid King Antiochus IV enraged the Jews by burning their scriptures and sacrificing an unclean pig inside their Second Temple. In the following year, a Jewish leader named Judah Maccabee led a successful revolt and ejected the Seleucids from Jerusalem and its surrounding kingdom, Judea. Maccabees' descendants established the Hasmonean Dynasty and ruled Judea for about a century, serving as Judea's kings and high priests of the Temple. The years of the Hasmonean Dynasty brought the return of a nearly independent Kingdom of Israel for the first time in centuries.

But Judea could not maintain its independence for long. In 63 BC, Roman General Pompey conquered the Seleucid Empire, along with many of its former holdings. He divided the Hasmoneans' kingdom and placed it under a Roman governor.

Through all of this, Jewish worship still centered around the Second Temple in Jerusalem, although Jews were scattered throughout the known world. The scattering of the Jews has persisted into modern times, and is known as the *Diaspora*.

Brief Timeline of Jewish history after the Fall of Jerusalem

587 BC: Jerusalem and the Kingdom of Judah fall to Babylon
539 BC: Jews begin to return to Jerusalem under Persia's Cyrus the Great
516 BC: The Jews complete and dedicate the Second Temple
333 BC: Alexander the Great conquers Judea (along with the rest of the known world)
312 BC: Alexander's General Seleucus establishes the Seleucid Empire in the eastern part of dead Alexander's empire
167 BC: The Maccabean Revolt restores a semi-independent Israel under the Hasmonean Dynasty
63 BC: Rome conquers the entire region and places Judea under a Roman governor

INTERESTING INDIVIDUAL: Herod the Great

The area that included the former kingdoms of Israel and Judah came to be known as Palestine, a name that came from the Philistines, those hated enemies of Samson, King David and others. In 63 BC, Pompey defeated the Seleucids in Palestine and claimed the territory for Rome. When Julius Caesar defeated Pompey, he in turn assumed control of Palestine.

Caesar appointed Antipater, an Arab Sheikh who had helped him defeat Pompey, as governor of Judea, Samaria and Galilee. Antipater installed his two sons Herod and Feisal as governors of Galilee and Judea. This put an end to the Maccabean or Hasmonean dynasty that had ruled in Judea since the Maccabean revolt. In an effort to make himself more acceptable to the people of Judea, Herod married a Hasmonean princess.

When the Persians attacked Palestine again, Herod fled to Rome for help. The Roman Senate gave Herod a warm welcome and elected him "King of Judea" in 37 BC. Herod returned to Palestine backed by Roman legions and drove the Persians out again. After this he was free to reign in Judea, although he was still subject to Rome's authority. Herod became

Rome's "client king," a local governor under Roman control.

But while the Romans liked Herod, the Jews did not. Herod was an Arab, and even though his father had raised him to worship the Jewish God, his mother was an Arab. According to Jewish tradition, one received Jewish heritage through one's mother, so Herod was no Jew. Hoping to ease the Jews' concerns over this, Herod brought his Hasmonean wife's father into his court and gave him a prominent position. Somewhat later, when he had apparently forgotten the Jews' concerns, he had his father-in-law executed.

Herod set out to improve Judea with immense public building projects. He built cities, improved the roads, and restored fortresses. He also built a seaport and an amphitheater. Most importantly for the Jews, Herod restored Jerusalem's Second Temple.

FASCINATING FACTS: Herod's Temple

Jerusalem's Second Temple was built under Zerubbabel, a grandson of Judah's King Jehoiachin, after the Jews returned from exile in Persia. Herod wanted to enlarge and beautify that Temple, which was again growing old. Although Herod's reconstruction of the Temple was a huge project, equivalent to rebuilding it from scratch, Herod's Temple is not considered a third temple. The Second Temple remained in use throughout the rebuilding.

Herod's work on the Temple began in 19 BC and carried on until 63 AD, so it went on throughout the life and ministry of Jesus. The work inside the Holiest places was performed by Levites, since only they could enter these places. Others were allowed to work on the Court of the Israelites (where Jewish men observed their sacrifices), the Court of Women and the Court of the Gentiles. Ironically, the Romans would destroy the Temple for the last time in 70 AD, just seven years after its restoration was complete.

Surrounding the entire Temple was a wall, part of which still stands today. This surviving remnant is known as the "Wailing Wall" or "Western Wall." The Wailing Wall is famous as the closest place in the world to the original Holy of Holies, which contained the powerful Ark of the Covenant, the original tablets containing the Ten Commandments, and other reminders of God's power. Jewish and other people from all over the world gather at the Wailing Wall to pray, often slipping bits of paper containing their prayer requests into the spaces between the stones.

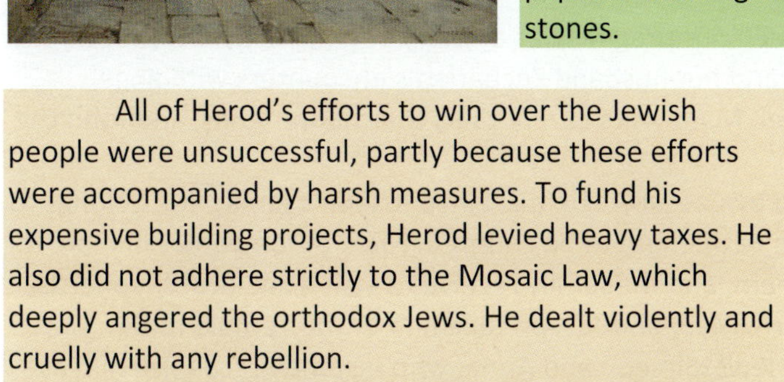

All of Herod's efforts to win over the Jewish people were unsuccessful, partly because these efforts were accompanied by harsh measures. To fund his expensive building projects, Herod levied heavy taxes. He also did not adhere strictly to the Mosaic Law, which deeply angered the orthodox Jews. He dealt violently and cruelly with any rebellion.

Herod the Great appears in the Bible story of Jesus' birth when he receives a visit from the Magi, or the Three Wise Men. They approached Herod as the ruler of the Jewish people, asking him for news of the one who was born to be King of the Jews. Herod was greatly concerned to hear that a challenger to his rule had been born, so he did what other kings had done before him: he ordered the executions of all male children born around Bethlehem at the time of Jesus' birth. Jesus, of course, escaped that purge, and the Wise Men avoided Herod on their return trip.

Upon Herod's death in 4 BC, Caesar Augustus divided Palestine between Herod's three sons. One of them, Herod Antipas, ruled in Galilee from 4 BC to 39 AD. He would be important in the life of Jesus of Nazareth. (If you are wondering how Herod the Great died in 4 BC, but was alive for the birth of Jesus, you should know that the accepted date for Jesus' birth is now about 6 BC!)

THE BIRTH OF JESUS

Take time this week to read the stories of Jesus' birth from the Bible books of Matthew and Luke. The Gospel of Mark begins with John the Baptist and does not mention the birth of Jesus. The Gospel of John does not mention Jesus' earthly birth, but John 1: 1-17 tells the story of Jesus from Creation to His Incarnation.

Matthew 1-2: Matthew begins with the genealogy of Jesus from Abraham to Joseph, Jesus' adoptive father. Matthew's genealogy includes five women: Tamar, Rahab, Ruth, Bathsheba and his mother Mary. Matthew's story then focuses on Joseph's encounter with an angel and his decision to raise the child as his own.

In Chapter 2, Matthew details the story of the Wise Men (Magi) who approach Herod about the baby. After their visit, Joseph takes his family to Egypt to avoid Herod's wrath. Upon their return, Jesus' family makes their home in the town of Nazareth in the province of Galilee.

Luke 1-2:1-40: The first chapter of Luke tells of the miraculous pregnancies of Mary and her cousin Elizabeth, the mother of John the Baptist. Luke begins with Elizabeth and her husband Zechariah's encounters with angels. Then he tells of Mary's encounter with the angel Gabriel. Mary visits Elizabeth as the chapter ends, and John the Baptist is born.

Chapter 2 begins with a Roman census decreed by Caesar Augustus. Since Joseph's family line belongs to the tribe of Judah, he must return to his family home in Bethlehem to be counted. Mary accompanies him on the journey. Jesus is born in a barn or a cave at Bethlehem, and the family receives a visit from local shepherds who hear of the birth from angels. After the baby is born, Mary and Joseph take him to the Temple to be dedicated. At the Temple they encounter two wise old Jews, Simeon and Anna, who instantly recognize him as the promised Messiah and prophesy about him.

FASCINATING FACTS SURROUNDING JESUS' BIRTH

- The birth of Jesus was foretold nearly seven hundred years before it happened. Over fifty prophecies concerning his birth, life and resurrection were fulfilled.
- The Shepherds visited Jesus soon after He was born, but the Magi did not arrive until weeks or months later.
- Mary may have been only fourteen to fifteen years old when she delivered Jesus.
- The sheep kept by the visiting shepherds may have been the sacrificial sheep used by the priests in the Temple.
- Joseph named the child Jesus, as the angel directed him. *Jesus* is the Greek form of the Hebrew *Joshua,* which means "the Lord saves."

FASCINATING FACTS: Jesus' Ancestors

Abraham - Isaac - Jacob - Judah and Tamar - Perez - Hezron - Ram - Amminadab - Nahshon - Salmon and Rahab - Boaz and Ruth - Obed - Jesse - King David and Bathsheba - Solomon - Rehoboam - Abijah - Asa - Jehoshaphat - Jehoram - Uzziah - Jotham - Ahaz - Hezekiah - Manasseh - Amon - Josiah - Jeconiah - Shealtiel - Zerubbabel - Abiud - Azor - Akim - Eliud - Eleazar - Matthan - Jacob - Joseph and Mary - JESUS

Chapter 30

Jesus' Life, Death and Resurrection

ANCIENT HISTORY AND BIBLE FOCUS
(This week the Ancient and Bible history are woven together)

DASTARDLY DICTATOR: Tiberius Julius Caesar Augustus (42 BC - 37 AD)
Second Emperor of Rome

Tiberius Claudius Nero was a stepson of Caesar Augustus, but he was not his stepfather's first choice to succeed him. Tiberius' real father had sided with Marc Antony against Caesar Augustus before the formation of the Second Triumvirate (see Chapter 29). But then Tiberius' mother divorced his father and remarried to Augustus, making Tiberius Augustus' stepson. He was further tied to Augustus' family when he married Augustus' daughter Julia. Tiberius hoped that he was being groomed as Augustus' successor. But Augustus lived on, and Tiberius began to see that succession would bypass him in favor of one of Augustus' two grandsons, Lucius and Gaius. Discouraged in his ambition, and angered by a wife who publicly humiliated him by seeking the company of other men, Tiberius went into a voluntary exile. But when first Lucius, then Gaius died prematurely, Augustus quickly recalled Tiberius and made him his heir. By 13 AD, he shared equal powers with Augustus. When Augustus died in 14 AD, the Senate conferred upon Tiberius all of the powers granted to Augustus.

Tiberius never enjoyed Augustus' popularity. He ruled like a Spartan, using a heavy fist and cruel tactics. He used secret police and intimidation to control the Senate, and he grew more and more paranoid as time went on. His last years were marked by the trials of many of his enemies, followed by their executions. When he died in 37 AD-- according to one account, he was smothered to death by a supporter of his successor, Caligula-- the Roman people celebrated in the streets.

Tiberius reigned throughout Jesus' adult life, ministry, death and resurrection.

JESUS' LIFE, DEATH AND RESURRECTION

The goal this week is to give a very brief overview of Jesus' life, ministry, death and resurrection. For family reading, read the Easter story from Matthew, Mark or Luke (Matthew 26-28, Mark 14-16 or Luke 22-24). For an added bonus, read John's version (John 12-21).

FASCINATING FACTS: The Four Gospels

The Bible books of Matthew, Mark, Luke and John are the first four books of the New Testament. Together they are known as the four *gospels*, because each relates the good news of salvation by faith in Jesus (gospel is an Old English word meaning "good news.")

The Gospels of Matthew, Mark and Luke are each written in a narrative style. These three are known as the *synoptic gospels* because they give an overall, summary view of Jesus' life story. The Gospel of Mark is the shortest of the three, and is believed to be the oldest. Some believe that both Matthew and Luke referred to Mark's Gospel while writing their own. The three synoptic gospels have a great deal in common, but each has its own focus and highlights different things. Their common witness serves to add credence to the stories of Jesus.

The Gospel of John differs from the other three in style and focus. John omits most of Jesus' many parables and instead focuses on the words and prayers of Jesus heard only by his closest disciples. John presents a highly developed theology of Jesus as the incarnate Word of God.

Early Life

Jesus spent his earliest years in Egypt, where his parents fled to protect Him from Herod the Great's infant massacre (see Chapter 29). After Herod died and his kingdom was divided between his three sons, Joseph felt that it was safe to return home to Nazareth. Joseph set up a carpentry shop there, and Jesus and his brothers probably apprenticed in the trade under their father.

INTERESTING INDIVIDUALS: Herod Antipas

When Herod the Great died, Caesar Augustus divided his kingdom between his three sons: Archelaus, Philip and Herod Antipas. Herod Antipas was set over Galilee and an area to the east called Peraea, and he ruled there from 4 BC - 39 AD. His reign coincided with the ministries of John the Baptist and Jesus.

Like his father before him, Herod Antipas was raised to practice Judaism, but true Jews disdained him. One of his many missteps was to build his capital city Tiberius, named to honor the new Roman emperor, over a Jewish graveyard. A second was to arouse the ire of John the Baptist, whom many Jews revered.

Herod Antipas divorced his first wife so that he could marry Herodias, the former wife of one of his brothers. The divorce was against the Law of Moses, and because Antipas claimed to practice Judaism, John the Baptist spoke out against the divorce and remarriage. Herodias hated John the Baptist for preaching against her marriage, and Antipas imprisoned John for speaking out against him. Later, Herodias took her own revenge. When Herodias' daughter Salome danced at her stepfather's birthday party, pleasing him and his guests, Antipas offered to grant her anything she asked. Salome consulted her mother, then asked for the head of the prisoner John the Baptist on a plate! Perhaps reluctantly, Antipas granted her request by killing John the Baptist.

Herod Antipas comes into the Bible story again during the trial of Jesus. After Jesus was arrested, the regional governor Pontius Pilate sent Jesus to Herod Antipas for questioning. Jesus refused to answer Herod's questions, so Herod mocked Jesus, then sent him back to Pilate.

Antipas' marriage to Herodias continued to cause trouble for him: his former wife's father attacked and defeated him. Later, Herodias' brother Agrippa accused Antipas of opposing the new Emperor Caligula, and Antipas had to spend the rest of his life in exile.

Jesus' ministry began when he was about thirty years old. One of his first recorded acts was to visit John the Baptist. As John baptized Jesus, he acknowledge Jesus as the long-awaited Jewish Messiah. Soon after this, Jesus spent forty days in the desert being tempted by Satan, but never giving in to sin. Over the following three years, He traveled all over Palestine healing the sick, teaching and confronting the Jewish leaders of his day.

FASCINATING FACTS: Pharisees and Sadducees

The Jewish religious leaders of Jesus' day were primarily divided into two groups, the Sadducees and the Pharisees. These were two Jewish sects with some important differences.

The Sadducees: The Sadducees were typically wealthy and highly-placed Jewish citizens, including the Temple's chief priests and the High Priest. They were generally less strict than the Pharisees, less insistent upon following the Law of Moses perfectly. The Sadducees' religious life centered around the Temple rituals and sacrifices. They did not believe in heaven or any afterlife, and they denied the existence of angels and demons. Because of this, they saw no need to pay any penalty for their sins.

The Sadducees were more conservative than the Pharisees in one area: they considered the written Scriptures to have the highest authority. The Pharisees placed oral traditions on the same level as the written Word of God, but the Sadducees believed only in the written Scriptures.

The Sadducees were not well regarded among common Jewish people. Although they held the majority of the seats in the Sanhedrin (Jewish local court), the Pharisees held more sway with the common people. Because the Sadducees were highly placed, they suffered the most when Rome grew tired of Jewish unrest and destroyed Jerusalem in 70 AD (see Chapter 31). The end of the Temple was the end of the Sadducees as well.

The Pharisees: While the Sadducees were generally wealthy, the Pharisees were generally middle-class businessmen. They were much closer to the common man's level than the Sadducees. They were a minority of the Sanhedrin, but still had much power because they were closer to the common people.

The Pharisees added oral traditions to the written Scriptures. Among these were highly detailed commentaries on how to keep God's Law perfectly. For example, where God commanded that his people "remember the Sabbath to keep it holy," the Pharisees added practical rules restricting how far one might walk on the Sabbath without violating the command to rest. The Pharisees were very strict about keeping these laws, and highly critical of any Jew who failed to do so. This brought them into conflict with Jesus, who was interested in the spirit of God's Law and not in the legalistic rules added by the Pharisees.

Unlike the Sadducees, the Pharisees believed in an afterlife and that God would punish the wicked. They believed in the prophecies of the Messiah, and were waiting for Him; but they believed that when He came, there would be world peace, and they never accepted Jesus.

FASCINATING FACTS: Torah and Talmud

Modern Jews rely on two written works: *Torah* and *Talmud*. *Torah* usually refers to the first five books of what Christians know as the Old Testament, the Books of Moses: Genesis, Exodus, Leviticus, Numbers and Deuteronomy. Torah may also mean the entire Old Testament.

Talmud is a collection of ancient Jewish oral traditions that have been set down in writing. The first set was compiled around 200 AD in a document called the *Mishnah*. Later, around 500 AD, additional commentaries were compiled as the *Gemara*. The Mishnah and the Gemara together make up the Talmud, and the Jews study Talmud as faithfully as they do Torah.

Like other rabbis (religious teachers) of his time, Jesus had followers or disciples (talmidim); but he did not choose his disciples as other rabbis did. The usual way was for a gifted student in his teens to approach a rabbi and ask to be taken on as a student. The rabbi either accepted or rejected him. Jesus broke this pattern by hand-picking each of his disciples. Most of Jesus' disciples were not top students, but young tradesmen. Their ages probably ranged from early teens (John) to early twenties (Peter). While most rabbis' disciples trained for 12-16 years, Jesus' disciples had just three years to sit at His feet. Despite this handicap, the work of Jesus' disciples after his resurrection changed the world forever.

GIANTS OF THE FAITH: The Twelve Disciples
(See Chapter 32 for more detailed information on each disciple)

1. Andrew: A fisherman, brother of Simon Peter
2. Simon Peter: A fisherman, brother of Andrew
3. James, son of Zebedee: Another fisherman, brother of John
4. John, son of Zebedee: Another fisherman, brother of James
5. Phillip: Yet another fisherman, close friend of Andrew
6. Bartholomew (Nathanael)
7. Matthew (Levi): Despised tax collector, author of the Gospel of Matthew
8. Thomas: Best known as "Doubting Thomas" for doubting Jesus' resurrection, but still a faithful disciple
9. James, son of Alpheus
10. Thaddeus, son of James
11. Simon the Zealot: Known as a "zealot," a Jewish patriot
12. Judas Iscariot: Jesus' ultimate betrayer

The more Jesus taught, the more the common Jewish people loved him and the more the Jewish establishment hated him. Jesus' criticism of the Pharisees and Sadducees was direct and harsh. After three years, the establishment reached its limit and set in motion a plan to eliminate Jesus. One of Jesus' own disciples, Judas Iscariot, helped them achieve their goal.

Timeline of Jesus' last week (Passion Week)

- Sunday (Palm Sunday): Jesus enters Jerusalem from Bethany, riding on a donkey. The Jewish crowds greet him enthusiastically, laying down palm branches in his path and treating him like their king.
- Monday: Jesus enters the Temple and drives out the money changers who have turned his Father's house into a "den of thieves."
- Tuesday: Judas Iscariot meets with the Jewish establishment leaders and agrees to betray Jesus. His price: thirty pieces of silver.
- Thursday: Jesus holds the Last Supper in the Upper Room (see Seder Meal below). Jesus prays into the night at the Garden of Gethsemane (see below). Late Thursday night, he is arrested at the garden by a group of soldiers led to him by Judas.
- Friday (Good Friday): Jesus is accused, tried and crucified (see The Trial below).
- Sunday (Easter): Jesus rises from the dead.

FASCINATING FACTS: The Passover Seder Meal

The Seder meal is the traditional Jewish Passover meal, and each element of the meal symbolizes something from the Jews' Exodus from Egypt. *Seder* means *order,* and the order of the Seder meal helps tell the story of the Passover.

During Passion Week, Jesus celebrated the Seder with His disciples in the Upper Room. What follows is a simple version of a Seder Meal:

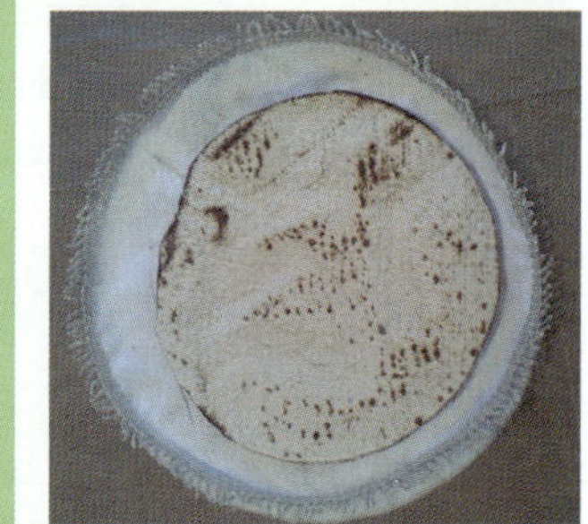

1. **LEAVEN**: Before the Passover, the house is cleaned from top to bottom and all leaven (yeast) is removed. Just before the meal, the father gives the house a final cleaning to be certain that not a speck of leaven remains. Leaven has a dual symbolism. Because leavened bread takes time to rise, the Jews of the Exodus could take only unleavened bread in their haste. Also, just as a tiny bit of leaven permeates the whole loaf, sin permeates one's entire being. Removing the leaven symbolizes the way God removes sin when He forgives.
2. **LIGHTING THE CANDLES**: The woman of the house lights the candles and says a blessing. The candles symbolize God's presence at the ceremony.
3. FIRST CUP OF WINE: Four times in the Seder, a blessing is recited over a cup of wine. In the Upper Room, Jesus blessed the cup and declared that He would not drink again until the Kingdom of God came (Luke 22 17-18).
4. **HAND WASHING**: There are several hand washings during the Seder. The first comes after the leaven has been removed and the candles are lit. Each person sits and washes his or her hands at the table using a basin and towel. Instead of washing His hands, Jesus took this time to wash the disciples' feet, in order to demonstrate that He was their servant and that they must serve one another.
5. **GREENS**: The first item eaten in the Seder meal is the *karpas* (greens). They are dipped in salt water as a symbol of the tears shed in the Exodus.
6. **HAGGADAH**: *Haggadah* means *telling*, and during the Seder, the story of the Passover is told in response to four questions asked by the children.
7. **BREAKING OF THE BREAD**: On the table is a bag divided into three sections. Inside each section is a piece of *matzo* (unleavened bread). At this point in the meal, the middle piece of matzo is removed and broken in half. One half is returned to the bag, and the other is hidden in a napkin. Later, the children will hunt for it. It was at this point in the meal that Jesus may have broken the bread and told the disciples that it was His body, broken for them.
8. **SECOND CUP OF WINE**: The second cup of wine is a reminder of the ten plagues and the suffering of the Egyptians.
9. **SECOND HAND WASHING**

10. **EATING OF THE BITTER HERBS**: So that the Jews will remember the bitterness of slavery, they eat Matzo with strong horseradish-- enough to bring tears to the eyes.
11. **EATING OF THE CHAROSET**: *Charoset* is a sweet mixture of apples, nuts, honey, cinnamon and wine (see picture). It symbolizes the mortar the slaves used to build with bricks in Egypt. Although the memory is bitter, the reminder that God will redeem is sweet.
12. **THE MEAL**: Matzo is the foundational food for the meal, but it may be served with fish, soup, vegetables, fried onions, chicken, potatoes, fruit and dessert.
13. **SEARCHING FOR THE BREAD**: After the meal is finished, the children are sent out to find the bread (Akifomen) that was hidden in the napkin. The meaning of this custom is uncertain, but the children look forward to it. Jesus may have shared the broken bread at this point in the meal.
14. **THE THIRD CUP**: The third cup of wine reminds the Jews that the shed blood of an unblemished lamb bought them redemption from Egypt. After the third cup, a child is sent outside to see if Elijah the Prophet has arrived to announce the coming of the Messiah. Throughout the meal, a place setting has been left empty

for Elijah. Jesus may have shared the wine that symbolized his blood at this point in the meal.

15. **SONGS OF PRAISE**
16. **THE FOURTH CUP**: The final cup of wine is a cup of praise. At this point in the meal, Jesus praised God and prayed over the disciples and all of the believers who would follow them (John 17). When the fourth cup is finished, the Seder meal is over. After the fourth cup, Jesus left the Upper Room and went to the Garden of Gethsemane to pray.

FASCINATING FACTS: Gethsemane

The Garden of Gethsemane lay at the foot of the Mount of Olives in Jerusalem. It was a peaceful garden full of olive trees and other plants, surrounded by a wall. Jesus and his disciples may have gone there often when they visited Jerusalem, because Judas knew where to find Jesus when he brought the group of soldiers to arrest him.

On the night of his arrest, Jesus went to the Garden of Gethsemane to pray. He told his disciples to pray and wait for him, while he himself prayed in such agony over what was to come that his sweat became like blood (Luke 22:44). His disciples did not understand what was coming or how much Jesus was suffering, and so they fell asleep waiting for him.

THE TRIAL

After Jesus' arrest, He had to suffer through several trials. The first three were mere show trials before Jesus' accusers, the very ones who wanted Him out of the way; the outcome of each was determined before it began. The **first trial** was before the former High Priest Annas, and the **second trial** was before the High Priest at the time, Caiaphas. Jesus was found guilty of several violations of Jewish law, including blasphemy because He said He was the Son of God. Both of these trials were conducted in the dead of night, and both were illegal by the laws of the time.

The **third trial** was before Caiaphas, the Sanhedrin and all of the Temple scribes, and Jesus was again pronounced guilty. Under Roman law, however, local courts did not have the power to execute, so they had to ask the Roman government to execute Jesus.

FASCINATING FACTS: The Sanhedrin

The Great Sanhedrin was the highest Jewish court. Its 71 members were responsible to interpret Jewish law as revealed in the Torah. The Great Sanhedrin met daily, except on the Sabbath, and the High Priest served as its Chief Justice.

Jesus' trial before the Sanhedrin was conducted at night because the Jewish leaders wanted to conceal it from the public, whom they feared might protest. This was illegal and highly irregular. Any trial before the Sanhedrin involving a capital crime (the death penalty) was to be conducted during the day.

For his **fourth trial**, Jesus was brought before the Roman Governor of Judea, Pontius Pilate. Pilate didn't understand Jesus' supposed crime. He could find no fault with Jesus, so he sent him to Herod Antipas, his subordinate in charge of Galilee.

In his **fifth trial**, Jesus was questioned by Herod Antipas, whom Pilate expected would know more about Jesus' supposed crime because Herod claimed to practice Judaism. But Jesus refused to answer Herod's questions, so Herod returned Jesus to Pilate without lifting the sentence of death. Herod may have known that Jesus was the cousin of his old enemy John the Baptist.

In his **sixth trial**, Jesus again appeared before Pilate. Pilate still could find no fault with Jesus and offered to release him under a custom that allowed the release of a Jewish prisoner during Passover. But the crowds chose another prisoner named Barabbas as the one they wanted released. So Pilate washed his hands of the matter and condemned Jesus to death by crucifixion.

INTERESTING INDIVIDUALS: Pontius Pilate

Pontius Pilate was the Roman Governor of Judea from 26 - 36 AD. As governor, one of his jobs was to administer Roman law throughout his province. Local courts had some authority, but the power of life and death was in Roman hands. Only the Romans had the authority to execute anyone.

Pilate is best remembered for "washing his hands" of responsibility for Jesus' execution. He was not Jesus' accuser, nor did he call for Jesus' execution. In fact, he offered to release Jesus because he found no fault with him. When the Jewish leaders and their supporters continued to demand death for Jesus, Pilate called for a basin of water and literally washed his hands before Jesus' accusers, in order to demonstrate that it was they, not he, who wanted Jesus dead. Nevertheless, Pilate granted the crowd's demand and executed a man he believed to be innocent; so Jesus' blood was on his hands whether he admitted it or not.

The Roman soldiers forced Jesus to carry His own cross to Golgotha, the place of His crucifixion.

A sign on Jesus' cross read **"Jesus of Nazareth, King of the Jews"** (abbreviated in Latin as I.N.R.I., "Iesus Nazarenus Rex Iudaeorum").

INTERESTING INDIVIDUALS: Barabbas

According to the gospels, a Roman custom allowed a Jewish prisoner to be released during Passover. This custom is not recorded anywhere outside of Scripture, but it may have been a concession the Romans made to the Jews in the hope that they would behave themselves. Pontius Pilate offered to release Jesus under this custom, but instead, the crowd chose Barabbas.

The little that is known of Barabbas indicates that he was a Jewish rebel, possibly a political prisoner and a murderer. Barabbas may have been fighting for Jewish freedom from the Romans, which would have made him popular with the Jews. No one knows what happened to Barabbas after his release.

INTERESTING IDEAS: **The Seventh Trial**

The number seven often indicates completion in Scripture. Jesus underwent six earthly trials, three before the Jewish authorities and three before the Romans. But he also underwent a seventh trial, the most important trial of all. **The seventh trial took place in heaven, where Jesus bore the penalty for the sins of all mankind**. In this trial, as in the others, Jesus was convicted and condemned. God the Father turned away from his Son Jesus Christ and allowed Him to suffer the penalty for all of our sins:

From the sixth hour until the ninth hour darkness came over all the land. About the ninth hour Jesus cried out in a loud voice, "***Eloi, Eloi, lama sabachthani***?" which means, "My God, my God, why have you forsaken me?" (Matthew 27: 45-46)

Jesus was crucified on a hill named Golgotha ("place of the skull") or Calvary. As he died, the earth shook, and the veil in the Temple that separated the Holy of Holies from the Holy Place was torn from top to bottom. The significance of the rent veil is at least twofold. One, the presence of God left the Temple forever upon Jesus' death, tearing the veil in the process, so that Temple worship was at an end. Another is that believers in Jesus are no longer separated from the presence of God by any veil.

FASCINATING FACTS: Crucifixion

Deuteronomy 21:23b "...anyone who is hung on a tree is under God's curse."

To *crucify* a person is to hang him from a cross until he is dead. The word comes from the Latin *crux*, meaning *cross*; but "crucifixion" can now refer to any severe punishment or pain. The word "excruciating," which means "exceedingly painful," comes from the same root because crucifixion was such a painful way to die.

The Persians were the first to use crucifixion as a means of execution. Alexander the Great adopted the practice, and from him it passed to the Romans. As a rule, the Romans reserved crucifixion for non-citizens. At first they used it primarily on slaves, but later they used it to punish robbers and any who rebelled against the Roman government. The Romans chose their crucifixion sites along main highways or near busy parts of cities so that plenty of people would see the victims. The horror of crucifixion was intended as a powerful deterrent to any who considered disobeying the Romans.

Crucifixion was a wretched way to die. The process began with a severe flogging, which weakened the condemned to speed his death. Jesus was both flogged and beaten during some of his trials (see Matthew 26:67, 27:26-31, Mark 14:65, 15:16-20). Next, the condemned was forced to carry the crossbeam of his cross to the crucifixion site, where the upright was already standing. Jesus was so weak from his beatings that he needed help to carry his crossbeam (see Mark 15:21).

Next, the condemned was fastened to the crossbeam, usually with ropes, but sometimes with nails through his hands and feet. Then the executioners raised the beam and attached it to the upright, and the condemned was left to hang until he died. This could take more than a day. To speed up the process, sometimes the executioners broke the condemned's legs. Because Jesus was beaten so badly and had lost so much blood from his floggings, His death came relatively quickly. When the Roman executioners were certain that He was dead, they removed his body from the cross.

Jesus' body was laid to rest in the tomb of Joseph of Arimathea. Because he died on Friday night, just as the Sabbath began, his body could not be treated with spices according to Jewish custom, because to do so would have violated the Sabbath. The women who wanted to do this had to wait until the Sabbath was over. So on Sunday morning, the women walked out to the tomb planning to care for Jesus' body. Instead, they discovered something that stunned them all and changed the course of history.

SCRIPTURE SPOTLIGHT: The Resurrection

(Matthew 28, Mark 16, Luke 24 and John 20-21)

The tomb was empty! The stone over the tomb's entrance was rolled back. The soldiers guarding the tomb had fled.

In all four Gospels, the first witnesses to the Resurrection were the women who came to anoint Jesus' body. To their amazement, they found that it was gone. Then Jesus appeared to the women. Even though the women of those days had few rights and could not bear legal witness in court, the risen Lord appeared to them first and instructed them to tell the disciples that He was risen.

The disciples, who were hiding in fear of suffering Jesus' fate, did not believe the women immediately. Peter and John ran to see for themselves, while others remained in hiding or set off for home and safety. But as the risen Lord appeared to them, they transformed. Over the next 40 days, Jesus prepared them and commissioned them to tell the world that He had conquered sin and death. Then He ascended into heaven, and the disciples began the ministry that spread the Good News of Jesus' resurrection to every corner of the world.

He is Risen Indeed!

Chapter 31

The Early Church and the End of the Jewish Nation

ANCIENT HISTORY FOCUS

FASCINATING FACTS: AD

The world has long used the year of Jesus' birth as a starting point for calendar years. BC is an abbreviation of the English "Before Christ." The years after Christ's birth are denoted AD, which is an abbreviation of the Latin *Anno Domini, "In the year of our Lord."* In light of this translation, it is technically more correct to place AD before the date: "In the year of our Lord 2010" is best abbreviated AD 2010, not 2010 AD. However, it is common to see AD after the date, and either is fine.

Those who don't like to be constantly reminded of Christ have proposed alternative abbreviations. In the place of BC, they use BCE to mean "Before the Common Era." Instead of AD, they use CE to mean "Common Era." The numbers are the same, so the dates are still counted from the birth of Christ.

To add to the confusion, it is now believed that the original calculations for the year of Jesus' birth were off. Jesus was actually born around 6 BC, so the calendar is probably off by about 6 years. By that dating, Jesus began His ministry around 24-26 AD and died around 28-30 AD.

Over the next two weeks we will focus on the Early Church, the destruction of the Temple in Jerusalem, the Diaspora of the Jews and the persecution of early Christians. All of these events took place simultaneously. As the Early Church was taking root and spreading across the Roman world, the Jewish people revolted against Roman rule.

THE ROMAN EMPERORS FROM 27 BC - 96 AD

Caesar Augustus (27 BC - 14 AD)	Rome's first and most beloved Emperor (see Chapter 29).

Tiberius (14 - 37 AD) 	Reigned during Jesus' ministry, death and resurrection. This hated tyrant was smothered to death in 37 AD (see Chapter 30).
Caligula (37 - 41 AD) 	Began as a decent emperor, but changed after an illness during his second year in power. Caligula became cruel and mentally unstable. He declared himself to be a god, then began to dress himself as a god and parade through the streets to receive worship. He was assassinated in his palace in 41 AD.
Claudius (41-54 AD) 	An able leader despite his delicate health. His accomplishments included conquering Britain for Rome and some major building projects. Claudius himself rode into Britain after the initial assaults were over, then returned to Rome as a conquering hero. Claudius groomed two young men as potential successors, his stepson Nero and his own son Britannicus. When Claudius began to promote Britannicus over Nero, Nero's mother Agrippina poisoned Claudius, and he died. Nero claimed the throne and poisoned 14-year-old Britannicus.

FASCINATING FACTS: Britain Conquered By Rome

In 55 BC, Julius Caesar crossed the English Channel and attempted to conquer Britain for the Roman Empire. Britain's native inhabitants were the Celts, a collection of separate, often warring tribes. Caesar had victories in Britain, but he was forced to retreat when storms prevented his reinforcements from joining him.

A year later, Caesar crossed the Channel a second time and had more victories. But again, he had to leave Britain, this time because of trouble back in Gaul. Over the next hundred years, Roman influence increased in Britain and trade opened up between the island and the mainland.

But Rome was never satisfied to leave the next territory unconquered. Unconquered territory always served as a haven for defeated enemies, who escaped beyond the borders and lived on to make trouble for Rome. In 43 AD, Emperor Claudius sent four legions of soldiers to defeat the Britons. By 47 AD, Emperor Claudius claimed South Britain for Rome. In typical Roman fashion, he built military outposts and roads throughout southern Britain. One such outpost, which the Romans called Londinium, grew into the city of London.

Nero (54- 68 AD)	Nero was an unpopular emperor, a tyrant and a persecutor of Christians. He killed his own mother Agrippina, who had poisoned Claudius in order to set Nero on the throne, because she interfered with his affairs. Nero was driven out of office by a military coup. Upon his death, civil war broke out (see Chapter 32).
Galba (68-69 AD) 	In the chaos after Nero's death, Galba reigned for just six months. Galba's army transferred its allegiance to Otho and assassinated Galba. Civil war continued.
Otho (69 AD) 	Otho reigned for just three months. Soon after he became emperor, German troops attacked. When his defeat appeared certain, Otho committed suicide.
Vitellius (69 AD) 	Vitellius did not last much longer than Otho. The civil war that had erupted after Nero's death continued. Vitellius' enemies captured him, dragged him through the streets and killed him.
Vespasian (69-79 AD) 	When the civil war broke out, Vespasian was stationed in Judea with an oversized army trying to quell the Jewish rebellion in Galilee. Vespasian was loved by his troops, and they declared him to be Rome's emperor instead of Vitellius. Otho's supporters joined in on Vespasian's side, and he quickly gained the support of the rest of the Empire. When he became emperor, he left his son Titus in charge of Judea. Vespasian restored order and civility to the Empire, and the ten years in which he reigned were peaceful ones. When he died, his son Titus succeeded him. Vespasian's reign was the end of the Julian Dynasty and the beginning of his own Flavian Dynasty.

Titus (79-81 AD) 	Titus is most famous for his 70 AD defeat of the Jewish rebellion in Galilee. Titus sacked Jerusalem, killing almost half a million Jews in the process. He also destroyed the Second Temple, which had stood since 516 BC. This was the end of the Jewish Temple worship practiced from the time of Solomon, more than a thousand years before. After Vespasian died, Titus took over as emperor and enjoyed the same popularity his father had. The cataclysmic eruption of Mount Vesuvius, which destroyed the cities of Herculaneum, Stabiae and Pompeii, happened while Titus was emperor. Titus died in 81 AD.
Domitian (81- 96 AD) 	Domitian became emperor after his brother Titus died. He was a cruel tyrant with an exalted opinion of himself. He asked to be addressed as "Lord and god." He took delight in devising horrific torture methods for his enemies. Under Domitian, no one was safe: Christians were murdered by the thousands, senators were tried for treason and even consuls were executed. Jews throughout the empire were forced to pay heavy taxes. When Domitian's Praetorian commanders realized that they were on his enemies list, they hatched a plot to overthrow him. Such was the general hatred for Domitian that his own wife was part of the plot. When Domitian was assassinated in 96 AD, his name was obliterated from all public buildings. Domitian was the last of the Flavian dynasty.

THE RISE OF THE EARLY CHURCH

Before Jesus ascended into heaven, he told the disciples to wait in Jerusalem for the baptism of the Holy Spirit:

"Do not leave Jerusalem, but wait for the gift my Father promised, which you have heard me speak about. For John baptized with water, but in a few days you will be baptized with the Holy Spirit." (Acts 1: 4-5)

The Festival of Weeks, or *Shavuot*, was an annual Jewish celebration that fell seven weeks and one day after Passover. Because this was a period of fifty days, the festival day was also known as *Pentecost.* This festival celebrated the giving of the Torah to Moses and the children of Israel at Mount Sinai. According to the Law of Moses (Leviticus 23:15f), all Jewish males were required to attend the Pentecost celebration at the Temple in Jerusalem each year. These Jews came from all over the Roman Empire, and some spoke in different languages.

All of Jesus' disciples were Jewish men, so they gathered for the celebration as usual. But in the middle of their celebration, tongues of fire appeared and rested on the disciples, and they began to praise God in different languages-- languages the disciples could not have known. Jewish people from all over the Roman Empire heard and understood their speech as if it were in their own languages. Some accused the disciples of being drunk, until Peter stood up and told the story of Jesus' life, death and resurrection. Three thousand believed the disciples' message that day, and the early Christian church began to grow.

At first the believers remained in Jerusalem and formed a small community. They sold their possessions and gave what they had to any believer who was in need, sharing everything. Soon, however, the same Jewish leaders who had worked to silence Jesus began to move against his disciples. When they stoned a believer named Stephen, who became the first Christian martyr (Acts 7), the Christians in Jerusalem scattered. One Pharisee who led the attacks against the Christians was a young man named Saul, later known as Paul (see below).

FASCINATING FACTS: Good News for the Samaritans

The City of Samaria was the capital of the northern Kingdom of Israel before Israel was overrun by Assyria. Later, "Samaritans" referred to the people of the region around Samaria, who traced their roots to Israel's ten lost tribes. True Jews regarded Samaritans as second class citizens, because their faith was a blend of Judaism and the Baal worship introduced by Jezebel and her kind.

But Jesus was not like other Jews. During his ministry, Jesus traveled to Samaria and ministered among the Samaritans. His willingness to mingle with Samaritans shocked and dismayed his disciples, but Jesus rubbed off on them. After the stoning of Steven and the scattering of the Jerusalem Christians, the first place the disciples ministered was Samaria. The Samaritans received the disciples' message with joy, and many Samaritans were saved.

The Good News of Jesus spread from Samaria to Judea, Phoenicia, Syria and the island of Cyprus. At first the message went only to the Jews, but as Gentiles (non-Jews) heard the gospel, they too began to believe and be baptized. The story of the disciples' missions to spread the gospel is continued in Chapter 32.

FASCINATING FACTS: "Christian"

The first recorded use of the word "Christian" is in Acts 11. When the Greeks of Antioch began to believe the good news about Jesus, a Christian convert named Barnabas went to Antioch to minister to them. It was in Antioch that believers first received the name "Christian," or "Christ follower."

GIANTS OF THE FAITH: The Apostle Paul

A Hebrew named Saul stood among those watching the stoning of Stephen, guarding the coats of those who participated. As a strict Pharisee and an enemy of the Christians, he very much approved of what he saw. Saul's Hebrew credentials were impeccable: born into the tribe of Benjamin, he was raised as a Pharisee and taught by the famous Jewish rabbi Gamaliel. He was in his teens when Jesus was crucified, and he participated in the persecution of the early Christians.

INTERESTING INDIVIDUALS: Gamaliel

Rabbi Gamaliel the Elder was a grandson of Rabbi Hillel, who was regarded as one of the greatest teachers in the history of Judaism. Gamaliel is honored in both Jewish and Christian traditions. He believed that the Law of Moses came directly from God, but he was more compassionate than others in its interpretation. Gamaliel was not so quick to seek death for heretics (those who disagreed with accepted Jewish beliefs).

Gamaliel sat on the Sanhedrin when Peter and the other apostles were arrested (Acts 5). Peter angered the Sanhedrin when he accused its members of killing Jesus. The Sanhedrin was ready to kill all of the apostles, until Gamaliel intervened:

"When they heard this, they were furious and wanted to put them to death.
But a Pharisee named Gamaliel, a teacher of the law, who was honored by all the people, stood up in the Sanhedrin and ordered that the men be put outside for a little while. Then he addressed them:

"Men of Israel, consider carefully what you intend to do to these men. Some time ago Theudas appeared, claiming to be somebody, and about four hundred men rallied to him. He was killed, all his followers were dispersed, and it all came to nothing. After him, Judas the Galilean appeared in the days of the census and led a band of people in revolt. He too was killed, and all his followers were scattered. Therefore, in the present case I advise you:
Leave these men alone! Let them go! For if their purpose or activity is of human origin, it will fail. But if it is from God, you will not be able to stop these men; you will only find yourselves fighting against God." (Acts 5:33-39)

Gamaliel's argument won the day. The apostles were flogged and released, and they were even happy that they were considered worthy to suffer in Jesus' name.

Saul believed strongly that the Christians were heretics who deserved punishment. He was in the forefront of the violence against Christians. He went from house to house, looking for believers and dragging them off to prison. When he learned that the Christians were spreading their message beyond Jerusalem, Saul set out for Damascus (Syria) hoping to stop them.

But something unforeseen happened on the road to Damascus: the Lord intervened, and Saul had a life-changing vision.

"As he neared Damascus on his journey, suddenly a light from heaven flashed around him. He fell to the ground and heard a voice say to him, "Saul, Saul, why do you persecute me?"
"Who are you, Lord?" Saul asked.
"I am Jesus, whom you are persecuting," he replied. "Now get up and go into the city, and you will be told what you must do." (Acts 9:3-6)

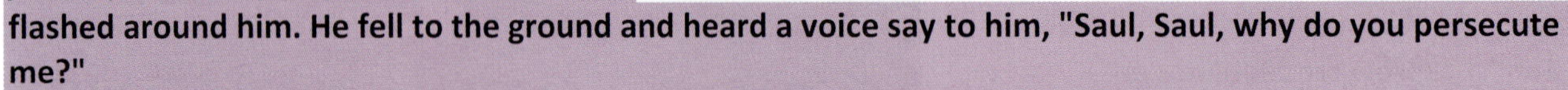

The vision struck Saul blind for three days. While he waited to regain his sight, he underwent a radical transformation: he came to faith in Christ and developed a single-minded focus on spreading the gospel throughout the Roman world.

The Christians did not quickly forget their persecution at Saul's hands, and they did not trust him at first. It was only when Barnabas brought Saul back to Jerusalem to minister to the Greek converts that the apostles begin to trust Saul. As his ministry to the Gentiles grew, Saul began to use his Greco-Roman name, Paul.

Simple Timeline of Paul's Life (dates are rough estimates):

- **33 AD**: Saul's conversion on the road to Damascus
- **33 - 36 AD**: Saul goes to Arabia to study
- **36 - 40 AD**: After a brief time in Jerusalem, Saul goes to Syria
- **40 AD**: Saul and Barnabas minister to the Christians in Antioch (Syria)
- **44-46 AD**: Paul's first missionary journey

From Antioch in Syria, Paul, Barnabas and John Mark journeyed to the island of Cyprus, across to Asia Minor and back (red line on map).

- **46 - 49 BC**: Paul preaches and ministers in Antioch (Syria)

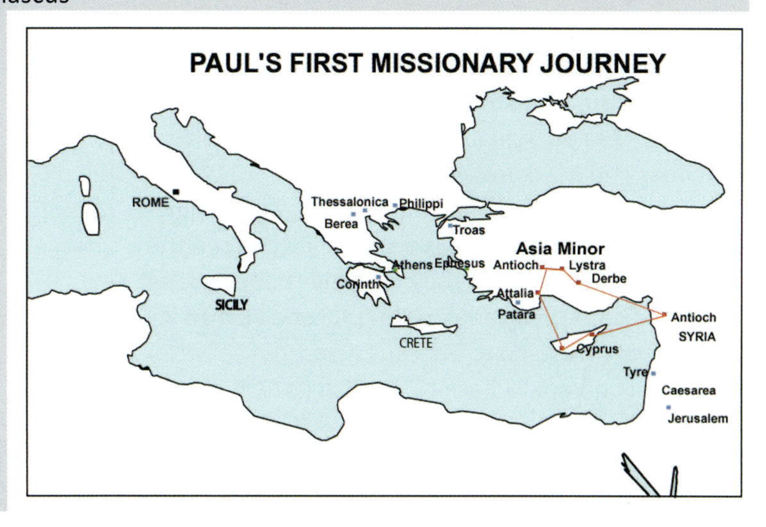

SCRIPTURE SPOTLIGHT: The Question of Circumcision

As more and more Gentiles came to faith in Jesus, some began to wonder whether they should all convert to Judaism. Since Jesus was a Jew and the Christian faith was explained as the fulfillment of the Jewish Scriptures, some insisted that all Christians should also be Jews. Since one mark of the Jew was circumcision, some believed that new male believers should also undergo circumcision.

The early church leaders, including Paul and Barnabas, gathered in Jerusalem to discuss the matter. After much debate, they decided that other things were more important than circumcision:

"Instead we should write to them, telling them to abstain from food polluted by idols, from sexual immorality, from the meat of strangled animals and from blood." (Acts 15:20)

To the modern reader, this sounds like a strange list; but in fact, these four rules were all chosen for a very specific reason: because these were the things that separated a Christian from a worshipper of idols.

A worshipper of idols:
- Offered food and worship to idols
- United with prostitutes in the temples of idols
- Ate meat from the sacrifices made to idols
- Drank blood from the sacrifices made to idols

A worshipper of God:
- Worshipped God alone
- Was united with Christ and the body of believers
- Symbolically ate the body of Christ, the ultimate sacrifice, in Holy Communion
- Symbolically drank the blood of Christ, the ultimate sacrifice, in Holy Communion

- **49 - 50 AD**: Paul's second missionary journey

Paul and Barnabas could not agree on their next destination, so Paul took Silas instead. The pair departed from Antioch (Syria) and returned to visit the churches Paul had established on his first trip. Barnabas and Mark traveled to Cyprus.

In Lystra, Paul met Timothy and added him to their group. Led by Paul's vision, they crossed the waters for Greece. Then they traveled to Philippi, Thessalonica, Athens and Corinth. After a year in Corinth they traveled to Ephesus, Caesarea, Jerusalem and finally back to Antioch (green line on map).

- **50 - 51 AD**: Paul writes his Epistles (letters) to the Thessalonians (Thessalonians I and II)
- **52-53 AD**: Paul confronts Peter about his treatment of the Gentile Christians. Paul writes the Epistle to the Galatians
- **53 - 57 AD**: Third missionary journey

Paul traveled to Antioch and then to Asia minor, revisiting his churches. He traveled to Ephesus and ministered there for three years. He then traveled to Macedonia and Corinth.

During this period he wrote the Epistles to the Corinthians (I and II) and the Romans. Paul then backtracked to Berea, Thessalonica, Philippi and Troas, traveled around the coast to Patara, across the Mediterranean Sea to Tyre and then to Caesarea. His journey ended with a visit to Jerusalem (blue line on map).

- **58 AD**: Roman soldiers arrest Paul in Jerusalem after he brings Jewish converts into the Temple area, causing a riot.

The soldiers threatened to whip Paul until Paul surprised them by letting them know that he was a Roman citizen. It was unusual for a Hebrew to have Roman citizenship, but Paul had it through his father. Paul's citizenship was a key factor in his treatment for the rest of his life. He was a member of two classes of people who caused trouble for the Romans, the Christians and the Jews; yet as a Roman citizen, he was entitled to certain protections.

Paul was taken to the Roman governor in Caesarea, and he spent the next several years as a Roman prisoner. Because of his privileged status as a Roman citizen, he spent most of his time under house arrest (confined to a house) rather than behind bars. Paul appealed his case to Caesar (Emperor Nero).

- **60 - 61 AD**: Paul is taken to Rome as a prisoner. His transport ship wrecks near the island of Malta, but everyone survives. Paul is also bitten by a poisonous snake, but he survives that as well. He is delivered to the captain of the guard in Rome.

- **61 - 63 AD**: Paul spends two years in Rome under house arrest. Here he writes the epistles to the Hebrews, Ephesians, Philippians, Colossians, I Timothy and Titus as well as the Book of Philemon.

- **63 - 67 AD**: Some believe that Paul is released from Roman prison during this time and makes another journey to Crete, Macedonia, Spain and possibly Britain. Others believe that he spends all of these years as a prisoner.

- **68 - 69 AD**: Paul is again a prisoner in Rome, if in fact he ever left. He writes his last letter to Timothy (II Timothy), and then dies a martyr's death during the reign of Nero. Paul's Roman citizenship probably saved him from crucifixion, and he was probably executed by the more "humane" means of beheading.

AMAZING ANCIENTS: Josephus (37 - 100 AD)

Around the time that Paul was studying in Arabia, a Jewish boy named Josephus was born in Jerusalem (37 AD). Born the son of a Sadducee, Josephus grew into a brilliant student. He studied in the schools of the Sadducees, the Pharisees and the Essenes before deciding to join the Pharisees.

In 64 AD, Josephus traveled to Rome to negotiate the release of some Jewish priests taken hostage by Nero. This was his first exposure to the awesome power of Rome, and he was much impressed.

When he returned to Jerusalem, he found that Judea was in the throes of a revolt. Josephus joined the resistance against the Roman legions (who were commanded by Vespasian, soon to be the Roman emperor). Eventually, Josephus found himself trapped in a cave with forty companions, with the Romans outside calling them to come out. Instead of surrender, Josephus and his companions decided on a bizarre form of mutual suicide, a "Roman Roulette." The 41 men stood in a circle. They drew lots to begin, then counted around the circle, killing every third man. The last man standing was Josephus. But instead of killing himself, Josephus surrendered and was carried off to prison.

Somehow, Josephus flattered his way into the favor of Vespasian. When Vespasian became Emperor, he freed Josephus. From then on, Josephus served as an advisor and historian on Jewish affairs, first to Vespasian, then to his sons Titus and Domitian.

Josephus published two major works: a history of the Jews entitled *Jewish Antiquities,* and an account of the war between the Jews and Rome entitled *The Jewish War*. These two works are an invaluable source of information about the culture, geography, history, customs, people and events of those days. Josephus' writings provide a profound extra-Biblical account of Jewish history after the exile. He also tells of New Testament characters such as Pontius Pilate, Herod, John the Baptist and even Jesus Himself. For centuries, Josephus' works were more widely read around the world than any other work except the Bible itself.

A passage from the *Jewish Antiquities* about Jesus: "Testimonium Flavianum," translated by William Whiston:

"Now there was about this time Jesus, a wise man, if it be lawful to call him a man; for he was a doer of wonderful works, a teacher of such men as receive the truth with pleasure. He drew over to him both many of the Jews and many of the Gentiles. He was [the] Christ. And when Pilate, at the suggestion of the principal men amongst us, had condemned him to the cross, those that loved him at the first did not forsake him; for he appeared to them alive again the third day; as the divine prophets had foretold these and ten thousand other wonderful things concerning him. And the tribe of Christians, so named from him, are not extinct at this day."

THE END OF THE JEWISH NATION

In **70 AD**, the Romans drove the Jewish people out of Judea, ending their centuries-long association with Abraham's Promised Land. They scattered into a Diaspora that carried Jewish communities all over the world.

Review

This was not the first scattering of the Jews. When Joshua first brought the Israelites into the Promised Land, they established a great nation in Canaan. This nation survived through the time of the Judges and on through the reigns of Saul, David and Solomon. Then the nation divided into the split kingdoms of Israel and Judah. The Assyrians conquered the Kingdom of Israel in 722 BC, and that kingdom disappeared. The Kingdom of Judah continued until 586 BC, when the Babylonians destroyed Jerusalem.

Within 70 years, the remnant of Judah was allowed to return to Jerusalem under Persia's Cyrus the Great. Under Cyrus and his successors, the Jews were able to rebuild their Temple and Jerusalem's city walls. Over the next 400 years, the Jews continued to live in their homeland as it passed through the hands of first the Persians, then the Seleucid Greeks, and finally the Romans. This last change was the hardest, because Rome had strict laws and levied heavy taxes. The Jews began to rebel against the harsh rule of Rome.

Herod the Great, the Roman governor of Galilee, tried to placate the Jews by restoring their Temple. But Herod's harsh methods and immoral lifestyle made him unpopular with true Jews. When Herod died, Rome divided his kingdom between his sons and gave them even more power, but the Jewish rebellion continued to grow. The more restrictive the Romans became, the more the Jews rebelled. In response to continued Roman oppression, a new group of Jews known as the Zealots formed around 6 AD.

FASCINATING FACTS: Zealots

The Zealots were Jewish patriots who resisted the rule of Rome. Zealots believed that Jews should be governed by God's Law alone, and were willing to rebel violently against Roman control. Josephus described the Zealots as a fourth "sect" of Judaism, like the Pharisees, Sadducees, and Essenes.

Under the Roman Emperor Caligula, there was an incident that sparked even greater unrest. Perhaps as a result of an illness, Caligula was suffering delusions of godhood, and he ordered that a statue of himself was to be set up in the Holy of Holies of the Temple of Jerusalem. He sent a military commander named Petronius to fulfill this order and slay anyone who stood in the way.

Naturally, the Jews resisted. The Holy of Holies was such a sacred place that even the Jewish High Priest himself could enter only once a year, with a rope tied to his ankle so that his fellow priests could drag him out if he somehow offended the Lord and was struck down. Commander Petronius was impressed with the Jews' faith and the fact that so many were willing to die before they would see Caligula's statue in the Holy of Holies. He didn't enforce the order, and Caligula died before he could put Petronius to death for his disobedience.

Still, Caligula's death did not make life any easier for the Jews under Roman rule. Heavy taxation left many Jews in poverty, and the Romans continued to show disrespect for Jewish faith and traditions.

First Jewish-Roman War (66 - 70 AD)

In **66 AD**, Emperor Nero ordered the confiscation of all of the Temple's treasures. This was the spark that set off the First Jewish-Roman War, one of the greatest catastrophes in Jewish history. Jesus Himself had predicted the destruction of the Temple almost 40 years before:

"Jesus left the temple and was walking away when his disciples came up to him to call his attention to its buildings. "Do you see all these things?" he asked. "I tell you the truth, not one stone here will be left on another; every one will be thrown down." (Matthew 24: 1-2)

When a Roman procurator (tax officer) arrived in Jerusalem to confiscate the Temple treasures, the Jewish masses rioted and wiped out a small Roman garrison stationed in Jerusalem. When more Roman soldiers arrived, they too were routed. Many Jews fled the violence in Jerusalem at this time, including the Jewish Christians.

In **67 AD**, Nero sent a new commander to the region, the future Emperor Vespasian. Vespasian's son Titus came along as one of his lieutenants. With them came numerous legions of Roman soldiers ready to put down the rebellion. They launched their first attack in Galilee, killing or capturing 100,000 Jews. The refugees from Galilee fled to Jerusalem, where a civil war broke out between the Zealots and the moderate Jewish leadership that still wanted to appease the Romans.

In **68 AD** the Romans were preparing to attack Jerusalem when the news arrived that Nero had committed suicide. Chaos erupted in Rome, and the Jewish-Roman War was temporarily on hold. But the Jews continued to fight among themselves, as Zealot leaders executed any who wanted to surrender to Rome. They foolishly destroyed the stockpiles of food that had been set aside in case of a Roman siege, perhaps because they believed that a siege could only end in capitulation. Starvation became as great an enemy as the Romans.

In **69 AD**, Vespasian became Rome's new Emperor. With matters in Rome back under control, Vespasian gave his son Titus the task of finishing the Jewish-Roman War.

On April 14, **70 AD**, during the Jewish Passover, Titus laid siege to Jerusalem. Armed with battering rams and catapults, Titus' legions were able to break through the city walls. The Jews were completely unprepared for the level of violence the Romans unleashed. Over a million Jews lost their lives in the fighting and its aftermath, in which the Romans slaughtered thousands more in a depraved victory celebration. As for the Temple, it was burned to the ground, and its foundation was torn down stone from stone by pillaging Romans seeking melted gold and silver from the horrific fire. Some of the few Jewish survivors were sent to work in mines around the empire, the worst form of hard labor punishment available. Others went to die in the arena as gladiators.

FASCINATING FACTS: Masada

After Rome destroyed Jerusalem, the surviving Zealots fled to the nearby fortress of Masada. Masada was situated atop an enormous mountain plateau in the desert near the Dead Sea. It was originally fortified by Herod the Great so that he would have a retreat if the Jews ever rebelled against him. A group of Jewish Zealots recaptured Masada from the Romans shortly after the Jewish-Roman War began in 66 AD.

After the fall of Jerusalem, 960 Jewish men, women and children holed up inside Masada. These Zealots used Masada as a base of operations for harassing the Romans, holding out against Roman assault for three years. Finally, Rome sent a force against Masada large enough to overwhelm the fortress. When it became clear that the Romans would breach the walls, the Jews inside decided to commit suicide rather than surrender to the Romans.

Modern people may question this desperate decision, but none of them lived through the sack of Jerusalem. Roman soldiers were not merciful in victory. Part of the Roman soldier's reward for risking his life in battle was the plunder that followed victory. Chaos erupted after a Roman victory, and the soldiers ran wild through the streets, recklessly raping and stealing. The women and children inside Masada would have faced unimaginable brutality at the hands of the vengeful Roman troops. Faced with two evil options, the Jews of Masada chose what seemed to them the lesser evil.

FASCINATING FACTS: The Essenes and the Dead Sea Scrolls

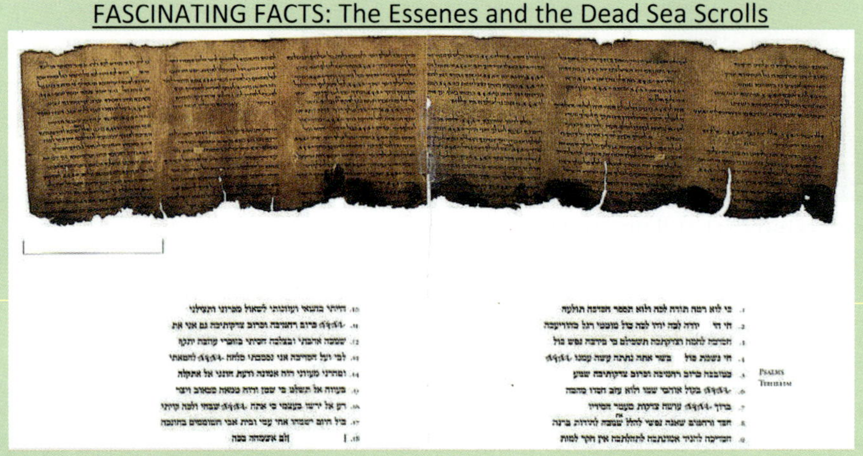

The Psalms scroll

Living alongside the Sadducees, Pharisees and Zealots were a smaller, quieter Jewish sect known as the Essenes. Because they believed in simple, communal living and in self-denial, the Essenes received less attention than the other groups.

Today, the Essenes are best known for preserving the Dead Sea Scrolls. These are scrolls containing the Jewish Scriptures and other sacred writings, rediscovered in eleven different caves along the Dead Sea between 1947 and 1956. Almost 900 separate scrolls were preserved there, containing both Biblical and extra-biblical writings.

Here are a few interesting items about the Dead Sea Scrolls (DSS):

- Every Old Testament Bible book except the book of Esther is preserved in the scrolls.
- The scrolls contain additional prophecies attributed to Ezekiel, Daniel and Jeremiah that are not included in the Bible. They also include additional Psalms attributed to King David.
- The scrolls are the oldest group of Old Testament manuscripts ever found.
- The extra-Biblical writings include liturgy, rules for living, war books, commentaries and hymns.
- Most of the scrolls are written in Hebrew or Aramaic, but some are in Greek.
- The Essenes may have hidden the scrolls during the First Jewish Revolt.
- The scrolls were made of animal skins or papyrus. One was made of copper.
- The scrolls do not mention Jesus.

FASCINATING FACTS: The Dreidel Game

The dreidel is a spinning top used as a game piece for a very old Jewish game. According to the legend, during the time of the Maccabees, the Greek King Antiochus refused to allow the Jews to worship or study the Torah. So in order to hide what they were doing whenever soldiers appeared, young Jewish students quickly hid their books and pulled out their dreidels so that they could appear to be involved in a game. In this way they could continue to worship and study under the nose of the Greek king.

GEOGRAPHY FOCUS

The Dead Sea

Did you know...

- The Dead Sea's shores are the lowest dry land elevation on earth, about 1380 feet below sea level.
- It is landlocked. It receives water from the Jordan River and has no outflow (except evaporation).
- Because it has no outflow, it is extremely salty. The Dead Sea's water contains over 8 times as much salt as typical ocean water.
- Its extreme saltiness means that no fish can survive in its water (hence the name, "Dead" Sea).
- Its extreme saltiness also makes its water more dense, so that objects float higher in the Dead Sea. A person doing the back float in the Dead Sea lies near the water's surface as if he or she were lying in bed.
- The minerals in the Dead Sea's water help people with skin or muscle ailments. The high atmospheric pressure (due to its low elevation) helps people with breathing ailments.
- White salt encrusts parts of the Dead Sea's shores.

Chapter 32

The Christians and Rome

ANCIENT HISTORY FOCUS

PARENT/TEACHER WARNING: The persecution of the Christians was a ghastly period in Church history. Please be discerning in what you choose to allow your children to read in the Companion this week. Some of the information may frighten or upset them.

THE ROMAN EMPERORS FROM 27 BC - 96 AD

- Caesar Augustus (27 BC - 14 AD): Rome's first and most beloved Emperor (see Chapter 29).

- Tiberius (14 - 37 AD): Reigned during Jesus' ministry, death and resurrection. This hated tyrant was smothered to death in 37 AD (see Chapter 30).

- Caligula (37 - 41 AD): Began as a decent emperor, but changed after an illness during his second year in power. Caligula became cruel and mentally unstable. He declared himself to be a god, then began to dress himself as a god and parade through the streets to receive worship. He was assassinated in his palace in 41 AD.

- Claudius (41-54 AD): An able leader despite his delicate health. His accomplishments included conquering Britain for Rome and some major building projects. Claudius himself rode into Britain after the initial assaults were over, then returned to Rome as a conquering hero. Claudius groomed two young men as potential successors, his stepson Nero and his own son Britannicus. When Claudius began to promote Britannicus over Nero, Nero's mother Agrippina poisoned Claudius, and he died. Nero claimed the throne and poisoned 14-year-old Britannicus.

- Nero (54- 68 AD): Nero was an unpopular emperor, a tyrant and a persecutor of Christians. He killed his own mother Agrippina, who had poisoned Claudius in order to set Nero on the throne, because she interfered with his affairs. Nero was driven out of office by a military coup. Upon his death, civil war broke out.

TERRIBLE TYRANTS: Nero (54- 68 AD)

Out of all of Rome's hated emperors, the one with the very worst reputation is probably Nero. Nero was sixteen year old when his mother Agrippina secured the throne for him by poisoning his stepfather, Emperor Claudius. Agrippina never allowed Nero to forget that he owed his position to her, and she constantly meddled in his affairs. The two began to quarrel so bitterly that Agrippina threatened to support Claudius' son Britannicus in Nero's place. Nero avoided that danger by poisoning Britannicus. Five years later, he executed Agrippina herself. Reportedly, he never got over the guilt he felt for killing his scheming mother, and she haunted his dreams for the rest of his life.

Another well-known story about Nero concerns a terrible fire that burned the city of Rome in 64 AD. The popular saying is that Nero "fiddled while Rome burned," which leaves the impression that a mad Nero obliviously continued to saw on his fiddle, ignoring the flames all around him. In fact, most believe that he was actually in the country entertaining some friends with music when the fire broke out, and not in Rome at all. And he was certainly not playing a fiddle, because that instrument would not be invented for another thousand years. Nero's instrument was the lyre. Nevertheless, Nero took advantage of the fire to confiscate the burned-out parts of the city, most of which had belonged to the poor. He replaced these poor homes with magnificent public buildings, a palace, gardens and groves of trees-- but no homes for the poor. Nero also used the fire as an opportunity to persecute Christians, whom he hated. He accused the Christians of starting the fire, then had them thrown to the lions, crucified, tortured, and burned to death. He even used their bodies as torches to light his gardens, covering them in tar and setting fire to them. During this part of Nero's reign, the Apostle Paul was beheaded and the Apostle Peter was crucified upside down.

Nero had another unfortunate turn of character: he thought he was good at everything. He considered himself an exceptional musician, and required audiences to sit uncomplaining through his long public performances. It was a deadly mistake to criticize his musicianship. He also believed himself to be an excellent actor, writer, chariot racer and athlete. When he participated in an Olympic Games in Greece, it is perhaps not surprising that he won all of his events, since death awaited anyone who crossed the finish line ahead of Nero.

Needless to say, such childishness made Nero widely unpopular. In 65 AD, a large group of prominent Romans conspired to get rid of Nero. Their plot was discovered and they were put to death, but from that time on, Nero grew ever more paranoid. Terror reigned in the Roman Empire as Nero accused and executed anyone he believed to be a threat.

Finally, in 68 AD, a Roman governor withdrew his allegiance from Nero. Other governors followed suit, and Nero was unable to punish them all at once. When his defeat became inevitable, Nero committed suicide. Civil war broke out as Nero's government collapsed.

- Galba (68-69 AD): In the chaos after Nero's death, Galba reigned for just six months. Galba's army transferred its allegiance to Otho and assassinated Galba. Civil war continued.

- Otho (69 AD): Otho reigned for just three months. Soon after he became emperor, German troops attacked. When his defeat appeared certain, Otho committed suicide.

- Vitellius (69 AD): Vitellius did not last much longer than Otho. The civil war that had erupted after Nero's death continued. Vitellius' enemies captured him, dragged him through the streets and killed him.

- Vespasian (69-79 AD): When the civil war broke out, Vespasian was stationed in Judea with an oversized army trying to quell the Jewish rebellion in Galilee. Vespasian was loved by his troops, and they declared him to be Rome's emperor instead of Vitellius. Otho's supporters joined in on Vespasian's side, and he quickly gained the support of the rest of the Empire. When he became emperor, he left his son Titus in charge of Judea. Vespasian restored order and civility to the Empire, and the ten years in which he reigned were peaceful ones. When he died, his son Titus succeeded him. Vespasian's reign was the end of the Julian Dynasty and the beginning of his own Flavian Dynasty.

- Titus (79-81 AD): Titus is most famous for his 70 AD defeat of the Jewish rebellion in Galilee. Titus sacked Jerusalem (see art), killing almost half a million Jews in the process. He also destroyed the Second Temple, which had stood since 516 BC. This was the end of the Jewish Temple worship practiced from the time of Solomon, more than a thousand years before. After Vespasian died, Titus took over as emperor and enjoyed the same popularity his father had. The cataclysmic eruption of Mount Vesuvius, which destroyed the cities of Herculaneum, Stabiae and Pompeii, happened while Titus was emperor. Titus died in 81 AD.

- Domitian (81- 96 AD): Domitian became emperor after his brother Titus died. He was a cruel tyrant with an exalted opinion of himself, which he demonstrated when he asked to be addressed as "Lord and god." He took delight in devising horrific torture methods for his enemies. Under Domitian, no one was safe: Christians were murdered by the thousands, senators were tried for treason and even consuls were executed. Jews throughout the empire were forced to pay heavy taxes. When Domitian's Praetorian commanders realized that they were on his enemies list, they hatched a plot to overthrow him. Such was the general hatred for Domitian that his own wife was part of the plot. When Domitian was assassinated in 96 AD, his name was obliterated from all public buildings. Domitian was the last of the Flavian dynasty.

BIBLE AND CHURCH HISTORY FOCUS

THE TWELVE DISCIPLES

Jesus' resurrection and the gift of the Holy Spirit at Pentecost transformed his twelve disciples. After the crucifixion, they cowered in fear; but after Pentecost, they found their courage. Even when the persecution of Christians began, all of the disciples ministered boldly, even though it meant their deaths. Of the twelve disciples, only one was spared a martyr's death. John died on the island of Patmos, where the cruel emperor Domitian exiled him.

DISCIPLE	MINISTRY	DEATH
Simon Peter	• Chief spokesman on the Day of Pentecost • Wrote Bible books of I and II Peter • Regarded as the First Bishop of Rome, First Pope by Roman Catholics	Crucified upside down by Nero

James, son of Zebedee	• Preached throughout Judea	Beheaded by Herod
John, brother of James, son of Zebedee	• Known as the "beloved disciple" • Wrote Bible books of John, I, II and III John and Revelation	Banished to the Island of Patmos by Emperor Domitian, where he died of old age.
Thomas	• Preached in Babylon and India	Killed by a spear in India
Andrew	• Preached in the area of modern Georgia and Bulgaria	Crucified on an olive tree in Greece
Bartholomew	• Preached in India	Beheaded or crucified with his head down

James, Son of Alphaeus 	• First Bishop of Jerusalem • Possibly wrote the Bible Book of James	Stoned to death after preaching in Jerusalem
Matthew 	• Wrote the Gospel of Matthew • Preached to the Ethiopians	Burned, stoned or beheaded
Philip 	• Preached in Asia Minor	Crucified upside down
Simon the Zealot 	• Possibly preached in Britain, Africa, Egypt and Persia	Crucified
Thaddeus (Jude) 	• Wrote the Bible book of Jude • Preached in Asia Minor	Clubbed to death

Judas	• Betrayed Jesus	Committed suicide
Matthias	• Elected by the other disciples to replace Judas	Stoned to death in Jerusalem

THREE POINTS ON THE WITNESS OF THE TWELVE DISCIPLES

- All twelve disciples saw Jesus die on the cross, and all saw Him alive again after His resurrection. These two things became part of the distinguishing marks of an "apostle," as Jesus' twelve hand-picked disciples were later called. Paul is also considered an apostle, because he too saw the risen Lord on the road to Damascus.
- Despite brutal persecution, none of Jesus' disciples changed his story about Jesus' resurrection. As long as they lived, they all continued to proclaim that Jesus was risen from the dead. Most people are not willing to suffer death merely to preserve a lie. The fact that ALL of them stood by their story affirms the truth of what they saw and heard.
- The early church took root and grew because so many people believed the testimony of the people who saw Jesus alive. If the apostles had appeared to be mentally unstable or deliberately dishonest, then no one would have believed them, and their story would have died with them.

THE PERSECUTION OF THE EARLY CHRISTIANS

Art: Caravaggio-Crucifixion of Peter

The Romans worshipped numerous gods, and were usually tolerant of other nations' religions. Sometimes they incorporated other nations' gods into their own worship, as they did with the Greek gods. In their polytheistic thought, this kept their spiritual bases covered. They were not surprised to find that each new territory they conquered had its own gods, and they wanted to keep these gods happy and gain their good will.

As long as their subjects were polytheists, this tolerance worked out fine. Other polytheists were not opposed to adding Roman gods to their lists, and would willingly bow down to the Roman emperor as a god. The Jews and the Christians were different. Both believed in one God, and bowed to no one else. When emperors like Caligula tried to force Jews and Christians to worship them, it was a cause for revolt. Jews rioted when Caligula tried to erect a statue of himself inside the Temple's Holy of Holies.

In the time of Nero, Rome's anger began to focus on the Christians as well. After Nero accused the Christians of starting Rome's great fire in 64 AD, Rome began to persecute Christians mercilessly. The Romans hated Christians for several reasons:

- Christians refused to assimilate into Roman culture, keeping themselves separate.
- Christians refused to worship the emperor as a god.
- Christians' teaching on the Lord's Supper shocked the Romans. The idea of "eating Christ's flesh" and "drinking Christ's blood" sounded like cannibalism, something the Romans did not tolerate.
- The idea that Christians called one another "brother" and "sister" also upset the Romans. It seemed to elevate women and slaves to the level of men, something the Romans never did.
- Christians were not tolerant of other religions, but insisted that Jesus was the only way to salvation. They insisted that new converts completely abandon the gods of their pasts. This was a negative judgment on Rome's gods.

Another thing that made Christians vulnerable was their practice of sharing their wealth with one another. If a new believer had any wealth, then he or she often shared it with his church group. When the Romans broke up a church group and killed its members, they could confiscate whatever wealth the group had.

The persecution of the early church sent Christians underground, both literally and figuratively. Christians began to hold their meetings in secret places. One such place was the catacombs of Rome.

FASCINATING FACTS: The Catacombs

The Romans had little respect for a person's earthly remains, so their practice was to cremate (burn and crush) their dead. The Christians believed that their bodies would be raised from the dead one day, just as Christ's had been raised. This belief gave them more respect for the remains of their dead, so they preferred to bury them. Because Christians had to do everything in secret, they also needed secret burial places. Their solution was the *catacombs*-- underground tunnels which they lined with the tombs of their dead.

Over time, the Christians found more uses for their catacombs. They began to hide in them during times of intense persecution, and they also held worship services in them. Some early Christian art is preserved in the catacombs.

The rising of Lazarus

Good Shepherd

Christ with Beard

Their walls were decorated with inscriptions, graffiti and fresco paintings depicting Bible stories and symbols. The image most often found on the walls of the catacombs is of the scene in which Jesus raises Lazarus from the dead. Resurrection is the hope and belief of every Christian who buries a loved one.

The persecution of Christians in Rome continued from the time of Nero and Domitian (see above) all the way through Emperor Constantine (306-337 AD), Rome's first "Christian" emperor. Some of Rome's notoriously Christian-hating emperors and their evil deeds are listed here:

Trajan (98-117 AD) 	Outlawed Christianity, along with all secret meetings. Trajan officially sanctioned (approved) the persecution of Christians. Thousands of Christians were put to death under Trajan.
Hadrian (117-138 AD)	Continued Trajan's policies against Christians with just a bit more leniency. The Jewish Bar Kokhba Revolt happened during Hadrian's reign.

INTERESTING INDIVIDUALS: Simon Bar Kokhba

Art: Expulsion of the Jews from Jerusalem

Fig. 357.—Expulsion of the Jews in the Reign of the Emperor Hadrian (A.D. 135): "How Heraclius turned the Jews out of Jerusalem."—Fac-simile of a Miniature in the "Histoire des Empereurs," Manuscript of the Fifteenth Century, in the Library of the Arsenal, Paris.

The Jewish Scriptures predicted the coming of a Jewish Messiah, or Savior/Deliverer. Most Jewish people believed that when he came, their Messiah would overthrow Rome and restore the Kingdom of Israel. When Jesus allowed Himself to be crucified, most Jews saw this as a failure and assumed that Jesus couldn't be their Messiah, the fulfillment of their Scriptures' promises. Jewish people continue to look out for their Messiah even today. Over the centuries, several candidates have presented themselves.

One such "messiah" was Simon bar Kokhba, who rose up during the time of Roman Emperor Hadrian. Under Bar Kokhba, the Jews began a three-year revolution against Rome. They declared a new, independent state of Israel in the part of Judea they managed to capture and hold. The Roman army eventually crushed the revolt, killing thousands of Jews in the process. Hadrian banned Jews from Jerusalem after the Bar Kokhba Revolt.

GIANTS OF THE FAITH: Polycarp (70-155 AD)

Polycarp was a disciple of the Apostle John, whom he knew late in John's life. He served as bishop of the church at Smyrna. He was an early defender of the Christian faith against some of the many heresies (false teachings) that threatened the church.

Polycarp is best known for the manner of his death. He knew well the warnings of Jesus about what would happen to those who denied Him, and he absolutely refused to deny his faith in Christ. When he was 86 years old, Polycarp was arrested for being a Christian. A Roman proconsul took pity on the old man and offered to release him if he would only agree that "Caesar is Lord" and burn incense before Caesar's statue. But to Polycarp, any form of idol worship was a denial of his Christian faith. Because he refused, Polycarp was burned alive at a stake.

Marcus Aurelius (161-180 AD):	
	Emperor Marcus Aurelius was a Stoic, a member of a Greek school of philosophy that emphasized the intellect instead of faith. Aurelius hated Christians, and their persecution under his reign was particularly bloody. One notable Christian who suffered death at Aurelius' hands was Justin Martyr.

GIANTS OF THE FAITH: Justin Martyr (100-165 AD)

Justin Martyr came to the Christian faith as an adult after years as a Stoic. He learned the good news of Christ from an old man walking on a beach. From that time on, Justin dedicated his life to defending Christianity. He even took the dangerous step of founding a Christian school in Rome, where he taught "the true philosophy." He died a martyr's death in Rome during the reign of Marcus Aurelius.

GIANTS OF THE FAITH: Blandina (martyred 177 AD)

Blandina was a slave girl who refused to renounce her faith, even after terrible torture. She was arrested along with her Christian master and several other slaves. The Christians of Blandina's day had already watched the bloody persecutions of many of their Christian brothers and sisters. Blandina was frail, and her companions were afraid that she would quickly renounce her faith when she was tortured.

Blandina proved them wrong. Her persecutors tied her to a stake and set wild beasts on her, but the beasts did not harm her. This went on for some days. Finally, they forced her to watch her companions die, then burned her, threw her to the wild bulls, and killed her with a dagger. Blandina remained true to Christ until the end.

Septimius Severus (193-211 AD)	
	Emperor Severus' reign was marked by cruel persecutions of Christians. Any who refused to curse God and worship the emperor were burned at the stake, beheaded or mauled by wild beasts. Two who suffered martyrdom under Severus were Perpetua and Felicity.

GIANTS OF THE FAITH: Perpetua and Felicity (martyred 203 AD)

Perpetua and Felicity lived in Carthage (modern Tunisia) during the reign of Emperor Severus. Perpetua was the daughter of a wealthy nobleman, and Felicity was her slave. Both loved the Lord and were strong in their faith. When Perpetua and Felicity were arrested, the pressure on them to renounce their faith was high because both had small children. Nevertheless, both refused to deny Christ, and they died hand in hand facing the wild beasts.

Maximinus (235-238 AD)	After a period of relative calm, persecution of Christians flourished again under Emperor Maximinus. Countless Christians were dragged through streets, slain without trial and buried in pits.
Decius (250-251 AD)  	Emperor Decius employed a new tactic to smoke out the Christians he hated: He issued an edict requiring all citizens to make a public sacrifice to the emperor. As each citizen made the sacrifice, the government issued a certificate to prove that he or she had done so. Anyone who refused to make the sacrifice or who could not produce his certificate was put to death.

FASCINATING FACTS: The Early Church's Dilemma over the Edict of Decius

The Edict of Decius required all citizens to make a public sacrifice to the emperor. The government issued a certificate of proof to each person who made the sacrifice, a sort of "get out of execution free" card. The Edict posed a terrible problem for Christians, because for them, to make a public sacrifice to any idol was to deny their faith.

The Edict sent shock waves through the church. Church leaders had to grapple with the problem of how to deal with Christians who made the sacrifice to save their own lives, but still considered themselves Christians. Another thing that muddied the waters was the corruption of public officials: It was possible to avoid death by purchasing a certificate of proof without actually making the public sacrifice. A synod (meeting of church officials) decided on the following policies for dealing with Christians who compromised on the Edict of Decius:

1. Christians who purchased a certificate of proof, but did not actually sacrifice to the emperor, could be readmitted to the church.
2. Christians who sacrificed to the emperor, but then repented, could be readmitted to the church only on their deathbeds. They could also be readmitted if they proved their loyalty to the faith at a later persecution.
3. Christians who sacrificed to the emperor, and did not repent, could never be readmitted to the church.

In setting this policy, the church did something it had never done before: it set manmade rules for inclusion in the family of God. Over the years, the church set more and more of these rules, until it had established a system of "penance," duties or punishments doled out by priests to restore believers to God's favor. Centuries later, the Protestant Reformation began primarily as a reaction against the church's penance system.

Valerian (257-259 AD) 	After a brief respite between emperors, Emperor Valerian reinstated the edict of Decius requiring that all Christians make a public sacrifice to the emperor. At first the punishment for refusal was exile, but after 258 AD, the punishment was death. Fortunately for the Christians, Valerian was taken captive by the Persians, and his son revoked the edict.

Emperors Diocletian and Galerius (303-324)	The last Roman emperors to persecute Christians were Diocletian and Galerius. Their time became known as the "Great Persecution" (read more about Diocletian in Chapter 33).

FASCINATING FACTS: The Great Persecution

The Great Persecution of Christians under Emperors Diocletian and Galerius began in the Roman military. First, Diocletian issued an edict that required all Roman soldiers to make a public sacrifice to the gods. Christian soldiers could not make this sacrifice in good conscience, so they tried to resign from the military. Christians who were not yet in the military refused to join so that they wouldn't have to make the public sacrifice.

The uproar over all of this raised Diocletian's anger against Christians, so in 303 AD, he ordered the burning of all Christian buildings, books and Bibles. What followed was bloody chaos. Many Christian leaders were arrested. Any who refused to sacrifice to the emperor were abused, starved, tortured, burned, mutilated or killed by gladiators in the arena.

Perhaps surprisingly, the Great Persecution did not reduce the number of Christians. Instead, the church flourished under persecution, and Christianity continued to spread throughout Rome. This is one of many historical examples of the way Christian churches grow under persecution and die when their faith goes untested.

The Great Persecution lasted through the last days of Galerius' reign, until he ended it on his deathbed in 311 AD.

AMAZING ANCIENTS: Constantine and the Christians (306-337 AD)

Emperor Constantine is known as Rome's first Christian emperor, but little is known about his personal faith. He learned about Christianity as a boy from his mother, Helena, but he was 42 years old before he publicly acknowledged his faith, and he was only baptized on his deathbed. Along the way, Constantine experienced a vision that affected him profoundly.

In Constantine's day, the Roman Empire was divided into the Western Empire and the Eastern Empire. There were several would-be emperors, all fighting among themselves for supremacy. Constantine dove into this mess when he gathered his forces in Gaul (modern France), marched across the Alps and headed for Rome on a quest to conquer the Western Empire. On the way, he had a vision in which he saw a cross above the sun with the inscription "By this sign thou shalt conquer." Constantine was familiar with the cross and whom it represented. Believing that his vision was a sign from God, Constantine ordered his men to paint the vision on their shields. Thus protected, they took the field against the larger and stronger army of Maxentius at the Battle of Milvian Bridge and won.

Constantine became the first Roman emperor to endorse Christianity, and he issued the Edict of Milan granting the religious freedom that allowed Christians to come out of hiding. But his behavior as emperor led some to doubt his commitment to the faith. Christians lived simply and practiced self-denial, but Constantine lived lavishly and denied himself nothing. He executed his oldest son, his second wife and his brother-in-law. And he never subjected himself to any church leader, as later Christian kings would do.

But to some, Constantine was the model of the Christian king. He built churches and enacted laws that encouraged Christianity. He appointed Christians to high positions in government, and he established Sunday as the official day of worship. Constantine's official promotion of Christianity legitimized the faith and enabled the church, especially the Roman church, to become a powerful political force in the years to come.

Raphael's Baptism of Constantine

FASCINATING FACTS: The Edict of Milan (313 AD)

The Edict of Milan, issued jointly by Emperors Constantine of the Western Empire and Licinius of the Eastern Empire, granted religious freedom throughout the Roman Empire. It went farther than the edict issued by Galerius on his deathbed, which only ended the official policy of persecution of Christians. The Edict of Milan returned property confiscated from Christians during the Great Persecution and made it possible for Christians to hold meetings in public places without fear.

It was not, however, an official endorsement of Christianity. It granted freedom of religious practice to everyone, Christian and non-Christian alike. Under the Edict of Milan, official sacrifices to idols continued, and Constantine did nothing to stop them. Only decades later, under Emperor Theodosius I, did Christianity become Rome's official state religion.

FASCINATING FACTS: Ichthys (Ichthus)

Persecuted Christians had to be wary of strangers, so they developed a means to identify themselves to one another as Christ followers. When a Christian spoke to a stranger and wanted to know if this person was a Christian, he would discreetly draw an arc on the ground with his foot. If the stranger recognized the arc, he would draw a second arc to complete the ichtys symbol. Then both knew that they were in safe company.

The Ichthys symbol had a double meaning for the early Christians. The letters of the Greek word for "fish" spell out an acronym for "Jesus Christ God Son Savior." The fish also reminded believers that when Jesus called the disciples, He said that He would make them "fishers of men" (Mark 1:17).

Chapter 33

Rome Weakens

ANCIENT HISTORY AND CHURCH HISTORY FOCUS
(This week the Ancient and Church history are woven together)

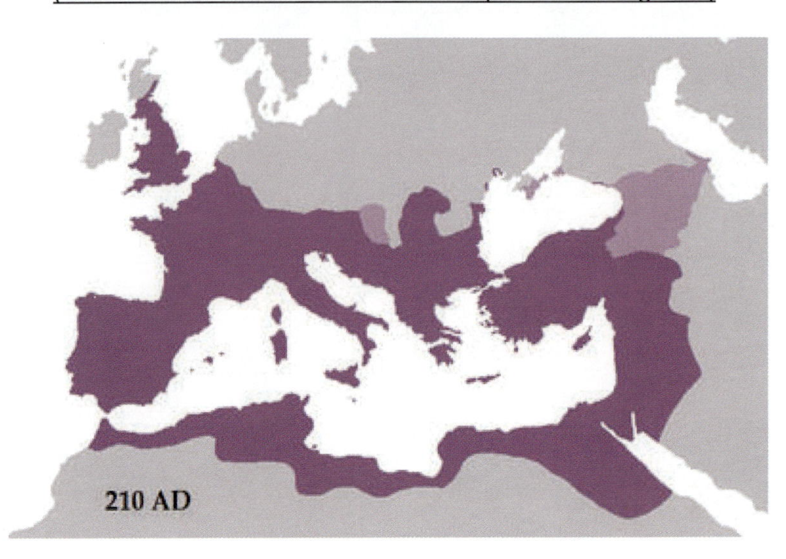

Our final two lessons will focus on some highlights and lowlights of Roman history from the conquest of Britain in 43 AD to the end of the Western Roman Empire in 476 AD.

In 43 AD, Emperor Claudius sent four legions of Roman troops into Britain and secured southern Britain for Rome. Rome built roads and established outposts throughout southern Britain, including an outpost called Londinium, which grew into the city of London. But the Celtic tribes of Britain did not give in to the Romans willingly. One tribe that resisted Roman domination was led by a woman name Boudicca.

INTERESTING INDIVIDUALS: Boudicca (Boadicea)

Queen Boudicca was the wife of King Prasutagus, the sovereign of a Brittanic tribe of Celts called the *Iceni*. When Rome moved into southern Britain, Prasutagus allied himself with Rome and became a *client king*, a local king who was allowed to keep his territory under a special arrangement with Rome (Herod the Great was a client king in Judea). Client kings were expected to leave their kingdoms to the Roman emperor when they died, but sometimes their male heirs were allowed to become client kings in their place. Prasutagus had no male heirs, so he tried to leave his kingdom to his wife and daughters (along with the emperor) when he died. But Roman law did not allow women to inherit property, so the Romans ignored Prasutagus' will. In brutal fashion, the Romans seized control of Prasutagus' land just as if they had conquered it. They made slaves of his nobles, flogged his wife Boudicca, and assaulted his daughters.

Boudicca decided to fight back against Rome's cruelty. She took her story to the neighboring tribes and showed them clearly what fate awaited them if they allowed Rome to dominate Britain. She convinced her neighbors to support a revolt, and she was able to lead a force of 100,000 against Rome's occupying force of about 10,000. She had some victories, including one in Londinium, and she showed the defeated Romans no more mercy than they had shown her.

Unfortunately, Boudicca was battling a ruthless and crafty foe with centuries of experience in dominating other cultures. The Romans abandoned their settlements and burned the food supplies behind them, leaving Boudicca's large force to starve. When the last battle came, Rome's well-trained legionnaires defeated Boudicca's underfed, ill-trained local troops. Preferring death to life under Roman domination, Boudicca fled from the battle and committed suicide by drinking poison.

INTERESTING INDIVIDUALS: Joseph of Arimathea (contemporary of Jesus)

Joseph of Arimathea was a member of the Jewish Sanhedrin (high court and council), but left it to become a disciple of Jesus. After Jesus was crucified, Joseph offered his personal tomb to Pilate as a burial place for Jesus' body. Jesus didn't need it for long. The tomb was sealed and guarded from Good Friday until Easter, when Jesus rose again. Joseph's tomb was the site of the resurrection and the place where Jesus' disciples found the empty tomb.

After Jesus' ascension, it is believed that Joseph of Arimathea traveled to Gaul and later to Britain, preaching the gospel of Christ. Around 63 AD, he built the first church in all of Britain at Glastonbury.

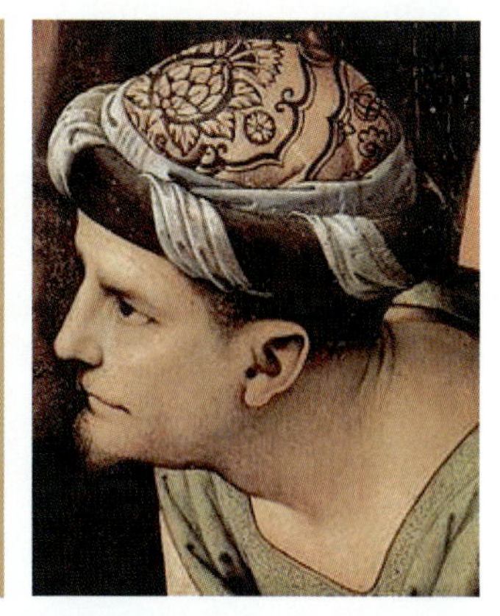

Between 75 and 85 AD, the Romans conquered Wales and Scotland as well as southern Britain. Parts of northern Britain were still unconquered, and they would remain so. Rome had reached its peak in Britain, and held as much territory as it would ever hold.

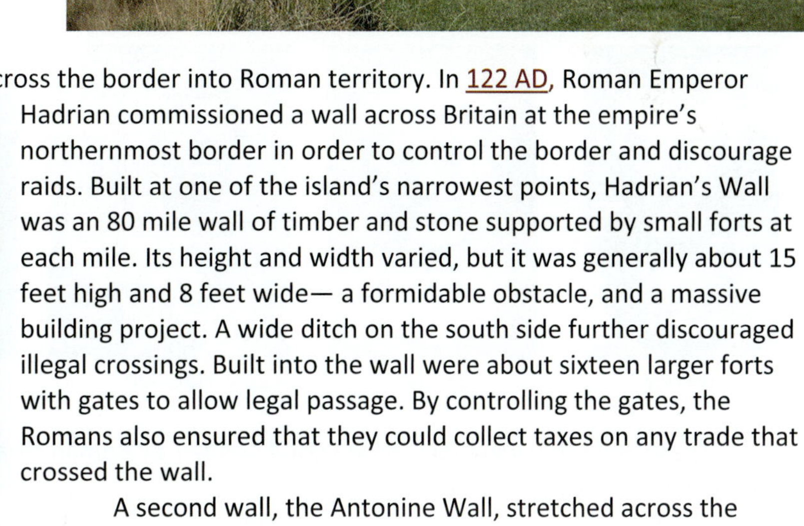

Back on the Italian Peninsula, in 79 AD, Mount Vesuvius erupted and destroyed the city of Pompeii (along with some other cities). See Geography focus below.

Hadrian's Wall

Even after Rome conquered southern Britain, northern Britain remained in the hands of native tribes such as the Picts. Sometimes these tribes conducted raids across the border into Roman territory. In 122 AD, Roman Emperor Hadrian commissioned a wall across Britain at the empire's northernmost border in order to control the border and discourage raids. Built at one of the island's narrowest points, Hadrian's Wall was an 80 mile wall of timber and stone supported by small forts at each mile. Its height and width varied, but it was generally about 15 feet high and 8 feet wide— a formidable obstacle, and a massive building project. A wide ditch on the south side further discouraged illegal crossings. Built into the wall were about sixteen larger forts with gates to allow legal passage. By controlling the gates, the Romans also ensured that they could collect taxes on any trade that crossed the wall.

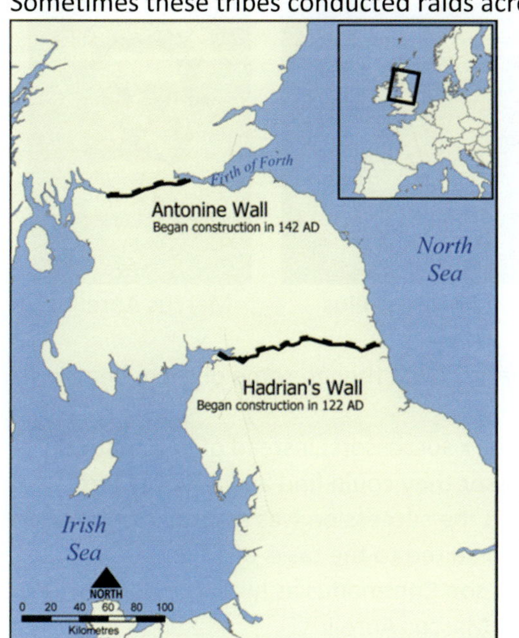

A second wall, the Antonine Wall, stretched across the island farther north beginning in 142 AD. However, the Romans failed to conquer the Pictish tribes who lived north of this shorter wall, and so abandoned it after only twelve years. Hadrian's Wall remained the Roman Empire's northernmost border until the declining empire withdrew from Britain around 410 AD.

FASCINATING FACTS: The Apostles' Creed

Around 150 AD Roman Christians developed a "symbol of faith," or creed, that condensed the essentials of the Christian faith into a single brief statement. They began to teach the Apostles' Creed to new converts and to use it in meetings as a statement of faith.

THE APOSTLES' CREED

I believe in God, the Father Almighty,
The Maker of heaven and earth,
And in Jesus Christ, His only Son, our Lord:
Who was conceived by the Holy Ghost,
Born of the Virgin Mary,
Suffered under Pontius Pilate,
Was crucified, dead, and buried;
He descended into hell.
The third day He arose again from the dead;
He ascended into heaven,
And sitteth on the right hand of God the Father Almighty;
From thence he shall come to judge the quick and the dead.
I believe in the Holy Ghost;
The holy catholic church;
The communion of saints;
The forgiveness of sins;
The resurrection of the body;
And the life everlasting.
Amen.

The Five Good Emperors

From 96 - 192 AD Rome prospered under the reigns of five "Good Emperors":

Nerva

Trajan

Hadrian

Antonius Pius

Marcus Aurelius

These emperors were considered good and fair by Roman citizens, even though some of them heavily persecuted Christians and Jews.

These five emperors all used an improved method to choose their successors: instead of automatically naming their own sons or stepsons as heirs, they chose the best successor they could find and adopted him. Under Roman law, adopted sons had the same rights as natural sons, so the succession was assured. Such hand-picked successors were less likely to be underage, inexperienced, and ill-suited to the tasks of an emperor. Finally, Marcus Aurelius broke this new pattern when he chose his own son Commodus as his successor. Some historians trace the fall of Rome back to this one bad decision made by Marcus Aurelius.

FASCINATING FACTS: The End of the Pax Romana

The Pax Romana (Roman Peace) was a 200 year period of internal peace that began under Caesar Augustus in 27 BC. Rome's wealth and prosperity reached its peak during the Pax Romana. The empire's borders were mostly secure, so Rome could spend its wealth improving roads and public buildings.

Marcus Aurelius, who reigned from 161-180 AD, was the last emperor of the Pax Romana. Aurelius faced more problems than his predecessors: internal problems such as famines, earthquakes and plagues, and external problems such as invasions from the Germans and the Parthians (from old Persia). Under Aurelius, the borders of the mighty Roman Empire began to crumble, and the end of his reign is considered the end of the Pax Romana.

In 180 AD, Marcus Aurelius's son Commodus became Emperor.

TERRIBLE TYRANTS: Lucius Aurelius Commodus

Marcus Aurelius was the last of the five Good Emperors. Aurelius' son Commodus was his father's opposite in many ways. Commodus was a bloodthirsty, cruel, power hungry and paranoid tyrant. He killed anyone who stood in his way. He was so hated that his own family joined in a failed conspiracy to assassinate him. Commodus cared little for his duties as emperor, preferring to spend his time partying and playing at being a gladiator in the arena.

Commodus was finally assassinated on New Year's Eve 192 AD. His weak government collapsed, and chaos erupted in Rome.

The Year of the Five Emperors

Pertinax

Didius Julianus

Pescennius Niger

Claudius Albinus

Septimius Severus

After the assassination of Emperor Commodus on New Year's Eve, the new year of 193 AD dawned in chaos. Because five different men made their bids for the throne of Rome, 193 became known as the "Year of the Five Emperors."

The first, Pertinax, reigned for only eighty-six days until he was killed by the Praetorian guard (the emperor's bodyguards). These soldiers then auctioned off the throne to the highest bidder. The winner was Didius Julianus, who offered each Praetorian Guard soldier 25,000 sestertii (the sesterce was a Roman coin). This was 5,000 more per soldier than the next bidder offered.

But the position of emperor was not the property of the Praetorian Guard to sell. The legions of soldiers stationed out in Rome's provinces had different opinions about who should be emperor, and bribes paid to the Praetorian Guard meant nothing to them. Three commanders led three different armies in their bids for the throne: Claudius Albinus led the army from Britain, Septimius Severus led the army from north and east of the Danube River, and Pescennius Niger led the army from the east.

What followed was a complicated mess. Pescennius Niger was proclaimed Emperor by his army of the east, which opposed the appointment of Didius Julianus. Meanwhile, Septimius led his army into Rome and disarmed the Praetorian Guard, deposing Didius Julianus. With Didius out of the way, Claudius Albinus' army proclaimed him Emperor. Septimius Severus defeated first Pescennius Niger, then Claudius Albinus to become Emperor himself in 197 AD. This was the beginning of the Severus Dynasty.

The Severus Dynasty

The emperors of the Severus Dynasty reigned from 193 - 235 AD. The first, Septimius Severus (193 - 211), stripped the central Roman government of most of its power. He dissolved the Praetorian Guard and raised a new one in its place, and he executed a number of senators. This left nearly all of the powers of government in his hands and in the hands of the military. Rome was essentially a military dictatorship. Severus' dying advice to his two sons who succeeded him was to trust the soldiers and no one else.

The two sons, Caracalla and Geta, shared the emperor's throne only briefly. They considered splitting the empire, but their hatred for one another boiled over, and Caracalla assassinated his brother Geta.

As emperor, Caracalla quickly earned a reputation for brutality. He made a notorious visit to Alexandria, Egypt, in which he unleashed his army on groups of defenseless civilians. He supposedly did this to control rioting, but one report suggests that he did it because the Alexandrians refused to believe that he had killed his brother Geta in self-defense.

Acting on his father's advice, Caracalla always remained close to his army, marching with them and sharing their meals. His close-cropped hair marked him as a military man. He gave his soldiers a substantial pay raise, which required him to raise taxes in order to pay for it.

Caracalla is also remembered for granting Roman citizenship to all free people who lived in the Roman Empire. This was a major departure from the policy of the past: Back in 91-88 BC, the Social Wars erupted because Rome refused to grant the benefits of citizenship to its allies on the Italian Peninsula. But the times had changed, and Rome's priorities were different. Caracalla granted citizenship to so many not because he wanted to be fair, but because it allowed him to collect more taxes.

FASCINATING FACTS: The Baths of Caracalla

For the free Roman, a trip to the public baths was a daily ritual, a bit like a visit to a modern golf, tennis or fitness club. A typical routine began with payment of a small fee. In the dressing room, the bather would exchange his everyday clothes for a light exercise garment, leaving a slave to guard his possessions. Then he would exercise in any of a number of ways: swimming, wrestling, running, playing ball games or lifting weights. After he had worked up a sweat, slaves would scrape the bather's body with a curved instrument called a *strigil*, giving him a thorough cleaning. Then he could move on through a series of rooms kept at different temperatures: a cold room (*frigidarium*), a warm room (*tepidarium*), and a hot room (*caldarium*). After this series of baths, the bather would get an oil massage and a final scraping with the strigil. He might then choose to finish in the cold room or swimming pool. Afterwards, the bather could visit the public galleries or libraries, or he could socialize in the restaurants. Public bath facilities were social and cultural centers as well as bath and exercise centers.

The Baths of Caracalla was a particularly lavish public bath facility in Rome. Beginning in 212 AD, Caracalla authorized and funded a 33 acre bath complex including gardens, art galleries, libraries (both Greek and Latin), fitness rooms, a swimming pool, a cold room, a hot room, and eateries.

Caracalla was assassinated by a soldier in 217 AD, probably at the suggestion of the next emperor, Macrinus. Macrinus interrupted the Severus Dynasty until he was defeated and replaced by Elagabalus the following year. Elagabalus has a reputation as one of Rome's very worst emperors. He concentrated on his depraved lifestyle and left the running of the empire to his mother and grandmother. When his assassination came in 222 AD, his nephew, Alexander Severus, assumed the throne in his place.

INTERESTING INDIVIDUALS: Alexander Severus (222-235 AD)

Emperor Alexander Severus was a breath of fresh air after the horrific reigns of Caracalla and Elagabalus. Apparently sympathetic to the Christian faith, the honest and just Severus inscribed the motto "Do unto others as you would have them do unto you" on buildings throughout Rome. He removed all of his predecessors' edicts against the Christians, allowing them to practice their faith freely.

After Alexander Severus was assassinated by some discontented soldiers, the empire fell back into chaos.

Chaos in the Empire: The Crisis of the Third Century (235-284 AD)

After the assassination of Emperor Alexander Severus, a 50 year civil war erupted. Almost all of the next 20 emperors were assassinated, and their average reigns lasted only 2-3 years. On Rome's borders, Persians, Goths and Vandals took advantage of Rome's internal chaos to reclaim territory lost to Rome. During this time, the Roman Empire split into three different states: Gallic (modern France, Spain and south Britain), Palmyrene (from Syria to Egypt) and Rome (Italy, Greece, Asia Minor and North Africa).

The credit for reuniting the Roman Empire goes to Emperors Claudius II and Aurelian, the first two in a succession of military emperors. Claudius defeated the Goths in 268 AD, and Aurelian reclaimed the Gallic and Palmyrene Empires for Rome. But the ravages of 50 years of chaos could not be quickly undone, and the empire showed the signs of strain.

AMAZING ANCIENTS: DIOCLETIAN (reigned 284-305 AD)

Diocletian was born into a poor family, but rose through the ranks to a high position in the military. He was the commander of the Praetorian Guard, the emperor's bodyguard, when Emperor Carus and his son Emperor Numerian died within a year of one another. Diocletian's troops declared him emperor. Soon after Diocletian's election, Carus' elder son Carinus marched against Diocletian, but he was defeated and killed.

Diocletian is best remembered as the emperor who divided the Roman Empire. In 285 AD, he elevated his senior army general Maximian to the rank of "Caesar" and set him over the western half of the empire. Diocletian himself retained control in the East. He argued that the huge Roman Empire was too vast for one man to control, and that he was returning to the two-consul system of the old Roman Republic.

In 293 AD, Diocletian further divided the empire by establishing the first *tetrarchy*, or rule by four emperors. Each emperor adopted as a son a "junior Caesar" to assist him: Diocletian adopted Galerius in the east, and Maximian adopted Constantius (father of Constantine) in the west. Diocletian retained veto power as emperor over all. The Roman Empire was now divided as follows:

Eastern Empire
Diocletian: Asia Minor, Egypt and Thrace (modern Bulgaria)
Galerius: Area around the Danube River

Western Empire:
Maximian: Italy and northern Africa
Constantius: Britain, Spain and Gaul

The divided empire was better able to protect itself. Goths, Vandals and other barbarians were all successfully repelled during Diocletian's time. On the other hand, the new system was heavy with military and administrative costs, so Roman taxes continued to rise.

Diocletian was a hero to Romans worried about the threat of invasion, but he was no hero to the Christians of his day. With Galerius' strong support, Diocletian mounted the fiercest persecution of the Christians so far. Any who refused to bow to the Roman gods were imprisoned, tortured and killed (see Chapter 32).

In 305 AD, Diocletian again shocked the empire by abdicating his throne and convincing Maximian to do the same. The two junior Caesars, Galerius and Constantius, took over as emperors of the empire's two halves. Within a year, civil war erupted.

(story continues in Chapter 34)

FASCINATING FACTS: Togas and Stolas

The *toga* was a formal robe worn by male citizens of Rome. It consisted of a long piece of heavy wool cloth that was draped carefully around the body with the help of a slave. Under the toga was only a loincloth or apron. Togas were heavy and cumbersome, and not terribly practical for everyday wear. They were, however, the required dress for formal occasions such as weddings, funerals, gladiator games, and parties, as well as in the assemblies and the senate. The toga was a mark of Roman citizenship, denied to all non-citizens. It was also a mark of peace, since military men wore other garments.

Instead of the toga, married Roman women wore their own garment, the *stola*. The stola was a long, often pleated dress, with or without sleeves, that was worn over a tunic. The Statue of Liberty in New York Harbor wears a stola.

FASCINATING FACTS: The Roman Standard

A Roman *standard* was a tall pole with a military unit's symbol affixed to its top. The Romans used standards to help keep their army units together. In battle, the standard was the rallying point to which a unit's soldiers automatically returned, and it was also used for signaling. The pole's height allowed the standard to be seen from all over the battlefield. Units also set up camp around the standard. Each legion had its own distinctive standards. They were carried by standard bearers (*signifier*), who often wore animal heads as headdresses to set them apart on the battlefield.

The first Roman standard was a handful of straw lashed to the top of a spear. The straw was later replaced by any of five animals: the eagle, the wolf, the minotaur, the horse or the boar. Around 100 BC, the eagle became Rome's most important power symbol. It was a terrible disgrace for a legion to lose its eagle in battle. Along with the eagle, the standard often included a portrait of the emperor molded of metal.

FASCINATING FACTS: S.P.Q.R.

S.P.Q.R. is an acronym for the Latin phrase "Senatus Populusque Romanus" and means "The Senate and the People of Rome." After Rome became a republic, sovereign power belonged to these two bodies, the senate and the Roman people (through their representatives). The SPQR sign appeared everywhere: on unit standards, armor, coins, documents, public streets and buildings, statues and monuments. Its use continued even under the emperors, who were considered the people's representatives. It is used in the city of Rome even today.

FASCINATING FACTS: Saturnalia and CHRISTMAS

At the end of each year's harvest the Romans celebrated Saturnalia, a holiday in honor of Saturn, the god of agriculture. Saturnalia was a time of intense partying. Celebrants exchanged gifts, especially wax candles, and decorated their houses with garland and green trees lit with candles. Schools and businesses were closed. Slaves ate at a banquet served by their masters and wore the hats of freedmen. Saturnalia was originally a day-long celebration, but because it grew so popular, it was stretched from three days to a week or even a month, depending on the emperor. Usually the celebration began on December 17 and lasted through December 24. A second celebration commemorating the birth of Mithras, the Persian god of light, followed from December 25 through January 1st.

There are no early historical records of a date for the celebration of Jesus' birth. When Christians first celebrated Christ's birthday, they chose January 6 (now the day of Epiphany). During Constantine's reign (336 AD), Rome added December 25 to its official calendar as Jesus' birthday in an effort to unify the Christian and pagan traditions. In 350 AD Julius I, the bishop of Rome, established December 25 as the official day for the observance of Christmas. From its beginning, the Christmas celebration mirrored the Saturnalia celebration with its feasts, gift exchanges, and decorated trees.

GEOGRAPHY FOCUS

Volcanoes

Did you know...

- The word "Volcano" comes from the name of Vulcan, the Roman god of fire.
- A volcano is an opening (vent) in the Earth's crust.
- The pressure of the earth's great weight creates movement, friction and heat beneath the earth's surface. Volcanic eruptions release hot gases, molten rock, ash and debris generated by that heat.
- Hawaii's Mauna Loa is the world's largest volcano.

FASCINATING FACTS: Mount Vesuvius

Mount Vesuvius is an active volcano that lies near Naples, Italy. It has been active since before human memory, but the long decades between its eruptions have sometimes allowed people to forget the danger of living in its shadow. As the Roman Empire reached the peak of its wealth and success in the first century AD, many people lived on the fertile ground around the slopes of Vesuvius, and its last eruption had been so long ago that it was no longer even recognized as a volcano.

On August 24, 79 AD, Mount Vesuvius exploded in its worst eruption in recorded history. An almost unimaginable volume of lava, ash and rock burst from its blasted top and buried several nearby towns in as much as 50-60 feet of debris. The eruption did not happen all in one day, but the local people were still caught by surprise. Some died when the weight of the volcanic debris collapsed their roofs, while others were trapped by lava flows. The largest towns destroyed were Pompeii and Herculaneum. Both vanished without a trace, completely buried under thick layers of mud, ash and volcanic rock. Both have since been rediscovered, excavated and studied; each contained well-preserved rooms, artifacts and even human remains.

Vesuvius continued to erupt about once every hundred years until 1000 AD. Then it had a centuries-long quiet spell, and the region again grew heavily populated. When it erupted again in 1631, it was another catastrophe, though not as large as the one in 79 AD. Despite the frequent eruptions, today over 3,000,000 people still live in the danger zone around Vesuvius.

Chapter 34

The Fall of the Roman Empire

ANCIENT HISTORY AND CHURCH HISTORY FOCUS
(This week the Ancient and Church history are woven together)

This week we will cover the highlights and lowlights of the Roman Empire from 305 AD, when Diocletian and Maximian abdicated their thrones to their junior Caesars, through 476 AD, when the Western Roman Empire fell for the last time.

THE CONSTANTINIAN DYNASTY (285-364 AD)

In 285 AD, Emperor Diocletian divided the Roman Empire to form the Eastern Roman Empire and Western Roman Empire (see Chapter 33). **Diocletian** elevated his favorite general, **Maximian**, to the rank of Caesar and made him Emperor of the Western Roman Empire.

Diocletian

Maximian

Galerius

Constantius

In 293 AD, Diocletian and Maximian elevated their adopted heirs **Galerius** and **Constantius** to the rank of Caesar and established the first tetrarchy (rule by four emperors, see Chapter 33).

Then in 305 AD, Diocletian and Maximian shocked the Roman world by abdicating (voluntarily giving up) their thrones and passing them down to their two adopted heirs, Galerius and Constantius. Galerius ruled the Eastern Roman Empire, while Constantius ruled the Western Roman Empire. Constantius appointed **Flavius Severus** as his junior emperor, and Galerius appointed **Gaius Maximinus** as his.

Both selections were surprises, because both of the new emperors had sons of their own: Constantius had **Constantine**, and Maximinus had **Maxentius**.

The two senior emperors retired to the countryside, believing that they had managed a peaceful transfer of power. Unfortunately, Constantius died in the very next year (306 AD). Constantius' troops proclaimed his son Constantine as their emperor, ignoring Constantius' chosen heir, Flavius Severus. Almost immediately, civil war broke out as different factions fought for the right to rule in Constantius' place.

The situation grew complicated. Constantine sent word to Galerius that he had been named Caesar by his father's troops in Severus' place. Hoping to prevent a war, Galerius agreed that Constantine could be emperor over Britain, Gaul and Spain. Maxentius, no doubt jealous of Constantine, also set himself up as emperor in Rome. Maxentius needed help defending himself, so he called his father Maximian out of retirement. By 308 AD there were as many as six different men trying to position themselves as emperor, and civil war spread throughout the empire.

In 312 AD, Constantine decided to move against Maxentius, who was in control of Rome.

FASCINATING FACTS: The Battle of Milvian Bridge

Milvian Bridge is a major bridge over the Tiber River near Rome. As Constantine advanced towards Rome, Maxentius brought his larger army out to meet him, possibly because he feared that if Constantine entered Rome, the senate would support Constantine's claim to the throne. In a further attempt to keep Constantine out of the city, Maxentius destroyed at least part of the Milvian Bridge. He built a pontoon bridge for his own use, which could be destroyed easily if necessary.

When Constantine attacked, Maxentius was still close to the river. Constantine pushed so near the river that Maxentius ran out of room to maneuver, forcing his men to retreat across the pontoon bridge. But the large number of desperate men and horses, all trying to cross at once, was too much for the hastily built pontoon bridge. It collapsed, and most of the men and horses trying to cross it drowned, including Maxentius himself.

Constantine made easy work of the remainder of Maxentius' army, then took control of Rome and the entire Western Roman Empire.

After his victory over Maxentius at the Battle of Milvian Bridge, the Roman Senate formally acknowledged Constantine as emperor of the Western Roman Empire. At the time, two men were contending to be emperor of the Eastern Roman Empire: Licinius and Maximinus Daia.

Constantine hoped to reunite the empire, but he was patient. Instead of attacking immediately, he allowed Licinius and Maximinus to wear each other down. In the next year, 313 AD, Licinius was married to Constantine's half-sister; and at the same time, Constantine and Licinius jointly issued the Edict of Milan granting religious freedom and returning confiscated property to Christians (see Chapter 32). The following month, Licinius decisively defeated Maximinus, sealing his place as Emperor of the Eastern Roman Empire.

But neither Constantine nor Licinius was content to remain emperor of only half of the Roman Empire. After a series of battles followed by brief reconciliations, Constantine finally eliminated Licinius in 324 and reunited the Roman Empire. For the first time since Diocletian, a single emperor ruled the entire Roman Empire, both East and West.

Constantine moved his empire's capital to Byzantium, which he would soon rename Constantinople, and reigned there for thirteen more years. These years were a time of growth and rebuilding for the empire.

FASCINATING FACTS: Constantinople

The capital of the Eastern Roman Empire was the city of Byzantium, strategically located on the border between Europe and Asia. Byzantium sits astride the Strait of Bosporus (picture at right), which links the Black Sea to the Sea of Marmara. The Sea of Marmara in turn links to the Aegean Sea via the Strait of Dardanelles; and of course, the Aegean Sea is open to the Mediterranean Sea. Thus, Byzantium guarded a key waterway for trade between central Europe, Asia and the whole area around the Mediterranean.

Constantine had come to believe that Rome was no longer a practical capital city for the defense of the empire. Immediately after Constantine defeated Licinius, he set about rebuilding the city of Byzantium into the Roman Empire's new capital city. He expanded its borders and moved statues from around Rome to public areas in Byzantium. He built a palace for himself there, as well as public baths, churches, and other buildings.

Although Constantine was careful not to take too much away from the city of Rome, moving the capital to Byzantium was a step down the road to the end of the Western Roman Empire. When barbarians eventually overran the Western Empire in 476 AD, Constantinople became the center that kept the Eastern Roman Empire alive for the next thousand years. The Eastern Empire would be renamed the Byzantine Empire, after the city of Byzantium (see Year 2). Byzantium itself would be renamed Constantinopolis ("city of Constantine"), or Constantinople. In modern times, it lies in the nation of Turkey. It is no longer a Christian city and now bears the name Istanbul.

After he issued the Edict of Milan (along with Licinius) in 313 AD, Constantine gradually began to change the nature of the relationship between the church and the empire. He added more and more laws favorable to Christians: he made their churches exempt from taxes, allowed churches to inherit property, and elevated Christians to high positions in his government. He also made Sunday an official day of worship. He also grew very interested in the details of Christian theology. In 325 AD, when a council of church elders met to make decisions on some important issues, Constantine presided over it personally. This was the First Council of Nicaea.

FASCINATING FACTS: First Council of Nicaea (325 AD)

From the very beginning, Christians struggled to define the theology of their new faith. Christianity was a new thing, unlike any other faith the world had ever known. Christians had to decide who Christ was and what His life, death and resurrection meant. Almost immediately, the early church's teachings about Christ were challenged by people with different ideas. Some of these challenges appear in the Acts of the Apostles and throughout Paul's letters.

The theological issue at the Council of Nicaea was posed by Arius, a leader in the church at Alexandria. Arius came to believe that Jesus was a created being: that He was the son of God, but not of the same essence as God Himself. As such, He was not present with God at creation, but was part of God's creation. In other words, Jesus was something less than God.

Arius' position drew him into conflict with his bishop, Alexander of Alexandria, who believed that Jesus was fully God. Alexander condemned Arius' beliefs in public and removed him from his position of leadership. Arius appealed to church leaders in Rome, and the whole church became embroiled in the Arian controversy. Constantine, who had just defeated his rival Licinius for the final time, stepped in and called an assembly of church leaders from all over the empire to resolve the issue.

The council was set for the city of Nicaea, not far from Byzantium, in 325 AD. About 300 church leaders attended, and Constantine himself presided. Because Arius was not a bishop, he was not invited to attend. One of the chief churchmen who argued against Arius was Athanasius, also from Alexandria, who went on to become a great father of the church. The council utterly rejected Arius' teaching and proclaimed that Christ was of the same essence as God. In order to solidify its position, the council produced and approved the Nicene Creed, which remains the most universally accepted Christian creed.

The Nicene Creed

We believe in one God,
the Father, the Almighty,
of all that is, seen and unseen.
We believe in one Lord, Jesus Christ,
the only Son of God,
eternally begotten of the Father,
God from God, Light from Light,
true God from true God,

begotten, not made,
of one Being with the Father.
Through Him all things were made.
For us and for our salvation
He came down from heaven:
by the power of the Holy Spirit
He became incarnate from the Virgin Mary,
and was made man.
For our sake He was crucified under Pontius Pilate;
He suffered death and was buried.
On the third day He rose again
in accordance with the Scriptures;
He ascended into heaven
and is seated at the right hand of the Father.
He will come again in glory to judge the living and the dead,
and His kingdom will have no end.

We believe in the Holy Spirit, the Lord, the giver of life,
who proceeds from the Father and the Son.
With the Father and the Son He is worshipped and glorified.
He has spoken through the Prophets.

We believe in one holy catholic and apostolic Church.
We acknowledge one baptism for the forgiveness of sins.
We look for the resurrection of the dead,
and the life of the world to come. Amen.

All but a few bishops signed the new creed. To affirm the Nicene Creed's correctness and importance, Constantine banned from their cities all bishops who refused to sign it.

The nature of the relationship between the church and the Roman Empire was now completely reversed. A few years before, Rome had encouraged open persecution of Christians. Now, under Constantine, Rome was deciding matters of Christian theology and exercising political power over church matters. The Roman government was linked to the church in a new and powerful way.

FASCINATING FACTS: Easter

(6th century depiction of the crucifixion and resurrection of Jesus)

Another issue decided at the First Council of Nicaea was the proper day to celebrate Easter, the day of Jesus' resurrection from the dead, each year. Because Jesus was crucified during Passover week, the date of the resurrection was linked to Jewish Passover; but the Jews had their own calendar, different from that of the Romans. The Council of Nicaea decided that Easter would fall on the Sunday following the first full moon after the spring equinox (March 21). Thus Easter became a moveable feast, celebrated each year between March 21 and April 25.

Constantine was baptized into the Christian faith on his deathbed, just before he died in 337 AD. The Roman Empire was divided between **three of his sons**, all of whom he had already elevated to the position of Caesar. All other potential heirs were killed in a purge, reportedly by the supporters of Constantine's son Constantius II.

- **Constantine II** controlled Spain, Gaul and Britain. He died in an attempt to seize his brother Constans' realm in 340 AD.
- **Constans** controlled Italy and Africa. A revolt in his kingdom led to his death in 350 AD.
- **Constantius II** controlled Greece, Constantinople and the Eastern Empire. When his two brothers were gone, he assumed control of the entire Roman Empire.

As emperor, Constantius II was faced with two simultaneous crises: border attacks from Persia and rebellion in Gaul. Constantius had two cousins who had survived the purge of Constantine's heirs, Gallus and Julian. He appointed Gallus to lead one army against the Persians, while he himself confronted the rebellion in Gaul. But Constantius began to believe that Gallus was disloyal, so he arrested him and ordered his execution. That left only the younger cousin, Julian. Constantius sent Julian to fight in Gaul this time, while he himself turned to the east.

In Gaul, Julian proved such an effective commander that his army proclaimed him Caesar. Ever paranoid about challenges to his throne, Constantius II set off in a panic to quell this new rebellion. Unfortunately, he grew seriously ill along the way. He followed his father Constantine's example and received baptism on his deathbed, then proclaimed Julian as his official heir.

In 361 AD, **Julian** became the new Roman Emperor. Like so many of his predecessors, Julian hated Christians and tried to reverse Constantine's policies favoring them. Fortunately for the Christians, Julian's reign lasted only two years, until he died in battle against the Persians. His successor, **Jovian**, negotiated an uneasy peace with the Persians that would last for about forty years. Jovian himself lasted for just one year.

The deaths of Julian and Jovian brought the Constantinian Dynasty to an end.

THE FALL OF ROME

SIGNS OF THE END: The Wandering Capital of the Western Roman Empire

One of the reasons Emperor Diocletian divided the Roman Empire was that he was dissatisfied with the location of its ancient capital city, Rome. The city of Rome was simply too far south to allow its armies to respond quickly to threats along the empire's borders far to the north.

In 285 AD, when Diocletian divided the empire into East and West, he moved the capital of the Western Roman Empire from Rome to Mediolanum (modern-day Milan), a city in the northern Italian Peninsula near the Alps. Rome remained a great and honored city, but it was no longer the empire's capital. The demotion of the City of Rome was a sign of the end for the Western Roman Empire.

In 402 AD, Emperor Honorius moved the capital a second time, from Mediolanum to Ravenna. Ravenna was a city on the Italian Peninsula's Adriatic Sea coast, largely surrounded by swamps and the sea. Ravenna's natural defenses meant that it was well positioned to defend itself, but poorly positioned to defend the rest of the empire. The move to Ravenna was another sign of the end.

Emperor Valentinian I

The next emperors were **Valentinian I** and his brother **Valens**, two sons of a prominent general. Valentinian I came to power in 364 AD, and soon elevated his brother to the rank of Caesar so that they could reign as co-emperors. Valentinian I ruled in the West, while Valens ruled in the east. However, Valentinian retained power over all as senior emperor. Valentinian I would be the last great Western emperor.

The Barbarian Invasions

Unfortunately for the Romans, the peace Jovian negotiated with Persia did not mean peace throughout the empire. During Valentinian's time, tribes of uncultured foreigners whom the Romans dubbed "barbarians" began to break through Rome's borders from all directions. The movement of foreign tribes was so large that it became known as the Great Migration, and it was a major cause of the Western Roman Empire's fall. Beset on every front, the Roman army was powerless to prevent the flood of Barbarian Goths, Huns and Vandals from overrunning the empire.

BENIGHTED BARBARIANS: The Goths

Along the Roman Empire's northern borders lived the *Goths*, who had often harassed the Romans over the years. The Goths were originally from Sweden, but later migrated down into Europe. They were divided into two groups, the *Visigoths* (western Goths) and the *Ostrogoths* (eastern Goths). Around 370 AD, the Huns (see below) swept down into Europe and drove the Visigoths out of their homes and across the Roman borders. The Romans were left with a choice between trying to wipe out the Goths or assimilating them into the empire. Roman and Visigoth coexisted peacefully for a time; but in 378 AD, the Visigoths revolted against Roman rule and murdered Emperor Valens. His successor, Emperor Theodosius, managed to secure another temporary peace with the Visigoths.

Emperor Theodosius I

Emperor Theodosius I succeeded Valens in the Eastern Roman Empire in 378 AD. He reunited the empire's two halves in 392 AD and ruled until his death in 395 AD. Theodosius would be the last emperor to rule the entire Roman Empire. In 380 AD, Theodosius became the first emperor to proclaim Christianity as the empire's official state religion.

Through a combination of military victories and negotiations, Theodosius succeeded in controlling the threat of the Goths throughout his reign. Nevertheless, that threat continued to grow.

Emperors Arcadius and Honorius

When Theodosius died, his two young sons **Arcadius** and **Honorius** divided the empire once again. Arcadius ruled the Eastern Roman Empire, and Honorius ruled the crumbling Western Roman Empire.

SIGNS OF THE END: The Visigoths Sack Rome (410 AD)

After Theodosius died, the Visigoths elected Alaric I as their king. Under Alaric, the Visigoths once again rebelled against Roman rule and attacked the Western Roman Empire. The Roman defense was led by a German-born general named Stilicho.

AMAZING ANCIENTS: Stilicho (359-408 AD)

Stilicho was part Roman and part Vandal, but he was fully loyal to the Roman Empire. Stilicho became one of Emperor Theodosius' most trusted generals, and on his deathbed, Theodosius appointed Stilicho as guardian over his young heirs Honorius and Arcadius. This meant that the crumbling Western Roman Empire's many military problems fell entirely on Stilicho's shoulders.

Stilicho was forced to repel invasions from Alaric the Goth no less than four times. The able Stilicho defeated Alaric each time, but Alaric always managed to do great damage before escaping once again. Rome grew frustrated with Stilicho's inability to end the threat of the Goths once and for all.

Stilicho and his wife Serena and son Eucherius

Around 407 AD, Stilicho convinced the Roman Senate to forestall yet another Alaric invasion by paying Alaric off with gold. Stilicho's opponents considered this traitorous. The Roman Army was already filling up with hired barbarians, and Stilicho's opponents believed that Stilicho wanted the gold so that he could hire Alaric and his band of barbarians as well. In the eyes of the still-proud Roman Senate, Stilicho's star began to fall.

In 408 AD, Stilicho's enemies arrested him and charged him with treason. He did not defend himself against the charges, and he was soon executed. His son Eucherius was also killed shortly thereafter. After Stilicho's execution, the Western Roman Empire was left without a strong commander to lead its armies.

Alaric took advantage of the leadership vacuum left by Stilicho's execution to launch a long invasion of the Western Empire. Honorius had moved his capital from Mediolanum (now Milan) to Ravenna in 402 BC. Ravenna was protected from invasion by the swamps that surrounded it, but the swamps also made it difficult for Rome's armies to respond to threats quickly. So Alaric simply bypassed Ravenna and ransacked cities throughout the Italian Peninsula.

In 410 AD, Alaric and the Visigoths sacked the City of Rome itself. They plundered the proud city for three days, then turned to southern Italy and ravaged the countryside there.

When Alaric died later that same year, his successor resettled the Visigoths in Gaul and Spain.

<u>BENIGHTED BARBARIANS: Attila and the Huns</u>

The Huns were nomads from somewhere in Asia (their origins are mysterious). Their fierce warriors fought with bow and arrow from horseback, causing terror wherever they went. Over the centuries, the Huns had invaded China, India, Persia and finally Europe. Around 400 AD, the Huns established themselves in Europe and conducted raids against both the Western and Eastern Roman Empires.

In 432 BC the Huns united under one king, Rugila. When he died two years later, perhaps killed by his brother, his nephews Bleda and Attila succeeded him. In 445 AD, Attila killed his brother and became sole ruler of the Huns.

Attila the Hun earned his nickname "the Scourge of God" by leading a series of attacks against Roman holdings across central and eastern Europe. One of these campaigns almost toppled Constantinople itself n 447 AD.

Just when Attila's fearsome reputation reached its peak, a new emperor rose to power in the Western Roman Empire: Valentinian III, a nephew of Honorius. Valentinian III's sister Honoria gave him a great deal of trouble, so he confined her to a monastery while he planned to marry her off to a senator. But Honoria was not content to be shut up inside a monastery. Instead, she sought a rescue from her brother's notorious enemy, Attila the Hun. Honoria sent Attila a ring and a letter begging him to break her out of her prison.

Attila interpreted the letter and ring as a proposal of marriage. Such a marriage would have given the barbarian Attila a chance to join Rome's proud royal family. So in 450 AD, Attila demanded that Valentinian give him his sister Honoria's hand in marriage. When Valentinian refused, Attila attacked Gaul and Italy. Only by a bribe payment negotiated by Pope Leo I saved Rome itself from Attila's ravages.

Attila died in the following year, and the Hun Empire was divided between his three sons. The Huns eventually mixed with the Germans and Slavs and settled throughout Europe.

BENIGHTED BARBARIANS: The Vandals and the Second Sack of Rome (455 AD)

The Vandals hailed from what is now eastern Germany. Around 400 AD, the Vandals moved down into Roman territory in an effort to escape the Huns. They arrived in Spain around 409 AD, and from there they moved into North Africa. By 439 AD they controlled Carthage. Then they began to raid the coasts of both the Eastern and Western Roman Empires, gaining control of the western Mediterranean Sea.

In May 455, the Vandals approached Rome. Pope Leo I interceded for the city once again, begging the Vandal leader not to burn the city. His efforts were only partly successful: the Vandals spent two weeks ransacking the city and stealing all of its treasures, but they didn't burn it. The Vandals left Rome, carrying along the empress and her two daughters, and sailed back to North Africa.

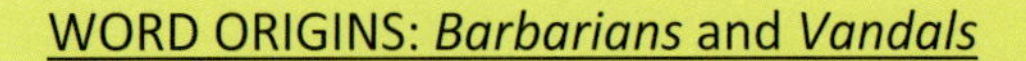

WORD ORIGINS: *Barbarians* and *Vandals*

In modern English, a *vandal* is someone who willfully or maliciously destroys property. This word comes directly from the Vandals, the Germanic tribe that sacked Rome in 455 AD. The Vandals wrecked the city and carried off a great deal of treasure, including some of the treasures from Jerusalem's Temple brought back to Rome by Emperor Titus in 70 AD. Their name became synonymous with wanton destruction.

Similarly, a *barbarian* is any uncivilized, uncultured foreigner. This word comes directly from the Greek, and its first two syllables are meant to mimic the chatter of the unschooled rabble the Greeks so despised. Greeks and Romans alike were highly proud of their refined culture and education, and looked down on less developed cultures. To Rome's shame, it was these unschooled barbarians and vandals who ultimately brought their lofty culture down.

THE END

After the Vandals left Rome, the Western Roman Empire was left under the control of barbarian generals who took orders from a chieftain named Ricimer the Goth. Because he was a barbarian, his pedigree would never allow him to call himself "emperor"; but even so, Ricimer controlled the Western Roman Empire through puppet emperors whom he chose or eliminated at will for the next seventeen years. After Ricimer's death in 472, chaos ensued.

In 475, a barbarian named Orestes, who had been Attila the Hun's secretary, took control of the capital city of Ravenna. Orestes placed his six year old son Romulus Augustulus on the throne of the empire. Romulus would be the last emperor of the Western Roman Empire, such as it was. Thus Rome both began and ended under a leader named Romulus.

Romulus' reign lasted for just one year. At the end of that year, a band of mercenaries led by a German barbarian named Odoacer or Odovacer marched into Ravenna. Odacer killed Orestes, and deposed Romulus Augustus (see picture).

What was left of the Western Roman Empire officially ended on September 4, 476 AD. This was the famous, final "Fall of Rome." The Eastern Roman Empire was to continue as the Byzantine Empire for centuries to come.

FASCINATING FACTS: Trigon

Trigon was a Roman ball game for three players, played on a triangular field with a hard ball called a trigon. The rules of the original Trigon game are, unfortunately, lost; but apparently, players passed the trigon around the circle by catching it with the right hand and throwing it with the left.

Sample Ancient History Timelines

The different books that BiblioPlan uses for its spine differ in their early timelines. There is little agreement on dates before 3,000 BC, and little enough for dates after 3,000 BC. The major events of the different timelines from Story of the World and Mystery of History for the period from 10,000 - 1,000 BC are listed below for your reference:

Story of the World Timeline

7,000 BC: Nomads roam the Fertile Crescent
6800: Jericho is built
3800 - 2400: Sumerians and Egyptians
3100: Iron Age
3000: Upper and Lower Egypt united
3000 - 1200: Gilgamesh Myth composed
2690: Huang Di rules China
2550: Great Pyramid built
2334: Sargon becomes king of Kish
2200 - 1450: Peak of Minoan Civilization
2166: Abraham leaves Ur
2040 - 1720: Middle Kingdom of Egypt
1980 - 1926: Amenemhet becomes pharaoh of Egypt
1792: Hammurabi becomes king of Babylon
1766: T'ang becomes King of China
1766 - 1122: Shang Dynasty
1750: Exodus of Indus Valley
1524: Thutmose I becomes Pharaoh
1473 - 1458: Hatshepsut becomes Pharaoh
1450: Mycenaeans settle in Crete
1446 - 1200: The Exodus (the date span is because of the difficulty in determining exactly when the Exodus took place and under which Pharaoh)
1357: Tutankhamen born
1352 - 1336: Amenhotep IV rules as Egypt's Pharaoh
1339: Tutankhamen dies
1300 - 1200: Assyrian Empire spreads
1260: The Battle of Troy
1200 - 900: Olmec flourish
1200 - 700: Phoenician civilization flourishes and Greek Dark Ages

Mystery of History Timeline

6,000 - 4000 BC: Creation
4000 - 3500: Noah and the Flood
3500 - 2500: The Ice Age
3500 - 2500: The Sumerians
3500 - 3000: The Tower of Babel
2750: The Epic of Gilgamesh
2700: Stonehenge
2575 - 2500: Early Egyptians
2200: Minoan Civilization
2100 - 1900: Abraham, Jacob and Joseph
1792: Hammurabi
1875 - 1730: Israelites in Slavery
1600 - 1066: Shang Dynasty
1525 - 1270: The Exodus (the date span is because of the difficulty in determining exactly when the Exodus took place and under which Pharaoh)
1470: Jericho falls
1353: Amenhotep IV

1333: Tutankhamen
1304 - 1237: Ramses II
1250: Legend of the Trojan Horse
1122: Zhou Dynasty
1000: The Phoenicians

Time chart on the earliest civilizations around the world from J. M. Robert's *Ancient History*

8000: Jericho is built
3500: Mesopotamia civilization (around the Fertile Crescent)
3100: Egyptian civilization appears (Africa)
2500: Civilizations in India appear (India - Asia)
2100: Minoan civilization - (Crete)
1500: Chinese civilization appears (China - Asia)
1400: Civilizations in the Americas appear (North and South America)

Kingdom of Priests - A History of Old Testament Israel by Eugene H. Merrill

3000-1200 BC: Bronze Age
2371-2316: Sargon
2166: birth of Abraham
1792-1750: Hammurabi
2066: Birth of Isaac
2006: Birth of Jacob and Esau
1929-1895: Egyptian Pharaoh Amenemhet II
1916: Birth of Joseph
1876: Jacob's descent to Egypt
1526: Birth of Moses
1504-1450: Thutmose III
1486: Moses flees to the desert for 40 years
1446: Moses returns to Egypt, The Exodus from Egypt
1450-1425: Amenhotep II, Egyptian pharaoh during the Exodus
1361-1352: Tutankhamen
1304-1236: Ramses II
1115-1077: Tiglath-Pileser I
1041: Birth of David
966: Solomon's temple

The following is the standard timeline that most archaeologists use for the Ancient Near East:

Stone Age (Neolithic and Chalcolithic)	8500 - 3300 BC
Early Bronze Age	3300 - 2000 BC
Middle Bronze Age	2000 - 1550 BC
Late Bronze Age	1550 - 1200 BC
Iron Age	1200 - 586 BC
Persian Period	586 - 330 BC
Hellenistic (Greek) Period	330 - 63 BC
Roman Period	63 BC - 330 AD
Byzantine Period	330 AD - 640 AD

Kings of the Northern Kingdom, Israel

(The dates listed below are from John Bright's *A History of Israel* and are one of many options. Some scholars have the divided kingdom beginning in 931 BC)

Jeroboam - 922-901 BC	Bad - chosen by God - reigned 22 years
Nadad - 901-900 BC	Bad - inherited the throne - reigned 2 years Assassinated
Baasha - 900-877 BC	Bad - reigned for 24 years
Elah - 877-876 BC	Bad - inherited the throne - reigned 2 years Assassinated
Zimri - 876 BC	Bad - reigned 7 days Assassinated
Omri - 876-869 BC	VERY BAD - chosen by army - reigned 12 years
Ahab - 869-850 BC	THE WORST - inherited throne - reigned 22 years

ELIJAH THE PROPHET
ELISHA THE PROPHET

Ahaziah - 850-849 BC	Bad - inherited the throne - reigned 2 years

ELIJAH IS TAKEN UP TO HEAVEN IN A CHARIOT

Jehoram - 849-843 BC	Bad - inherited the throne - reigned 8 years Assassinated

Jehu - 843-815 BC	Decent - chosen by God - reigned for 28 years

Jehoahaz - 815-802 BC	Bad - inherited the throne - reigned 17 years
Jehoash - 802-786 BC	Bad - inherited the throne - reigned 16 years
Jeroboam II - 786-746 BC	Bad - inherited the throne - reigned 41 years

AMOS, JONAH AND HOSEA

Zechariah - 746-745 BC	Bad - inherited the throne - reigned 6 months Assassinated
Shallum - 745 BC	Bad - reigned one month Assassinated
Menahem - 745-737BC	Bad - reigned 10 years
Pekahiah - 737-736 BC	Bad - inherited the throne - reigned 2 years Assassinated
Pekah - 736-732 BC	Bad - reigned 20 years Assassinated
Hoshea - 732-724 BC	Bad - reigned 9 years Conquered by Assyria

THE END OF THE KINGDOM OF ISRAEL - 722 BC

Kings of the Southern Kingdom, Judah

(The dates listed below are from John Bright's *A History of Israel* and are one of many options. Some scholars have the divided kingdom beginning in 931 BC)

Rehoboam - 922-915 BC	Bad - inherited the throne - reigned 17 years
Abijah - 915-913 BC	Bad - inherited the throne - reigned 3 years
Asa - 913-873 BC	Good - inherited the throne - reigned 41 years
Jehoshaphat - 873-849 BC	Good - inherited the throne - reigned 25 years
Jehoram - 849-843 BC	Bad - inherited the throne - reigned 8 years

Joel

Ahaziah - 843 BC	Bad - inherited the throne - reigned 1 year	Killed
Athaliah - 842-837 BC	Bad - (mother of Ahaziah) -reigned 6 years	Killed
Joash - 837-800 BC	Good/Bad - inherited the throne - reigned 40 years	Assassinated
Amaziah - 800-783 BC	Okay - inherited the throne - reigned 29 years	Assassinated
Uzziah - 783-742 BC	Good - inherited the throne - reigned 52 years	

Isaiah (end of Uzziah's reign)

Jotham - 742-735 BC	Good - inherited the throne - reigned 16 years

Micah

Ahaz - 735-715 BC	VERY BAD - inherited the throne - reigned 16 years
Hezekiah - 715-687 BC	THE BEST - inherited the throne - reigned 25 years
Manasseh - 687-642 BC	THE WORST - inherited the throne - reigned 55 years

Nahum

Amon - 642-640 BC	VERY BAD - inherited the throne -reigned 2 years	Assassinated
Josiah - 640-609 BC	THE BEST - inherited the throne - reigned 31 years	Killed

Jeremiah, Zephaniah

Jehoahaz - 609 BC	BAD - inherited the throne - reigned 3 months	Kidnapped/died
Jehoiakim - 609-598 BC	BAD - inherited the throne - reigned 11 years	

Habakkuk

Jehoichin - 598 BC	BAD - inherited the throne - reigned 3 months	taken into exile
Zedekiah - 598-587	BAD - inherited the throne - reigned 11 years	taken into exile

THE FALL OF JERUSALEM - 587 BC

Synchronized Chart of the Two Kingdoms

Kingdom of Judah	Judah's Prophets	Kingdom of Israel	Israel's Prophets
Rehoboam		Jeroboam	
Abijah			
Asa			
		Nadad	
		Baasha	
		Elah	
		Zimri	
Jehoshaphat			
		Omri	
		Ahab	**Elijah and Elisha**
		Ahaziah	
Jehoram	**Joel**	Jehoram	**Obadiah**
Ahaziah			
Athaliah		Jehu	
Joash			
		Jehoahaz	
Amaziah		Jehoash	
Uzziah	**Isaiah**	Jeroboam II	**Amos, Jonah, Hosea**
Jotham	**Micah**	Zechariah	
		Shallum	
		Menahem	
		Pekahiah	
Ahaz		Pekah	
		Hoshea	
		END OF ISRAEL	**END OF ISRAEL**
Hezekiah			
Manasseh	**Nahum**		
Amon			
Josiah	**Jeremiah, Zephaniah**		
Jehoahaz			
Jehoiakim	**Habakkuk**		
Jehoiachin			
Zedekiah			
THE FALL OF JERUSALEM 587 BC	**THE FALL OF JERUSALEM 587 BC**		
	Ezekiel (ministered to the exiles in Babylon)		

	Daniel (ministered to the exiles in Babylon)
	Haggai (ministered to the Jews who returned to Jerusalem during Darius the Great's reign)
	Zechariah (followed Haggai's message to the Jews who returned to Jerusalem)
	Malachi (ministered to the returned Jews after the rebuilding of the Temple)

Bibliography

Allen, Leslie C., et al. *Old Testament Survey: The Message, Form, and Background of the Old Testament.* Grand Rapids, Michigan: Wm. B. Eerdmans Publishing Co., June 1996.

Alexander, T. Desmond, David W. Baker, and Bruce Waltke. *Obadiah, Jonah and Micah: Tyndale Old Testament Commentaries.* Leicester, England: IVP Academic, 19 Oct. 2009.

"Ancient Board Games and the Nabataeans."*Nabataea.net.* 31 May 2011 <http://nabataea.net/ games3.html>.

"Ancient Civilizations." *Mr. Donn's Ancient History Page.* 20 April 2011<http://www.mrdonn .org/ancienthistory.html>.

"Ancient Egyptian History and Peoples." *Washington State University.* 31 May 2011 <http:// public.wsu.edu/~dee/EGYPT/HISTORY.HTM>.

Ancient Greece. 31 May 2011 <http://www.ancientgreece.com/s/Main_Page/>.

"Ancient History." *BBC History.* 20 April 2010 < http://www.bbc.co.uk/history/ancient/>.

"The Ancient World." *F. Smitha.com.* 31 May 2011 <http://www.fsmitha.com/h1/>.

Anderson, Gerald, Ed., and James Norman Dalrymple Anderson, Ed. *The World's Religions.* Grand Rapids, Michigan: Wm. B. Eerdmans Publishing Co., Feb. 1976.

Archer, Gleason. *A Survey of Old Testament Introduction.* Chicago: Moody Publishers, 1 Oct. 2007.

Barrett, Matt. *A History of Greece.* 30 May 2011 <http://www.ahistoryofgreece.com/>.

Bauer, Susan Wise. *The History of the Ancient World: From the Earliest Accounts to the Fall of Rome (1st Ed.).* New York: W.W. Norton & Co., Mar. 2007.

---. *The History of the Medieval World: From the Conversion of Constantine to the First Crusade (1st Ed.).* New York: W.W. Norton & Co., 22 Feb. 2010.

Bergen, Robert D. 1, 2 Samuel: The New American Commentary Volume 7. U.S.A. Broadman and Holman Publishers, 13 Dec. 1996.

Blenkinsopp, Joseph. *Ezra-Nehemiah: A Commentary.* Philadelphia: Westminister John Knox Press, 1 Dec. 1998.

Boling, Robert G. *Judges: The Anchor Yale Bible Commentaries.* Garden City, N.Y.: Yale University Press, 7 March 2005.

Bromiley, Geoffrey W. Ed. *International Standard Bible Encyclopedia: A-D (Revised Edition).* Grand Rapids, Michigan: Wm. B. Eerdmans Publishing Co., July 1979.

---. *International Standard Bible Encyclopedia: K-P (Revised Edition).* Grand Rapids, Michigan: Wm. B. Eerdmans Publishing Co., Feb. 1994.

---. *International Standard Bible Encyclopedia: E-J (Revised Edition).* Grand Rapids, Michigan: Wm. B. Eerdmans Publishing Co., March 1982.

---. *International Standard Bible Encyclopedia: Q-Z (Revised Edition).* Grand Rapids, Michigan: Wm. B. Eerdmans Publishing Co., June 1995.

Brownrigg, Ronald, and Joan Comay. *Who's Who in the Bible.* New York: Bonanza Books, 2004.

Bruce, F. F. *The Book of Acts (New International Commentary on the New Testament).* Grand Rapids, Michigan: Wm. B. Eerdsmans Publishing Co., 30 June 1988.

Budd, Philip J. *Word Biblical Commentary: Numbers, Vol. 5.* Waco, TX: Thomas Nelson, 15 Feb. 1984.

Bulliet, Richard, W. et al. *The Earth and Its People: A Global History, Vol. I: To 1550.* Boston: Houghton Mifflin, 20 Oct. 2006.

Bush, George. *Commentary on Exodus.* Grand Rapids, Michigan: Kregel Publications, Dec. 1993.

Cassuto, Umberto Moshe David. *A Commentary on the Book of Exodus.* Jerusalem: The Magnes Press, 1997.

Chadwick, Owen. *A History of Christianity.* Great Britain: Barnes and Nobles Books, 2005.

Chadwick, Henry. *The Early Church (The Penguin History of the Church) Vol. 1.* Great Britain: Penguin, 1 Oct. 1993.

Cook, Jean, et al. *History's Timeline Revised and Updated: a 40,000 Year Chronicle of Civilization.* New York: Barnes and Nobles Books, 1981.

Corbishley, Mike. *Ancient Rome: Cultural Atlas for Young People.* New York: Chelsea House Publications (3rd Ed.), 30 June 2007.

Creative Commons. 18 June 2011 <http://creativecommons.org/licenses/by-sa/2.5/>.

Cundall, Arthur E, and Leon L. Morris. *Judges and Ruth: Tyndale Old Testament Commentaries.*
Leicester, England: IVP Academic, 9 Sept. 2008.

Denault, Leigh T. "Life in Ancient Egypt." *Watson.org.* 31 May 2011 <http://www.watson. org/~leigh/egypt.html>.

Dorsey, David. A. *Literary Structure of the Old Testament: A Commentary on Genesis-Malachi.* Grand Rapids, Michigan: Baker Books, 1999.

"Egypt, a Brief History."*Mid East Web.* 31 May2011 <http://www.mideastweb.org/egypt history.htm>.

Elwar, Eliot. "Islamic Empires." *Military History.* 23 April 2011< http://www.suite101.com/ content/the-spartans-a367334>.

---. "The Spartans." *Military History.* June 2010< http://www.suite101.com/content/ the-spartans-a367334>.

Fensham, Charles. *The Books of Ezra and Nehemiah, New International Commentary on the Old Testament.* Grand Rapids, Michigan: Wm. B. Eerdsmans Publishing Co., Feb. 1983.

Ferguson, Everett. *Backgrounds of Early Christianity.* Grand Rapids, Michigan: Wm. B. Eerdsmans Publishing Co., Sept. 2003.

"Foundations." *Teaching the Middle East, A Resource for Educators.* 31 May 2011 < http://teachmiddleeast.lib.uchicago.edu/index.html>.

GNU Operating System. 18 June 2011 <http://www.gnu.org/licenses/fdl.html>.

Gonzalez, Justo L. *Story of Christianity: The Early Church to the Dawn of the Reformation Vol. I.* New York: Harper One, 10 August 2010.

Grant, Robert M. *Formation of the New Testament (University Library).* New York: Harper and Row Publishers, 1 Oct. 1965.

"Greco-Persian Wars 492-449 BC." *Emerson Kent: World History for the Relaxed Historian.* June 2010 <http://www.emersonkent.com/maps.htm>.

"Greece History: A Brief Description of the history of Greece and the Greek Islands."*Greeka .com, the Greek Islands Specialists.* 20 June 2011 <http://www.greeka.com/greece-history.htm>.

"Greek History." *Ancient Greece.* 30 May 2011 <http://www.ancient-greece.org/history.html>.

"Greek History." *History for Kids.* 10 April 2010 <http://www.historyforkids.org/learn/ greeks/history/history.htm>.

Hamilton, Victor P. *The Book of Genesis Ch.1-17 (1st Ed.).* New International Commentary on the Old Testament Series. Grand Rapids, Michigan: Wm. B. Eerdsmans Publishing Co., Nov. 1990.

---. *The Book of Genesis Ch.18-50 (1st Ed.).* New International Commentary on the Old Testament Series. Grand Rapids, Michigan: Wm. B. Eerdsmans Publishing Co., Oct. 1995.

Hayes, John H. *Amos, The Eigth-Century Prophet: His Time and His Preaching.* Nashville, TN.: Abingdon Press, Dec. 1988.

Hecht, Richard D., Ed., and Ninian Smart, Ed. *Sacred Texts of the World: A Universal Anthology.* New York: The Crossword Publishing Co., 2002.

Hemminger, Bill. "Why Study Ancient World Cultures?"*Exploring Ancient World Cultures.* 31 May 2011 <http://eawc.evansville.edu/>.

Hesse, Hermann. *Siddhartha.* New York: New Directions Publishing Corp., 1951.

Hill, Andrew E., and John H. Walton. *A Survey of the Old Testament.* Grand Rapids, Michigan: Zondervan, 10 Feb. 2009.

"History of Ancient Greece." *Oracle Think Quest.* 20 June 2011 <http://library.thinkquest.org /10805/history-g.html>.

"Historical Perspective." *Teaching the Middle East, A Resource for Educators.* 31 May 2011 < http://teachmiddleeast.lib.uchicago.edu/index.html>.

"Historic Figures." *BBC History.* 20 April 2010 < http://www.bbc.co.uk/history/ancient/>.

"History Map Archive." *Emerson Kent: World History for the Relaxed Historian.* June 2010 <http://www.emersonkent.com/maps.htm>.

"History of Ireland."*History World.* 31 May 2011 <http://www.historyworld.net/>.

"History of Mesopotamia."*History World.* 31 May 2011 <http://www.historyworld.net/wrldhis /PlainTextHistories.asp?historyid=aa53>.

Hobar, Linda Lacour. *The Mystery of History Vol. I.* Dover, Delaware: Bright Ideas Press, 2 July 2007.

---. *The Mystery of History Vol. II.* Dover, Delaware: Bright Ideas Press, 2 July 2007.

Hogan, Maggie., and Cindy Wiggers. *Ultimate Geography and Timeline Guide.* U.S.A.: Geo Creations Ltd., 31 July 2000.

Holmberg, Bengt. *Sociology and the New Testament: An Appraisal.* Minneapolis, MN.: Fortress Press, August 1990.

House, Paul R. *The New American Commentary Vol. 8: 1 & 2 Kings.* Grand Rapids, Michigan: Holman Publishers, 21 Feb. 1995.

Hubbard, David Allan. Joel and Amos: Tyndale Old Testament Commentaries. Leicester, England: IVP Academic, 23 Sept. 2009.

Hubbard, Robert L. *The Book of Ruth: The New International Commentary on the Old Testament (2nd Ed.).* Grand Rapids, Michigan: Wm. B. Eerdsmans Publishing Co., March 1989.

Hunter, Erica C. D. *First Civilization: Cultural Atlas for Young People.* Facts on File by Mike Corbishley. New York, June 2003.

Hyma, Albert, et al. *Steams of Civilization: Earliest Times to the Discovery of the New World (Vol. I—2nd Ed.).* United States: Christian Liberty Press, 1992.

Hyper History Online. 10 April <http://www.hyperhistory.com/online_n2/History_n2/a.html>.

Illustrated History of the Roman Empire. 31 May 2011 <http://www.roman-empire.net/>.

"Introduction to the Greek History." *In 2 Greece.* 30 May 2011 <http://www.in2greece.com /english/historymyth/ancient_hist_and_myth.htm>.

Jeffers, James S. *The Greco-Roman World of the New Testament Era: Exploring the Background of Early Christianity.* Downer's Grove, IL: IVP Academic, 7 Oct. 1999.

King, Philip J. *Amos, Hosea, Micah: An Archaelogical Commentary.* Philadelphia: Westminister Press, 1988.

Knappert, Jan. *Kings, Gods, and Spirits from African Mythology.* New York: Peter Bedrick Books, 1986.

Kuiper, B. K. *The Church in History.* Grand Rapids, Michigan: Wm. B. Eerdsmans Publishing Co., 1 June 1988.

Lewis, Brenda Ralph. "Africans in Ancient Rome: When African Emperors Rules." *Ancient History Suite 101.* 31 May 2011 < http://www.suite101.com/content/africans-in-ancient-rome-when-african-emperors-ruled-a366794>.

---. "Royal Ghosts of Medieval England." *UK Irish History Suite 101.* 10 May 2011 <http://www.suite101.com/content/royal-ghosts-of-medieval-england-a366945>.

Malina, Bruce J. *The New Testament World: Insights from Cultural Anthropology.* Louisville, KY: Westminister John Knox Press, March 2001.

Martin, Goldsmith. *Islam and Christian Witness.* Illinois: Intervarsity Press, 1982.

Merrill, Eugene H. *Kingdom of Priests: A History of Old Testament Israel.* Grand Rapids, Michigan: Baker Academic, 1 March 2008.

"Mesopotamia."*History-World International.* 1 June 2011 <http://history-world.org/mesopot amia_a_ place_to_start.htm>.

Milgrom, Jacob. *JPS Torah Commentary: Numbers, The Traditional Hebrew Text within the New*

JPS Translation Commentary. Philadelphia: The Jewish Publications Society of America, May 1990.

---. Leviticus 1-16: A New Translation with Introduction and Commentary, Anchor Bible Vol. 3. New York: Bantam Doubleday Publishing Co., 1 Dec. 1998.

Motyer, J. Alec. *Isaiah: Tyndale Old Testament Commentaries (Reprint Ed.).* Grove, Illinois: Drowners, 10 July 2009.

New International Bible. Colorado Springs, CO: International Bible Society, 1984.

New Living Translation. Wheaton, IL: Tyndale House Publishing, 1996.

Nielson, Paula L. "Alexandria, the Light of the Ancient World." *Anthropology, Suite 101.* 23 April 2011 < http://www.suite101.com/content/alexandria-the-light-of-the-ancient-world-367405>.

Powell, Anton. *Ancient Greece: Cultural Atlas for Young People.* New York: Chelsea House Publications (3rd Ed.), 30 June 2007.

Pritchard, James B., Ed. *The Ancient Near East: An Anthology of Texts and Pictures.* Princeton, N.J.: Princeton University Press, 8 Nov. 2010.

Richardson, Cyril. *Classics (Paperback Westminister).* New York: Macmillan Publishing Co., 1 Dec. 1995.

Ridpath, John Clark. *1-490 Egypt Babylonia, Ancient World Greece Vol. I.* Cincinnati, OH: History of the World Ridpath Historical Society, 1941.

---. *490-970 Greece, Macedonia, Rome Vol. II.* Cincinnati, OH: History of the World Ridpath Historical Society, 1941.

Roberts, J. M. *Ancient History.* London: Duncan Baird Publishers, 16 Sept. 2004.

"Roman History."*UNRV History.* 31 May 2011 <http://www.unrv.com/empire/roman-history.php>.

"Rome." *Internet Ancient History Sourcebook.* 20 April 2011<http://www.fordham.edu/ halsall/ancient/asbook09.html>.

"Rome." *Washington State University.* 31 May 2011 <http://public.wsu.edu/~dee/ROME/ CONTENTS.HTM>.

Sarna, Nahum M. Exodus: The Traditional Hebrew Text with the New JPS Translation Commentary. Philadelphia: The Jewish Publications Society of America, Mar. 1991.

---. *Exploring Exodus: The Heritage of Biblical Israel (1st Ed.).* New York: Schocken Books, 1987.

---. *JPS Torah Commentary: Genesis, The Traditional Hebrew Text within the New JPS Translation Commentary.* Philadelphia: The Jewish Publications Society of America, 1989.

Scheidel, Walter, et al. "Working Papers by Subject: Greece." *Princeton-Stanford: Working Papers in Classics.* 20 June 2010 <http://www.princeton.edu/~pswpc/papers/subject /subject/greekhist.html>.

Simon, Uriel. *JPS Bible Commentary on Jonah.* Philadephia: Jewish Publication Society, 1 August 1999.

Smith, Ralph L. *Word Biblical Commentary Vol. 32: Micah and Malachi.* Waco, TX: Thomas Nelson, 15 March 1984.

Stuart, Douglas. *Word Biblical Commentary Vol. 31, Hosea and Jonah.* Waco, TX: Word Book Publishers, 1987.

Tigay, Jeffrey H. *The JPS Torah Commentary: Deuteronomy, The Traditional Hebrew Text with the New JPS Translation (1st Ed.).* Philadelphia: Jewish Publication Society of America, June 1996.

"Timeline: Ancient Rome."*Exovedate.* 31 May 2011 <http://www.exovedate.com/ancient _timeline_one.html>.

US Copyright Office—Fair Use. 18 June 2011 <http://www.copyright.gov/fls/fl102.html>.

Vermes, Geza. *The Complete Dead Sea Scrolls in English.* New York: Penguin Classics, 30 Nov. 2004.

Walton, Robert C. *Chronological and Background Charts of Church History.* Grand Rapids, Michigan: Zondervan, 13 Sept. 2005.

Wenham, Gordon J. *The Book of Leviticus: New International Commentary on the Old Testament.* Grand Rapids, Michigan: Wm. B. Eerdsmans Publishing Co., Dec. 1994.

---. *Leviticus: New International Commentary on the Old Testament.* Grand Rapids, Michigan: Wm. B. Eerdsmans Publishing Co., Oct. 1994.

---. *Numbers: Tyndale Old Testament Commentaries.* Leicester, England: IVP Academic, 7 July 2008.

---. *Word Biblical Commentary, Vol. I: Genesis 1-15.* Dallas, Texas: Thomas Nelson Publishing, 9 Oct. 1987.

---. *Word Biblical Commentary, Vol. I: Genesis 16-50.* Dallas, Texas: Thomas Nelson Publishing, 28 June 1994.

Whiting, Edward, Ed. *Atlas of European History.* New York: Oxford University Press, 1957.

"World History." *Info Please.* 20 July 2010 <http://www.infoplease.com/ipa/A0001196.html>.

Woudstra, Marten H. *The Book of Joshua: New International Commentary on the Old Testament.* Grand Rapids, Michigan: Wm. B. Eerdsmans Publishing Co., Dec. 1994.

Yamauchi, Edwin M. *The Archaeology of New Testament Cities in Western Asia Minor (Baker Studies in Biblical Archaeology). Grand Rapids, Michigan: Baker House Publishers, 1980.*

Wikimedia Commons. 20 June 2010 <http://commons.wikimedia.org/wiki/Main_Page>.

Wikipedia Encyclopedia. 31 May 2011 <http://en.wikipedia.org>.

World History.com. 10 July 2010 <http://worldhistory.com/>.

Zacharias, Ramona. "Masada National Park." *Middle Eastern History.* 20 April 2011 <http:// www.suite101.com/content/masada-national-park-a367000>.

PHOTO AND ILLUSTRATION CREDITS:

Public Domain Creative Commons License:

Chapter 1: Creation of Light, by en:Gustave Doré (1832–1883), Creation Scene, Creación de Adán, Dwelling foundations at Tell es Sultan in Jericho, Flavio.Biondo.HistorieDolina-Pano-3 (Archeological dig), Shaduf - Romania, Nomad, 20,000 Year Old Cave Paintings Hyena, The Globe of Crates of Mallus

Chapter 2: Molnár Ábrahám kiköltözése 1850, Construction of the Ark: Nuremberg chronicles, Ivan Yendogurov (1861-1898): Rain, Noah's Ark, oil on canvas painting by Edward Hicks, Olive trees on Thassos, Joseph Anton Koch 006 (rainbow), NarmerPalette ROM-gamma, Europe in the ice age, Pharaoh by Jeff Dahl, Mummy in Vatican by Joshua Sherurcij, Photo Courtesy of Captmondo: CanopicJarsOfNeskhons-British Museum

Chapter 3: Brueghel-tower-of-babel, Photo Courtesy of garethwiscombe: Stonehenge, Kew gardens papyrus plant, Sumerian 26th c Adab, Cylinder seal Shamash Louvre, Sargon of Akkad

Chapter 4: Abraham and Sarah to Promised Land, Woodcut for "Die Bibel in Bildern, Hagar, Hagar and the Angel, Expulsion of Ishmael and His Mother by Abraham, part of art by Gustave Doré, laughter, World ocean map

Chapter 5: The sacrifice of Abraham, Ram, Eliezer, Rebecca at the well, Prologue Hammurabi Code, Hammurabi marble bas-relief

Chapter 6: Isaac, Gustave Doré: Isaac Blessing Jacob, Jacob's Ladder to heaven, Rachel by William Dyce, Jacob Wrestling with Angel, Enkidu leon

Chapter 7: Joseph telling his Dream to his Father, Joseph sold by his brothers, Joseph and Potiphar // getty museum, Joseph interpreting the dreams of the baker and the butler, Joseph made ruler in Egypt, Joseph Forgives His Brothers, Tissot Joseph and His Brethren Welcomed by Pharaoh, Jacob's bones to Egypt

Chapter 8: Ramses II at Kadesh, Luxor Nativity Sharpe, Nile Delta

Chapter 9: Tuthmosis III, Pharaoh Seti I - His mummy - by Emil Brugsch

Chapter 10: Moses takes his leave of Jethro by Jan Victors, c. 1635, Moses Rescued From The Nile, Moses Pluchart, Moses and Aaron Appear before Pharaoh, Plague of First Born, Moses Leads the Israelites, Pillar of fire, parting of the red sea, Bridgman Pharaoh's Army Engulfed by the Red Sea, A Pleasant Sukka

Chapter 11: Edward John Poynter, Israel in Egypt, 1867, Tissot The Gathering of the Manna, Victory O Lord! by John Everett Millais, Moses on Mount Sinai by Jean-Léon Gérôme (1824–1904), Altar of Burnt Offering, Laver of Brass, Table of Shewbread, Golden Candlestick, Altar of Incense, Veil in Temple Torn, Mercy Seat with Cherabims, Worshipping the Golden Calf, The Grapes of Canaan, c. 1896-1902, by James Jacques Joseph Tissot, Moses striking the rock by Pieter de Grebber, Moses with the Ten Commandments by Rembrandt

Chapter 12: Ghanghro location, Fuxi and Nüwa, Shennong, Yellow Emperor, Emperor Yao, Emperor Shun, King Yu, pictograms, Joshua, Rahab of Jericho, Sun Stands Still, Gideon, Samson and lion, Samson in the Treadmill, Ruth, 1795-William-Blake-Naomi-entreating-Ruth-Orpah, Ruth in Boaz's Field

Chapter 13: Brown Spider, Br'er Rabbit and Tar-Baby, Infant Samuel, Relief, Auch Cathedral, France: the Ark of the Covenant, Nuremberg chronicles f 41r 2, casting lots, Saul defeats Ammonites, David anointed, David playing the harp, Dagon, Osmar Schindler David und Goliath, Michal Gustave Doré, Saul and the Witch of Endor

Chapter 14: Hippos 2, Phoenician alphabet, Phoenician Oinoichoe, David King Over All Israel, David and the ark, David and Nathan, Absalom by Albert Weisgerber, King-Solomon-Russian-icon, Solomon's Wealth and Wisdom, Solomon's temple, Solomon dedicates the temple

Chapter 15: Strait, Monte Alto "Potbelly", San Lorenzo head, Nazca monkey, Jeroboam's Idolatry, Elah, Omri, Ahab Rex, Elijah Resuscitating the Son of the Widow of Zarephath, Elijah and Ahab, Ahaziah, Jehoram, Elijah taken up in a chariot, Elisha raising the Shunammite Son, Elisha at Dothan, Obadiah

Chapter 16: Jehoahaz, Jehoash, Jeroboam II, Zechariah, Sargon II and dignitary, Gerizim2, Russian icon - Amos, Russian icon - Hosea, Menahem, Pekahiah, Pekah, Hoshea, Assurbanipal op jacht, Samaritan Passover prayer, Mosaic Tribes, Kinadshburn, Jonah Painting by Jan Brueghel the Elder, Jonah catacomb, Russian icon - Nahum

Chapter 17: Inferno Canto Minos, Akrotiri minoan town, Daedalus und Ikarus, Knossos bull, Rehoboam, Abijah, Asa, Jehoshaphat, Ahaziah, Athaliah, Joash, Amaziah, Uzziah, Jotham, Ahaz, Fragment of Wall Painting from Basel Town Hall Council Chamber, by Hans Holbein the Younger, Joel (Michelangelo), Isaiah's Lips Anointed with Fire, Russian icon - Micah

Chapter 18: The Procession of the Trojan Horse in Troy, Mycenaean stirrup vase, Homer British Museum, Achilles Penthesileia, Portrait of Eratosthenes, Hezekiah, Sennacherib, Åhus kyrka, Manasseh, Manasseh's sin and repentance, Amon

Chapter 19: Rigveda, Jainism vows, Vishnu vishvarupa, Josiah, Josiah tears his robe, Russian icon - Nahum, Russian icon - Zephaniah

Chapter 20: Jehoiakim, Jeconiah, Russian icon - Habakkuk, Nebuchadnezzar II, Zedekiah, exile, Daniel refusing food, Simeon Solomon - Shadrach Meshach Abednego, Nebuchadnezzar's dream, fiery furnace, William Blake - Nebuchadnezzar, Jeremiah, Hanging Gardens of Babylon, City model of the main procession street towards Ishtar Gate in Babylon

Chapter 21: Ezekiel by Michelangelo, Ezekiel vision, Rembrandt-Belshazzar, Daniel's Answer to the King by Briton Rivière, Portrait of Cyrus the Great. By a 21st century Iranian artist, Magi, Emperor Cyrus the Great of Persia, who permitted the Hebrews to return to the Holy Land and rebuild God's Temple, Haggai, Zacharias (Michelangelo), fire temple

Chapter 22: Hop2, Athena Parthenos, Theater of Dionysus, Beached Ships Marathon, Xerxes, Xerxes lash sea, Trireme, Esther Haram, Megillat Esther, Purim gragger

Chapter 23: Zeus, Hera, Poseidon, Aresm Hermes, Hephaestus, Aphrodite, Apollo, Athena, Artemis, Hestia, Demeter, Hades, Parthenon, Socrates, Plato, Aristotle, Pericles, tesserae, Artaxerxes I, Rebuilding the temple, Nehemiah, Building the walls, Malachi

Chapter 24: Alexander and Aristotle, Alexander, Battle of Issus, Hippocrates Rubens, Domenico-Fetti Archimedes, Giza, Hanging Gardens, Zeus, Artemis, Halicarnassus, Colossus of Rhodes, Pharos of Alexandria, Greek mask, Spartan Hoplite

Chapter 25: Departure Herald-Detail, Confucius Tang Dynasty, Taoism, Shi Huangdi, Xu Fu expedition's for the elixir of life, Diamond Sutra from Cave 17, ancient Chinese watchtower from the Han Dynasty, Opening detail of a copy of "Preface to the Poems Composed at the Orchid Pavilion"(ACE353) by Wang Xizhi, Great wall

Chapter 26: She-wolf suckles Romulus and Remus, Fasces lictoriae, Jupiter, Cupid, Neptune, Pluto, Apollo, Mercury, Vulcan, Minerva, Venus, Juno, Vesta, Diana by Rembrandt, Ceres, Bacchus, Borghese gladiator 1, Segovia Aqueduct, Codex vaticanus

Chapter 27: Hannibal The Carthaginian, Ebro River, Hannibal (elephants), Carthaginian war elephants engage Roman infantry at the Battle of Zama, Scipio Africanus the Elder, Jungfrau seen from near Interlaken, Alps, Carthage destroyed

Chapter 28: Rome: Ruins of the Forum, Boulanger Gustave Clarence Rudolphe The Slave Market, Roman Slave Market, Fedor Andreevich Bronnikov Place of execution in ancient Rome, Julius Caesar - Wall painting in Acre, Israel, Looking towards the Capitol, Spartacus, CaesarTusculum, Wreath, Marcus Licinius Crassus Louvre, Pompey, Vercingetorix Throws Down his Arms at the Feet of Julius Caesar, Carl Theodor von Piloty Caesars Death, The Triumphs of Caesar, IX - Julius Caesar on his triumphal chariot, Caesar coin: RSC 0022, Brutus Eid Mar, Painting of Roman Calendar before the Julian reforms - about 60 BC
Chapter 29: Bust of Emperor Augustus wearing the Corona Civica, Mark Antony, Cleopatra-VII.-Altes-Museum, Lawrence Alma-Tadema- Anthony and Cleopatra, Herod the Great, Wailing Wall by Gustav Bauernfeind, Brooklyn Museum - The Magi Journeying, Gerard van Honthorst, Adoration of the Shepherds
Chapter 30: Resurrection art, First Page of the Gospel of Mark, Brooklyn Museum - Herod (Hérode) - James Tissot, Sustris Baptism of Christ, Jesus silences the Pharisees and Sadducees, Mihaly Munkacsy Head of a Pharisee, Bloch-Sermon On The Mount, Gethsemane Carl Bloch, Munkacsy - Christ before Pilate, Give Us Barabbas, PALMEZZANO, Marco Crucifixion, Rubens: The Descent from the Cross, Resurrection of Christ
Chapter 31: Tiberius, Claudius, Otho, Domitian, Pentecostés (El Greco, 1597), The High Priest of the Samaritans, Paul T, Conversion of Saint Paul, Bouveret Last Supper, Josephus bust, Ercole de Roberti Destruction of Jerusalem Fighting Fleeing Marching Slaying Burning Chemical reactions, Sack of Jerusalem, Ninth Av Stones Western Wall
Francesco Hayez, The massive earthen ramp at Masada, constructed by the Roman army to breach the fortress' walls, The Psalms scroll
Chapter 32: Caligula, Remorso de Nero, The destruction of the Temple of Jerusalem, Saint Peter, Saint James the Greater, John the Apostle, Thomas the Apostle, Saint Andrew the Apostle, Bartholomew the Apostle, Saint Matthew and the Angel, Philip the Apostle, Saint Simon the Zealot, Saint Jude the Apostle, Brooklyn Museum - Judas Iscariot (Judas Iscariote) - James Tissot, Caravaggio-Crucifixion of Peter, The Christian Martyrs Last Prayer, The rising of Lazarus, Good Shepherd, Christ with Beard, Trajan, Hadrian, expulsion of the Jews from Jerusalem, Burghers Michael Saint Polycarp, Justin Martyr, Santa Blandina, Maximinus, Decius, Valerian, Diocletian, Galerius, Raphael Baptism Constantine, Ichthys
Chapter 33: Queen Boudicca by John Opie, Josef von Arimathea, Hadrian's wall at Greenhead Lough, Nerva, Trajan, Hadrian, Antonius Pius and Marcus Aurelius, Bust of Commodus as Hercules, Pertinax, Didius Julianus, Pescennius Niger, Claudius Albinus, Septimius Severus, Septimius Severus, Caracalla, Alexander Severus, Diocletian, Toga, Stola, The Standard-Bearer of the Tenth Legion
Chapter 34: Battle of the Milvian Bridge by Giulio Romano, 1520-24, Nicaea icon,6th century depiction of the crucifixion and resurrection of Jesus, Young Folks' History of Rome - Goths, Sack of Rome by Alaric - sacred vessels are brought to a church for safety, Stilicho and his wife Serena and son Eucherius, Attila and his Hordes Overrun Italy and the Arts, The Sack of Rome by the Vandals, Genseric sacking Rome 455, Romulus Augustus resigns the Crown before Odoacer

Creative Commons Attribution-Share Alike 2.5 Generic/GNU Free Documentation License/Copyright Free Use:

Chapter 1: Creación de Adán
Chapter 2: Egyptian hieroglyphs-Iteru, Narmer Palette-Close Up Of Narmer
Chapter 3: Ancient Egyptian funerary stela, Ashmolean Museum by ChrisO, Europe topography map courtesy of San Jose
Chapter 4: Photo courtesy of Hardnfast: Ancient ziggurat at Ali Air Base Iraq
Chapter 5: Photo courtesy of Georgezhao: Code of Hammurabi, Photo courtesy of Hansueli Krapf: Portugal-Porto Moniz
Chapter 6: Photo courtesy of Samantha from Indonesia: Gilgamesh, photo courtesy of Deror Avi: A Senet game from the tomb of Amenhotep III - the Brooklyn Museum, Photo courtesy of Chris 73: Old Backgammon, Pergamonmuseum Inanna, Photo courtesy of Dr Marian Muste, University of Iowa: Amazon River
Chapter 7: Photo courtesy of Jason De Donno: Paddle Doll
Chapter 8: Photo courtesy of Jon Bodsworth: Mastaba, Mastaba, Photo courtesy of Wknight94: The Pyramid of Djoser in Saqqara, Egypt, Photo courtesy of Nina Aldin Thune: Kheops pyramid, Great Sphinx of Giza, Egypt, Photo courtesy of John Campana: Funerary relief of Amenemhet I from El-Lisht
Chapter 9: Photo courtesy of Keith Schengili-Roberts: Ahmose I-Statue Head Metropolitan Museum, Photo courtesy of Keith Schengili-Roberts: Amenhotep I -Statue Head Metropolitan Museum, Photo courtesy of Captmondo: Colossa l Sandstone Head Of Thutmose I – British Museum, Photo courtesy of Postdlf: Hatshepsut, Amenhotep II -Statue Head Brooklyn Museum, Thoutmôsis IV Louvre, Photo courtesy of אליבאבא: P1020665, GD-EG-Caire-Musée 061, Photo courtesy of Bjørn Christian Tørrissen: Tutankhamun Egyptian Museum, Photo courtesy of Keith Schengili-Roberts: Portrait Study Of Ay, Photo courtesy of Jean-Pierre Dalbera: Statue of Horemheb with Amun, Photo courtesy of Keith Schengili-Roberts: Statue Head Of Paramessu -Titled Frontal View - Ramesses I, Photo courtesy of Hajor: Ramses II Egypt, Photo courtesy of Captmondo: Merenptah, Photo courtesy of Keith Schengili-Roberts: Amenmesse - Statue Head Metropolitan Museum, Photo courtesy of Roberto Venturini: Turin statue of Seti II, Photo courtesy of John D. Croft: Siptah, Photo courtesy of Nikola Smolenski: Valley of the Kings
Chapter 10: Photo courtesy of Ian Sewell: Mount Sinai View, Photo courtesy of Kamalnv: Indian cobra, Pile of pitas
Chapter 11: Photo courtesy of Steve F-E: CAMERON, EGYPT, Photo courtesy of Ruk7: Model of the tabernacle, as seen in Israel, Timna Park, Schematic courtesy of Gabriel Fink: Top view, parallel projection, of tabernacle
Chapter 12: Photo courtesy of Mountain: Liu Ding, Shang Dynasty Bronze Battle Axe, Photo courtesy of Tamago915: Meshi (Rice), CMOC Treasures of Ancient China exhibit - oracle bone inscription, Photo courtesy of Luc Viatour: cinnamon bark
Chapter 14: Assyrian Warship, Photo courtesy of José-Manuel Benito: Rey David por Pedro Berruguete, Photo courtesy of Gilabrand: View of David's Citadel from Hinnom Valley, April 2007
Chapter 15: Photo courtesy of Brian Stansberry: Paleo-Indian point, Photo courtesy of Tim Kiser: Grave Creek Mound, Cahuachi, Sheshonq II mask 2004, Elijah, Photo courtesy of Guérin Nicolas: Asiatic Black Bear
Chapter 17: Photo courtesy of Marsyas: Children boxing
Chapter 18: Photo courtesy of Leo2004: Funeral mask also known as “Agamemnon Mask, Photo courtesy of DANIEL WONG: Hezekiah's Tunnel, Siloam Inscription
Chapter 19: Photo courtesy of JM Suarez: Ganges river at Varanasi in India, Photo courtesy of Luca Galuzzi: Mount Everest North Face as seen from the path to the base camp, Tibet, Akshardham Temple, Jainism Symbol, Mangalsutra, Buddha in Sarnath Museum, Dharma Wheel, Chakravatin, Asokan pillar, The "Great Stupa" at Sanchi, Necho-Kneeling Statue Brooklyn Museum
Chapter 20: Nebuchadnezzar, Ish-tar Gate detail, Berlín - Pergamon - Porta d'Ishtar - Lleons, Pergamonmuseum Ishtartor
Chapter 21: Photo courtesy of Jona lendering: Nabonidus Photo courtesy of Ariely: The Second Jewish Temple. Model in the Israel Museum, Standard of Cyrus the Great, photo courtesy of PHGCOM: Polylobed decorated weapons
Chapter 22: Leonidas statue, Athens, AGMA Hérodote, Hoplites, Homemade hamantaschen
Chapter 23: Mytikas summit
Chapter 25: Terracotta Army, Terracotta Army, Photo of an officer of the Terracotta Army, Terracotta army 5256, 20090529 Great Wall 8185
Chapter 26: Etruscan walled town, Servian Wall-Termini Station, The Constitutional Structure of the Roman Republic: A graphical representation of

the checks and balances of the Constitution of the Roman Republic, A view of part of the Forum Romanum, Rome, Mars, Civita di Bagnoregio, Photo courtesy of David Iliff: Colosseum in Rome, Italy, Douris Man with wax tablet, Couple with child, Pompeii Street
Chapter 27: Penteres, Quinquereme-and-corvus, Hannibal Crossing the Alps; detail from a fresco ca 1510, Pincer, Hannibal route of invasion, Scutum, Helmet centurion end of second century, Pugio, Uncrossed gladius, Photo courtesy of heather@etrusia.co.uk: Pilum, Hanukia
Chapter 28: Roman trireme on the mosaic in Tunisia image taken by user:Mathiasrex Maciej Szczepańczyk, Roman boy wearing bulla
Chapter 29: Marcus Aemilius Lepidus, Statue-Augustus, Photo courtesy of Kamalnv: Indian cobra, Second Temple
Chapter 30: Tiberius Ny Carlsberg Mirrored, Torah inside of the former Glockengasse Synagogue in Cologne. Twelve Disciples, Seder table, Hand-baked shmurah matza, Charoset, Photo courtesy of Andreas Praefcke: Ellwangen St Vitus Vorhalle Kreuzaltar (Crucified Christ, Ellwangen Abbey, Germany)
Chapter 31: Vexilloid of the Roman Empire, Statue-Augustus, Caligula, Nero, Galba, Vitellius, Vespasian, Titus, Photo courtesy of David Shankbone: The Dead Sea
Chapter 32: Nero, Statue of the apostle Saint James the Less, Septimius Severus, MMA bust - Constantine
Chapter 33: Panorama of the Thermae of Caracalla (Baths of Caracalla) in Rome, Roman SPQR banner, Saturnalia by Ernesto Biondi (1909), at the Buenos Aires Botanical Gardens, Volcán Chaitén-Sam Beebe-Ecotrust
Chapter 34: Diocletian, Maximum, Galerius, Constantius, Flavius Severus, Gaius Maximinus, Constantine, Maxentius, Constantine II, Constans, Constantius, Julian, Jovian, Valentinian, Valens, Theodosius I, Arcadius, Honorius, Istanbul and Bosporus

MAP CREDITS:

Public Domain Creative Commons License:

Chapter 1: Map of Fertile Crescent
Chapter 5: Map courtesy of Map Master Hammurabi's Babylonia
Chapter 6: Map courtesy of Map Master Hammurabi's Babylonia
Chapter 8: Africa in 400 BC
Chapter 10: Map Red Sea
Chapter 11: Deserts of the Earth
Chapter 12: Indus Valley Civilization, Jordan River
Chapter 13: Sahara Satellite Views, Early-Historical-Israel-Dan-Beersheba-Judea
Chapter 14: Mediterranean Relief, Phoenician Trade
Chapter 15: Bering Strait, Formative Era sites, Map of the southern Levant
Chapter 16: Map of the southern Levant, Map of the near east circa 1400 BCE, Urartu, Map of Assyria
Chapter 17: Map Minoan Crete
Chapter 19: Himalayas Map, Nanda Empire, Maurya Dynasty in 265 BCE
Chapter 20: Neo Babylonia Empire, World map with equator
Chapter 21: Neo Babylonia Empire, Persian Empire, 490 BC, Persia - Cyrus, Prime meridian
Chapter 22: Sparta territory, Attica map, Persia, North Pole, South Pole
Chapter 23: Prime Meridian
Chapter 24: Macedon Empire, Danube River, World map torrid
Chapter 25: Warring States 350 BC, Great Wall of Qin Dynasty, Silk route
Chapter 26: Via Appia map
Chapter 27: Map of Tunisia, Carthage Map, Hemispheres
Chapter 29: Roman Empire 117, Mediterranean Sea political map
Chapter 31: Roman Roads in Britannia
Chapter 33: Roman Empire Severus 210AD, Hadrian's Wall map, Mt Vesuvius 79 AD eruption
Chapter 34: Roman Empire Map, Byzantion

Julia Nalle:

Chapter 2: Ancient Egypt
Chapter 3: The Sumerians
Chapter 4: Abraham's travels
Chapter 7: Jacob's family in Hebron
Chapter 8: Egypt
Chapter 10: The Exodus
Chapter 12: Asia, Yellow and Yangtze Rivers, Dividing the Land
Chapter 17: Around the Mediterranean Sea
Chapter 18: Mycenaeans
Chapter 19: India
Chapter 22: Halicarnassus, Scythians, Battle of Marathon
Chapter 23: Peloponnese, Peloponnesian War
Chapter 24: Seven Ancient Wonders
Chapter 25: China
Chapter 27: First Punic War
Chapter 31: Paul's First Missionary Journey, Paul's Second Missionary Journey, Paul's Third Missionary Journey, Paul's Journey to Rome

Cover and Logo Design by Poppies Blooming, London, England
www.poppiesblooming.co.uk

Index

1

2

A

B

C

D

E

F

G

H

I

J

K

L

M

N

O

P

Q

R

S

T

U

V

W

X

Y

Z